Speaking Pittsburghese

OXFORD STUDIES IN SOCIOLINGUISTICS

General Editors:
Nikolas Coupland
Copenhagen University, University of Technology, Sydney, and Cardiff University
Adam Jaworski
University of Hong Kong

Recently Published in the Series:

Speaking Pittsburghese

THE STORY OF A DIALECT

BARBARA JOHNSTONE

OXFORD
UNIVERSITY PRESS

OXFORD
UNIVERSITY PRESS

Oxford University Press is a department of the University of Oxford.
It furthers the University's objective of excellence in research,
scholarship, and education by publishing worldwide.

Oxford   New York
Auckland   Cape Town   Dar es Salaam   Hong Kong   Karachi
Kuala Lumpur   Madrid   Melbourne   Mexico City   Nairobi
New Delhi   Shanghai   Taipei   Toronto

With offices in
Argentina   Austria   Brazil   Chile   Czech Republic   France   Greece
Guatemala   Hungary   Italy   Japan   Poland   Portugal   Singapore
South Korea   Switzerland   Thailand   Turkey   Ukraine   Vietnam

Oxford is a registered trade mark of Oxford University Press
in the UK and certain other countries.

Published in the United States of America by
Oxford University Press
198 Madison Avenue, New York, NY 10016

Library of Congress Cataloging-in-Publication Data
Johnstone, Barbara.
Speaking Pittsburghese : the story of a dialect / Barbara Johnstone.
   pages cm.—(Oxford Studies in Sociolinguists)
Includes bibliographical references and index.
ISBN 978-0-19-994570-2 (pbk. : alk. paper)—ISBN 978-0-19-994568-9 (hardcover : alk. paper)
1. English language—Dialects—Pennsylvania—Pittsburgh (Allegheny County, Pa.)
2. Americanisms—Pennsylvania—Pittsburgh (Allegheny County, Pa.)
3. Sociolinguistics—Pennsylvania—Pittsburgh (Allegheny County, Pa.)
4. Pittsburgh (Allegheny County, Pa.)—Languages. I. Title.
PE3101.P4J64   2013
427′.974886—dc23   2013019337

YINZ

Yinz, as in *you all*. Like a big bathroom
we're all politely sharing. The name of an old friend
from school you've lost touch with. The sound of a zipper
after good sex. The tiny washing machine part
you stamped out on the assembly line.
That record album you wore out playing
in 1971. An open invitation—no rsvp necessary.
The nickname of your son's best friend. The secret word.
A $2 winning lottery ticket someone slipped
in your birthday card. A friendly wrong number.
The shortcut through the South Side. Two girls
in matching outfits at Kennywood—their private laugh
in the bathroom. A child's sticky fingers—the sound
they make wiping on your pant leg. A late-night beer
on a barstool in Carrick. The TV clicking off
after a Steelers' win. The first bird of spring
reminding you you're from Pittsburgh, PA.
Yinz coming outside to play?
                    You bet.

                                        —*James Daniels*

Contents

Preface and Acknowledgments

Pittsburgh is a medium-sized city located on the Allegheny Plateau in the southwestern part of the US state of Pennsylvania. In many ways, it is a typical city of the US northeast. Pittsburgh's economy, once dependent on manufacturing, changed dramatically during the last decades of the twentieth century and the first decade of the twenty-first century. Rust-belt, deindustrializing cities like Pittsburgh, Buffalo, or Cleveland have fewer inhabitants than they once did, and many of those who remain have family roots or personal experience as unskilled or skilled-on-the-job industrial laborers. Like those in other rust-belt cities, Pittsburgh's economic planners have tried to capitalize on the city's universities and healthcare infrastructure to create a new "eds and meds" economy. As in other rust-belt cities, buildings and natural resources once devoted to industry are being refashioned for recreation, tourism, and other forms of consumption: there are bicycle trails and parks along the rivers where there were once steel mills and coal depots, and pleasure boats in the once-toxic water. One large steel-mill site now contains a shopping center, another an upscale apartment complex, another a high-tech economic incubator.

Sociolinguistically, however, Pittsburgh is unlike most other US cities. Students of regional variation in American English such as Hans Kurath (Kurath 1949; Kurath and McDavid 1961), William Labov and his colleagues (Labov, Ash, and Boberg 2005, 271–275), and others have found the Pittsburgh area interesting because it is linguistically distinctive. Laypeople from southwestern Pennsylvania have also noticed this. Most people from the Pittsburgh area are aware of, and many are interested in, the idea that Pittsburgh has a unique way of speaking and that speaking this way is a key element of a Pittsburgher's identity. In fact, Pittsburghers talk about "Pittsburghese"—their word for what they think of as their dialect—a great deal. "Authentic" Pittsburghers speak Pittsburghese or can at least talk about it. People play with Pittsburghese, performing bits of it to show that they have the knowledge associated with being local. Pittsburghese is represented in written form on coffee mugs, T-shirts, shot glasses, and other souvenirs, often in connection with the city's image or one of the city's sports teams. Bits of Pittsburghese are used to form new words such as *Yinzer*: a person who says *yinz* instead of *you guys* or *y'all*, hence a person who is authentically local. Pittsburghese appears in YouTube videos, in the names of rock bands and museum exhibits, in sports-fan ballads, in graffiti tags. Sounding like a Pittsburgher means different things to different people, and these meanings have changed over time. Pittsburgh is thus a compelling site for studying how, why, and when language, place, and identity can come to be related and how these relationships evolve.

This book explores how the meanings of Pittsburgh speech and Pittsburghese are created, contested, and circulated, and what kinds of work these meanings can do. I trace the history of linkages between linguistic form and social meaning in Pittsburgh, showing how sounds, words, and bits of grammar that once did no social work became linked with social class, and then increasingly with Pittsburgh the place. I show how these processes have been shaped by local historical, economic, and ideological conditions, primarily over the course of the second half of the twentieth century. I then explore the particular activities and experiences during which linguistic forms become linked, for particular speakers, with particular ways of being and acting. These activities include face-to-face, everyday conversation, which is the speech genre to which sociolinguists typically devote most of their attention. But ideas about how linguistic forms and meanings are linked are also formed in other genres of talk and writing, for various purposes, and different ideas are made possible and likely in different ways by the existence and availability of different communications media. People link linguistic forms to social identities when they talk or write about Pittsburgh or Pittsburghese; when they design or use artifacts that represent local speech; when they listen to or argue with experts on the subject of sociolinguistics; and when they put on performances, fleeting or carefully staged, of local characters.

The story of Pittsburghese provides a number of lessons for sociolinguists. In order to understand the history of Pittsburghese, I have had to build a model of social meaning and its shifting relationship to linguistic form over time. Trying to describe a city, rather than a smaller, more homogeneous community, has led me to see how important it is to think about the sociolinguistic world from multiple perspectives, as it is experienced by different people, positioned differently in the social and economic world, living in different kinds of neighborhoods, and at different times. The resulting picture is more disorderly, more layered in social space and in time, than models that involve orders of indexicality or indexical fields tend to suggest. It is also, I think, more interesting in some ways.

The story of Pittsburghese also encourages sociolinguists to reimagine what we call "dialect awareness" as a set of interrelated social and rhetorical processes rather than just a mental state. The fundamental first step in becoming aware of anything is noticing it, and noticing is a social process, a process that takes two (or more). People notice things because other people point to them in one way or another, sometimes by talking about them. People become aware that (for example) *yinz* is "a Pittsburgh thing" not just by hearing Pittsburghers say *yinz*, but by having it pointed out that Pittsburghers say *yinz*. (In fact there are lots of people—including readers of this preface—who now know that *yinz* is a Pittsburgh thing without ever having heard a Pittsburgher say *yinz*.) Furthermore, the phenomena we have often gathered under the rubric of dialect awareness can range from having the sense that one particular friend uses one word or sound differently ("You know, Ann always says that") all the way to "knowing" that there is a "dialect" with a name and a semiofficial dictionary.

Further, the story of Pittsburghese has something to tell us about language change, sociolinguists' first concern. The story of Pittsburghese shows us something important about why linguistic features that are "stereotyped"—features that people are aware of, talk about, try to avoid in everyday speech—drop away over time and about the relationship between socially marked speech features and social identities. It turns out that the people who use stereotyped features in everyday speech are not, on the whole, the people who attribute meaning to these features, so such people cannot be projecting social identities associated with those features. Pronouncing words like *downtown* and *out* with a monophthongal /aw/ sound ("dahntahn" or "aht") is one of the most stereotyped features of Pittsburgh speech: it sounds more Pittsburghy, to put it another way, than almost anything else. Young Pittsburghers are less likely to monophthongize the /aw/ in words like *downtown* and *out* ("dahntahn" and "aht") than their parents or grandparents are, and younger people may think older people sound more Pittsburghy. But the older people may not be aware that they are saying "dahntahn" or "aht," and even if they wanted to stop, they might not be able to. Using local variants may, in other words, sound local, but possibly not as much to the people who use them as to people who do not. Sociolinguistic stereotyping and the loss of stereotyped features are related, but not because people who once used stereotyped features stop using them.

The story of Pittsburghese is also important for Pittsburghers, and I have tried to write this book in such a way that people who are not sociolinguists can make sense of it. This is not easy when we are talking about speech sounds and details of the structure of phrases, and it might require some patience on readers' part. Linguists will have to put up with the eye dialect spellings I have used to make my arguments accessible to nonlinguists, and nonlinguists will have to agree not to worry about the details that are hidden in the phonetic transcriptions. Mainly, what is required is an open mind to all the things language does for us besides just being a way of packaging facts. Think what you like about Pittsburghese—it's fun, it sounds like home, it's what makes us special, it's an embarrassing relic of the past, it's ugly, it's a bad joke—it is an indelible part of Pittsburgh's cultural heritage. I would not want children of mine to have no choice but to speak in a way that can sound uneducated and unintelligent, but I would want them to appreciate the role of Pittsburghese in the history of Pittsburgh. If I am making an argument to my fellow Pittsburghers, it is that we should be taking the story Pittsburghese as seriously as we take the story of steelmaking or the stories of immigrants, because they are all intertwined.

The story of Pittsburghese is predictable in many ways. Once we see how linguistic variation, history, and identity can become connected to each other in settings like Pittsburgh, we can see this happening in other places in similar ways, and we can see that it has happened before and might happen again. At the same time, the story is a patchwork of coincidences. Pittsburghese is the phenomenon it is and plays the role it does because all sorts of contingencies have come together here over the last 250 years: because Pittsburgh is hilly, because Sam McCool's in-laws suggested he put his money where his dialectological mouth was, because the steel industry boomed at the turn of the twentieth century and busted toward the end of the twentieth century, because of YouTube, because American baby boomers became adults in the 1970s and 1980s, because Robert Parslow was at the University of Pittsburgh when he was, because personal computers became available in the 1980s, because I moved to Pittsburgh when I did, and because of a thousand other things. For me, discovering that all these things came together exactly as they did, when they did, has been the most exciting part of this project. I hope people who decide to use what I have found to explain what is happening in other settings will be alert to the fact that the details will inevitably be different in interesting ways.

The story of Pittsburghese is a story about people noticing language in particular ways, so it seems only fair to describe how I noticed Pittsburghese. Like the history of Pittsburghese, the history of this project is full of contingency, full of little things that just happened to come together when and where they did. Before moving to Pittsburgh in 1997 to teach at Carnegie Mellon, I spent ten years at Texas A&M University. I had had no particular interest in regional speech before moving to Texas, but being for the first time in my life a linguistic outsider in the United States (the fact that I was a Yankee—a northerner—was apparent from my accent), I began to notice the consequences regional accents could have. At the same time, my Texas A&M colleague Guy Bailey opened my eyes to the richness of the data from the *Linguistic Atlas of the Gulf States*, for which he had been a fieldworker, and the power of variationist sociolinguistic methods, which he was using in his research on African American speech in Texas. By the time I left Texas, two graduate students and I had launched a study of the linguistic styles of a dozen Texas women, focused on the combinations of sociolinguistic resources that came together in their public voices (Bean 1993; Johnstone 1995; Johnstone and Bean, 1997).

Moving to Pittsburgh meant moving much closer to my hometown in central Pennsylvania. On earlier visits to State College I had often changed planes in Pittsburgh, where I heard the vowel that made the airport announcements sound like home. If I had given the matter any consideration, I would have guessed that people in Pittsburgh sounded like the "locals" in the area I grew up in. Arriving at Carnegie Mellon to teach in the rhetoric program, which is oriented toward standard English in institutional settings, I had no particular plans to study Pittsburgh speech. Then, at a used-book sale on campus, I came across a copy of *Sam McCool's New Pittsburghese: How to Speak Like a Pittsburgher* (McCool 1982). The little book struck me as problematic, and I thought that at some point I would need to address some of what I then saw as errors in it. I started collecting newspaper and magazine articles that mentioned Pittsburghese, surprised at their frequency and curious why people talked about local speech so much. But other work was more pressing, and it was not until the fall semester of 2000 that I was able to work such a project into a class I was teaching on rhetoric and place. The work we did as a class (Johnstone, Bhasin, and Wittkofski 2002) suggested that monophthongal /aw/, the phonological feature of Pittsburgh speech that turned out to be the most prevalent in the newspaper and magazine corpus, may have dated only from the beginning of the twentieth century, and that it was not disappearing from working-class men's speech as quickly as might be expected. We thought there might be a relationship between the attention paid to this feature and its persistence but realized that it would take a great deal more work to figure out what the relationship was. In the meantime, I was coming to see that my initial reaction to Pittsburghese had been wrong. It would be a lot more interesting (and a lot more likely to accomplish something) to try to figure out why there was a dictionary of Pittsburghese than to try to explain what was wrong with it from a linguist's point of view.

Without the impetus of a colleague, I might not have pursued the project beyond the 2002 article. In the meantime, however, Scott F. Kiesling had been hired by the University of Pittsburgh as an assistant professor of Linguistics. Kiesling's background in quantitative variationist sociolinguistics complemented my background in qualitative approaches to linguistic style, and we shared an interest in the study of language in use, so we teamed up to organize a research-planning workshop and apply for grants. We were lucky to secure generous seed funding at this stage from the University of Pittsburgh and through a Berkman Fellowship and a grant from the Department of English at Carnegie Mellon. This enabled us to bring together a group of sociolinguists who had done projects like the one we envisioned or who had worked on features of midland American speech, several historians of the Pittsburgh area, a University of Pittsburgh sociologist, a folklorist with the Rivers of Steel National Heritage Area, a British geographer who was studying Braddock, Pennsylvania, and a communication designer.

At the 2002 planning workshop, I expected my colleagues to tell us how to carry out a standard sociolinguistic survey of Pittsburgh aimed at correlating the usage of local-sounding variants with demographic facts like age, gender, and socioeconomic class. And so they did, but they also encouraged us to think about Pittsburghese, the funny-spelled words on coffee mugs and T-shirts, the jokes, and the dictionary. They helped us frame research questions about how the Pittsburghese phenomenon intersected with the facts about Pittsburgh speech, questions which turned out to be the most fruitful ones we asked.

In the fall of 2003, funded by a University-Supported Professional Leave from Carnegie Mellon University, I began to conduct interviews in two of the four Pittsburgh-area neighborhoods we had settled on: Forest Hills and Lawrenceville. In the meantime, Kiesling and I successfully reapplied for grant funding for the Pittsburgh Speech and Society Project (PSSP), each of us receiving support for collaborative work from the US National Science Foundation. I was able to continue interviewing in Forest Hills and Lawrenceville and start in Cranberry Township. In 2005, I applied for and received supplemental funding from the National Science Foundation for interviews in the primarily African American Hill District.

By 2006, interviewing was mostly over, although other kinds of research continued. As we started to analyze the material we had collected, we also brought together a Community Advisory Board (CAB) to help us decide on the best ways to disseminate our results to Pittsburghers. The CAB consisted of some of the people I had interviewed, representatives of local archives, a retired steelworker, educators, and a web designer. Talking to Pittsburghers about what we were finding was a crucial part of the work that is represented in this book. In the course of planned efforts to spread the word, via a website, a set of podcasts, in media interviews, and in presentations to community groups, I got to hear Pittsburghers talking about Pittsburghese and reacting to how I talked about it, and this has fed back into the story I tell here in many ways.

This book represents only one outcome of the Pittsburgh Speech and Society Project, but it is impossible to disentangle the story of this book from the story of the PSSP as a whole. Nor is possible to separate the people who helped with the PSSP from the people who helped with this book. Over the course of ten years of research, thinking, talking about, presenting my work in public, and writing, I have asked a lot of people for help, a lot of people have offered help without my asking, and a lot of people have helped without even knowing it. I wish I could be sure that this list is complete, but I am sure it is not, and I thank the people who are not on it but should be as well as the people who are.

From beginning to end, my sometimes-collaborator and always-advisor Scott Kiesling has been a source of ideas and encouragement. I can't thank Scott enough for all the work he has put into this project since that lunch at the Thai place on Craig Street where I asked if he wanted to be involved. Scott has worked with me both in publicly visible ways (we have coauthored a journal article, a book chapter, and a number of presentations at conferences and colloquia) and in ways that have been visible only to me and other coworkers. Scott has fitted the PSSP in among his many other projects and obligations for the last ten years, and I am counting on him to continue to do so.

Another key player in the story of this book has been Joan Beal. I met Joan at a conference in 2001, where she presented some of her research on language and identity in the north of England, showing how the "Geordie" dialect was evoked in spellings like < the Toon> (' the town') for a Newcastle soccer club. The things she described sounded very familiar. Furthermore, Joan had just moved from Newcastle to Sheffield, the steel-producing center of England and one of Pittsburgh's sister cities. Over dinner, we hatched plans for a conference on "Steel Cities." The interdisciplinary conference took place in 2006, in Sheffield; Joan did all the organizing work. By then, Joan had visited Pittsburgh, and I had visited Sheffield. We took each other on tours only we could love: we searched for dialect-themed T-shirts, visited shopping malls on steel-mill sites, looked at Bessemer furnaces and other remnants of the steel industry now repurposed for tourist experiences, drove through nearly abandoned mill towns, and talked about how the hilly topography of both cities shaped local speech and local identities. Unlike me, Joan is a historian of English, and her work on eighteenth-century pronouncing dictionaries and nineteenth-century dialect literature opened my eyes to the fact that the dialect-enregisterment process I was studying had happened before. In addition to her friendship and hospitality, Joan gave me the crucial insight that what was happening in Pittsburgh in the late twentieth century was not unique to Pittsburgh or to the twentieth century.

For funding, I am grateful to the Berkman Fund and the Department of English at Carnegie Mellon, and to National Science Foundation (award numbers BCS-0417684 and BCS-0417657). Time for research and writing was provided by Carnegie Mellon University, via University-Supported Leaves in 2003–2004 and 2010–2011, and by the Freiburg Institute for Advanced Studies (FRIAS) at Albert-Ludwigs University in Freiburg, Germany, for a very generous six-month fellowship in 2011. The FRIAS fellowship was facilitated by Peter Auer, and I think him and everyone else who was affiliated with FRIAS in the spring of 2011 for new ways of thinking about language and dialect, some of which are apparent in this book.

Participants in our planning workshop in 2002 included (in addition to Kiesling and me) Sharon Ash, Susan Berk-Seligson, Sabine Deitrich, Doris Dyen, Maeve Eberhardt, Beverly Flannigan, Peter Gilmore, Joan Guerin, Kirk Hazen, Daniel Ezra Johnson, Paul Laxton, Bonnie McElhinny, David Miller, Michael Montgomery, Richard Oestreicher, Beth Lee Simon, and Walt Wolfram. Neeta Bhasin coordinated things so I didn't have to. Without these people's advice, I don't think I would have pursued the line of thinking that led to this book.

For helping me find interview contacts in Forest Hills, I am grateful to Ron Placone, Ken Gormley, Jane Freund, Vivian Broz at the Forest Hills Senior Center, Betty Evans, and Susan Lawrence and Toby Yanowitz, who had rowing friends everywhere. In Lawrenceville, I got leads from Michael Witmore, Kelly Delaney, my across-the-street neighbor Bonnie Isacke, Christiane Leach at Lawrenceville United, Barbara Thompson, Tim Haggerty, Allan Becer, Susan Gilpin, and Thora Brylowe. I am also grateful to the Lawrenceville branch of the Carnegie Libraries of Pittsburgh for space to conduct interviews. In Cranberry Township I got a huge amount of help from Marilynn McElhinny, who seems to know everyone, as well as from the staff of the Cranberry Township Community Center, who, among other things, let me use the library to talk to two retired teachers who were at the Community Center for Silver Sneakers class.

Jennifer Andrus helped with some of the Cranberry Township interviews and conducted some of them herself. She also helped me think through the basic structure of the argument I make in this book, transcribed parts of most of the interviews, and put up with a TV-less basement dorm room in Wales when I dragged her along to present part of the project at the University of Cardiff. Jenny did all this while working on her dissertation on a completely unrelated topic and enlarging her family by two active little girls. I can't thank her more. Trista Pennington is one of the most gifted fieldworkers I have ever encountered: resourceful, dependable, and an absolutely wonderful interviewer. I don't say much in this book about the African American Pittsburghers she talked to, but her work has led to a PhD dissertation by Maeve Eberhardt and several scholarly articles, and sociolinguists will continue to draw on it.

For giving me access to and helping me find archival material, I am grateful to Ron Baraff at Rivers of Steel National Heritage Area and Steven Doell at the Western Pennsylvania Historical Society. Alan Fried talked to me about his Pittsburghese.com website and, without my asking, put a link on it to my work. Sam McCool has been extremely generous, helping me fill in crucial details about his book, *How to Speak like a Pittsburgher*, and talking to me about the project more generally. I am very grateful to Sam, and to Twyla McCool, who got us together finally. Priscilla Parslow generously shared the papers of her late husband Robert Parslow.

The members of the Community Advisory Board, who advised us about how to take this project back to the people who made it possible, were Suzie Ament, Ron Baraff, Karen Billingsley, Mary Estep, Joan Guerin, Connie Placone, Ginger Placone, Lois Sharpe, Roy Smith, Jude Wudarczyk, and Mary Young. The graduate students who facilitated discussion were Jennifer Andrus, Dan Baumgardt, Maeve Eberhardt, and Trista Pennington. I am grateful to all of you.

I got help with transcription from Jennifer Andrus, Bill Blake, Roxana Botezatu, and Kate Hough. Scott Kiesling, Dan Baumgardt, Anna Schardt, and Neeta Bhasin helped with coding and analysis. Members of Chris Neuwirth's

Online Information Design course provided the initial template for the Pittsburgh Speech and Society website; Mark Thompson maintained and edited the site for several years; and Ed Galloway and other members of the staff of the University of Pittsburgh Archives Service Center relocated the site to where it is now, updated the visual design, and integrated it with the archived PSSP interviews. The podcasts that are part of that website were performed by Allan Becer, Kelly Delaney, Scott Kiesling, Connie Placone, and other participants in the PSSP. They were produced, pro bono, by my friends Don and Barbara Neumiller, and Don advised me on microphones and other recording equipment. Dan Baumgardt wrote the scripts, and Tom Mitchell helped me direct. The Newlanders let us use some of their music. Many journalists have also helped me spread the word about the PSSP. Chris Potter of the *Pittsburgh City Paper* has been an especially regular correspondent. Potter's intelligent questions helped me articulate ways to talk about the trickier parts of my story. Thank you to all these people, too.

I have talked to many scholarly audiences about this project, in the United States and elsewhere, and I have received a lot of useful feedback from those audiences. No matter where I am, there always seems to be someone from Pittsburgh in the room, and it is always especially interesting to hear their reactions. My main audience throughout the process, though, has been the members of SMiLe, our reading group on Social Meaning in Language. The group's membership has changed from year to year, but with Scott Kiesling and me providing the University of Pittsburgh and Carnegie Mellon anchors, respectively, SMiLe has meet almost every week, every academic semester but one, for over a decade. The seeds of this book were planted the semester we spent working through Michael Silverstein's oeuvre, and our reading of Asif Agha's book and some books on working-class discourse helped me see how the characterological figure of the Yinzer works. Pittsburghese has been my test case for trying out everything we've read, and fellow SMiLers have listened to each step in my thinking about it (in addition to sharing some delicious food at our end-of-semester potlucks). Here is to all of you!

Many people have helped in the actual production of this book. John Oddo, Sam McCool, and Scott Kiesling read and commented on the manuscript. MAPW student Amanda Cardo copyedited it before I submitted it to Oxford University Press. Nik Coupland and Adam Jaworski, the editors of the Oxford Studies in Sociolinguistics, welcomed the idea of this book and then the book itself. At Oxford University Press, Hallie Stebbens's enthusiasm for the project was a huge incentive. Thanks also to production editor Erica Woods Tucker and copy editor India Gray.

Finally, thank you to the magician outside the August Wilson Center on New Year's Eve, 2010, who performed a special trick to thank me for the work I was doing. I hope he reads this book, and I hope he likes it.

A Note on Transcriptions and Typographic Conventions

There is no such thing as a completely accurate transcript of speech. Any written transcription of talk can provide only a rough approximation of the experience of being part of a conversation. Extremely detailed transcriptions, full of special symbols and conventions for font and spacing, can be useful for making certain kinds of arguments, but they can also be distracting and so difficult to read that people don't bother to try. Since I am aiming for a readership that includes both language specialists and laypeople, I have tried to keep transcriptions in this book as simple and readable as they can be while still including the details that are necessary for illustrating the points I make. This means that I have not hewed to a single set of transcription conventions. In particular, some of the transcribed extracts in this book include no detail about how words are pronounced, others include only informal spellings meant to give a rough sense of the sounds of words, and others include technical phonetic transcription. Likewise, some transcripts include more detail about things like overlap (when two or more speakers talk at once) and things like laughter and voice quality, and others include less. When I have used conventions that differ from those of playscript dialogue, I describe and explain them as they come up.

In a book about language, it is inevitable that words get used in different ways. Most of the time, I use words the way they are normally used with their normal meanings. Often, however, I will be talking about particular words rather than simply using them, and sometimes I need to indicate what a word means. Sometimes I want a particular word to stand in for a whole category of words. I also quote people and texts, and I talk about how words are spelled. If I simply used quotation marks for all but the first of these ways of using words, it would quickly become unclear what I was doing. Thus I use typography to indicate how I am using a word. Here are the conventions I have tried to adhere to. (Sometimes it is impossible to tell whether someone is citing a word or quoting it, for example, so there are judgment calls involved.)

For phonetic and phonemic transcription, I have employed the International Phonetic Alphabet (IPA) with two exceptions: the diphthongs that would be [au] and [ai] or [aj] in the IPA are represented in this book as [aw] and [ay]. This usage, borrowed from William Labov, is conventional in representing these sounds in American varieties of English, and it is consistent with how I have represented these sounds in almost all my previous published work about Pittsburgh speech.

Typographic convention	Meaning	Examples
italic type	Words and phrases being referred to rather than having their usual function.	The verb *redd up* comes from Scotch-Irish English. So does *slippy. Yinz* and various forms of the verb *jag* have long been included in glossaries of Pittsburghese.
"double quotation marks"	(1) Words and phrases taken from actual speech or written material.	(1) "It never occurred to me," says Molly G., "that *needs ironed* wasn't proper English."
	(2) Letters and sets of letters that are informal spellings to suggest to nonlinguists what a phonetic transcription sounds like. They are meant to be helpful, particularly to readers with North American accents, but they are not as precise as the phonetic transcriptions.	(2) Some Pittsburghers do not hear the difference between the sound of [da:nta:n] ("dahntahn") and the sound of [dawntawn] ("downtown").
'single quotation marks'	Definitions.	Still in use are *slippy* for 'slippery'; *redd up* for 'tidy, clean up'; *nebby* for 'inquisitive, nosey'; and other derivatives of *neb* (an older English word for the snout of an animal) like *nebnose,* 'inquisitive person'.

Typographic convention	Meaning	Examples
SMALL CAPITAL LET-TERS	Represents a category of words that include the same vowel sound.	Words with the OUT *vowel include town, found, crowd, down, out,* and *around.* They hear people pronouncing CAUGHT and COT words the same way.
<angled brackets>	Illustration of how a word is spelled.	A word spelled <dahntahn> This pronoun is typically spelled <yinz> or <yunz> in Pittsburghese.
/slashes/	Used in the standard linguistic sense: a phonemic transcription.	This happens in syllables that do not end in /l/. So that /haws/can sound like [ha:s]
[brackets]	Used in the standard linguistic sense: a phonetic transcription. For nonlinguists, I use double quotation marks to suggest roughly what these transcriptions sound like.	Some Pittsburghers do not hear the difference between the sound of [da:nta:n] ("dahntahn") and the sound of [dawntawn] ("down-town").
((double parentheses))	In transcribed excerpts from interviews, they indicate who the speaker(s) was talking to, whether the speech was inaudible, voice quality, and the like.	((indistinguishable)), ((speaking to John K.)), ((sighs))

Permissions

The poem "Yinz" is used with the permission of the author, James Daniels.

The photograph entitled "Yinz Float" is used with the permission of the photographer, David Kent.

The two skits from the WDVE Morning Show discussed in chapter 8, and my transcription of them, are used with the permission of WDVE Radio.

I have discussed many of the ideas in chapter 2 at greater length in Johnstone, Barbara. 2004. "Place, Globalization, and Linguistic Variation." In *Sociolinguistic Variation: Critical Reflections*, ed. Carmen Fought, 65–83. New York: Oxford University Press; Johnstone, Barbara. 2010. "Locating Language in Identity." In *Language and Identities*, ed. Carmen Llamas and Dominic Watt, 3–26. Edinburgh: Edinburgh University Press; and Johnstone, Barbara. 2010. "Language and Geographical Space." In *Language and Space: An International Handbook of Linguistic Variation*, ed. Peter Auer and Juergen Erich Schmidt, 1: Theories and methods: 1–18. Berlin: De Gruyter Mouton. Parts of chapter 3 are adapted from Johnstone, Barbara, Jennifer Andrus, and Andrew E. Danielson. 2006. "Mobility, Indexicality, and the Enregisterment of 'Pittsburghese.'" *Journal of English Linguistics* 34 (2): 77–104. Parts of chapter 4 are adapted from Johnstone, Barbara, and Scott F. Kiesling. 2008. "Indexicality and Experience: Exploring the Meanings of /aw/-monophthongization in Pittsburgh." *Journal of Sociolinguistics* 12 (1): 5–33. Parts of chapter 5 are adapted from Johnstone, Barbara, and Dan Baumgardt. 2004. "'Pittsburghese' Online: Vernacular Norming in Conversation." *American Speech* 79: 115–145; Johnstone, Barbara. 2007. "Discursive Sources of Linguistic Diversity: Stancetaking and Vernacular Norm-formation." In *Diversity and Universals in Language: Perspectives and Implications*, ed. Yoshiko Matsumoto, David Oshima, Orrin Robinson, and Peter Sells, 167–196. Palo Alto, CA: Center for the Study of Language and Social Interaction, Stanford University; and Johnstone, Barbara. 2007. "A New Role for Narrative in Variationist Sociolinguistics." In *Narrative: State of the Art*, ed. Michael Bamberg, 57–67. Amsterdam/Philadelphia: John Benjamins. Parts of chapter 6 are adapted from Johnstone, Barbara. 2011. "Making Pittsburghese: Communication Technology, Expertise, and the Discursive Construction of a Regional Dialect." *Language and Communication* 31:3–15. Part of chapter 7 is adapted from Johnstone, Barbara. 2009. "Pittsburghese Shirts: Commodification and the Enregisterment of an Urban Dialect." *American Speech* 84 (2): 157–175. Part of chapter 8 is adapted from Johnstone, Barbara. 2011. "Dialect Enregisterment in Performance." *Journal of Sociolinguistics* 15 (5): 657–679.

Speaking Pittsburghese

1

Pittsburgh Speech and Pittsburghese

The first English-speakers to settle permanently in southwestern Pennsylvania were the Scotch-Irish, who arrived mainly during the 1700s.[1] Not surprisingly, they brought their English with them, a way of speaking influenced by the English of the northern counties, Scots (one of the related languages of Scotland) and Irish Gaelic. We know almost nothing about their pronunciation, but we know that they employed words that were different from those used by people who came from other parts of Britain to America: they "redd up" instead of tidying, called noses "nebs" and nosy people "nebby," and said the road was "slippy" when some English-speakers might have said "slippery." They used "whenever" for "when" sometimes and "needs done" for "needs to be done," and they called thorns "jaggers." Over the generations, Scotch-Irish words and grammatical features continued to be used in the Pittsburgh area, and, because the area was isolated from the East Coast, some of these features persisted for longer than they did elsewhere. In ways we cannot exactly trace, their pronunciation evolved differently than did the pronunciation of people in New York or Maryland, and they ended up with some distinctive sounds as well as distinctive words and bits of grammar. Newcomers, or at least their children, learned to talk the way the local people did. As a result, there is a distinctive set of language forms that can be heard in southwestern Pennsylvania.

Dialectologists studying the regional vocabulary of southwestern Pennsylvania in the 1940s noted the Scotch-Irish origin of many of the local words. A recent map of the dialect areas of American English shows a small circle in western Pennsylvania surrounding an area that differs from any other when it comes to how a particular set of speech sounds are related to one another and how they are pronounced (Labov et al. 2005, 271–275). Other visitors have sometimes noted peculiarities of Pittsburgh speech. A 1910 article in the *Pittsburg Dispatch* discusses distinctive "sayings and proverbs" from the Pittsburgh area (Carrell 1910), and, starting in the 1950s, writers for the *Post-Gazette* and the *Pittsburgh Press* regularly listed quirks of local speech that visitors remarked on.

For most of the city's history, however, Pittsburghers barely noticed the local way of speaking, if they were aware of it at all. Even today, many older Pittsburghers—including some who sound like Pittsburghers—say they never noticed anyone with a Pittsburgh accent when they were growing up. Some of them observe that they must have been exposed to the accent but that they were unaware of it, because it was the way they themselves spoke and because they were surrounded by people who talked the same way. When it is suggested that they have an accent, many Pittsburghers are not sure what it is about their speech that people notice. Is it that they pronounce *north* as "nort"? That they drop the *g* in words that end with *ing*? That they use the word *downtown* to refer to the city's central business district, or that they pronounce it "dahntahn"? There were and are Pittsburghers who pronounce sounds and use words this way, a way that an outsider might find odd. But if there was a Pittsburgh-dialect area before the later decades of the twentieth century, it was only from the point of view of outsiders such as dialectologists. On the whole, Pittsburghers did not notice that their speech was different from anyone else's, and they did not talk about how they talked. A Pittsburgher who moved away in the early 1960s might have identified Pittsburgh accents with the working-class residents of the neighborhood down the hill; some teachers might have corrected students who used *you'uns* as the plural of *you*, and some (though by no means not all) might have flagged sentences like *My hair needs brushed* as incorrect. The terms *Pittsburghese* and *Yinzer* had not yet been coined.

When the emigrant of the 1960s returned to Pittsburgh in 2004, however, things were very different. By the early 2000s, Pittsburghese was hard to miss. Pittsburghese was no longer how the steelworkers in the next neighborhood talked; it was, if you believed what you heard, how all Pittsburghers talked. More and more, this way of talking was thought of as a unique dialect associated with being a Pittsburgher, not just with being uneducated or incorrect. In 2011, representations of Pittsburgh pronunciations, words, and bits of unusual grammar could be seen everywhere: on souvenir items like T-shirts and coffee mugs, on billboards and protest banners ("Yinz' Live in a Police State"), in museums and on the radio, in the names of city-betterment initiatives (Redd up Pittsburgh), rock bands (Enemiesofyinz), even literary magazines (*The New Yinzer*). A Subway sandwich shop welcomes "yinz" to Pittsburgh in its airport signage. Today, younger Pittsburghers are less likely to have strong Pittsburgh accents in their everyday speech than their parents are, but they are much more likely to be able to imitate a Pittsburgh accent in a self-conscious performance, sometimes very accurately. People agree about what words and structures are Pittsburghese, and they use a common set of words and structures to evoke Pittsburghese and Pittsburgh identities. According to them, and to the artifacts they are surrounded by, Pittsburghers say "dahntahn" instead of "downtown." They use *yinz* as the plural of *you*. On Sunday afternoons they cheer for the Pittsburgh "Stillers," not the Steelers, and they shop at the Giant "Iggle" (Giant Eagle).

As we will see, many of the words and bits of grammar that people think of as Pittsburghese can be traced to the English of the Scotch-Irish, and most can be found in many other places besides Pittsburgh. Others have different sources, and some are representations of habits all English-speakers possess. How, then, did this particular set of words, phrases, and pronunciations become an icon of Pittsburgh, and why? What happened during the second half of the twentieth century to reshape a largely unnoticed way of speaking in southwestern Pennsylvania into a highly visible urban dialect called Pittsburghese? How has Pittsburghese come to be linked to local identity so strongly that Pittsburghese is alluded to almost every time people talk about what Pittsburgh is like or what it means to be a Pittsburgher? How do language, place, and identity get linked in this way? Why has this happened in Pittsburgh, and what characterizes cities around the world where similar processes are in play? What is it about a city's history, geography, and economy that leads people to make links between a particular set of linguistic forms, a geographical site, and a way of being? How are the links forged? More generally, how is it that local ways of speaking that are clearly in the process of homogenizing with neighboring ones come simultaneously to be celebrated more than ever before?

These are the questions that students of place, language, and identity across disciplines need to ask in the context of current social and economic change, and they are the questions I try to answer in this book. I show how a particular set of geographic, economic, ideological, and linguistic circumstances came together in Pittsburgh during a particular span of time to create the milieu in which Pittsburghese emerged into people's consciousness and gave it the shape and meaning it has. In the process, I show that the only way to piece together the story of Pittsburgh speech and Pittsburghese is to combine theory and method from linguistics, history, social theory, anthropology, rhetoric, and geography.

Although my aim is to trace the history of a dialect, what I am doing is not historical sociolinguistics in the usual sense. I am not primarily interested in reconstructing how different groups of people may have spoken in earlier times or in using archival sources to trace language change in the past. My project has more in common with what have been called "social histories" of language and dialect (Leith 1997; Wales 2006; T. Crowley 2012). Social histories of languages and dialects explore how historical events might have put people in contact with people who spoke differently, what historical facts led to language standardization, and what sorts of social and material facts caused languages and dialects to spread.

Whether they study remote times or recent ones, sociolinguists are often more interested in how people actually speak than in how they think they speak. However, I am not interested in Pittsburghers' everyday, vernacular speech as my primary focus. Rather, I want to understand how Pittsburghers' everyday accents are shaped by Pittsburghers' conceptions of how they talk, and, conversely, how people's actual speech shapes their conceptions. In this respect, this project shares some aims and methods with scholars of "folk linguistics" or "perceptual dialectology" (Long and Preston 2000; Niedzielski and Preston 1999; Preston 1989), who take seriously what nonlinguists say about ways of talking and about particular linguistic variants. More explicitly than most perceptual dialectologists, however, I am interested in Pittsburghese, and dialects in general, as cultural products; that is, as the outcomes of complex chains of ideological and material conditions and social activities. Pittsburgh speech, as it is actually used and heard, is just one part of the material context that gave rise to Pittsburghese.

Like other research about how people perceive and talk about variation in language, the work I describe in this book has important implications for my colleagues in sociolinguistics and linguistic anthropology. Dialect awareness, linguistic focusing and standardization, the stigmatization and stereotyping of particular forms, and whole ways of speaking all arise from complex sets of social and historical circumstances and processes of meaning making that we cannot take for granted. We will not have a full picture of how and why language changes unless we think more systematically about the particular circumstances that give rise to larger scale patterns of variation. This book provides some conceptual tools for doing this. These tools are drawn mainly from recent work on semiotics that originates in the American pragmatist philosophical tradition, although some of these tools have been talked about in other terms in other strands of sociolinguistic research. I describe and then illustrate the idea of enregisterment, together with the related concepts of metapragmatics, reflexivity, and indexical meaning. I show how, using these tools, we can trace how particular ways of pronouncing sounds and particular choices among words and patterns of grammar become linked with social meaning, and we can explain when and why this happens. Using these tools, I show that dialect awareness is better conceptualized as a process than as a mental state. Dialect awareness is something that happens in social interaction as a result of social and rhetorical exigencies that can be described in detail. The detailed historical work that I model in this book also provides a way to understand why certain linguistic variants become stereotyped, in Labov's (1972c, 180) sense, and why stereotyped features tend to disappear from the speech community. I will show that, contrary to our usual understanding of this process, stereotyped features do not disappear because people who employ them stop doing so. Instead, stereotyping and the loss of stereotyped features result from two different though interrelated processes that involve two different sets of people.

My project is situated between city-scale explorations of urban speech like those of William Labov (1972a, b) and others (Kerswill and Williams 2000; Milroy 1987) and community of practice-scale studies like those of Eckert (2000) and others (Alim 2004; Mendoza-Denton 2008). I bring the ideas of practice and phenomenology to bear to highlight how the social meanings of linguistic forms vary among Pittsburghers in ways some larger scale studies have missed. Pittsburgh is not a community of practice in any but the most vacuous sense of the term. But in order to understand Pittsburgh sociolinguistically, I join community-of-practice scholars in looking carefully at particular instances of talk among people who are engaged in mutual endeavors, sometimes with an eye to seeing when and why local-sounding forms are used. And along with scholars of linguistic landscapes and soundscapes (Gorter 2006; Jaworski and Thurlow 2010; Landry and Bourhis 1977), I am interested in how ways of talking are experienced in a variety of modes and media, not just in face-to-face talk. Interactions with visual and aural representations of dialect (on signs, for example, or in YouTube videos) help shape how people talk and think about the dialect, which in turn helps shape vernacular speech.

My project also draws on linguistic anthropology—the study of language and culture—both in its traditional concern with how language functions in social life and in its newer concern with language ideology (Gal and Irvine 1995; Joseph and Taylor 1990; Schieffelin, Woolard, and Kroskrity 1988) and semiotics (Agha 2006; Silverstein 1993, 1995, 2003). I explore how US-wide discourses (ways of thinking, talking, and acting) about correctness, place, class, and ethnicity shape the particular ways Pittsburghese is evoked, created, and used in local discourse.

Finally, this project draws on and contributes to the study of style in language. In the history of oratorical and literary study, style has sometimes had to do with the ornamentation of prose, sometimes with the linguistic characteristics of a particular writer's unique voice, and sometimes with how speech or writing is or should be adapted for different audiences or purposes. Sociolinguistic approaches to style (Coupland 2007; Eckert and Rickford 2001; Rampton 1999) generally take the third of these approaches, focusing on why and how a person's language may vary from situation to situation. I draw on research on style in language both when I talk about why some people move in and out of Pittsburgh-accented speech in daily life and when I talk about imitations and performances of Pittsburghese.

Pittsburgh Speech

Ideas about how Pittsburghers speak are obviously related to how Pittsburghers actually speak. The existence of linguistic features that can be heard in the Pittsburgh area and not everywhere else is, in other words, an essential material building block for Pittsburghese. If at least some people in southwestern Pennsylvania did not, at least sometimes, sound different from people elsewhere or employ different words or bits of grammar, no one could ever have linked a person's use of local speech features with any kind of social identity. However, we cannot rely on descriptions of Pittsburghese to tell us about Pittsburgh speech. This is because not all ideas about speech are accurate reflections of the facts about how people talk. Research in perceptual dialectology (Niedzielski and Preston 1999; Preston 1989) shows this clearly. Northerners in the United States think southern speech sounds "nasal" and "ugly"; southerners think northern speech sounds "nasal" and "ugly." Nasal turns out to mean something like ugly, and there is no objective way to measure ugliness. In other words, Americans often notice the ways other Americans talk, but what they say about how other Americans talk is more evaluation than description.

In order to describe how Pittsburgh speech and Pittsburghese are related, we need a description of Pittsburgh speech that is independent of descriptions of Pittsburghese: a scientific description to contrast with the folk description that is the focus of this book. This poses a methodological conundrum, however. As we will see in a later chapter, scientific and folk descriptions of Pittsburghers' speech have always been intertwined. Linguists have drawn on folk ideas about Pittsburgh speech to decide what to describe, and folk ideas have been shaped and legitimated by linguists. While linguists do have a systematic way of describing an accent—for example, since there are relatively few distinct speech sounds in a language, we can provide a complete phonemic and phonetic inventory as part of such a description—we do not have a systematic way of describing the set of words (or lexicon) that a group of people employs or their grammar system. Of the hundreds of thousands of words Pittsburghers use and grammatical choices they make, only a tiny percentage are not words and structures that all English-speakers use. Because of this, linguists inevitably pay the most attention to the words and bits of grammar that are different from those heard elsewhere. In other words, linguists tend to be more interested in the Pittsburgh pronunciation of words like *house*, for example, than in the Pittsburgh pronunciation of words like *mansion*, because we have noticed that the Pittsburgh pronunciation of *house* is distinctive, while the Pittsburgh pronunciation of *mansion* is more or less the same as how people elsewhere pronounce it. The trouble is that linguists notice that the Pittsburgh "hahs" pronunciation is distinctive because other people have suggested that is. Linguists' noticing of distinctiveness is channeled by the conventions of our discipline, for one thing. We might start with a chart of American-English vowel phonemes and describe how each of these vowels sounds in the dialect we are interested in, or we might be motivated by a previous linguistic analysis of the dialect to focus on a particular subset of vowels that might be related via chain-shifting. Alternatively, the other people who tell us that "hahs" is distinctive might be the laypeople who write Pittsburghese dictionaries and shoot Pittsburghese videos for YouTube. In other words, linguists know which local sounds, words, and structures are distinctive because we have been told so, through a process that is parallel to the process that gives rise to folk ideas about what is distinctive: people tell each other what to listen for. Short of engaging in a very different kind of research (looking at the regional distributions of *all* the variable features of English, and seeing which variants cluster around Pittsburgh), there is no way to avoid this methodological circularity.

I have tried to minimize the risk by including in this description of Pittsburgh speech only linguistic features that have been described as characteristic of southwestern Pennsylvania by linguists other than myself. This technique is obviously not perfect. To add an extra methodological wrinkle, older descriptions of western Pennsylvania speech, like those of Newlin (1928) and Maxfield (1931), are based on a combination of literary sources (mainly dialect literature, in which unconventional spellings represented the sound of local ways of speaking) and personal observation. These descriptions likely exaggerate the degree to which early settlers sounded Scottish, Irish, or "backwoods," depending on who was being described. In the case of personal observation, the observer's own linguistic background may shape what is noticed. Maxfield, for example, appears to have contrasted the speech of southwestern Pennsylvania with New England speech, which made him note things like people pronouncing *aunt* and *ant* the same way.

Linguists have, in fact, paid repeated attention to forms of language that can be heard in the speech of people from southwestern Pennsylvania. As we will see, only a minority of these features—in fact, depending on what we count, possibly only one—is actually unique to the area, in the sense that it does not function the same way anywhere else. In this section, I describe these features the way linguists have described them, adopting the conventional order of exposition and vocabulary of descriptive linguistics. This section will inevitably seem technical—perhaps too much so—to readers who are not linguists, although I have tried to provide some guidance where possible.

We will begin with phonology, the repertoire of speech sounds that can be heard in the speech of some western Pennsylvanians, and how these sounds are related to one another. My focus here is primarily on the speech of white people, although I will discuss what is known about Pittsburgh African Americans' speech compared to whites' speech. This is because Pittsburghese is largely associated with whites, as we will see, and Pittsburghese, not Pittsburgh speech, is the focus of this book. Then, after a brief methodological excursus into how tricky it is to tell exactly where words and phrases come from, we will turn to lexis, or the study of distinctive local vocabulary items. Finally, we turn to morphosyntax, the internal structure of words and what sorts of grammatical patterns particular words appear in. Lexical and morphosyntactic features are more likely than phonological ones to be shared by local whites and African Americans, but I will point out exceptions to this tendency.

PHONOLOGY

One key feature of the phonological system for people who speak with a Pittsburgh accent is that the vowels in words like CAUGHT and words like COT can be merged, or pronounced identically and perceived as identical. This feature is thought to have originated in the speech of Slavic-speaking immigrants who did not have this contrast in their home language (Herold 1990, 1997). While the merger probably originated in the eastern United States, it is also found throughout Canada and the far western United States, and it is spreading quickly throughout the country. What is distinctive in the Pittsburgh area is not that CAUGHT and COT sound alike but that they are both pronounced with a backed, somewhat rounded vowel which, to speakers who do not merge these two vowels, sounds more like the vowel in CAUGHT than like the vowel in COT. Of the fifty-seven white Pittsburghers whom I asked in a field experiment whether CAUGHT and COT sounded the same or different, fifty-six said they sounded the same. (The fifty-seventh was an elderly woman who may not have understood the question.) Their pronunciation of the vowels also sounded merged, although I did not analyze the production data acoustically. Interestingly, African American Pittsburghers also tend to merge these two sounds, unlike African Americans in other US cities (Eberhardt 2008).

People for whom two vowels are merged are not likely to be able to hear or produce the difference between them without considerable difficulty, and this is true of the CAUGHT-COT merger for Pittsburghers. If speakers cannot produce or perceive the difference between two sounds, they cannot use that difference to show that they are being more or less careful or to show that they are more or less local. Furthermore, they will not notice the difference between the two sounds if another speaker is using the difference to convey social meaning. The feature is likely, in other words, to be stylistically invariable, that is, used to the same degree no matter what the speaker is doing. One way to see this is to examine the speech of someone who is speaking as carefully and self-consciously as possible (W. Labov, 1972a, 2001a).

On December 27, 2000, one of Pittsburgh's public TV stations, WQED, broadcast an interview with the owners of three Pittsburgh sports teams. One was Dan Rooney, then owner of Pittsburgh's American-football team, the Steelers. Rooney is from Pittsburgh and has a Pittsburgh accent. In the formal situation of the interview, he could be expected to use local features less than in other, less formal situations, assuming he had any control over his use of the local features. In the interview, however, Rooney invariably pronounced words like CAUGHT (*Los* in "Los Angeles," *also*) and COT (*problem, not, beyond, impossible*) with the Pittsburgh variant of the merged vowel, [ɔ]. This suggests that he does not hear and cannot produce the difference even in his most careful speech.

People who do *not* merge the CAUGHT and COT vowels *do* hear the difference, however, and they may notice it when they hear people pronouncing CAUGHT words and COT words the same way. Many outsiders notice the Pittsburgh variant of the merged CAUGHT-COT vowel and comment on it, sometimes calling it "the Pittsburgh *o*," since the sound in question is often spelled with an <o> in English. The moderator of the WQED program on which Dan Rooney was interviewed was a former basketball player from Baltimore. At the beginning of the interview, to warm up the audience, he talked about Pittsburgh speech. "I know I'm in Pittsburgh when I hear the *o*," he said. As examples, he used *dollar* and *college*, pronouncing both with the backed, rounded vowel sound that is characteristic of Pittsburgh speech. By the same token, parents who are from other places sometimes notice their Pittsburgh-educated children calling their mothers *Mom* or *Mommy* with the Pittsburgh *o*.

Another phonological feature that people often notice is the pronunciation of the vowel in words that rhyme with *out* as a monophthong rather than a diphthong. Diphthongs are vowel sounds that have two parts: a nucleus and a glide. During the glide portion of the diphthong, the speaker's tongue moves from its original position to a new position. The resulting sound is often spelled with two letters to reflect the fact that the vowel starts with one sound and ends with another. Common English diphthongs are [ay], as in the standard, news-anchor pronunciation of *my* or *side*; [ɔy] as in *boy* or *lawyer*; and [aw] as in *sound* or *down*. In Pittsburgh, the word spelled <house> (linguists would transcribe it phonemically as /haws/) can sound like [ha:s] ("hahs"), with a longer vowel nucleus and little or no gliding (Kurath and McDavid 1961; McElhinny 1999).[2] Monophthongization of /aw/ may not have been present in Pittsburgh-area speech until the twentieth century (Johnstone, Bhasin, and Wittkofski 2002). This suggests that that this feature may be due to contact between English and European-immigrant languages. The diphthong /aw/ can be monophthongized in any word, but it appears to be somewhat more likely for this to occur before the liquid consonants /r/ and /l/ (which sound like the letters they are transcribed with) and the nasal consonants /m/, /n/, and /ŋ/ ("ng") than before other consonants, and less frequent at the ends of words than elsewhere.

Monophthongal /aw/ is stylistically variable in the speech of many Pittsburghers with local accents. That is, they can produce words like OUT with the diphthong [aw] or the monophthong [a:] depending on what situation they are in or what personal style they are projecting. For example, in the WQED interview, Dan Rooney monophthongized /aw/ very little, despite the fact that /aw/-monophthongization is a feature of his speech in other contexts. Of ten words containing the OUT vowel, he pronounced eight with the diphthong sound [aw] (*out, town, found, crowd, crowd, down, out,* and *around*), one with an intermediate-sounding vowel (*how*), and only one with a clear monophthongal pronunciation (*Cowher*). Bill Cowher was the coach of Rooney's football team at the time, a Pittsburgher in a job with a very local identity. Perhaps Rooney pronounced Cowher's name with a Pittsburgh accent for that reason.

On the other hand, there are Pittsburghers who pronounce the *out* vowel as a monophthong invariably, in every context. One was John K., who, in my interview with him, used an erudite phrase from the title of a nineteenth-century English novel, *Far from the Madding Crowd* (Hardy 2000). Although doing his best to sound as educated as he was (he had a PhD in chemistry), he pronounced *crowd* with a monophthongal vowel, so that the phrase sounded like "the madding crahd."

These two features, the CAUGHT-OUT merger and the monophthongization of the OUT vowel, may be related via a chain-shifting process to a third: the lowering of the vowel in words like CUT, so that this vowel sounds a bit more (to non-Pittsburghers) like the vowel in COT. Chain-shifting is the process by which a change in the pronunciation of one vowel leads to a change in the pronunciation of another, which in turn leads to a change in how a third vowel is pronounced, and so on. The "Pittsburgh chain shift" was proposed by William Labov and his colleagues (W. Labov, Ash, and Boberg 2005, 271–275), who describe it in more detail. The lowering of the CUT vowel is not stylistically variable in the speech of Pittsburghers who do it. That is to say, if a person's accent includes this feature, it will appear all the time, no matter what situation they are in or what style they are projecting.

Some Pittsburghers monophthongize /ay/ before some consonants, so that the vowel in FIRE sounds somewhat like the vowel in FAR. The process is similar to the process that produces "the madding crahd": the glide from [a] to [y] in the diphthong is reduced and the nucleus vowel becomes longer. When /ay/ is monophthongized, it is usually before /r/ and /l/. A Pittsburgher who monophthongizes both /aw/ and /ay/ may pronounce words like FOWL and words like FILE the same way. This can be very noticeable to non-Pittsburghers, because it can lead to misunderstandings: a Pittsburgher can be heard as talking about an *owl* when he or she is actually talking about an *aisle*, or about a *towel* rather than about a *tile* or a *tower* rather than a *tire*.

Particularly when it is at the ends of words, /l/ can be vocalized in some Pittsburghers' speech, sounding somewhat like /w/. This happens when there is little or no contact between the top of the tongue and the top of the mouth. Several sets of vowel sounds may be merged when they occur before /l/, perhaps in part because /l/ is vocalized (McElhinny 1999). The front vowel /i/ (the vowel in words like SEAL) can be pronounced the same as the vowel in words like SILL, so that *steel* is pronounced [stɪl], or "still." Other sets of vowels can also be merged before /l/ (and sometimes before /r/): /e/ and /ɛ/, so that words like BALE and words like BELL sound the same, and /u/ and /ʊ/, which means that words like POOL and words like PULL can sound the same (Dickey 1997).

Another characteristic of some Pittsburghers' vowel systems is that the vowel in words like COAT is fronted. That is to say, this vowel can be pronounced with the tongue further forward in the mouth than in other accents of English, so that *coat* sounds a bit like "kewt" or *home* like "hewm." This happens in syllables that do not end in /l/, because the presence of the vocalized /l/ tends to result in a vowel that is farther *back* in the mouth rather than forward. Thus, a word like COAL would have quite a different vowel sound for someone with a Pittsburgh accent (something like "co," with a bit of a "w" sound at the end) than would a word like COAT (something like "cewt") (W. Labov 2001b, 494).

Three other features of Pittsburghers' pronunciation have also received comment, though relatively little study. One is the presence of an "intrusive" (or extra) /r/ before /ʃ/ in the words *wash* and *Washington*. Another is an intrusive /l/ in a word like *drawing*, making it sound like *drawling*. This may be a result of the fact that /l/-vocalization can make it impossible to tell, without seeing it in writing, whether a word like DRAW has an /l/ at the end or not. Finally, some Pittsburghers add a /g/ sound to /ŋ/ (the "ng" sound at the end of *sing*) when it appears word-finally before a word beginning with a vowel. Thus, *going out* can sound like [goɪŋgawt] (something like "going gout"). This seems to be relatively rare.

LEXICON

The vast majority of the words used in the Pittsburgh area are also used throughout the English-speaking world, and, as we will see, many of the words Pittsburghers think of as local are actually widespread in the United States. There is, however, a small set of words that are regional in distribution (that is, they can be heard in the Pittsburgh area and not, for the most part, elsewhere in the United States). In general, it is hard to be absolutely sure where words come from, and in some cases there is influence from two or more sources. However, many of the words that linguists have noted in the speech of people in the Pittsburgh area are likely to have been brought to the area by early immigrants.

Early English-speaking settlers in southwestern Pennsylvania spoke a mix of language varieties, but many of the earliest English-speaking immigrants belonged to the group who later came to be called Scotch-Irish. While many of these people came from the northern counties of Ireland and would have thought of themselves as Irish, in many cases they were descendants of people from Scotland, northern England, and elsewhere. (Some had French Huguenot names, for example.) The language of these immigrants was shaped by a variety of influences, including Scottish Gaelic, Scots, Scottish English, English English (both through print and through contact with its speakers), Irish Gaelic, and Irish English (Montgomery 1989, 236). Furthermore, the persistence of some Scotch-Irish words may have had to do with how they resonated with German words, since Germans also settled in the area early on.

Words traced to the language of the Scotch-Irish immigrants include some that can still be seen on street signs and in Pittsburghese dictionaries but are no longer in regular use, such as *diamond*, in the sense of 'town square' and *hap*, 'comfort' or 'comforter' (on a bed). Still in use are *slippy* for 'slippery'; *redd up* for 'tidy' or 'clean up'; *nebby* for 'inquisitive, nosey'; and other derivatives of *neb* (an older English word for the snout of an animal), like *neb-nose* for 'inquisitive person'.

Also common are various derivatives of the verb *jag*, meaning to prick or poke, such as *jagger* for 'thorn'; *jaggerbush* for 'briar'; *jag around* for 'fool around'; *jag someone around* to mean 'tease, trick'; and *jagoff* for 'annoying person'. *Gumband*, for 'rubber band, elastic fastener' is also regional in distribution and heard in Pittsburgh, although the earliest attestation of this word in the *Dictionary of American Regional English* is from Vermont (von Schneidemesser 2003). As von Schneidemesser points out, the origin of *gumband* is not clear, but it is probably not German. (Most German immigration to the United States predated the invention of the rubber band, for one thing.)

Another small subset of Pittsburgh-area words are coinages that name commercial products produced and/or sold in the area. Among these are *Klondike*, a brand of ice cream bar, and *chipped ham*, a kind of thinly sliced ham, both of which were invented by Isaly's dairy-bar chain (Buttko 2001). *Jumbo*, a kind of inexpensive bologna sausage, may also have been a commercial coinage.

MORPHOSYNTAX

Morphosyntax means the shapes of words and how particular words articulate with particular grammatical structures. To Pittsburghers, as we will see, the most salient morphosyntactic feature of local speech is a form of *you'uns* (a contraction of *you ones*) used as the second person plural pronoun, where standard written English uses *you* and other colloquial varieties use forms like *you all* or *y'all*, *youse*, *you guys*, *you lot* (in the United Kingdom) and other such forms. This pronoun is typically spelled <yinz> or <yunz> in Pittsburghese; in everyday speech, it is pronounced in a range of ways, from [yuʌnz] ("you'unz") to [yunz] ("yunz") to [yɪnz] ("yinz"). This particular way of forming a plural pronoun corresponding to *you* singular was probably Scotch-Irish (Montgomery 2002). Variants of *you'uns* are still in use throughout the Appalachian Mountains, which were settled predominantly by Scotch-Irish immigrants. It is possible that the need for such a form was a result of their earlier contact (in northern Ireland) with Irish Gaelic, which has distinct singular and plural pronouns in the second person.

Another Scotch-Irish feature has to do with clauses like *the car needs washed* (Murray, Fraser, and Simon 1996; Murray and Simon 2002; Tenny 1998). This structure also occurs with the verb *want*, as in *the cat wants petted*. For convenience, we can refer to it as the *need/want + X'ed* construction. Because the standard way to express this meaning in written American English is to use a passive infinitive (the car needs *to be washed*), linguists and Pittsburghers alike sometimes suppose that something has been deleted to produce the regional form. Linguists call this something the infinitival copula; laypeople think of it as the words *to be* and joke that Hamlet's best-known line would consist of "or not" had Hamlet been a Pittsburgher. But to describe the *need + X'ed* in terms of deletion is to suppose that people who use this construction start with the standard form and then drop something from it. This seems unlikely in light of the fact that a perfectly standard alternative in British English is *need/want X'ing* (*The car needs washing*). The *need/want + X'ed* construction is frequent in both spoken and written speech in Pittsburgh. A neurologist can talk about whether a particular symptom "needs treated" or not, and a plumber's invoice may include the formula represented in "found the faucet needs replaced" and "found the circulating pump needed replaced." This construction is also common in the speech of African American Pittsburghers, as in this newspaper quote from an African American community leader: "There were things that happened in this neighborhood that really needed tended to" (Mock 2005).

Two other morphosyntactic features characteristic of Pittsburgh speech have to do with the usage of the adverbials *anymore* and *whenever*. "Positive *anymore*" is the use of *anymore* in sentences without negative grammar or meaning, with a meaning somewhat like that of *these days* (*It's quite warm anymore*; *Anymore Wal-Mart has almost everything I need*). This feature has been documented both east and west of Pittsburgh (Hindle and Sag 1973; Hindle 1975; Murray 1993). "Punctual *whenever*" is the use of *whenever* where speakers of other language varieties would use *when*: to locate a single event in time rather than a repeated one. Examples are "I was diagnosed with leukemia whenever I was fourteen," and "He was in the bank, standing in line to deposit his Social Security check, whenever he dropped dead of a heart attack." Montgomery and Kirk (2001) suggest that punctual *whenever* is Scotch-Irish in origin.

H. L. Mencken, the early twentieth-century journalist and language aficionado, claimed that the *need/want + X'ed* construction was the result of German influence (Mencken 1962, 202–203). It is unlikely that German is the source of the construction, but it is possible that the similarity (in some instances) of the German way of constructing clauses like these, or the fact that German-speakers may have produced something like the *need/want + X'ed* construction in their second-language English, may have made the English *need/want + X'ed* construction more likely to be adopted in the Pittsburgh area. Likewise, nonstandard usage of the verbs *leave* and *let* may be the result of dialectal English reinforced by German second-language usage, with *leave* sometimes meaning 'allow' and *let* sometimes meaning 'leave', as *Let the bag on the table*, *Leave me be*, or *Leave the dog go out* (Adams 2000; Maxfield 1931). The same can be said of other features of Pittsburgh speech: *redd up* sounds somewhat like the German verb *retten*, although one with a different meaning ('to save'), and *gumband* looks as if it could be a German word. In fact, vernacular English in some parts of Pennsylvania has clearly been influenced by German (Kurath 1945; Shields Jr. 1985; Tucker 1934), as illustrated by the use of *all* where other varieties of English have *finished* (*The soup is all*); the use of *dare* rather than *may* (*Dare I go out?*); the use of *once* in the expression *come here once*; and the use of verbs made from

English stems and the German verb-marker -en, like *outen* 'turn out' in *Outen the light*.

Although Germans were among the early settlers of western Pennsylvania, they were more likely to have settled farther east, where the land was better for farming. (German town names are much more common in central Pennsylvania than in the western part of the state.) Members of the German-speaking Anabaptist groups, the Amish and Mennonites, likewise originally settled farther east, the Amish particularly in Lancaster County. Today, bits of German-influenced English can sometimes be heard in the agricultural counties north of Pittsburgh but rarely in the Pittsburgh metropolitan area, where the descendants of German immigrants have lost most of the linguistic evidence of their origin.

There is, however, one feature of Pittsburgh speech that is almost indubitably the result of German influence. This is a pattern that has been referred to as "Pennsylvania Dutch question intonation" (Fasold 1980). While Fasold's observations were made in south-central Pennsylvania, this feature has been described in the southwestern part of the state as well (Maxfield 1931), and it occurs a number of times in my interview data. Maxfield described what was most likely this pattern in his comments about intonation more generally: "characterized by odd curves of pitch and tone, a question, for example, rising when one would expect it fall, and descending at the most unexpected places" (18). Fasold's discussion is considerably more systematic than Maxfield's. Pennsylvania Dutch question intonation occurs only in some yes/no questions (questions to which the answer could be simply "yes" or "no," such as "Is it raining?" or "Have you eaten lunch yet?"). In questions with Pennsylvania Dutch question intonation, the speaker's voice rises in pitch and then falls abruptly, starting with the last syllable with primary stress, or a syllable with contrastive stress. Figure 1.1 shows Fasold's graphic representation of such a question, "Are you looking for a new car, Ralph?"

A more convenient convention for representing questions like these is to indicate where the Pennsylvania Dutch question intonation begins, as in this version of the question in figure 1.1: Are you looking for a !new car, Ralph? The exclamation point indicates the point at which the pitch starts to rise.

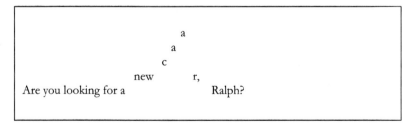

Figure 1.1 Pennsylvania Dutch Question Intonation. (Fasold, 1980, p. 1)

For the speakers Fasold studied, Pennsylvania Dutch question intonation appeared to be used in cases in which the answer to the question was not an issue for the questioner, either because the answer would not be consequential in the social interaction or because the speaker wanted to suggest this. So, for example, Fasold's speakers could use Pennsylvania Dutch question intonation in a question like, "What are we going to watch, the Giants and the !Jets?" if they did not care which game would be viewed but not if they did care and might argue with the answer. They could use Pennsylvania Dutch question intonation in "Is !dinner ready?" to avoid the implication that could be read from the non-Pennsylvania Dutch intonation question, "Is dinner ready?" that dinner should be ready. Fasold's Pennsylvania Dutch question intonation-users were completely unaware of the fact that they had two intonation patterns for yes/no questions and seemed to have no intuitive sense of when they used the Pennsylvania Dutch pattern.

Pittsburghese

Pittsburgh speech is local language as linguists would describe it. Pittsburghese is local language as it is locally imagined. The set of linguistic features that is represented when people talk about, perform, or otherwise invoke Pittsburghese overlaps with the set of features a linguist might describe as characteristic of the area. But it is not the same. For one thing, Pittsburghese is associated almost exclusively with white people. It draws very little on the speech of southwestern Pennsylvania's African Americans, except where their distinctive speech patterns overlap with those of whites. The set of linguistic features included in descriptions or uses of Pittsburghese is continually evolving. People continue to suggest and to use new Pittsburghese items and to argue about what should be included and why, and the visibility of particular Pittsburghese items waxes and wanes. For example, *yinz* and various forms of the verb *jag* have long been included in glossaries of Pittsburghese, but *yinz* and *jagoff*, 'a stupid or annoying person', have become much more visible since around 2005; *grinnie* ('chipmunk') used to show up on such lists but no longer does.

In this description of Pittsburghese, I draw on a set of newspaper and magazine articles about local speech and on a folk dictionary of Pittsburghese to show which forms are most commonly represented as examples of Pittsburghese and how they are represented. My two corpora, or sets of examples, represent two time periods. The first corpus is *Sam McCool's New Pittsburghese: How to Speak like a Pittsburgher* (McCool 1982), a folk dictionary that was first published in 1982 and has been in print ever since. Like other folk dictionaries (Hilliard and Wolfram 2003; Schneider 1986), this 39-page booklet contains words and phrases listed in alphabetical order. Here is an example entry:

Cahch: a piece of furniture usually found in the living room.
"Dad's asleep on the *cahch* again."

In the analysis that follows, I consider not only the words being defined but also the definitions and example sentences, which often include additional representations of local speech.

The second corpus consists of 190 print representations of features of Pittsburgh speech intended as fleeting evocations of local speech in the context of talk and writing about other subjects. Most of these are respellings like <dahntahn> or <Stillers>. Others are words spelled standardly in contexts which make it clear they are intended as examples of local speech (as when a memoirist describes her mother's use of the word *poke* for bag). My sampling technique consisted of collecting every written representation of local speech to which I was exposed over the course of three years, from August 1997 through August 2000. Items come from newspapers and magazines, a Pittsburghese website, the memoirs of a Pittsburgh author, and a number of other artifacts (see Johnstone et al. 2002). There is thus a fifteen-year gap between the two corpora, which allows us to see some of the ways Pittsburghese changed over that period.

Table 1.1 shows which of the linguistic features of Pittsburgh speech I described earlier are represented in each of the two corpora of Pittsburghese and how often.

As we can see in table 1.1, Pittsburghers have noticed many of the same things about Pittsburgh speech as linguists have noticed, including most of the phonological features linguists describe, all of the words on linguists' lists, and all but one of the grammatical features. The features that do appear on linguists' lists but do not appear in the Pittsburghese corpora tend to be ones that are infrequent, like the insertion of an /l/ in *drawling* ('drawing').

However, the object of linguists' descriptions is quite different from the object of laypeople's descriptions. In fact, the two ways of describing Pittsburgh speech do fundamentally different things and have fundamentally different effects. When linguists describe a feature of Pittsburgh speech, they provide an abstract characterization of it, using a technical vocabulary that includes terms like *monophthongization*, *merger*, and *vocalization*. Lay representations of Pittsburghese, on the other hand, are lists of particular words and phrases, not abstract descriptions of how the pronunciations and structures these words and phrases represent were produced. So, for example, while linguists talk about the monophthongization of /aw/, lay representations of this feature include particular words like *dahn*, *dahntahn*, *clahdy*, and *haus* and phrases like *Git aht a tahn* ('Get out of town') and *Car par* ('Cowher power'). While linguists describe the *need/want X'ed* construction or the punctual use of *whenever*, lay representations are sentences like *The car needs washed* and *Whenever I finish the car I'll take you for a ride*. When people experience lay representations of Pittsburgh speech,

Table 1.1 **Pittsburgh Speech Compared with Pittsburghese**

Feature of southwestern Pennsylvania speech, in descriptions by linguists	How this feature is represented in McCool	How often this feature is represented in McCool	How this feature is represented in the print representations corpus	How often this feature is represented in the print representations corpus
phonetic/phonological features				
pronunciation of the low back vowel resulting from the COT-CAUGHT merger	Dawn ('Don')	2	Bawdy Shop (play on 'Body Shop'), kiel-BAWsa ('kielbasa'), "wahch" ('watch'?)	2
monophthongization of /aw/	dahntahn ('downtown')	11	abaht ('about'), aht, ahht ('out'), arahnd ('around'), brahn ('brown'), caach ('couch'), car ('Cowher'), clahds ('clouds'), clahdy ('cloudy'), dahn, dahntahn, dahntaan ('downtown'), haus, haas ('house'), paht ('pout'), par ('power'), pond ('pound'), prahd ('proud'), sar ('sour'), shahrs ('showers'), tahn ('town'; used twice in "Git aht a tahn!," 'Get out of town', an expression associated with former mayor Sophie Masloff), thah-sand, ('thousand'), trot ('trout'),	40
lowering of /ʌ/		0		0
monophthongization of /ay/	Arn ('iron')	5	Imp'n Arn ('Imperial and Iron')	1

(continued)

Table 1.1 (continued)

Feature of southwestern Pennsylvania speech, in descriptions by linguists	How this feature is represented in McCool	How often this feature is represented in McCool	How this feature is represented in the print representations corpus	How often this feature is represented in the print representations corpus
vocalization of /l/	cawd ('called')	3		
merger of /i/ and /ɪ/ before /l/	still ('steel')	12	filled ('field'), ill ('eel'), mills ('meals'), rill ('real'), rilly ('really'), Stiller, Stillers ('Steeler(s)')	13
merger of /e/ and /ɛ/ before /l/	felled ('failed')	1	well ('whale')	1
merger of /ʊ/ and /u/ before /l/		0		0
fronting of /o/		0		0
intrusive /r/ in wash, Washington	worsh ('wash')	1		0
intrusive /l/ in drawling		0		0
/ŋ/ → [ŋg] /#_V		0		0
lexical features				
diamond, hap, other archaic words	carbon oil ('kerosene'), cup-board ('closet'), gommed up (?), onion snow ('early spring snow'), reverend ('extreme')	1 each*		0
slippy	slippy ('slippery')	1*	slippy	2
redd up	redd up ('tidy'; 'clean')	1*	redd up	2
nebby, other forms with neb	nebby ('nosy')	1*	nebby	3

jag, other forms with jag	jaggers ('thorns')	1*	jaggin' around, jagging around ('fooling around'), jagoff, jagoffs ('annoying people, idiots')	5
gumband	gumbands ('rubber bands')	1*	gumband, gummy band ('rubber band'), 3 gumball (possibly a mistake?)	3
Klondike	Klondike ('ice cream bar')	1*	klondike	1
chipped ham	chipped ham ('thinly sliced ham')	1*	chipped ham	4
jumbo	jumbo ('bologna sausage')	1*	jumbo	2
morphosyntactic features				
yinz (2nd person pl.)	yunz	1*	younz (1), yunz (8), yinz (4)	13
need/want X-ed	needs washed	3	Winter driving needs relearned.	6
positive anymore	Anymore there's so many new buildings . . .	1		0
punctual whenever	Whever I finish the car I'll take you for a ride.	1		0
uses of leave, let	leave ('let')	1		0
Pennsylvania Dutch question intonation	0			0

*These are words that are being defined.

they are experiencing words and phrases, not abstract features, and these words and phrases are selected not because they represent abstract features of Pittsburgh speech but because they are imagined to be actual examples of Pittsburgh speech. To put it another way, readers of a folk dictionary like McCool's do not learn that Pittsburghers monophthongize /aw/. Instead, they learn that Pittsburghers say "dahntahn." They do not learn that Pittsburghers merge /i/ and /I/ before /l/ but rather that Pittsburghers say "still" and "Stillers." And so on.

Pittsburghers do sometimes talk about Pittsburghese in abstract terms, as we will see. However, the underlying logic of laypeople's categories in their descriptions of Pittsburghese is different than linguists' underlying logic. For linguists, speakers do things like vocalizing consonants, monophthongizing diphthongs, and merging vowels; for nonlinguists, speakers do things like slurring sounds together, speaking carefully or sloppily, and using words that people from other places don't understand. Furthermore, characteristics of Pittsburgh speech that linguists describe as abstract features, processes that happen the same way, for the same reason, in many different words or phrases, are sometimes experienced in lay representations as particular words and phrases. Pittsburghers who do not hear the difference between the sound of [da:nta:n] ("dahntahn") and the sound of [dawntawn] ("downtown"), but have been told over and over that Pittsburghers use a word spelled <dahntahn>, may quite reasonably believe that the word *downtown*, however it is spelled, is a Pittsburghese word and that people in other cities use some other word to label their central business district. It is a mistake, in other words, to assume that linguists' and lay descriptions of the speech of southwestern Pennsylvania are describing the same thing. They are not. For this reason I use the term "Pittsburgh speech" (or sometimes "the speech of southwestern Pennsylvania" or "the speech of the Pittsburgh area") to label what linguists try to describe, and I use the term "Pittsburghese" to label what laypeople try to describe.

Lay descriptions of Pittsburghese also include many words and phrases that do not represent linguistic features that appear on any linguist's list. These include words and phrases that represent linguistic features that a linguist would say are not regional or nonstandard at all, as well as words and phrases that represent linguistic features that a linguist would agree are either regional and/or nonstandard but which are widespread in the United States or in the English-speaking world at large. Table 1.2 lists examples, which I have categorized according to why they seem to appear in folk representations: either because they evoke a kind of casualness associated with working-class life or because they evoke Pittsburgh the place and how people in Pittsburgh experience the city.

The vast majority of the Pittsburghese represented in the two lay corpora (the McCool book and the collection of articles) relies on nonstandard spellings. But not all these nonstandard spellings represent the same thing, and they evoke

Table 1.2 **Forms Listed in Two Corpora of Pittsburghese, not in Linguists' Descriptions of Pittsburgh Speech**

Category	Sub-category	Explanation of sub-category	Examples in the McCool corpus (1982)	Examples in the print representations corpus (1997-2000)	Notes
REPRESENTATIONS OF CASUALNESS, CLASS	**Eye dialect**	words spelled in such a way as to make them appear non-standard, even though they are actually pronounced the way they are spelled.		jynt ('giant')	Occurs in "Giant Eagle," a Pittsburgh-area supermarket chain, so this is also part of a representation of place (see below).
				yer ('your')	
				ya ('you')	
				lookit ('look at')	
	Allegro forms	words spelled in such a way as to represent how they actually sound in connected speech.	sammiches ('sandwiches')	sammitch	
			'n ('and')	'n	In the print corpus, this spelling is ued in "Fifth 'n Forbes," a local address, and "Imp 'n Arn," a working-class bar order (see below), so it indexes casualness, place, and class all at once.

(continued)

Table 1.2 (continued)

Category	Sub-category	Explanation of sub-category	Examples in the McCool corpus (1982)	Examples in the print representations corpus (1997-2000)	Notes
			Jeet jet?/No, j'ew? ('Did you eat yet?/No, did you?')	Jeetjet?/Nodju?	
			Jaynell (J&L)		
				'lectric ('electric')	
				'bout ('about')	
				gotta ('got to')	
				getcha ('get you')	
				hafta ('have to')	
	Non-standard forms	These are spellings that represent pronunciations and word forms that sound casual and/or non-standard in large parts of the English-speaking world, if not throughout it. These pronunciations and word forms are not particular to Pittsburgh, although they are thought to be.		in' or in ('-ing')	

git ('get')	
a or 'a ('of')	
Ahz ('I was')	This spelling combines a non-standard pronunciation which is actually more common in the US South than in southwestern Pennsylvania, the pronunciation of *I* as [a], with an allegro form (the contraction of *was* to 's) and an example of eye dialect (the use of "z," which is actually the final sound in *was*, instead of "s," which is the standard spelling.
whatta ('what I')	This spelling represents a non-standard pronunciation which is actually more common in the US South than in southwestern Pennsylvania, the pronunciation of *I* as [a], as part of an allegro form.

(*continued*)

Table 1.2 (continued)

Category	Sub-category	Explanation of sub-category	Examples in the McCool corpus (1982)	Examples in the print representations corpus (1997-2000)	Notes
			Ahia ('Ohio')		Used in "Ohio River," so also a reference to a local place.
			'ats ('that's')	Norseside, Sauside, Souseside ('North Side, Southside'); up 'ere ('up there')	
				da, dem ('the, them')	
			filum ('film')	filum	
			how's about ('how about')	hauscome ('how come')	
			seen, et ('seen', 'eaten')		nonstandard past participle forms
				we got ('we have got')	nonstandard verb construction
				yunz is, yunz be	nonstandard subject-verb agreement
				real ('really')	nonstandard adverbial form
				Come here often? ('Do you come here often?')	deleted subject and do-support in yes/no question. (Could also be a reference to Pennsylvania Dutch question intonation.)

	you best ('you had better')	nonstandard, somewhat archaic, Appalachian/southern form
Alright (as a response to "How are you?")	There ya go, hon. (Said by waitress serving food to customer)	Represent something about interactional style, perhaps in the sort of community where high politeness is not necessary.
	'n 'at, 'n 'at, an 'at, n'at, an 'at ('and that')	"general extender" (Overstreet 1999) ('and stuff like that, and so on'). Presupposes that listeners are part of the same community so can recover the missing information. This form is widespread in Scotland, Northern Ireland, and Scots-Irish settlement areas worldwide.
	whatchamacallit ('what you may call it')	Also widespread, in this form and closely related forms, in the English-speaking world. Like an'at, presupposes that interlocutors can recover the information.

(continued)

Table 1.2 (continued)

Category	Sub-category	Explanation of sub-category	Examples in the McCool corpus (1982)	Examples in the print representations corpus (1997-2000)	Notes
	"Folk Formality" (Tannen 1986)	These are forms that suggest people trying to sound more sophisticated than they know how to.	in regards to ('with regard to')		hypercorrection (over-reaching for the correct form)
			crewsants ('croissants')		In the 1980s, when McCool wrote, croissants were new to the US. This respelling suggests that Pittsburghers did not know how to pronounce the French word.
	Forms linked to immigrant ethnicities	These items are found wherever many Eastern European immigrants settled.	babushka ('grandmother', 'a headscarf once worn by old women')	babushka	
				gutchy ('underwear,' also a nickname)	
				pierogie (filled dumpling)	

Forms linked to local lifestyle, nostalgia		boilermaker ('beer with a whiskey shot'), city chicken ('pork or veal'), chitchat, carline ('trolley, streetcar line'), scrub ('clean'), what the cat drug in ('dragged in')	
		stogie ('cigar')	Short for "conestoga." These cigars were produced in Pittsburgh, so the word "stogie" is claimed to have been invented in Pittsburgh.
REPRESENTATIONS OF PLACE, LOCAL EXPERIENCE	**Local toponyms** Toponyms are place names. Sometimes the way they are spelled appears to represent local usage and/or pronunciation.	Pixburgh," Pixburg ('Pittsburgh')	The pronunciation represented by this spelling is sometimes attributed to African-American Pittsburghers.
		Burgh, The Burgh ('Pittsburgh')	

(continued)

Table 1.2 (continued)

Category	Sub-category	Explanation of sub-category	Examples in the McCool corpus (1982)	Examples in the print representations corpus (1997-2000)	Notes
				Sliberty, 'sliberty ('East Liberty')	This spelling was apparently invented by a marketing agency in the 1950s (D. Josephs, P.C.)
				Kernigie, CarNAYgie ('Carnegie')	
			Skwirohill ('Squirrel Hill')		This spelling represents the 2-word phrase as one word. It also represents a vocalized /l/ in *squirrel.*
			Mon ('Monongahela River')		A local abbreviation for a local toponym.
			The Point, Strip District, etc.		These toponyms appear in their standard form and spelling.
	Regional forms	These are words and pronunciations that are different in different parts of the US, but not particularly linked to class or correctness. They are widespread in the US, not limited to the Pittsburgh area.		crick ('creek'), poke ('sack, bag'), wooly brush	older and/or more Southern/ Appalachian terms, some now infrequent.

		Notes
pop ('soda, soft drink')	pop	Widespread in the US and a topic of frequent note. Perhaps particularly salient in Pennsylvania, where the isogloss (dividing line) between *pop* and *soda* runs through the state.
worsh, wosh ('wash')		
keller ('color')	keller	
spicket ('spigot')		
What gives? ('What is going on?, What's up?')		Possibly a German loan-translation.
Playful uses of other Pittsburghese forms	The Yunz and the Restless, (play on 'The Young and the Restless') Yunzbonics (play on 'Ebonics'), Yunzby (play on the name of a popular toy bear)	

(*continued*)

Table 1.2 (continued)

Category	Sub-category	Explanation of sub-category	Examples in the McCool corpus (1982)	Examples in the print representations corpus (1997-2000)	Notes
Don't know, possibly idiosyncratic		These appear only in the McCool corpus, and I have not seen any of them represented anywhere else.	dittent ('didn't'), cout-tent ('couldn't')		
				to box ('to put into a box')	
				wait on ('wait for')	

different kinds of meaning. In the first category in table 1.2 are "eye dialect", that is, words spelled in such a way as to make them appear nonstandard. Eye dialect is actually pronounced the way it is spelled, even in the most careful speech. One example is spelling *your* as <yer>: for American English, <yer> is simply the most phonetic spelling of the standard pronunciation of *your*. Closely related are what Dennis Preston (1982; 1985) calls "allegro forms": words that are spelled in such a way to represent how they actually sound in connected speech, where words are routinely shortened and combined. *And,* for example, very rarely sounds like anything except <'n>, unless a person is reading aloud, word by word. Like eye dialect spellings, allegro-form spellings make words and phrases look less standard than they actually are. Two allegro forms that appear very often in representations of Pittsburghese are *sammiches* ('sandwiches') and this exchange: *Jeet jet?/No, j'ew?* ('Did you eat yet?/No, did you?'). Since laborers traditionally carry sandwiches in their lunchboxes, this spelling evokes (and helps create and reinforce) an image of working-class life as well as an image of casual speech. The *Jeet jet* exchange represents the question *Did you eat yet?* as a casual alternative for *Have you eaten yet?* It thus makes the imaginary conversation sound casual in two ways: through the nonstandard spelling and through the choice of how to phrase the question. Another interesting allegro form that appears in the McCool dictionary is *Jaynell*, for 'Jones and Laughlin'. Jones and Laughlin was a Pittsburgh steel company, so the item evokes social class in several ways: by referring to a place where many working-class Pittsburghers were employed; by being abbreviated (and requiring local knowledge to interpret); and by being reanalyzed as a single word, suggesting that users of the name may not have known, or needed to know, what it meant. In its full form, incidentally, the <gh> in *Laughlin* was pronounced with a fricative [x] sound (as in German *Bach* or Scots *loch*), which for some users pointed to the Scottish origin of the name.

A third category of respellings is comprised of spellings that represent pronunciations that are, in fact, nonstandard, but which are not regionally restricted in a way that would make linguists associate them with region. By far the most common of these is the spelling <in> or <in'> for the suffix *–ing*. In the print representations corpus, this accounts for 8 percent of the spellings that represent pronunciations, second only to monophthongal /aw/. Unlike monophthongal /aw/, however, the alveolar pronunciation of *–ing* as [ɪn] ("in'") rather than [ɪŋ] ("ing") can be heard everywhere where English is spoken around the world. This respelling thus provides a good example of how forms which are actually local and forms that are nonstandard but not local get conflated in representations of Pittsburghese. Another fairly frequent respelling that represents a nonstandard pronunciation is exemplified in <'ats> (*that's*) or <up 'ere> (*up there*). The sounds that are spelled with <th> are particularly difficult for many foreign learners of English, including many of the European immigrants who settled in Pittsburgh and other US industrial cities. Thus the dropping of these sounds, [ð] and [θ], is associated with working-class speech throughout the United States. Another response to the same pronunciation problem is to substitute /d/ for /ð/, which is represented in respellings like <da> and <dem> (*the, them*). Spellings that represent nonstandard word forms (like <seen> or <et> for *seen* or *eaten*) and grammar (like <yunz be> or <yunz is>) also fall into this category.

Other words that appear in lists of Pittsburghese can be associated not with immigrants' English but with European-immigrant ethnicities (and can be found wherever large numbers of Eastern European immigrants settled): *babushka* (the Slavic word for 'grandmother', also a 'headscarf once worn by older women'), *gutchy* ('long underwear,' also a nickname), and *pierogie* ('an Eastern European filled dumpling').

Other words on the two lists represent something about how Pittsburghers are thought to interact with one another: Pittsburghers are informal: they say "Alright" as a response to "How are you?" (McCool) and waitresses proffer restaurant orders with "There ya go, hon" (in a newspaper cartoon). They live in a world where people share a lot of knowledge: lists end with the phrase *n' at* (spelled various ways), so as to suggest that hearers already know the rest of the list; people substitute *whatchamacallit* for the exact names of things. When they do need to be formal and explicit, they sometimes overdo it or miss the mark—Deborah Tannen (1986) calls this "folk formality"—using "in regards to" for *with regard to* or "crewsants" for *croissants* (at least in the 1980s, when Sam McCool wrote his dictionary and when croissants were new to the United States).

Other words resonate with people's memories of the past, and some seem to appear on Pittsburghese lists almost entirely because of the way they invite nostalgia. For example, McCool lists the expressions *boilermaker* ('beer with a shot of whiskey'), *city chicken* ('pork or veal'), *chitchat* ('casual conversation'), *carline* ('trolley', 'streetcar'), *scrub* ('clean'), and *what the cat drug in* ('Look what the cat dragged in!', used to tease someone who looks disheveled). These all refer to the way a Pittsburgher might have lived a generation before McCool wrote his dictionary: going to the bar after work, eating inexpensive meat, taking the streetcar to work or shop, chatting with neighbors, cleaning the house and porch, and using folksy expressions. The lifestyle that is evoked is a working-class one.

Other items in the Pittsburghese corpora represent the experience of living in Pittsburgh. They are words that residents of the city are claimed to use or recognize independent of social class and in formal situations as well as casual ones. One large group of words in this category consists of toponyms (place names) sometimes respelled or abbreviated to suggest how they sound locally: *Pixburgh*, *The Burgh*, *Sliberty* ('East Liberty', a neighborhood), *Skwirohill* ('Squirrel Hill', represented with a vocalized /l/ sound), *The Point*, *The Strip District*, and *The Mon* (a nickname for the Monongahela River, which flows through the city). <Kernigie>

and <CarNAYgie> both represent *Carnegie*, for Andrew Carnegie, a founder of the steel industry in Pittsburgh, part of the name of a university there, and the name of a nearby town. The first spelling is probably intended to represent what the second spelling represents more clearly: the stress is on the second syllable of the name, not on the first, as it is elsewhere. Using <k> for <c> is also a conventional way of representing nonstandard speech in English orthography.

Both McCool, in the early 1980s, and the print corpus from the late 1990s and early 2000s include *pop* as the Pittsburgh word for 'soda' or 'soft drink'. The word *pop* is widespread in the United States and often comes up in talk about regional differences, along with other alternatives like *soda water* and *Coke*.[3] As Dan Baumgardt pointed out to me, people in Pennsylvania may be particularly aware that some people say *pop* and others say *soda*. Unlike any other state, Pennsylvania is more or less bisected by the boundary between *pop* and *soda*. *Pop* is the traditional form in the western half of the state and *soda* in the eastern half. This means that youth traveling in-state for competitions, camp, or college are likely to encounter peers who use the other word.

Also regional in distribution but not particularly tied to class are forms like *crick* ('creek'), *poke* ('sack', 'bag'), and *wooly brush*, as well as the pronunciations that are represented in <keller> for *color*, <spicket> for *spigot*, and <wosh> or <worsh> for *wash*. These are older, more southern or Appalachian-sounding forms, some of which are now infrequent. Many are tinged with nostalgia: these words and pronunciations, and in some cases the things they represent, are less common than they once were and more remote in history.

We see from this analysis that Pittsburghese is not just about how people are thought to talk, in the way linguists think about how people talk, but about how people act, how they interact, how they experience the world. If a linguist were to try to convince people that *sammich* or *yinz* or *worsh* are not really Pittsburghese words, the linguist would be missing the point. To use the philosopher Ludwig Wittgenstein's term, the "language game" that gives rise to the lists of words and phrases that comprise Pittsburghese is not the same as the language game that gives rise to linguists' lists of regional features of phonology, lexis, and morphosyntax. The two games are played by different people (for the most part) for different reasons. My goal in the rest of this book is to describe how the Pittsburghese game works. By what logics do the words and phrases of Pittsburghese belong there? And through what activities, when, and why do people come to share these logics?

Overview of the Book

In chapter 2, I turn to three concepts that are crucial for the study of linguistic variation across space in general and for understanding Pittsburghese in particular: dialect, place, and meaning making. I suggest that traditional ways of imagining what dialects are and what a place is, in sociolinguistics as well as in the common sense of the English-speaking world, need to be supplemented with some newer ideas from dialectology, anthropology, and geography.

Traditionally, linguists interested in finding and describing regional dialects started with relatively small sets of variables chosen in advance (different ways of saying the same word, different words for the same thing, and different grammatical patterns for the same purpose). They looked for dialect boundaries by finding the dividing lines between the variants of these variables and then looked for places where numerous dividing lines overlapped. Current dialectology, on the other hand, suggests that linguists need to look at how much larger numbers of data points cluster together, while trying to remain agnostic about what the clusters represent and paying attention not just to the centers of clusters but also to their peripheries. Once the aim shifts from finding and describing "dialects" or "languages" to finding and describing the kinds of patterns that emerge in large collections (or corpora) of examples of actual speech, we are led to reimagine dialects and languages not as empirical objects but as ideological ones, concepts that come into being in particular historical and material contexts via particular human activities.

To put this another way, the only linguistic phenomena we can actually observe are particular instances of particular individuals choosing particular sounds, words, and structures when English provides multiple options. If we make enough such observations (and computer power now allows us to assemble and analyze sets of millions of linguistic data points), we can detect patterns in the geographic distribution of particular forms. In the United States, for example, we could find more instances of /ay/ pronounced as /a:/ (as in "mah" for *my*) in the southeastern states than elsewhere. We could find other features as well whose distribution was different in the southeast than elsewhere. But the patterns are never exactly the same from one feature to another, and there are always exceptions to the rule, forms that occur unexpectedly. In order to claim that there is a southern dialect of US English, we must abstract from the facts we can actually observe, generalize over them, and ignore the exceptions. We may want to do this for one reason or another, but when we do, we are not simply describing something but creating it for some particular set of reasons. This is what it means to say that dialects are "socially constructed."

Places are also socially constructed. Like most laypeople, sociolinguists have typically thought of place in physical terms, as the location of speakers or varieties in space, on the globe or on a map. In order to understand the role of place in the sociolinguistic processes I am interested in, however, we need to conceptualize place not just as a demographic fact about speakers but also as an ideological construct created through human interaction. Newer ways of thinking about language and place have emerged in the context of widespread interest in how the social world is collectively shaped via talking, writing, and other aspects of social interaction and in how individuals experience language and linguistic variation. These new ways of thinking are useful in understanding the kind of sociolinguistic change that gives rise to Pittsburghese and makes it useful in Pittsburghers' lives and consequential for language change.

To do the sort of historical work I do in this book requires a model of how linguistic form—pronouncing a word one way or another, using one word or another, and so on—and social meaning come to be related. For this purpose, I begin with a model of meaning making developed by the American philosopher Charles Sanders Peirce (1960) and adapted for purposes like mine by anthropologist Michael Silverstein and others. This model helps us understand not just how words and phrases are related to the kinds of meanings that can be found in dictionaries (*denotation*, to use one common term) but also how elements of language on all levels can be linked to other kinds of meaning. It accounts for how using a particular accent can make a speaker sound sophisticated or uneducated, southern or northern, nerdy or hip; how a particular set of words and structures can evoke a professional or personal identity; and how some ways of using language can sound oppositional, others conciliatory, and so on.

The rest of the book explores how this process has worked in Pittsburgh—how the set of ideas that constitutes Pittsburghese has emerged over time, in the context of the set of ideas that constitutes Pittsburgh—and what we can learn from this. I do this in two steps. In chapters 3 and 4, I trace the history of Pittsburghese. I describe the sets of ideas about language, place, class, ethnicity, and identity that have come together in the Pittsburgh area to give rise to Pittsburghese and bond it with local identity. I show how material facts about Pittsburgh and southwestern Pennsylvania—topography, economic history, natural resources, and natural barriers—made this confluence of ideas if not inevitable, then likely. I show how Pittsburgh speech and Pittsburghese impact the sociolinguistic biographies of several generations of Pittsburghers in different ways, shaping how they talk, how they interpret other people's speech, and how they think about themselves, their speech, and their city. I show how the history of Pittsburghese is implicated in the history of Pittsburgh speech, focusing on the details of the processes that give rise to what has been called dialect awareness and the linguistic stereotyping that can lead to language change.

The model of meaning making I sketch in chapter 2 helps us see how links between social meaning and linguistic form are built on, and help build up, frameworks of cultural common sense. The sort of meaning that can link saying "dahntahn" with being an "authentic" Pittsburgher is not the kind of meaning found in a dictionary. Instead, it is a kind of meaning that is built up over time by experiencing two phenomena in the same context. This is referred to as "indexical" meaning, and it will be discussed in more depth in chapter 2. Sets of associations between linguistic forms and meanings that are built on the same framework of cultural common sense have been called "orders of indexicality"

(Silverstein 2003) or "indexical fields"(Eckert 2008). I will show that both these ways of imagining how indexical meanings are organized in the social world are useful, depending on the perspective we adopt. For painting a broad-brush picture of historical change, the idea of orders of indexicality is useful. For modeling how indexicality works in a particular community of speakers, the idea of an indexical field of overlapping frameworks of meaning is useful. I will also propose a third model, "indexical layering," to describe how multiple frameworks for making form-meaning links, arising in different historical contexts for various reasons, can be circulating in a particular speaker's sociolinguistic world at the same time, sometimes overlapping very little, if at all.

Chapters 5–8 explore how the set of ideas and habits that constitute Pittsburghese are transmitted from person to person, over time, and how this set of ideas and habits evolves. I describe a number of situations in which people show each other what they take Pittsburghese to be and what they take it to mean. These include situations in which people are talking about Pittsburghese, in face-to-face conversations of various sorts and in the media: instructing others about it; arguing about it; speaking as experts about it or as curious outsiders, often trying to draw a bright-line boundary between what counts as Pittsburghese and what does not. I also explore situations in which people consume Pittsburghese, in the form ofT-shirts, dolls, and other artifacts whose value lies in what they say about local speech and the people who speak it. Finally, I analyze highly self-conscious performances of Pittsburgh speech, performances that can creatively loosen the ties between linguistic forms and social meanings, shifting the meanings of Pittsburghese to make Pittsburghese useful in shifting ideological and material contexts. Pittsburghers often imagine that when they are talking about or using Pittsburghese they are describing or displaying something that already exists—a dialect. I suggest, on the contrary, that Pittsburghese is an activity, that is, a set of social practices—something people do as they interact.

Doing this requires a model of how indexical meanings are forged in human interaction. For this purpose I use the idea of "enregisterment" proposed by Asif Agha. When the use of a particular speech feature comes to have a particular social meaning for a particular speaker or hearer, it is because that feature has been linked with a particular "register," or way of being or acting. Enregisterment is the process by which people create and share these links. The idea of enregisterment is useful for understanding how people come to agree on the meanings of particular linguistic forms and set of forms and how ways of speaking can come to be more and more focused and consistent across speakers and time. Some of the activities I describe (arguments about Pittsburghese and the production and consumption of Pittsburghese shirts, to give two examples) serve this focusing purpose. As a result, Pittsburghese has, over time, come to consist of a smaller and smaller inventory of items, used in fewer and fewer ways. But Pittsburghese also changes. I show how this can happen in an analysis of performances of Pittsburghese, suggesting that we need to pay attention not just to the focusing functions of enregisterment but also to the ways it can be used creatively.

To make these arguments, I draw on ideas and materials from a variety of sources, assembled over more than a decade. In addition to drawing on the work of many other scholars, I have used a combination of data-collection methods from sociolinguistics, discourse analysis, and ethnography.

Describing the history of Pittsburgh speech has required bibliographic work, pulling together information from dictionaries, linguistic atlases, newspaper articles, and journal publications. To learn about the history of the city, I have relied on the work of historians, particularly historians of labor and economics. I have read accounts of life in Pittsburgh by memoirists and collected representations of Pittsburgh and Pittsburghers in novels and plays. I have also talked to colleagues in many disciplines. Together with Scott Kiesling, I organized a workshop in 2001 where we hosted academics and other professionals who helped us decide what questions to ask and how to go about finding answers. These people included historians, a sociologist, linguists, and museum curators.

Once the project was underway, we set up a Community Advisory Board of local people with a variety of stakes in the project: educational specialists, teachers, museum curators and archivists, a web designer, and six of the Pittsburghers I had already interviewed by then. They helped us decide how to take our research findings back to the community, and in the process showed us a lot about what they found interesting in our work.

To find out how Pittsburghers have talked since recorded speech became available, I was guided by the methods of dialectologists and sociolinguists. Looking for older voices, I viewed films and listened to tapes in the archives of the Western Pennsylvania Historical Society and the Rivers of Steel National Heritage Area and a CD produced by the Cranberry Township Historical Society. With students, I analyzed the voices in local history films produced for public television by Rick Sebak and in police-training films made in Pittsburgh. With assistance from Jennifer Andrus, I conducted forty-five-minute interviews with eighty-one European-American Pittsburghers aimed at eliciting a sample of their speech as well as their conscious beliefs and subconscious attitudes about speech. We also conducted small field experiments: we asked interviewees to read aloud, to tell us whether pairs of words sounded alike or not, and to react to sentences pronounced different ways. Fieldworker Trista Pennington conducted twenty similar interviews with African American Pittsburghers.

Pittsburghese is a multimodal and multimedia phenomenon. It exists in sound, but also in other modes such as pictures, writing, and physical stance; it circulates both face-to-face and via media that include clothing, radio, TV, and the Internet. To study the development of Pittsburghese and the social activities that surround and support it, I have drawn on the oral interviews. I have also assembled collections of print material in which Pittsburghese is the topic, including newspaper and magazine articles, websites, and an online discussion board. I have downloaded and transcribed podcasts and videos posted on the Internet. I have taken pictures of signs, graffiti tags, T-shirts, and bumper stickers. And I have taken notes about things fleetingly seen and overheard.

Throughout this period, I have been a participant observer in the tradition of ethnography. Except for six months in Germany while I was writing this book, I have lived in Pittsburgh the whole time, interacting with Pittsburghers in my job as a professor and in other activities such as dog walking in Frick Park, shopping at the Giant Eagle and in the Strip District, hiking and orienteering in the Allegheny Mountains, attending concerts by the Pittsburgh Symphony Orchestra, riding the bus, listening to local radio and TV, going to doctors' appointments, and living in Squirrel Hill and Downtown. I have also made systematic efforts to engage with Pittsburghers, particularly on the topics of Pittsburgh speech and Pittsburghese. This has been easy, because Pittsburghers love to talk about these things. I have agreed to almost every interview request from the local media, and I have kept track of Pittsburghers' responses to the resulting reports. I have also volunteered my time to speak to more than forty-five community history groups, service organizations, teachers' workshops, alumni reunions, and a retired steelworkers' club. With help from students and the staff of the University of Pittsburgh Libraries Archives Services Center, I mounted a website about Pittsburgh speech and invited readers to contact me. I have answered every one of the many hundreds of e-mails and phone calls I have received from Pittsburghers curious about their speech and my interest in it, or who had a correction or an addition to offer. The story I am about to tell may not be the only possible way of understanding the Pittsburghese phenomenon, but I hope it is a coherent one, and I know it is based on a lot of hard but rewarding work.

2

Yinz Are in Stiller Country: Dialect, Place, and Social Meaning in Language

In this chapter I lay some of the groundwork needed to answer the question I posed in chapter 1: What is the relationship between Pittsburgh speech and Pittsburghese? How does Pittsburgh speech—a set of phonological, lexical, and morphosyntactic features that, according to linguists, can each be heard in the Pittsburgh area, but also elsewhere—feed into Pittsburghese, a shifting set of words and sentences, generated mainly by Pittsburghers, used in stylized performances of Pittsburghers and to illustrate how Pittsburghers are perceived to talk? And how does Pittsburghese feed into Pittsburgh speech, if it does?

Since both Pittsburgh speech and Pittsburghese can be (and have been) referred to as dialects, I begin by exploring what we mean when we discuss dialects. I then introduce the concept of place that we need to see how Pittsburgh speech and Pittsburghese have come to be linked to the city of Pittsburgh. Finally, and crucially, I talk about meaning, asking how words and other signs are linked to objects, ideas, and identities. Doing this means first sketching a theory of semiosis, or meaning making, and describing how sociolinguists have talked about the ways linguistic choices are related to social meanings such as class, gender, and community. Finally, because saying something one way or another or using one word or another is not always meaningful in the social world, I talk briefly about the historical moments at which linguistic variation does tend to become meaningful—when linguistic difference becomes particularly noticeable and usable. Paradoxically (it seems), these are also the moments at which differences among ways of speaking start to level out.

What Is a Dialect?

In the preceding chapter, I talked about "dialect areas" and "dialect awareness." Both of these terms have technical definitions in dialectology and sociolinguistics. I used the term *dialect* much more sparingly, because dialect is not a term of art. Since the earliest days of dialectology, in fact, linguists have been skeptical about the possibility of actually finding ways of speaking that have geographical boundaries of the sort dialects are often thought to have, and the focus of dialectology has shifted away from the attempt to identify and describe regional dialects. Scholars interested in why different people speak differently now tend to pay more attention to reasons for variation that have to do with who people interact and identify with. Scholars with a particular interest in region now try to explain the patterns of usage that can be found in large-scale geographical surveys, without assuming that what they will find are dialects. A glance at the history of dialectology helps explain why regional dialects seem problematic these days.

Regional dialectology was shaped by the same intellectual environment as the geography of the nineteenth and early twentieth centuries was, that is, by nationalism, environmental determinism (the idea that people's behavior was genetically shaped by characteristics of the places they were from, also known as scientific racism), and nostalgia for a more "authentic" way of life (Johnstone 2010). During the nineteenth century, the idea that a nation was bound together by a shared language shaped philologists' search for earlier, perhaps purer, forms of language and dialectologists' search for the isolated, old-fashioned varieties that were thought to be throwbacks to the more authentic language of the "folk."

During the first half of the twentieth century, the focus of geographers, such as Carl Sauer (1925), on regions and regional exceptionalism was mirrored in dialectologists' work on the Linguistic Atlas of the United States and Canada projects, large-scale attempts to map dialect areas based on the words people used for a large number of things and how they pronounced these words (Allen 1973; Kurath, Bloch, and Hansen 1939; McDavid, O'Cain, and Dorrill 1979; Pederson, McDavid, and Leas 1986). Geographers' and dialectologists' idealization was the sort of region around which boundaries could be drawn and which could be identified with a single, labeled dialect such as "North Midland" or "Coastal Southern." It was the sort of region in which the ideal informant would be the most traditional and the least mobile, since this would be the person most likely to embody "indigenous modes of thought and action" (Zelinsky 1995, 110).

But dialectologists and sociolinguists have known since the earliest attempts to map variant forms that the world does not present itself to us with neat linguistic boundaries waiting to be discovered. If, like fieldworkers in the tradition of dialectology, we interview people in various locations about the words they use, and then map the locations where our interviewees use *pail* versus *bucket*, "greasy" versus "greazy," *frying pan* versus *skillet*, we can find places where multiple boundaries coincide. These bundles of "isoglosses," as they are called, may well coincide with cultural boundaries (in these examples, the US north versus the South). But it is never the case that everyone on one side of such a line talks one way and everyone on the other side talks another way. Dialects and dialect boundaries are idealizations. W. N. Francis, a fieldworker on the Survey of English Dialects, points this out on the first page of the introductory chapter of his textbook *Dialectology*: "The truth is that dialect boundaries are usually elusive to the point of non-existence. Very seldom does a traveler cross an imaginary line and suddenly find the people using a new and quite different dialect from that used on the other side of the line" (1983, 2–3). To support the point, Francis quotes nineteenth-century dialectologists like Gaston Paris and Louis Gauchat, likewise claiming that dialects do not really exist. In their textbook, J. K. Chambers and Peter Trudgill similarly point out that "the labels 'dialect' and 'accent' . . . are used by linguists in an essentially ad hoc manner" (1998, 5), since what can actually be observed are continua of variation rather than discrete varieties. Contemporary dialectologists stress the political, historically contingent reasons for dialectology's mapping of boundaries (Auer 2005) and the ways in which people's perceptions of regional dialect boundaries and regionally variable features are ideologically shaped (Niedzielski and Preston 1999; Niedzielski 1999; Preston 1989). What regional dialectologists study today are not dialects, but the distribution of regionally variable features, and what they find are not boundaries but continua—not neat bundles of lines between one way of saying something and another, but fuzziness.

Linguists have also started to wonder about why we are drawn to use the term *dialect* at all. Humans may be born with the tendency to pay attention to talk and to make certain kinds of generalizations and not others about order and form. This means that people who have similar linguistic experiences are likely to make the same generalizations about them and reuse the same words and phrases. Such people can be said to speak "the same" language or variety or to "share" a way of talking. But such sharing is never complete. It must be renegotiated in every interaction. We continually calibrate our language, and our explicit ideas about language, as we speak, write, or use signed languages. Languages and dialects exist as helpful, even necessary, ideas, not as objects that are objectively observable by an outsider. As has been pointed out often, associations between particular features of pronunciation, grammar, and vocabulary, on one hand, and what we think of "languages," "dialects," and (for linguists) "speech communities," on the other hand, arise in talk and other local activities.[1] These activities are both made possible and constrained by larger scale political and economic conditions. In other words, languages and dialects are cultural constructs, produced by a group of people using, orienting to, and/or talking about, a particular set of linguistic features, in a process that also constructs the group itself (Gal and Irvine 1995; Silverstein 1998b).

In general, the sociolinguistics of the later twentieth century moved away from explicit concern with the linguistic effects of space, turning instead to the study of language differences that could be systematically linked to class, gender, and formality (W. Labov 1972c). Early work in sociolinguistics was precisely about how and why speech patterns varied within areas like Martha's Vineyard or the Lower East Side neighborhood of New York, because geographically defined regions are almost never linguistically homogeneous. Language differences are not automatic reflexes of speakers' physical locations or places of origin. Large-scale statistical studies that rank the correlations between demographic variables and linguistic variables find, in fact, that speakers' locations and places of origin sometimes rank very low as predictors of language differences. (Szmrecsanyi 2010). Recently, however, some sociolinguists have turned their attention back to the relationships between language and space, conceptualizing space and place in some new ways and sometimes explicitly drawing on cultural geography as they do so.

PLACE AS LOCATION, PLACE AS MEANING

For most of the twentieth century, geographers envisioned place as "the relative location of objects in the world" (Entrikin 1991, 10). Place in this sense is physical, identifiable by a set of coordinates on a map; one place is different from another place because it is in a different location and has different physical characteristics. Places, in this sense of the word, can be seen objectively, on a map or out of an airplane window, for example. Place relates to human activity by virtue of being the natural, physical setting for it. From this perspective, place might affect human life via its physical characteristics, for example, by enabling a certain kind of agriculture or providing other natural resources or transportation arteries.

This is the concept of place that many people remember from school geography classes in which the world was presented as a set of clearly bounded places with physical characteristics that were reflected in different economic systems and ways of living. A physical concept of place might lead a geographer to describe the area in which Pittsburgh is located as the Allegheny Plateau; western Pennsylvania might be defined as the part of the state that is drained by the Ohio River system. Geographers working in this framework might also delimit regions on the basis of historical or economic criteria. The South in the United States might, for example, be defined historically, as the area of the former Confederacy, or economically, as an area that was once characterized by plantation agriculture and slave labor. Doing geography, in this framework of ideas, is like doing science. The focus is on the large scale and the general, and appropriate research methods are larger scale, often quantitative. Discourses about place, when place is seen as location, are expository: because they exist independently of humans' interpretations, places can be objectively described and explained. Places are, in other words, value neutral; a person is in a place if he or she is physically located there, from a place if he or she was born there. The epistemological underpinnings of this way of thinking about place, and the relationships of humans and places, are positivistic and modernist.

Beginning in the 1970s, some geographers suggested another way of thinking about place that provides a better account of the roles place plays in human life. Humanistic geography, as it is known, is the branch of human geography that is concerned with respects in which space and place are socially constructed.[2] Current humanistic geography, like other branches of postmodern social theory, is deeply influenced by phenomenology. Humanistic geographers investigate place as "the meaningful context of human action" (Entrikin 1991, 10). Seeing human experience as fundamentally "emplaced," these geographers are interested in such things as "sense of place," in the difference between being in a place and "dwelling" there, in the meaning of "home," and in the meanings and uses of ideas about region. According to Yi-Fu Tuan, one of the founders of humanistic geography,[3] "place is not only a fact to be explained in the broader frame of space, but it is also a reality to be clarified and understood from the perspectives of the people who have given it meaning" (1974, 213). Critical geographers in the Marxist and neo-Marxist tradition ask about how discourses about spatiality are produced and circulated and whose interests such discourses serve (Soja 1989).

People develop a sense of place by participating in the shaping of their world (Seamon 1979). That is to say that a SPACE becomes a PLACE through humans' interactions with it, both through physical manipulation, via such activities as agriculture, architecture, and landscaping, and symbolically, via such activities as remembering places, talking about them (Myers 2006; Schegloff 1972), depicting them, and telling stories about them. Places are thus known both sensually and intellectually. People experience places both as repeated, immediate everyday experiences, as "distinctive odors, textural and visual qualities in the environment, seasonal changes . . . how they look as they are approached from the highway" (1977, 152) and in more abstract, articulated ways, as "their location in the school atlas or road map . . . population or number and kind of industries" (153). As Tuan points out (ibid.,161–164), art, education, and politics systematize and focus our sense of place by articulating inchoate experience for the eye and the mind, making the place "visible" in the same way to all members of the group. Stories about places and experiences linked to places can have this function (Johnstone 1990; Finnegan 1998). So can such things as exhibitions in historical museums, tourist brochures, and advertisements, as well as public debate about community development (Crowley 2005; Modan 2007).

Popular labels for places often reflect the ways in which places are constituted through shared experiences and shared orientations. Pittsburgh's informal designations as "the 'Burgh" or "Steel City" reflect the social aspect of place. Because places are meaningful, place is normative, invested with a set of right and wrong ways to be. Being "from" the 'Burgh requires people to orient in one way or another to Pittsburgh practices (to root for the Steelers or to make a point of not doing so, for example). Similarly, being a "real" Pittsburgher can mean acting in certain ways and believing certain things. Being born in Pittsburgh can be less diagnostic of Pittsburgh-ness in this normative sense than wearing a Steelers jersey to work on football-season Fridays or displaying a bumper sticker that says, "Yinz Are in Stiller Country."

In geography, the debate over place in general has been felt in the study of geographical region. Regional geography has its roots in military planning and nationalism. It once consisted of the study of what has been called "traditional region." Regions as defined in this traditional sense are relatively self-contained, endogamous, stable, and long lasting:

> The individual is born into the region and remains with it, physically and mentally, since there is little in-or out-migration by isolated persons and families; and the accidents of birth would automatically assign a person to a specific caste, class, occupation, and social role. An intimate symbiotic relationship between man and land develops over many centuries, one that creates indigenous modes of thought and action, a distinctive visible landscape, and a form of human ecology specific to the locality. (Zelinsky1973, 110)

This is the idealized region on which nineteenth and much twentieth-century dialectology was focused; the sort of region around which a boundary could be drawn and which could be identified with a single, labeled dialect such as "North Midland." In geography, this way of imagining the prototypical region lost favor in the 1950s and 1960s because it encouraged regional exceptionalism (the idea that different regions are fundamentally different) and environmental determinism (the idea that physical characteristics of the environment are responsible for human behaviors).

Instead, in line with the approach to place which we have been exploring, many geographers have come to see regions as meaningful places which individuals construct, as well as select, as reference points. Contemporary regional geography pays attention not just to description but also to "ways of seeing." It highlights the historical contingency of traditional regional theory, which is based on an ideology about place and its relationship to humans that arose from and served nineteenth-century nationalistic politics. It pays attention to the cultural effects of (post-) modernity and to new modes of spatial experience, such as hyperspace. Rather than assuming that there are regions in the world to be discovered, regional historians and geographers now ask, "Where do *regions* come from, and what makes them seem so real?" (Ayers and Onuf 1996, vii). In this framework, borders and boundaries are seen as cultural constructs; regions are subjectively real but objectively hard to define (Meining 1978). The "traditional region" is replaced by the idea that regions are "voluntary"; that is, the results of humans' choices about how to divide the world they experience. Because studying voluntary regions means listening to how nongeographers talk about the world, socially defined regions are also "vernacular" regions. The process by which individuals ground their identities in socially constructed regions is seen as analogous to, or the same as, the process by which people construct, claim, and use ethnic identities (Reed 1982). Language is seen (though not often studied) as part of the process: languages, dialects, and "ways of speaking" create and reflect "at-homeness" in a region (Mugerauer 1985).

The most radically relativistic version of humanistic geography is that place can only be imagined as a social construction. But Tuan and Entrikin, among others, argue for a concept of place that incorporates both its material and its experiential aspects. This is the view I take. Sociolinguists have very rightly tried to get beyond the comparative linguistics of the nineteenth century, with its focus on rivers and mountains as causes of linguistic differentiation, and the naive regionalism of nineteenth and twentieth century dialect atlas projects. In the process, however, we may have turned our gaze too exclusively on the ways sociolinguistic meaning is shaped by language ideology, underplaying how ideology is shaped by people's experiences of the physical and economic world and by facts about what human language is like. To understand the development of Pittsburghese, we need to consider both material and ideological forces—facts about topography, economic history, and language, along with facts about beliefs, habits, and experiences.

Interaction, Experience, and Meaning: How Language and Identity Get Linked

Aspects of how people talk can be correlated with their sex, social class, ethnicity, and other demographic facts. Early dialectologists noted that people with less education, who had traveled less, tended to use older forms of words, and they sometimes sought such people out. In his groundbreaking work in New York in the 1960s, sociolinguist William Labov (1972c) showed that people with lower family incomes made more use of relatively "stigmatized" variants of New York whites' speech, such as the deletion of /r/ after vowels, than did people with higher incomes. His work also showed that men used stigmatized variants more than women did. Although the details are different (sometimes women sound more nonstandard than men, for example), findings like these have been replicated all over the world. But correlation is not the same as causation: the finding that class and language vary together does not imply that a person's class causes him or her to speak in a certain way.

What, then, does account for the sort of sociolinguistic patterns that Labov described? Why do speech patterns vary according to speakers' class and gender, and according to other demographic facts such as their age, place of residence, and level of education? It is tempting to think that different people, and different sets of people, use language differently because it can *mean* something to talk one way versus another. But how do linguistic forms become linked with meanings? To begin to answer this question, we need to first look at the process by which links between linguistic forms and meanings—including "social meanings" such as class and gender—are forged. Second, we need to look at how linguistic forms that have social meaning are deployed in actual social interaction and how social interaction creates opportunities for new meanings to be made. Third, we need to explore the historical factors that make people particularly likely to use language as a social differentiator.

WHAT IS "SOCIAL MEANING"?

As I have noted, facts about people's language are often correlated with facts about their social class, place, gender, social identity, genre, and the like. But such correlations are not always meaningful. Thus, we need a way of modeling the kinds of relationships that can exist between linguistic forms (words, ways of pronouncing words, and so on) and meanings, and we need a framework for understanding when and why linguistic forms can come to have particular kinds of meaning. For the first of these tasks, I draw on semiotic theory, or the theory of how phenomena (linguistic and otherwise) come to have meanings, and what kinds of meanings they can have.

A great deal of twentieth-century linguistics and philosophical language theory, at least in North America, focused on the "literal" meanings of words.[4] Denotation is the sort of meaning that is encoded in dictionaries. From the point of view of denotation, it is thought that the meaning of a sentence can be recovered by parsing its structure and by looking up its words in a mental dictionary. This level of meaning is thought not to vary across contexts; a sentence means the same thing, on this abstract level, no matter who utters it, in what situation. This view of language—that words have fixed meanings that can be looked up in a dictionary, whether the dictionary is a book or a mental list, and that the meanings of sentences can be computed on the basis of the meanings of their words and how the words are put together—is the dominant view in language teaching in the United States, be it the teaching of English or the teaching of foreign languages. Schoolchildren learn the correct meanings of words and how to diagram the structures of sentences. The view of meaning as denotation shapes some of the ways people talk about Pittsburgh speech, as we will see, so we will return to it later on. But denotation is not all there is when it comes to what people mean and what they take other people to mean in actual talk and writing.

Clearly, what a sentence is actually taken to mean varies according to the context in which it is uttered. A sentence that would be appropriate if uttered in one context can seem rude or crazy in another. To account for this, philosophers and linguists have developed theories of "pragmatic" meaning (see, for example, Levinson 1983) that purport to account for how people actually interpret each others' utterances. There are many versions of pragmatic theory, but the basic notion is that speakers and hearers add a layer of calculations about the context on top of calculations about lexical and structural meaning that are needed to figure out the utterance's literal, denotational meaning. For example, according to speech act theory (Searle 1969), in order to decide whether "it's chilly in here" is to be taken as a request to close a window or simply an assertion of fact, the addressee calculates whether the speaker would benefit from the addressee's taking action, whether the addressee is able to take action, whether the speaker really desires the action (or, alternatively, is being ironic), and so on.

However, whether one person can request another person's compliance in the first place has to do with power relations. It is easier for a superior to make a request of a social inferior than the other way around, and social superiority and inferiority are connected with identities like boss, teacher, sergeant, and sometimes male or white versus identities like employee, student, private, or female or black. It is easier to make a request of someone socially closer than someone socially more distant, and social closeness is connected with identities like spouse, neighbor, and friend. Some individuals are more intimidating, some more approachable. Because of this, linguists needed a way of thinking about how social and personal identities and linguistic forms are related. For this, we turn to semiotics, or the theory of meaning. We ask, in general, how things-that-mean-something (we call them SIGNS) work, whether the signs are words, ways of dressing, dance moves, or anything else that can have meaning to humans. In particular, we ask how linguistic choices can locate people in the social world.

The model of semiotics I sketch in what follows is based on the work of the American philosopher Charles Sanders Peirce. I borrow heavily from the interpretation of Peirce's semiotic theory that is associated with linguistic anthropologists Michael Silverstein and Asif Agha, though the use I make of Peircian semiotics differs from theirs in some ways. Pierce distinguished among three ways in which phenomena (including linguistic ones) could be taken as meaningful signs. A linguistic sign is ICONIC to the extent that it is taken to resemble what it means. When< Place pdf of pencil image >s used to refer to a pencil, it is functioning as an iconic sign. A sign is SYMBOLIC to the extent that it is related to its meaning by convention rather than by resemblance. The word *pencil* is functioning as a symbol when it is taken to refer to a pencil. Because the sign (the word *pencil*) does not resemble the thing it refers to, the word *pencil* can also be used for other things that may or may not actually involve a pencil: you can "pencil someone in" for an appointment via keyboard or pen rather than by using a pencil. INDEXICALITY refers to the way signs are related to meanings by virtue of co-occurring with the things they are taken to mean. When we hear thunder, we often experience lightning, rain, and a darkening sky, so the sound of thunder may lead us to expect a storm. Because the sound of thunder evokes storminess in this way, thunder noise can be used to evoke a storm in a staged play.

Likewise, if hearing a particular word is experienced in connection with a particular style of dress or grooming, a particular set of social alignments, or a particular social activity, that word may evoke and/or create the situation or social identity. To many Americans, the sentence "take out your pencils" evokes a situation in which a person whose relevant social identity is "student" is about to engage in an activity known as taking a quiz in school. The relationship between the word and the identity is an indexical relationship; we can say that the word INDEXES the situation or identity; the word can be called an INDEXICAL (or an INDEX) to the extent that it serves this purpose. Indexical meanings can be widely shared, the way the meaning of "take out your pencils" is. Indexical meanings can also be very particular. To me, pencils evoke my Aunt Barb, a writer who always had a can of freshly sharpened pencils at hand. As we will see, particular linguistic features can likewise index the identities of individuals and the identities of groups. Just as words can index situations and identities, by virtue of being experienced together with other evidence of them, so can any other kind of linguistic form: ways of pronouncing sounds, phrases, grammatical patterns, patterns of discourse, even linguistic consistency or inconsistency over a lifetime (Johnstone 2009).

All signs can have all three kinds of meaning, and signs that start out as indexicals may turn into conventionalized symbols that can sometimes come to seem as if they iconically depict what they mean. When a child hears a word for the first time, it is in the context of the thing the word refers to, and children learn to use words to create a context in which the thing exists. For example, a child hears "ball" when there is a ball in the environment—European-American children often have older people actually pointing to a ball as they say the word—and eventually this creates an indexical link between the thing and the word. The child learns both to label the ball and to use the word *ball* as a command, that is, to make a ball appear. The link between the word and the thing it refers to becomes symbolic when the child learns to read the word, spell it, and look it up in a dictionary. A schematic picture, like a two-dimensional drawing of a ball, is both iconic (it looks somewhat like a ball) and symbolic (in order to interpret a two-dimensional picture, we rely on conventional ways of visually translating two dimensions into three). The stick figures on the doors of airport bathrooms are as conventional (men and women do not look like stick figures) as they are iconic (yet there is some visual connection between the lines in the figures and the legs, arms, torso, and head of a human body, and the female figures often include lines that sketch something like a skirt.). Words can be both indexical and symbolic: words like *aleatory* or *lessor* are conventionally related to what they mean, and their use also indexes a specialized sort of discourse, scientific or musical in the case of *aleatory* and legal in the case of *lessor*. Using one of these words can both evoke and help create the context in which it usually appears.

The use of one pronunciation option versus another can also come to have social meaning of various kinds. If you hear people from the southern United States pronounce *time* as [ta:m] ("tahm") and *my* as [ma:] ("mah"), you may come to hear the monophthongal pronunciation of /ay/ ("ah") as an index of southernness. This form-meaning link can become symbolic, used when there are no southerners around as a conventional way of suggesting southernness (for example, by actors pretending to be southern). And it can seem iconic, such as when people describe this feature of southern speech as lazy, attributing the sound to a supposed temperamental characteristic of its users. This linguistic feature has different kinds of meaning to different people: some may hear it as southern but may not be able to use it in a conventional way to suggest south-ernness; some may hear it as southern but not hear it as lazy, and so on. And to some people (for example, English-speakers from other counties), the fact that a person pronounces *time* as [ta:m] rather than some other way may have no meaning at all—some people may simply not be able to hear the difference. Not all indexical meaning is social meaning, and not all social meaning is indexical; aspects of everything we do when we talk—both what we say and how we say it—can be correlated with speakers' social identities and can be taken up by others as signs of these identities.

SOCIAL MEANING IN INTERACTION: SOCIAL NETWORKS AND COMMUNITIES OF PRACTICE

I noted earlier that a child learns that the word *ball* means what it does by hearing the word in the context of an example of the object—a ball. This happens in the course of social interaction: other people have to interact with the child. A child in isolation could not make semiotic links between words and meanings. Like-wise, links between linguistic choices and social meanings, like *southerner*, are made in the context of social interaction. There are two major strands of research about how linguistic variation is related to patterns of social interaction. The two strands focus, respectively, on SOCIAL NETWORKS and COMMUNITIES OF PRAC-TICE. Both approaches share the basic assumption that language changes are sparked by people adapting their speech to the speech of people around them, although the interpretations of why they do this are different.

The social network approach was pioneered by Lesley Milroy (L. Milroy 1987) through research in three working-class neighborhoods in Belfast, Northern Ireland. Drawing on models of social networks and their effects proposed by sociologists (Boissevain 1974; Granovetter 1973), Milroy explored how people's networks of friends, acquaintances, and relatives were related to how and when they used features of the Belfast vernacular variety of English. The variants

Milroy looked at were ones that, in the wider world, were stigmatized: they sounded substandard or incorrect. And yet using these features clearly had social value for some speakers. Milroy used social network theory to model why.

Social networks differ based on their DENSITY and MULTIPLEXITY. An individual's social network is relatively dense if the people with whom the individual is linked tend to know each other. A typical US elementary school classroom in which teacher and pupils are together all day is a dense social network, because each pupil interacts with all the other pupils and with the teacher. A typical university classroom is likely to be a less dense social network, since, while each student interacts with the instructor and vice versa, the students may or may not interact with each other. An individual's social network is relatively multiplex if the individuals in it interact with each other in multiple ways—if, for example, the mail carrier is also a neighbor, or if your doctor's children go to school with your children.

Milroy found that people with denser, more multiplex social networks tended to use more Belfast vernacular speech features, despite the fact that these features were seen as lower status. This was true both of demographic groups of people and of individuals. Women tended to have lower scores for network density and multiplexity than men, partly because women were more likely to work outside their neighborhood. Accordingly, women used fewer vernacular features than men. Individuals with higher network scores were more likely to sound vernacular, like their neighbors, than individuals with lower network scores. According to Milroy, this is because social networks are norm-enforcement mechanisms. Networks that are dense and multiplex tend to enforce local norms, in speech as well as in other aspects of behavior. New ways of doing things are less likely to come into the system than is the case for looser, more open networks, and the same people interact with each other often, modeling the same ways of doing things.

Penelope Eckert (2000) draws on the idea of social networks and takes it a step further. Asking, with Milroy, why people would use stigmatized linguistic forms, Eckert explores the "linguistic marketplaces" (Bourdieu 1977, 1991) in which choices of one form or another have social value. Eckert proposed that some linguistic marketplaces could be characterized as communities of practice (Wenger 1998). A community of practice is "an aggregate of people who come together around some enterprise," coming to "develop and share ways of doing things, ways of talking, beliefs, values—in short, practices—as a function of their joint engagement in activity" (Eckert 2000, 35). A community of practice may be engaged, among other things, in the mutual creation and perpetuation of a "style," or a way of acting, appearing, and talking. In the urban US high school Eckert studied, communities of practice known as "jocks" and "burnouts" were organized in part around opposing styles. The school-oriented jocks dressed for success, participated in after-school activities, planned on attending a university, and chose standard"-sounding alternatives for the pronunciation of a number of vowels, alternatives that sounded more like teachers and newscasters. The school-alienated burnouts imagined a local, working-class future for themselves. They dressed differently than the jocks; their extra-curricular activities were city-oriented ones like "cruising" the city streets; and they chose the more local, more nonstandard-sounding (and in this case newer) variants of the vowels.

For Eckert, as for Milroy, people accommodate linguistically to the people they interact with. But in Milroy's social network model, accommodation is an automatic result of the fact that a social network creates de facto norms. If a social network is dense and multiplex, such that everyone talks to everyone else, in multiple contexts, members of the network have no other option but to sound alike. For Eckert, on the other hand, speakers are agents in the "continual construction and reproduction of [the linguistic system]" (43). People choose who to be in a particular situation by choosing what style to adopt. This does not mean that people are fully conscious of what such a choice implies at every level. Burnouts may be able to identify themselves explicitly as burnouts, but they cannot describe the phonological choices they make. People in a community of practice are agents in that they can bring new ways of doing things into the community's style, choose to adopt some aspects of the style and reject others, or choose to drop out of the community altogether.

When Does Language Matter?

Milroy and Eckert both did their work in settings where linguistic differences had social meaning: people's language choices showed how they were integrated into their communities, and sounding one way or another could have social consequences. There are situations, however, in which linguistic difference is *not* used as a local resource for mapping social difference. For example, Nancy Dorian (1994; 2010) studied the residents of several small, isolated fishing villages in northeast Scotland where Gaelic was spoken. She found a wide range of variation in the Gaelic of people who were, in demographic terms, alike: siblings, age mates, friends, and so on. Although people in these East Sutherland villages thought there was a correct way of speaking Gaelic, and suspected that they spoke it poorly, they had no access to the standard norms. (The language was used less and less frequently, and opportunities to hear other people speaking it were rare.) In this situation, small differences among speakers did not matter—variation did not do social work. As long as a person could sustain a conversation in Gaelic, he or she was treated as a Gaelic-speaker. People did not attend to details of pronunciation and grammar. This shows that links between linguistic options and social meanings are not inevitable. Whether people link linguistic variation to social variation at all, and how they make such links, depends on sets of ideas about what sorts of work linguistic variation can do and what social identities can be attached to linguistic options. These ideas are shaped, in part, by historical facts.

In 1962, American novelist John Steinbeck published a memoir about traveling in a camper truck across the United States, accompanied by his dog Charley. Noticing the increasing availability of radio and television, Steinbeck mourned the loss of the regional speech differences he remembered from his youth:

> It seemed to me that regional speech is in the process of disappearing, not gone but going. Forty years of radio and twenty years of television must have this impact. Communications must destroy localness, by a slow, inevitable process. I can remember a time when I could almost pinpoint a man's place of origin by his speech. That is growing more difficult now and will in some foreseeable future become impossible. It is a rare house or building that is not rigged with spiky combers of the air. Radio and television speech becomes standardized, perhaps better English than we have ever used. (1980, 106)

Steinbeck was not the first American to suppose that regional differences in speech were "in some foreseeable future" fated to disappear. His concern was to some extent justified. Sparked by Peter Trudgill's (1986) book *Dialects in Contact*, sociolinguists have arrived at an increasingly nuanced understanding of "dialect leveling," or the ways in which dialects can lose aspects of their distinctiveness when their speakers come into contact with speakers of other dialects. According to Trudgill, contact among speakers who use different linguistic forms might be expected to lead to linguistic accommodation by speakers needing to express solidarity or avoid miscommunication with others (Giles, Taylor, and Bourhis 1973). Over the long run, this might be expected to lead to a reduction in the number of differences between dialects.

In the United States, as in Europe, industrialization beginning in the eighteenth century led people to move from the countryside to the cities. Subsequent developments included the emergence of suburbs and "new towns" during the twentieth century and a current "urban revival" trend that in some cases is shifting poorer people outward from city centers as wealthier people move back in. The sociolinguistic consequences of these historical developments have included dialect leveling and the formation of "new dialects" when sets of simplified, mixed, and leveled forms are no longer identified with the source varieties (Kerswill 2005).

Dialect leveling has been documented in many geographic settings, including England (Kerswill and Williams 2000; Britain 2002; Watt 2002), the United States (Thomas 2003), and Europe (Auer, Hinskens, and Kerswill 2005), as well as in a number of colonial varieties of English (Trudgill 1986) and other languages (Trudgill 2006). However, according to Auer, Hinskens, and Kerswill, "It is too early yet to tell if the internationalisation of economic and administrative structures and the increase in international communication . . . will strengthen or weaken the traditional dialects" (2005, 36). For one thing, if only one variety is available in a speaker's environment, accommodation is not an option. When urbanization is accompanied by the formation of ethnic or working-class neighborhood enclaves, traditional distinctions may be enforced via the kinds of dense, multiplex social networks I discussed previously (L. Milroy 1987). Similar processes, in the context of residential and educational segregation, are responsible for the maintenance of substantial differences between the English of some African Americans and that of nearby whites.

Furthermore, leveling is not the only consequence of dialect contact. Research in the United States (Labov, Ash, and Boberg 2005) and in the United Kingdom (Watt 2002; Watt and Milroy 1999) suggests that leveling at the subregional level has been accompanied by the maintenance and even increase of dialect differentiation among larger "supra-local" dialects such as midland versus northern speech in the United States or northern versus southern speech in England. On a more local level, too, the linguistic effects of dialect contact are unpredictable. Schilling-Estes (2002) compares two once-isolated islands off the east coast of the United States whose residents are now in massive contact with outsiders. While the pronunciation of /ay/ (as in *tide*) on one of the islands is becoming more similar to the dominant, mainland pronunciation, the pronunciation of the same sound the other island is becoming more dissimilar to that of the mainland. Schilling-Estes suggests that there are linguistic, social, and attitudinal factors at work to differentiate the behavior of the two island varieties in the face of contact. The details of the sound's function in the linguistic system, how the local-sounding form is socially marked, and what kind of population shift is taking place all affect the outcome of dialect contact in these two places.

The fact that the social meanings of linguistic forms can change means that forms that once sounded nonlocal can be preserved if they come to have new meaning in the local context. Dyer (2002) shows, for example, that forms that migrating laborers brought from Scotland to an English steel town called Corby soon stopped sounding Scottish and instead came to signal Corby identity in opposition to a nearby English town. In Glasgow, Stuart-Smith, Timmins, and Tweedie (2007) show that, contrary to what we might expect, the people with the loosest social networks and the most ties to speakers of English English are maintaining distinctive Scottish features in their speech, while less mobile working-class adolescents are adopting nonlocal forms that distinguish them from other Glaswegians.

Further complicating the picture are people's attitudes about regional varieties vis-à-vis other varieties. Auer, Hinskens, and Kerswill (2005) discuss "sociolinguistic polarisation." Sociolinguistic polarization can be defensive, if people refuse to adopt new forms from elsewhere (in which case it inhibits the borrowing of new linguistic features from outside), or offensive, if people aggressively adopt outside forms. According to Auer et al., "It would seem that a precondition for sociolinguistic polarisation, be it defensive or offensive in nature, is a certain level of awareness of the spreading feature in the consciousness of speakers of the 'threatened' dialect" (2005, 9).

Joan Beal (2010) shows how contemporary popular discourse about the loss of regional speech differences echoes the discourse of the late eighteenth and early nineteenth centuries, when "the enclosure of common land, the mechanisation of agriculture, and the Industrial Revolution . . . caused people to move from the countryside into rapidly-expanding industrial towns and cities" (139). Many of the English dialects that are now considered endangered were themselves the result of leveling processes sparked by this previous era of geographic mobility. In England, a boom in dialect dictionaries in the nineteenth and early twentieth centuries was accompanied by a surge in dialect literature and the development of regional dialect societies. In the United States, nineteenth-century "local color" fiction featured respelled representations of regional dialects, and actors performing stereotypical regional characters were popular on the entertainment circuit. The American Dialect Society was founded in 1889, at the height of the Gilded Age of industrialization and the immigration and geographical mobility that accompanied it.

A similar burst of regional dialect awareness appears to characterize popular culture at the beginning of the twenty-first century. A British rock band, the Arctic Monkeys, who might once have wanted to sound American (Trudgill 1983, 141–60), now features words associated with Sheffield, their city of origin (Beal 2009). Advertisements feature representations of their target audiences' dialects, even if they are nonstandard or minority dialects (King and Wicks 2009). Internet sites now supplement folk dictionaries; one called Slanguage offers to help viewers "talk like the locals in cities around the world."[5] Groups on social networking sites emerge around regional identities, and membership often requires knowing or acting as if one knows the correct regional words for things.

To summarize, economic and cultural globalization and the attending social and geographical mobility and dialect contact seems to result in two contradictory trends: increased dialect leveling and increased talk about dialect. To put in another way, globalization both erases objectively visible linguistic difference via leveling and dialect loss, and creates ideological difference among imagined language varieties via increased popular attention to variation. This is because the noticing of difference that occurs as a consequence of dialect contact may lead to semiotic change of two sorts. Dialect contact can lead to accommodation by people who need to understand one another or who identify with one another. This can lead to dialect leveling. But dialect contact can lead people to notice, and sometimes to reinforce, differences among ways of speaking. Both of these things have happened in Pittsburgh.

3

From Pittsburgh Speech
to Pittsburghese

As we have seen, if the historical and ideological conditions are right, a set of linguistic features that can be heard in an area can become linked to one another as a dialect and ideologically associated with localness. This association happens when people start noticing these features and attributing meaning to them. People attribute indexical meaning to the features first and then symbolic or iconic meaning later, when the features and meanings are abstracted from the social interaction in which they were originally heard. The idea of a regional dialect can help create a place, in the sense of the term proposed by humanistic geographers: hearing features of the dialect can evoke and help shape the meaning of the place. So can simply knowing that there is such a dialect.

In this chapter, I explore how this process has played out in Pittsburgh. I begin by describing the key precondition for the development of Pittsburghese: the fact that there are linguistic features hearable in southwestern Pennsylvania that are not heard everywhere. If people in the Pittsburgh area were linguistically indistinguishable from people elsewhere, the idea of Pittsburgh speech would never have emerged. I trace the history of language in southwestern Pennsylvania, focusing on four periods, beginning with the Scotch-Irish immigrants, on whom later immigrants modeled their speech. I then turn to the industrial immigrants from Europe who arrived in the Pittsburgh area in the late nineteenth and early twentieth centuries. I describe how immigrants and their children learned English when they did. For these people, the identities that were noticeable and linked to ways of talking were ethnic identities linked with a variety of European languages, as well as identities linked with whether a person could speak English—such as whether one was a foreman or a laborer at work. Different ways of speaking English were not part of their sociolinguistic world, and so could not be heard as meaningful.

Around the middle of the twentieth century, differences among ways of speaking English started to become noticeable, due to social and geographic mobility that put working-class Pittsburghers into contact with people who spoke differently than they did. I describe how indexical meaning arises from correlations people notice between different ways of speaking and different ways of acting and being, and how this meaning-making process can recur over time, so that a particular feature or a way of speaking involving a number of features can have multiple meanings. I show why Pittsburgh speech came to have the meanings it did, when it did. I suggest that the baby-boom grandchildren of early twentieth-century immigrants played a key role in linking Pittsburgh speech with place and local identity, when traditional identities failed them and they had to reimagine themselves. Finally, I describe how young people experience Pittsburgh speech and Pittsburghese and what new meanings and uses they have created for it.

The Founders

When two groups of people are separated in space, not communicating with each other, their speech patterns will inevitably become increasingly different. Over many centuries, one language can evolve into many languages whose speakers can no longer understand the other languages. Classical Latin, for example, gave rise to French, Spanish, Portuguese, Italian, Catalan, and other languages when Romans moved to the provinces of their empire and out of easy touch with people in other provinces. Over the shorter term, communicative isolation can lead to dialect differentiation, the gradual formation of differences that are salient enough that people notice them and start treating the two varieties as different. North American varieties of English have diverged far enough from British varieties of English in the course of four hundred years or so that some American movies are subtitled for British audiences and vice versa.

In the United States, there are now three major dialect areas that correspond to early patterns of settlement and westward migration. The original English-speaking migrants to New England and the southern colonies tended to be from southern England. The settlers in the middle-Atlantic states tended to be from further north, and their English was different in many ways from that spoken in southern England. Many early settlers farmed, and as farmers moved west, they tended to stay at the same latitude, so that the seeds they brought with them would be able to grow in a similar climate. As figure 3.1 shows, the main dialect areas in the eastern United States still reflect the diverse origins of these migrants.

Pittsburgh is in the midland area, and most features of Pittsburghers' speech reflect midland usages. The first English-speaking settlers in eastern Pennsylvania were Quakers, mainly from the north of England. Southwestern Pennsylvania was, for a time, on the Virginia frontier, and early English-speakers in Virginia would have been from southern England. But the Virginians who explored and surveyed the area (including George Washington) tended not to settle there. The midland speech patterns common throughout Pennsylvania,

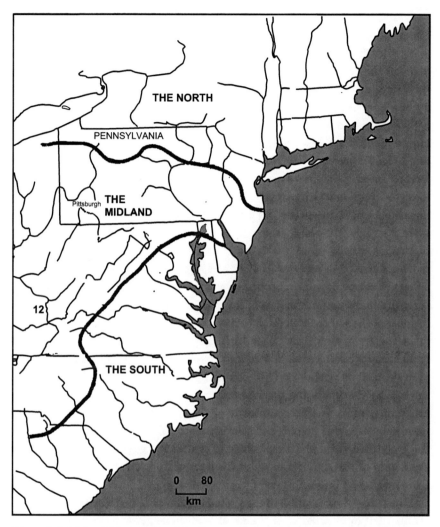

Figure 3.1 Major Dialect Areas of the Eastern United States. (Adapted from Kurath 1949, figure 3).

and, by now, throughout much of the United States, probably have their origins in the mixture of the varieties of English spoken by early settlers in the eastern part of the state, where the Quakers' tolerance for religious differences attracted immigrants from throughout the British Isles.

As I noted in chapter 1, the speech features that distinguish central and western Pennsylvania from the rest of the state have to do with the particularly heavy influence in this area of the speech of Scotch-Irish settlers. For the most part, the Scotch-Irish people's ancestors were from lowland Scotland, northern England, and the borderland in between.[1] In 1610, the King of England and Scotland, James Stuart, began to offer land in the northern counties of Ireland to these people, providing they would move there. This policy, known as the Ulster Plantation, was meant to pacify rebellious northern Irish Catholics by settling (or "planting") Protestants, who were loyal to the King, in their midst. Many of the people whose descendants were eventually known as Scotch-Irish were among these settlers. They settled mainly in the Irish counties of Armagh, Tyrone, Londonderry, and Farmanagh, and in parts of Donegal.

Life in Ireland was difficult for the English and Scottish Protestant immigrants, due, among other things, to religious hostility and poor harvests. Northern Ireland's growing population caused competition for land, which made land-rents rise, sometimes dramatically. There were periodic downturns in the linen industry on which many depended, some caused by trade restrictions on linen and wool. Between the 1680s and the American Revolution of 1775–1783, more than 250,000 people from northern Ireland emigrated to America, many of them descendants of the Scottish and English immigrants.[2] The largest numbers arrived in America in 1772 and 1773, when the Irish linen industry suffered a severe downturn because of competition with cotton fabric manufactured in America. After the Revolution perhaps half a million more arrived.

Most of the Scotch-Irish disembarked at the ports of the Delaware Valley and made their way west from there. In Pennsylvania, they settled mainly in the mountainous west-central and western parts of the state, because the better agricultural land farther east had already been claimed by English and German settlers. By the end of the American Revolution, the population of southwestern Pennsylvania was predominantly of Scotch-Irish ancestry, with a smaller number of people of English and German origin. Among the many town names the Scotch-Irish brought from Ireland to central and western Pennsylvania are the names of the counties many of them came from: Armagh, Tyrone, Derry, Farmanagh, and Donegal.

Scotch-Irish immigration to the United States continued into the nineteenth century, but by the middle of the century, most immigrants from Ireland were Catholics from the south, many of them victims of the potato-blight famine of 1845. In the meantime, many descendants of the early Scotch-Irish settlers had moved into the economic and social elite. The term *Scotch-Irish* had been in use during the colonial period (Leyburn 1962; Montgomery 2001), but many of the immigrants had referred to themselves simply as Irish. Scotch-Irish came into wider use toward the end of the nineteenth century, as a way for Americans of Irish Protestant ancestry to distinguish themselves from the newer, poorer, Irish Catholic immigrants. As T. G. Fraser describes it:

> At the first convention of the Scotch-Irish Congress, held at Columbia, Tennessee, in May 1898 "to preserve the history and perpetuate the achievements of the Scotch-Irish race in America," delegates had warmed to the message of how they had helped forge contemporary

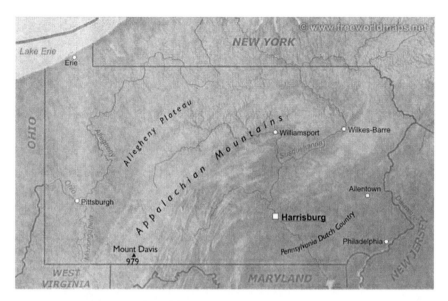

Figure 3.2 Relief Map of Pennsylvania (Source: http://www.freeworldmaps.net/
united-states/pennsylvania/pennsylvania-map.jpg).

America . . . Those descendants of the Ulster immigrants wished to
mark a clear division between themselves and more recent immigrant
groups, not least the Catholic Irish who had come in large numbers in
the wake of the Famine. (1997, vii–viii)

As figure 3.2 shows, the Pittsburgh area is separated from the rest of the eastern
United States by the Allegheny Mountains, part of the Appalachian range.
For early settlers, the journey across the mountains was long and difficult, so
there was little travel back and forth. Isolated from the linguistic influence of the
east, the speech of the Scotch-Irish settlement areas in central and western
Pennsylvania diverged in some respects from the speech of eastern Pennsylvania. In accordance with a well-known phenomenon known as the "founder
effect" (Mufwene 1996), or the "doctrine of first effective settlement" (W. Labov
2001b, 503–504), later immigrants, no matter what their background, tried to
adopt the speech patterns of the people who were already there.

Even as Pittsburghers of Scotch-Irish ancestry moved into the economic and
social elite, they remained relatively isolated from the outside world. According
to historian John Ingrahm (1989), the Pittsburgh elite were mostly Scotch-Irish
Presbyterians, both in the city's early mercantile days and in the later industrial
period. (While there were also wealthy Pittsburghers of German ancestry, the
German community was more fragmented than the Scotch-Irish community, in
part due to religious differences among the Germans.) The Scotch-Irish elite
tended to marry within their own community. The Pittsburgh upper class was

relatively provincial and not mobile well into the twentieth century, according to Ingrahm. Sons of the wealthy steel barons and merchants were sent east to prep schools and Ivy League colleges, but they often returned home to marry. Because they tended not to participate in the business mergers of the early twentieth century, many Pittsburgh businesses remained local.

To summarize, Pittsburgh's settlement history, the topography of Pennsylvania, and the inward-oriented culture of the Scotch-Irish-descended elite all came together with the desire of later immigrants to learn to speak like the locals to result in a distinctive southwestern Pennsylvania way of speaking. While the speech of the Pittsburgh area no longer sounds like that of the original Scotch-Irish settlers, its sounds have remained distinctive in some ways, and it carries traces of its Scotch-Irish origins in the words and grammatical patterns I described earlier.

Industrial Immigrants: Learning English in Pittsburgh in the Early Twentieth Century

There is very little evidence about how people talked in Pittsburgh before the middle of the twentieth century. Data about word choice and pronunciation from the *Dialect Atlas of the Middle Atlantic States* (Kurath and McDavid 1961; Kurath 1949; McDavid et al., 1979), collected in the 1940s, includes information about Pittsburgh-area English speakers born as early as the 1860s, but the project's focus on rural speakers means that it is not a good source for the study of urban speech, and it gives us no evidence about how newcomers to the area sounded. However, historical research about the social history of the city, and cities like it, provides enough clues to allow at least a tentative sketch of the linguistic lives of the European immigrants who came in droves to Pittsburgh at the end of the nineteenth century and the beginning of the twentieth. As was also the case elsewhere (T. G. Labov 1998), the shift from the European homeland language to English was usually complete in three generations.

In 1907, a group of Chicago sociologists (Byington 1974; Fitch 1989) conducted a survey of Pittsburgh. Writing about immigrants in Homestead, a steel-mill town across the Monongahela River from Pittsburgh, sociologist Margaret Byington described the isolation experienced by Eastern European immigrant families. They did not speak English and, as Byington noted, "to the better class of entertainments they are not welcomed" (151). This made them "keep up their own festivities" (151), which distanced them even further from the native-born residents of the town. Even once immigrant families were able to buy homes, English-speaking neighbors were not welcoming. To the native-born "Teutons" and "Celts" of Homestead, and to Byington herself, "the Slav" belonged to a different race.[3] Though Byington took pains to avoid racism in her account of Eastern European families, their neighbors often did not.

Until 1906, it was not necessary to know English to become an American citizen (Pavlenko 2002), and this may also have discouraged first-generation immigrants from making the effort. Widespread illiteracy, along with the need for constant work, made it difficult in any case to take advantage of opportunities to learn English like those offered by the Carnegie Libraries and at some workplaces. Furthermore, ethnic groups were often segregated from one another in the steel mills where they worked, reducing the need for a common language. In some cases this was because ethnic or national groups controlled the hiring in their divisions of the mills, bringing in friends and relatives. In other cases it was because the people of German, Irish, and English ancestry who managed the mills encouraged ethnic identification among the people who worked in them. Steel companies like the one in Steelton, Pennsylvania, studied by John E. Bodnar (1979) enforced rigid segregation by national group, partly to discourage collective action that might lead to unionization.

Ethnic fraternal organizations were founded early and also encouraged immigrants to keep themselves apart from American life and to continue speaking their homeland languages. According to labor historian Bodnar (1987, 120–130), many fraternal organizations started out as mechanisms for mutual financial aid, that is, to cover expenses such as burials. Some were founded explicitly as secular organizations "to mute the influence of religious . . . leaders with workers" (123), while others were founded by priests. These organizations served other functions as well, such as preserving ethnic history and culture. Some had rules stipulating that only the homeland ethnic language could be used for association business. Fraternal organizations also became crucial in immigrant politics. Membership in ethnic fraternal organizations was so central an expression of ethnic identity that one elderly woman I interviewed, whose children and grandchildren all identified themselves as Italian Americans, insisted that she was not Italian, since she did not belong to "any of the Italian clubs."

Ethnic churches also encouraged segregation among ethnic groups and the preservation of the homeland language. Describing Homestead in 1907, Byington noted that the church was the most important institution for the Slavic immigrants, offering social and educational services as well as religious ones. The priests did not speak English, and activities were conducted in the homeland languages (Byington 1974, 159). Describing the history of religion in Pittsburgh, Linda Prichard notes that, "between 1904 and 1931, a new church was founded every thirty days" (1989, 339). According to Prichard, most of these were ethnic, or "national," parishes organized by Poles, Slovaks, Hungarians, Croatians, and Italians and often funded by ethnic fraternal organizations. Earlier German immigrants had established the right of ethnic communities to their own parishes by arguing for parishes "populated by Germans, [led] by a

German priest, and stocked with German rituals" (339). Not all new parishes were Roman Catholic, however. At least seven Orthodox congregations were established in Pittsburgh after 1910, and Pittsburgh was a major center of the Byzantine Rite Catholic Church, which served Czech immigrants. Ethnic fraternal associations helped fund these churches.

Many ethnic parishes had parochial schools in which immigrants' children were taught at least partly in their parents' homeland language. The church hierarchy encouraged the establishment of parochial schools in Catholic ethnic parishes. Some fraternal organizations actually required members to send their children to ethnic parochial schools, fearing that children would lose their ethnic values and their religion if they did not. Bodnar (1987) notes that, in Chicago, all but two Catholic parishes had parochial schools by 1883, even though the people in most of these parishes were poor. In 1880, there were thirty-five Roman Catholic churches and forty-three parochial schools in Pittsburgh, with over twelve thousand children enrolled (Prichard 1989, 335). By 1921, there were 390 parochial schools. Describing a parochial school in Homestead in 1907, Margaret Byington noted that such schools kept immigrants' children segregated from others and discouraged the use of English: "The parochial schools not only fail to provide adequate instruction, but also hinder the work of amalgamation in which public schools are so potent a factor. If the foreign children played and studied with American children, barriers to mutual understanding would be overcome. Moreover, they do not come into contact with intelligent American women. Of the six teachers in the Slavic Roman Catholic school, three spoke English fluently, though not correctly, three spoke almost none" (1974, 159). Although the principal claimed that, except for religion and Slavic language, classes were taught in English, Byington observed that the teaching of English was "inadequate."

After World War I, however, immigrants came under increasing pressure to learn English. War in Europe brought to American attention the fact that there were many Europeans living in the United States, some of whom might not support American policies. Nationalism had always been partly based on the idea that a nation-state would be tied together by a national language, among other things, and, as Aneta Pavlenko puts it, "eventually, concerns about the 'immigrant invasion,' combined with the anti-German hysteria and xenophobia engendered by World War I, led to the convergence of Americanization, Anglicization, and Anglo-Saxonization and to the emergence of a hegemonic discourse which established English monolingualism as a constitutive part of American national identity" (2002, 174). Immigrants and their children were encouraged, and sometimes even required, to learn English, as a putative path to social mobility and acceptance in American society. English classes were offered at work, because companies such as U.S. Steel were afraid that "it was low proficiency in English that made their workers easy prey to socialist propaganda, and

that acquiring English would also make them internalize free-enterprise values"
(180). Ironically, labor unions were also interested in having immigrants learn
English, so they could understand the need for strikes and the details of disputes
with management. According to Bodnar (1987, 99–100), "On Chicago's South
Side unionization became a process of Americanization," and the same was no
doubt true in Pittsburgh.

English and acculturation classes were also offered elsewhere (McClymer
1982; Pavlenko 2002). For example, "Progressive International Institutes," at
first sponsored by the YWCA, provided immigrant women and girls with English
classes, recreation, clubs, and assistance with housing and legal matters (Mohl
1982). One of the International Institutes was in Pittsburgh. Settlement houses
also encouraged English-learning (Prichard 1989, 342–343). In Pittsburgh, the
Kingsley House opened in 1893 in the Strip District, backed by the elite from
Presbyterian, Unitarian, Episcopalian, and Roman Catholic churches. The goals
of the settlement houses were to improve living conditions for immigrants,
teach them better personal habits, and, sometimes, convert them to their own
religions.

Although public schools "were always interested in using the classroom to
inculcate American values and beliefs in the foreign-born" (Bodnar 1987, 190),
vocational training sometimes was seen as equally, if not more important, for
immigrant children. Even in this context, it was thought that "training in the
English language and American government would instill patriotism and loyalty
and reduce inclinations toward radicalism" (190). Some public schools forbade
the use of languages other than English (Pavlenko 2002, 184). But many immigrant children remained beyond the public schools' reach. Immigrants often
wanted their children to work instead of going to school, and ethnic harassment
at school meant that immigrants' children often stopped attending. Furthermore, "for many Catholic, Orthodox, and Lutheran newcomers, public schools
were still perceived as anathema to religious faith" (Bodnar 1987, 193).

As a result, immigrant children learned English on the street, not primarily in
school. There is no documentary evidence of this that I can find from Pittsburgh,
but a study of Jewish immigrant children in New York (Brumberg 1986) probably provides a parallel. One child who attended school in New York in the 1910s
said this: "All of [the children] in this kind of environment came from Yiddish-
speaking homes. But once you were out on the street, you spoke English."
According to another, who arrived in the United States in 1913 at the age of ten,
"I learned English in the street. I learned English hitching rides on the trolley car
and when the kids would call me greenhorn I'd say I'm not a greenhorn, I'm here
three months when I was actually here two days. So that you learn, [but] you
never really learned proper English." (9).

In order not to sound like "greenhorns," immigrant children and the children
of immigrants learned to speak English the way their peers did. Only if they were

beyond puberty, when it becomes more difficult to learn to speak a new language with native-like pronunciation, would they have had a foreign accent, and nobody would have wanted to have an accent. If they could, they would have adapted to the local norms for speech. Research in current immigrant communities supports the argument that second-generation immigrants are likely to have sounded more local than ethnic. In a study of speech in twenty-first-century Chinese and Italian communities in Toronto, Canada, Michol Hoffman and James Walker (2010) discovered that the children of immigrants were adopting local, Canadian variants of the two sounds they studied. People who had moved to Canada as speakers of Chinese or Italian transferred aspects of their native languages into their English, but "differences between generations suggest that transfer does not persist" (Hoffman and Walker 2010, 36). Second-generation immigrants did not sound Chinese or Italian, in other words. They spoke English the way other Torontonians did, and the only thing that might have indexed their ethnic identities was the use of fewer of the more local-sounding variants. In other words, people who oriented more to Chinese or Italian life than to life in Toronto sounded not more Chinese or Italian, but less Canadian.

Pittsburgh English to the Mid-Twentieth Century

Until World War II, Pittsburgh continued to be relatively isolated, and Pittsburghers relatively immobile, both socially and geographically. People remained in the same jobs all their lives, preferring security to social mobility (Bodnar 1977, xv), and their children followed in their footsteps. Unionization was a slow process in the steel industry, and there were several large, unsuccessful strikes during which strikers were replaced with African Americans brought from the South. Nonetheless, workers gradually became more secure financially, as they came to depend less on family and friends for jobs and job security and more on larger institutions like unions. Working-class solidarity began to supplement ethnic identity in the steel mills during the Depression of the 1930s, and in 1942, the United Steelworkers union was founded, in Pittsburgh.

Second-generation immigrants continued to live in their parents' neighborhood and marry within their own ethnic groups. In a review of research about community building in Pittsburgh, Michael Weber (1989) reports that the Poles, Italians, and Jews who immigrated between 1880 and 1920 formed strong ethnic neighborhoods and support institutions that lasted two and sometimes three generations. Although earlier German and Irish immigrants had tended to divide up based on their religious affiliation or province of origin, Jews, Poles, and Italians—along with other groups that were not studied—formed unified communities based on a common religion. Pittsburgh's topography, with rivers and ravines that separate the city into relatively isolated islands of habitation, also contributed to the maintenance of ethnic neighborhoods. Steel mills and related industries spread along the three rivers, while tightly packed residential areas separated from one another by cliffs and stream beds grew on the flood plains and hills behind them.

Ideologically, ethnicity has always been strongly linked with neighborhood for Pittsburghers. People who do not identify with any of the immigrant ethnic groups sometimes attribute this to not having grown up in the right part of the Pittsburgh area. For example, one interviewee from a newer suburb called Cranberry Township, twenty miles from downtown Pittsburgh, said, "I never celebrated ethnicity. If I did, it was Americanized. I think because we were never tied to ethnic neighborhoods."

During the 1920s and 1930s, Pittsburgh's white population moved steadily outward to new blue-collar suburbs across the rivers and to the east. However, few moved very far. A study conducted in 1939 showed that 70 percent of the people who moved outward from the inner city in 1936 moved less than half a mile. In fact, outward movement tended to help increase the concentration of racial and ethnic groups in some areas (Bodnar et al. 1983, 192–194). In the Bloomfield census tract in the 1930s, almost 70 percent of heads of families were Italian, as were 77 percent in East Liberty (195). The lower Hill District, Bloomfield, and East Liberty contained over half the city's Italians. Likewise, Polish Hill, the Strip District, and the Southside were heavily Polish, with more than three-fourths of the population of Polish Hill and some parts of the Southside being Polish in origin. On some streets, according to the census, everyone was Polish. Between the 1930s and the 1960s, two generations of Pittsburghers grew up in these neighborhoods, where ethnic churches, schools, fraternal organizations, businesses, and newspapers provided support and assistance. There were neighborhood scout troops, ladies clubs, sports teams, and holy-name societies, while "interneighborhood competition was often fierce" (201).

Because of the strong mutual dependence among people in ethnic neighborhoods, and because their homes were close to where they worked, children often stayed in the community where they grew up. According to Bodnar et al. (1983, 218), "almost none of the Polish or Italian families from the 1930 neighborhoods left the city after 1940 . . . Many had resided in the same neighborhood for twenty, thirty, or more years, and attractions from other locations were not strong enough to induce them to leave Pittsburgh" for the suburbs. On some streets, "40% of the homes were owned by sons and daughters of the original 1930 residents" (220). By the 1940s, the population in the ethnic neighborhoods was relatively young, and the neighborhoods had large schools. As in the 1920s, most of the adult residents had blue-collar jobs. When eventually these neighborhoods got too crowded, the third generation started having to move to the suburbs to raise their families. But "while the outward migration was perhaps inevitable, it was undertaken with mixed feelings and usually to a developing area as close as possible to the urban homestead" (219). This continues to be the case in neighborhoods like Bloomfield, where young adults who grew up there lament not being able to find homes in the city and move to a suburb as close and easy to reach as is practical.

Until the mid-twentieth century, it is likely that when Pittsburghers noticed differences among ways of speaking at all, they noticed foreign-sounding speech. For example, in a memoir of life in Pittsburgh during the nineteenth century, publisher William G. Johnston (1901) repeatedly calls attention to the speech of recent immigrants from Ireland, using nonstandard spelling to represent their accents.[4] Johnston describes an Irish night watchman who cries out "Two o'clock and a *foine, clare mornin*" (79; italics his) and Irish immigrants who complain of missing "the convaynyances lift behoind in the ould counthry" (298). German accents were also the butt of ridicule, according to Johnston. But their own accent would have been unhearable to most Pittsburghers, who did not notice that their speech differed from that of anyone else.

The use of local speech forms may have been correlated with social class and with localness, but, to the people who used them, nonstandard speech forms did not yet index social identity. Many people sounded like working-class Pittsburghers simply because they had no other way to sound. As we have seen, people growing up in working-class families tended to live in insular neighborhoods within walking distance of the steel mills and other factories where their parents worked, and they went to school and church with their neighbors. Their dense, multiplex sociolinguistic networks gave them access to local dialect features and little opportunity to become aware that they spoke differently from people elsewhere or that some people would consider the way they talked nonstandard. The kinds of social and geographical mobility that would give rise to varied linguistic repertoires were available to relatively few people.

Dottie X., born in 1930 and raised in the Irish ward of the inner-city neighborhood called Lawrenceville, reflected on this linguistic situation in my interview with her. Dottie grew up in a neighborhood that she identified as working class, where local speech was not talked about, joked about, or even noticed. "Everyone would have spoke the same, I guess," as she put it. Dottie went on to say that she "never even heard" a form she and others used regularly, the second-person plural pronoun *yinz*.

3.1 *"Yinz!"*

> DOTTIE X. And I never even like, I guess I just, when I hear the word *yinz*, I mean I never even heard that. I mean, maybe I did, but there were, everyone said it, so I never thought anything of it or something like that. But now, people are like, "Yinz!" and I'm like, "Well so what?"
>
> BJ So you grew up saying that, and everybody else did. I guess—

DOTTIE X. Well maybe they did, and I don't know. It just doesn't faze me. What's the, what's the big deal?

Dottie describes her neighbors in retrospect as having had an accent, but because the people she came into contact with on a daily basis sounded the same ("everyone said it"), she did not notice it. If using features of Pittsburgh speech went hand-in-hand with being a working-class Pittsburgher, nothing in Dottie's environment pointed the connection out. Now, she suggests, people notice local-sounding forms like *yinz* ("people are like, 'Yinz'!"). But for Dottie, sounding local is not, as she puts it, a "big deal." Another interviewee of Dottie's generation, when asked about local speech, said something similar: "I've never heard it; I just grew up in it."

Social Mobility and Enregisterment: Pittsburgh Speech, Class, and Correctness

The fact that there are linguistic features that that can be correlated (by scholars and other outsiders) with particular contexts is not enough to create indexical links between the features and the contexts in the minds of insiders. In order for a feature that is used in a particular context to evoke or create that context, people have to notice the correlation and attribute meaning to it. In other words, indexical links between forms and meanings are not an automatic result of the statistical frequency of the forms in particular contexts. Something has to happen to call attention to the statistical pattern. People who visit Pittsburgh may not notice that people there talk differently from people elsewhere in the United States. Because nothing has called their attention to the possibility that Pittsburghers might have a distinctive way of speaking, such people are simply not engaged in noticing the potential social meaning of local forms. Just as you have to learn to understand a language, you have to learn to hear an accent.

When people start to use correlations between forms and contexts to do semiotic work, we can say that the forms have been ENREGISTERED (Agha 2007a). This is to say that the forms have come to be associated with a "register" of speech. A speech register, in this sense, is a way of speaking linked with a social identity, a persona, or a situation. For Dottie, the use of *yinz* could only be enregistered as a feature of incorrect speech once she was in a position to notice that some people used *yinz* and others did not and that the people who used *yinz* were people whose speech was thought to be incorrect. This could have happened in school, if Dottie's teachers had discouraged their pupils from using *yinz*. But since the nuns who taught Dottie in her youth were also local (and also probably Irish in origin), they might not have thought of *yinz* as incorrect. Alternatively, *yinz* could have been enregistered as a feature of incorrect speech if Dottie had been in contact with people her age who did not use it, and if she had noticed that they did not use it. But this did not happen either. Only as an adult, coming into contact with people who *had* noticed *yinz* and had evaluative reactions to it, did Dottie become able to make this semiotic link herself.

To give another example, monophthongal /aw/ (as when people pronounce *downtown* as [daːntaːn] or spell it as <dahntahn>) is more common in the speech of Pittsburghers than in the speech of non-Pittsburghers and more common in working-class Pittsburghers' speech than in the speech of non-working-class Pittsburghers, and men pronounce /aw/ as a monophthong more often than women do (Johnstone et al. 2002; Kiesling and Wisnosky 2003). Because monophthongal /aw/ is statistically distributed the way it is, someone who has noticed this distribution can hear monophthongal /aw/ as indexing that the speaker is from southwestern Pennsylvania and/or working class and/or (in case of ambiguity) male. Accordingly, people who can use this feature variably may use it less when they are trying harder to sound educated or cosmopolitan, or more when they are trying harder to sound like working-class men or like other Pittsburghers. The social meanings of linguistic forms are shaped by correlations between forms and social contexts: a feature has to be correlated with a context before this correlation can be noticed and used to make meaning. At the same time, though, the fact that a form has been enregistered in a particular way can influence the statistical "facts on the ground," since the sociolinguistic value of a form affects the demographic distribution of its use. (People who hear monophthongal /aw/ as working class may start to use it less.)

In order for linguistic choices to become linked with registers of speech, there must be frameworks of ideas about the world in which it makes sense to create these links. People will notice that a particular word or pronunciation sounds "working class" only if it makes sense to them that working class people speak differently than other people. Likewise, people will notice that a particular form sounds "like a Pittsburgher" only if they have reason to suppose that people's speech varies depending on where the speakers are from. In other words, enregisterment is shaped by ideology. In Pittsburgh, indexical relations now link phonetic and lexical form with social meaning in several ways. Drawing meaning from several ideological schemas about language and identity, nonstandard forms heard in Pittsburgh can now, to different people and in different contexts, sound incorrect, working class, local, or some combination of these, and thus, they can be used or avoided in various contexts: when people are trying to sound correct (or not), when they are trying to sound working class (or not), or when they are trying to sound like Pittsburghers (or not).

Local linguistic features acquired social meaning when features that could be heard in the speech of working-class Pittsburghers were enregistered with social identities, personas, and situations, and taken up as sociolinguistic resources. This became possible in the context of social and geographical mobility, which gave Pittsburghers access to new variants of forms that had not been variable in their speech or that of their neighbors. Forms like *yinz* or monophthongal /aw/ became variable once working-class Pittsburghers started to come into contact with people who did not use *yinz* or monophthongize/aw/, and learned that they could choose to use *yinz* or *you* or to pronounce *house* as [haws] ("house") or [ha:s] ("hahs"). At this point, the choice among variants could, for some people, be invested with social meaning, such as class or correctness. People's speech started to vary depending on what they were doing or whom they were talking to.

Dr. John K., born in 1928, was the son of a firefighter. He grew up in the Mount Washington neighborhood, then a solidly working-class part of the city. Like Dottie X., John K. was not aware in his youth of the possibility that others might think he sounded like he was from Pittsburgh or that he sounded working class, and when I interviewed him, he was still almost completely unaware that he had what others might consider a local accent. John monophthongized /aw/ almost invariably in his own speech, but when asked to comment on alternative pronunciations of the word *house* ([haws] ("house") and the more local-sounding monophthongized [ha:s] ("hahs"), he associated the monophthongized "hahs" version with people from elsewhere, claiming never to have heard it in Pittsburgh. In the extract that follows, the recorded voice is on a recording that I played for John K. and Arlene C., whom I interviewed together. The recording contained the prompts for an experimental task meant to elicit participants' senses of the social meanings of variants of a number of sociolinguistic variables. In discussing the prompt and answering the ensuing questions, John K. and Arlene C. explicitly link local-sounding speech with social class and education and explicitly deny that it can index local identity.

3.2 *What does "hahs" sound like?*

1 RECORDED VOICE	a. We bought a [haws] ("house"). We bought a [haws] ("house"). b. We bought a [ha:s] ("hahs"). We bought a [ha:s] ("hahs").
2 ARLENE C.	We bought a what?
3 JOHN K.	A [ha:s] ("hahs").
4 ARLENE C.	[ha:s] ("hahs").
5 JOHN K.	A [ha:s] ("hahs").
6 ARLENE C.	[ha:s] ("hahs") **((sighs))**
7 JOHN K.	A [haw-] ("hou-"), [haws] ("house") and a [ha:s] ("hahs").

8 BJ	So you can tell, you can hear a difference.
9 JOHN K.	Oh my God, yes.
10 ARLENE C.	Mm-hmm.
11 BJ	Does one of them sound more correct than the other?
12 JOHN K.	[haws] ("house") is more correct than [ha:s] ("hahs").
13 ARLENE C.	((laughing)) It's not—
14 JOHN K.	[ha:s] ("hahs"), that sounds like Brooklyn or something.
15 ARLENE C.	Or some—yeah. **Or South Side**, somewhere.
16 BJ	Yeah. Southside. ((speaking to Arlene C.)) So, does that— So to you it sounds more Pittsburgh? [ha:s] ("hahs") than [haws] ("house")?
17 JOHN K.	**I've never heard of [ha:s] ("hahs")**. Not here ((indistinguishable)). Not anywhere in Pittsburgh, I never heard that. I heard it in Brooklyn.
18 ARLENE C.	I don't know.
19 BJ	Mm hmm. So, you wouldn't say it ((i.e., [ha:hs] ('hahs"))) sounds more Pittsburgh?
20 ARLENE C.	No.
21 BJ	((to John K.)) You wouldn't either. ((to both)) **Does it ((i.e. [ha:hs] ("hahs"))) sound more working class?**
22 ARLENE C.	Ohh.
23 JOHN K.	**Than [ha:s] ("hahs")?** Why yeah, it has to be.
24 BJ	Yeah, okay.
25 JOHN K.	They didn't go to school or else they didn't learn.
26 BJ	Mmm-hmm.
27 ARLENE C.	Or the teacher talked that way.
28 BJ	Or the teacher talked that way.
29 JOHN K.	That's right.

Although he was socially mobile, eventually earning a PhD, owning a medical laboratory, and living in a white-collar suburb, John had little reason to distance himself from potentially local-sounding forms, and thus little reason to notice or talk about them and little control over his choice of variants. In line 17 of the extract, he claims never to have heard the [ha:s] ("hahs") pronunciation, the one he in fact uses. In line 23, he produces [haːs] ("hahs"), apparently intending to say [haus] ("house"): in response to the question about whether the variant [haːs] ("hahs") "sounds more working class," (line 21), John queries, "Than [haːs] ("hahs")? Why, yeah." It seems likely that he means that [haːs] ("hahs") sounds more working class than [haws] ("house"), but because he cannot control whether he pronounces /aw/ as a monophthong, he produced [haːs] ("hahs") instead.

Particularly for men, using speech forms that sound working class can carry "covert prestige" (Trudgill 1972). This is to say that linguistic features that are stigmatized—ones that are enregistered with incorrectness or with lower class or uneducated speech—can also be enregistered with a particular kind of masculine identity. As such, features like these can carry social value in men's linguistic marketplaces. In a mine or a mill, for example, it can be both practically and socially useful for the foreman to talk like the laborers, because doing so can create a sense of solidarity which can lead to safer, more productive work. As a result, a man's use of stigmatized linguistic features might not sound as unusual as a woman's use of such features would. During John's travels to conferences and trade shows, nobody ever commented on his accent, he said. As a result, the link between features like /aw/-monophthongization and social identity is a simple correlation in John's speech production: he uses local features because he has no other option, not to express indexical meaning. When asked explicitly to reflect on the potential indexicalities of the monophthongal variant of /aw/ ("hahs"), John labels it as working class and adds that it signals a lack of education ("They didn't go to school or else they didn't learn," line 25), but he does not hear it as a local, Pittsburgh form.

For Arlene C., with whom John was interviewed, sounding local *was* a social liability, on the other hand (as is suggested by her sigh in line 6). Arlene has productive control of variable features that, for her, are indexical markers of class and incorrectness. With a working-class upbringing and an upwardly mobile professional, marital, and residential trajectory, Arlene exemplifies the upper-working-class pattern of "hypercorrection," or the use of even more standard-sounding speech than the people she aspires to be like (W. Labov, 1972d). She monophthongizes /aw/ at a much lower rate than does John K., using the nonlocal, diphthongal variant ("house") at the same rate as women two generations younger than she. Arlene is very sensitive to class differences, which (adopting a common strategy in Pittsburgh) she often points to through references to neighborhoods. In the extract, for example, she identifies local speech with the "South Side," a working-class neighborhood (line 15). She identifies herself with Forest Hills, the white-collar neighborhood she lives in now, preferring the awkward neologism "Forest Hillian" to "Pittsburgher" when I asked her for a list of words reflecting her sense of identity. If local speech forms can now index Pittsburgh identity as well as social stigma, Arlene does not hear them that way, answering "No" when asked whether monophthongal /aw/ ("hahs") "sounds more Pittsburgh" than the diphthongal variant.

Like Arlene C., many interviewees continue to link local speech forms to incorrectness. In the next extract, Dottie X. and her daughter Barb E. (born in 1954) talk about an accent-reduction course Barb has read about. Like Arlene, they use neighborhood names to encode class distinctions and draw on the potential linkage of local-sounding forms with incorrectness to construct a negative linkage between local speech and social class. Thus, people who don't "speak correctly" must be "from Lawrenceville," and such people are candidates for accent-reduction classes because they risk "misrepresenting" the companies they work for.

3.3 "So they wouldn't know that you were from Lawrenceville."

BARB E. There was an article in the *Business Times* a couple weeks ago about a—I guess it's a consulting firm, I think. Where they will, if you had a company, and you were hiring employees. They would go into your company and sort of counsel people on how to **speak correctly**, so that they wouldn't **misrepresent the company**, if you have—

DOTTIE X. So they wouldn't know that you were **from Lawrenceville**.

BARB E. Yeah.

DOTTIE X. So, 'cause they always say that Lawrenceville, they don't like the accent. The way people, you know. Their terminology, I guess the way they speak, you know, **they** ((indistinguishable)) **must be from Lawrenceville**.

BJ Yeah. Uh huh.

BARB E. Yeah.

As she suggested in the first extract (3.1), Dottie spent most of her life unaware of the value others might associate with the way she spoke, because she was not in social contact with many people for whom local speech features could carry indexical meaning. Becoming aware that she speaks with the local nonstandard accent has required learning to hear local forms as nonstandard and enregistering them as a socially stigmatized "accent." Dottie's daughter Barb, who grew up with an awareness that local forms can index a stigmatized class-based identity, talks about how their use can also signal social solidarity based on being from the same place. This can be seen in the following segment, where Barb describes talking differently (i.e., using more local-sounding forms) with a university maintenance worker ("someone in the service response center") than to "the assistant to the president" of the university. If she "knows it's a Pittsburgher" she is talking to and "they're talking to me in that sort of colloquial kind of this is how we talk," then local-sounding speech is appropriate. "I don't think it's a judgmental thing," as she puts it.

3.4 *"I don't think it's a judgmental thing"*

BARB E. And I will say this too. I think working in my job, I think there are certain people that I interact with that I, um, I will talk a little bit differently with them, just to, so that they'll feel, feel comfortable with me. But I think that goes back to, like I said earlier about what I do, and how I interact with all different kinds of people. I think that you, and **I don't think it's a judgmental thing**. I think it's just you should be aware of, you know, who you're talking with and you know sort of what their expectations are and what their perception of you is going to be. So, **if I am talking with someone in the service response center about needing a light bulb, I'm going to talk differently than I'm going to talk to the assistant to the president**. Yeah, I mean it's just, you know. And if it's, **if I know it's a Pittsburgher and they're talking to me in that sort of colloquial kind of this is how we talk**, then that's, yeah, that's you know, that's how we talk.

Unlike her mother, Barb E. came of age in an environment in which sounding local could have social consequences. It could create social solidarity with fellow Pittsburghers via its potential to index place, but it could also index class, occupation, or level of education. For people Barb's age, features that were once enregistered as indexes of class or correctness, or not enregistered at all, have come, during their lifetimes, to be enregistered as indexes of local identity and solidarity. As a result, people in this generation sometimes note that things that did not used to "sound Pittsburgh" now do. Another such person is Richard I., who was born in 1945. I asked him whether he had ever seen any media representations of Pittsburghese, and he said he knew the book *How to Speak Like a Pittsburgher* (McCool 1982) and in fact thought there was a copy in the house. The conversation proceeded as follows:

3.5 *"It was* normal*"*

BJ Do you remember stuff like that growing up? When you were growing up? Do you remember—

RICHARD I. N—

BJ jokes about Pittsburghese and little booklets and—

RICHARD I. No.

BJ cartoons and things? When did that start? Do you, do you have any idea of—

RICHARD I. Well, it had to be not before, not long before he ((i.e., Sam McCool)) wrote that book, because, you know, to us, back then, um, you know again I mentioned **Pittsburgh was like a, a little city unto itself and, and there was not a lot of movement in and movement out** and if it was, those people didn't live within the city. Most of them lived out, outside of the city limits.

BJ Mm-hmm.

RICHARD I. Um, so, **when we talked like that in high school and, it was normal**.

BJ Mm-hmm?

RICHARD I. You know I mean ((indistinguishable)).

BJ Nobody commented on it ((indistinguishable)).

RICHARD I. **There was nothing *wrong* with, with that**.

BJ Mm-hmm?

RICHARD I. You know. **And then when Pittsburgh started to really get, uh, to become more of a, you know, there were people coming into corporate headquarters, and, and, and people started to notice, "Boy, you guys really *talk* funny here."**

BJ ((laughs))

RICHARD I. You know. And 'at—that's when I think that came into being.

According to Richard, who would have been in high school in the early to middle 1960s, the way he and his friends talked then was "normal." "There was nothing *wrong* with it," he says. Since everyone talked that way, nobody commented on it. Richard attributes this to Pittsburgh's isolation and Pittsburghers' lack of mobility: "Pittsburgh was like a little city unto itself and there was not a lot of movement in and movement out," except by local commuters (people who "lived outside the city limits" like him and his high school cohort). But once people from elsewhere started to come into the city, saying things like, "'Boy, you guys really *talk* funny here,'" "people started to notice."

Geographic Mobility and Re-enregisterment: Pittsburgh Speech and Place

As Richard I. points out, Pittsburgh speech only started to be associated with Pittsburgh the place when people noticed the correlation between how Pittsburghers talked and how careful or cosmopolitan they were trying to sound, and attributed meaning to that. This did not happen until local social and economic history created a climate in which it made sense to re-enregister forms that could previously sound incorrect and working class (if they sounded like anything at all) as indexes of place. Only then did it make sense, in other words, to move from using and hearing features of Pittsburgh speech as signaling that a person was speaking incorrectly or in a working-class way to using and hearing features of Pittsburgh speech as signaling that a person was speaking like a Pittsburgher. Only at that point would the term *Pittsburghese* begin to make sense.

In general, an indexical meaning is formed when people notice a correlation between speech forms and social identities and attribute significance to it, thus making the speech forms usable to evoke or create a new social identity, situation, or persona. In the post–World War II decades, the indexicality of certain features (their potential to index correctness, class, and place) became usable. While the older indexical meanings of these forms continues to make them hearable and usable as markers of social class, education, and local orientation, the fact that these features could be used these ways became more and more noticeable.

During World War II, many working-class Pittsburgh men were geographically mobile, traveling in the military, and wartime demand enriched and enlarged Pittsburgh's steel industry. Previously, steelworkers and other industrial laborers were poor and unable to travel, but the steel boom that started during the war continued during the 1940s and 1950s as demand for consumer products replaced demand for war materiel. Since increased demand made labor more valuable, the United Steelworkers' collective bargaining efforts finally "created the tide that carried all steelworkers to higher-income ground and led to a significant increase in living standards" (Hoerr 1988, 175). Industrial workers in the post–World War II years made enough money to vacation at East Coast beaches and elsewhere, where they interacted with people who sounded different and noticed how the Pittsburghers sounded.

Demographic change at home also helped create the conditions for noticing local speech and using aspects of it to do identity work. During the 1960s, the baby-boom grandchildren of the immigrant industrial laborers who had arrived between 1880 and 1920 began to come of age. Two generations removed from the "old country," they did not speak the homeland language and had weakened ties to immigrant religions (Oestreicher 1989, personal communication). While their parents and grandparents thought of themselves mainly in ethnic or religious terms (as Polish, for example, or Eastern Orthodox), these third-generation Pittsburghers began to develop class and regional consciousness. The ground was thus fertile for ways of imagining what it meant to be a working-class Pittsburgher, and the existence of variable local pronunciations that could index class and place, forms that people elsewhere heard as different and Pittsburghers elsewhere identified with home, provided an easily available resource for doing this.

Pittsburgh's economic upheaval of the 1970s and 1980s meant vastly increased geographical mobility and resulted in new kinds of talk that led to dialect leveling, and at the same time, it led people to link dialect and social identity more explicitly. According to economic reporter John Hoerr (1988, 24–25), several things came together in the 1970s and 1980s to restructure the American steel industry. The oil crisis caused by the OPEC cartel meant that Americans switched to smaller cars and drove them less, and the fact that US cities and the American transportation infrastructure were essentially built out meant reduced demand for structural steel, rails, and the like. Due in part to high labor costs in the United States, new industrial powers began to emerge, producing steel in competition with the American companies. This in turn helped alter the balance of trade and made the US deficit grow. With little competition, companies like U.S. Steel had previously had little motivation to modernize, and in the economic conditions of the 1970s and 1980s they could not raise the capital they needed for this purpose. Meanwhile, computerization increased the speed at which capital could flow around the world, and this facilitated mergers and acquisitions by speculators interested mainly in short-term profit. According to Bensman and Lynch (1988, 80–91), environmental protection laws passed in the 1970s also played a role in decisions to shut down older mills, as did poor management, slow growth in the world economy, and declining yields from the Mesabi Range iron-ore mines in the United States, so that by the late 1950s, Venezuelan iron ore had become cheaper. Mini-mills that made steel by recycling scrap were also a threat to the large integrated mills that started with iron ore and other raw materials. Like other companies, U.S. Steel began to branch out into more profitable industries, purchasing Marathon Oil at the end of 1981. This put the company further in debt and further contributed to its weakness.

All this meant huge cutbacks in the US steel industry. In the Pittsburgh area, between 1980 and 1983 alone, 95,000 manufacturing jobs were lost, out of workforce of around 1 million. The steel mills that lined the rivers in the city were abandoned seemingly overnight and then sold for scrap, leaving only ugly brownfields. The Pittsburgh Community Food Bank opened in 1980 to help people who suddenly had no money. People whose families had lived in Pittsburgh for generations were forced to relocate to find work. Losing 6.9 percent of its residents between 1980 and 1990, the Pittsburgh metropolitan area shrank more during the 1980s than did the populations of Detroit and Cleveland combined, with the largest number leaving the city in 1984–1985 (Rotstein 2004).

Pittsburghers who grew up in the 1950s or before sometimes recall thinking of the city as the center of the world. Pittsburgh was one of the largest and one of the richest cities in the United States, and the smoke and flames from the mills, which spurred outsiders to think of Pittsburgh as "hell with the lid off" (in the words of a nineteenth-century journalist), had represented wealth and progress in local minds. Pittsburghers of that era are nostalgic, in a knowingly perverse way, for the times when streetlights were kept on all day due to the soot-darkened air. Steelworkers in particular were proud of their ability to get a dangerous, tricky, often sweltering job done. In a study of a steel town outside of Chicago, Bensman and Lynch (1988, 21) note the "camaraderie" and "sense of mutual responsibility" bred by the working conditions in a steel mill, where a false step could land a person in a trough of molten metal. Steelworkers seemed indispensable, and people could easily overlook the fact that their jobs were at the mercy of the steel companies. As Bensman and Lynch put it:

> Over time, the mills came to be seen not as appendages of giant corporations but as part of the local landscape. If the people of these neighborhoods still knew that they depended on the mills for their livelihoods, they had also come to believe that the mills depended on them to make one of the world's most important commodities—steel. There was a sense of pride and power in their view of the universe. (37)

The children of steelworkers were not pushed to be upwardly mobile. Their parents wanted to give them a good education and said they did not want them to be steelworkers. But the best-paying jobs were in the mills. As one former steelworker put it, "Your father didn't want you to, but when you were of age and ready to go to work, he was the guy that got you the job, for crying out loud" (Bensman and Lynch 1988, 28). Schools also reinforced the idea that children were destined to follow in their parents' footsteps. Sketching the culture of a Monongahela Valley steel town in the 1940s, John Hoerr (1988) describes a high school friend who recalled that "a counselor asked him, 'Why do you want to go to college, you're just the son of a steelworker?'" (173).

When the steel mills closed, young people were the first let go. Many felt cheated out of their inherited identities as steelworkers or as wives of steelworkers. If they were no longer Polish or Russian (except when it came to holiday food and rituals), no longer tied to their parents' churches and fraternal organizations, and now no longer working people, how were they to imagine themselves? On the basis of research conducted in 1985–86 in a high school in a steel town she calls "Freeway," educational ethnographer Lois Weis (1990) argues that working-class boys of that era defined themselves in contradistinction to girls and to African Americans. Their sexism, claims Weis, resulted partly from the fact that without a future in the steel plant they had lost access to the tough male identity associated with steelworkers. Their racism, she claims, although expressed as competition with black boys for girls, had deeper roots in the historical competition between black and white men for jobs. Both girls and boys claimed to be more open to education than earlier working-class youth, knowing that being educated was now the key to getting a job in the post-steel economy, but many failed to act on this knowledge.

Popular youth culture of the 1970s and 1980s reflected working-class youths' sense of being cheated out of an identity. Rock stars like Bruce Springsteen, Billy Joel, and John Mellencamp sang about alienated working-class kids, and movies like *Saturday Night Fever* (1977) and *Hoosiers* (1986) depicted their struggles to overcome what was suddenly the adversity of being working class. In a study of Springsteen's hit "Born in the USA," Jefferson Cowie and Lauren Boehm (2006) argue that the song was not just nostalgic, but rather an attempt to represent the lives of working-class males in the 1970s and 1980s. As working-class men's sense of identity based on work was undermined by inflation and plant closures that forced them to leave home, what was left, say Cowie and Boehm, was a sense of identity based on a kind of nationalism that resonated with Reagan-era politics. Cowie and Boehm argue that the identity crisis the song is about was specifically a white male crisis. At the same time as white males' economic security was being threatened, new equal-rights policies had them competing against African Americans and women for disappearing jobs.

Scholars like Weis and Cowie and Boehm consider gender and race the major sources of identity for working-class youth. As I have noted, though, the working class youth who came of age in the 1970s and 1980s in Pittsburgh were in large part third-generation immigrants. For them, having been "born in the USA" is what distinguished them from their grandparents and a metaphor for what had distanced them from the culture their parents inherited from their grandparents. For them, then, "Born in the USA" must have had ethnic overtones as well as political and nationalist ones.

Furthermore, and crucially for the story of Pittsburghese, many of the young people who left Pittsburgh in the 1970s and 1980s reacted against the loss of identity by creating new ways to be linked to place. The plot of Michael Cimino's 1978 film *The Deer Hunter*, set in a Pittsburgh-area steel-mill town, ties the older generation to the Russian Orthodox Church and immigrant traditions, and the younger generation to the mountainous local topography and a western-Pennsylvania way of life represented by deer hunting. The film begins with preparations for a wedding, which is held in a Russian church and church hall with food prepared by old women in babushkas and traditional music and dances. Afterward, the bride and groom and their friends pile into a car and head for the mountains on a deer hunt, metaphorically escaping from a European way of being to an American one.

Diaspora, Regional Exceptionalism, and the Emergence of Pittsburghese

Hundreds of thousands of young Pittsburghers left the city during the 1980s to find work. As sportswriter Wright Thompson notes, "If you meet ex-Pittsburghers [in Houston], odds are they left home between 1980 and 1985" (W. Thompson

2011, 124). Many have remained intensely loyal to the city. Although there has been no scholarly research about this group, the "Steeler Nation" has received considerable media attention. A reporter for the *Pittsburgh Post-Gazette* described this cohort in one of a series of articles based on interviews with its members:

> Blue-collar workers whose fathers and grandfathers had worked in the mills fled for readily available jobs in Sun Belt states like Texas, Florida, and Virginia. College graduates discovered that local openings were as scarce as Pittsburgh sunshine in February, and many of them ended up in Washington, D.C., California, the Raleigh, N.C., research triangle and other white-collar growth areas.
>
> Two decades later, this coast-to-coast diaspora of ex-Pittsburghers remains passionate in their loyalty to their hometown. They miss the tight-knit neighborhoods, the beauty of the hills and rivers, the small-town friendliness of a place with big-city amenities, the thrill of uniting in a crowd of thousands behind the professional sports teams. (Rotstein 2004)

Displaced Pittsburghers who visit and "gumbanders"[5] who eventually move back to Pittsburgh bring with them stories about being told they sound funny, and nostalgic talk about Pittsburgh and Pittsburgh speech has become common in diasporic communities of Pittsburghers. Now nearing retirement or already retired, members of Pittsburgh diaspora work to preserve the memory of a time that has long passed and a city that has changed:

> So they construct a sort of Renaissance fair for manufacturing America. They treat Pittsburgh in the same way their Italian ancestors treated Italy—a complex thing becoming simple, fighting assimilation, trying to keep a culture from diluting into nothing. What makes this unique is that they do it almost entirely by following a football team.
>
> "The ethnic enclaves of Little Pittsburgh exist most poignantly in tailgate parking lots of away [Steelers football] games," says Jim Russell, a Western Pennsylvania-born geographer who studies geopolitics and the relationship between migration and economic development. "That's where you see people doing the performances of culture. The blue-collar Pittsburgh that you see flashed on the screen during games exists only in Steeler bars and in the visitors' parking lot." (W. Thompson 2011, 126)[6]

Nostalgic reasons for talk about talk has meant that Pittsburghers, in Pittsburgh and elsewhere, became increasingly aware that features of their speech are local in geographic distribution and noticeable to others, and the potential for indexical linkages between local forms and social identities has been made increasingly explicit. In Pittsburgh, the monophthongal /aw/ and certain other forms that are sometimes indexically associated with class, correctness, or local identity have now acquired a new kind of meaning on a new level. Some features of Pittsburghese are now symbols, in the sense I described in chapter 2, in just the same way a word like *word* or *now* or *urban* is. That is, in some situations and for some people, *yinz* is no longer a second-person pronoun that suggests a speaker is a Pittsburgher, and features like *yinz* no longer have to occur together with other aspects of localness to evoke or point to localness. Instead, a word like *yinz* can now be used as symbol, meaning something like "Pittsburghy" even when it is not uttered by a Pittsburgher or otherwise semiotically linked to the city. As we will see later on, for some people *yinz* is now so disconnected from its history as a pronoun that some people use it as an adjective. Symbols of localness like *yinz* appear in explicit lists of local words and performances of local identities, in the context of widely circulating discourse about the connection between local identity and local speech. As we saw in chapter 1, only a subset of the features of Pittsburgh speech that can index correctness and class have been integrated into this new speech register, which consists of a highly codified repertoire of words and phrases that can, on their own and out of context, symbolize Pittsburgh, as well as index Pittsburgh and Pittsburgh identity in self-conscious performances of localness.

Using these features is now also a way for people who may have few of the local speech resources that people like Barb E. or Richard I. have—people who cannot actually shift into a Pittsburgh accent, for example—to show that they know how "authentic" Pittsburghers sound. This has occurred through overt representations of a subset of the forms that had been enregistered with class, localness, and correctness, re-enregistering this subset with a more stabilized social identity—the identity often linked with the persona of the "Yinzer"—and making these forms available for self-conscious, performed identity work. In the process, this subset of nonstandard forms has become increasingly linked to place and less, or more indirectly, to class.

As we have seen, the Scotch-Irish influenced founder variety on which later immigrants modeled their speech was shaped by the topographical and historical factors that gave rise to communicative isolation in southwestern Pennsylvania (the Allegheny Mountains, the relative infertility of the land west of them, the area's rivers and mineral resources, and so on). These material factors also helped give rise to the ideology of regional exceptionalism, the idea that the Pittsburgh area is unique, different from any other area. Along with the historical developments I have sketched, the ideology of regional exceptionalism is conducive to the idea that there is a unique regional dialect. Cultural geographer Wilbur Zelinsky (1988) explored the vernacular regions of the United States by looking for terms of "locational and cultural significance" in the business names listed in telephone books. Zelinsky's study showed that there was a very weak sense of regional identification in an area that included western Pennsylvania and parts of adjoining states. Terms such as *Midwest, mid-Atlantic,* and *East* tended not to be used in business names in this area (Zelinsky 1995, 151). The sense of not being part of any larger region is linked to the area's physical isolation from the eastern seaboard. (Pittsburgh is much closer to Cleveland, Ohio, than it is to Philadelphia, Pennsylvania.)

Pittsburghers' sense of regional exceptionalism is also linked to the existence of a number of political boundaries, in the form of state borders, which both trace historical distinctions and help create ideological ones. Pittsburgh is close to Ohio but not ideologically of the Midwest; close to Maryland but not southern; close to West Virginia but not, in Pittsburgh's collective mind, Appalachian. Pittsburghers' identity has always been linked to the city rather than to the state or the region. When I asked the people I interviewed to list a few terms they would use to identify themselves, most included "Pittsburgher" (and many said "American"), but no one listed "Pennsylvanian."

People from elsewhere in southwestern Pennsylvania know that some features of Pittsburghese are used where they live, too, but they nonetheless call this variety Pittsburghese, suggesting that its "best" or most "authentic" speakers are Pittsburghers. For example, one of a series of video sketches featuring two male characters who are supposed to be from Johnstown, Pennsylvania (a small city sixty-five miles east of Pittsburgh) shows the men realizing that they have "an accent" but identifying it as Pittsburghese rather than associating it with Johnstown (Yeager and Skowron 2009). The film's YouTube caption is "Dey say I got dat Pixburgh accent." In part, the belief that the accent is associated with Pittsburgh, rather than with the larger region in which many elements of it can be heard, might reflect the historical fact that at least one feature of Pittsburgh speech—monophthongal /aw/—may have originated in urban language contact. As we have seen earlier and will see again, the ideological and the material intertwine in the ways in which Pittsburghese (the idea) shapes Pittsburgh speech (the "facts on the ground") and vice versa.

Working-class Pittsburgh neighborhoods are less homogeneous than they once were. Many formerly mono-ethnic neighborhood parochial schools have been merged, and Pittsburgh-area public school systems are trying to increase racial integration by means such as specialized magnet schools meant to draw enrollment from all over the city. All this means that young Pittsburghers now come into contact with people who are unlike them at a much earlier age than before. Even among people who have not (or not yet) left the city, conditions are thus conducive to the discursive practices that give rise to explicit talk about the social meanings of certain forms. The medical and university sectors of the economy have grown, attracting students and professionals from elsewhere. The availability of inexpensive housing, studio, and office space in former industrial neighborhoods means that young artists, designers, musicians, and other "creatives" can stay in the city after graduating from local universities. These people notice local speech features (as often in mediated form as by actually interacting with locals) and use them in reflexive, self-conscious identity work.

Jessica H., who was twenty-five when Jennifer Andrus and I spoke to her in 2004, represents one of the ways the more stabilized set of ideas about local speech that have circulated since the 1980s can be deployed in self-conscious identity work. Jessica grew up with relatively little exposure to people with strong local accents, but aware of "Pittsburghese." (She remembers seeing T-shirts and other written representations of it in childhood.) Jessica H. does not use local-sounding speech features or claim local speech as central to family, community, or personal identity. During the interview, however, she narrated "one of the biggest games from freshman year," her first year at a university that draws students from all over the United States. The game involved performing and comparing regional accents.

3.6 "One of the biggest games from freshman year"

JESSICA H. It was the first opportunity that I had to be out of the area for an extended period of time. An–and, I mean, my, my close friends from school, from X University, were from New Jersey, New York, Buffalo again, Chicago, um, all over.

BJ Did people ever talk about the places they were from, like, compare and contrast their hometowns?

JESSICA H. Oh. **That was one of the, one of the biggest games from freshman year. To figure out who had accents from what areas,** and how we said things differently and that kind of thing.

BJ Really?

JESSICA H. It was like different colloquialisms and that kind of thing. Um, it was interesting.

BJ Were there really big differences, or?

JESSICA H. Um, my, my friend from New Jersey, she was from South Jersey near Philly, and, had a pretty serious South Jersey accent, so that was a fun one. Um. There was people with, with New York accents. And then there was a group of us actually who were from Pittsburgh, and got picked on for our Pittsburgh accents as well. So, it was interesting.

BJ ((laughs)) What were—what did people say? I mean, what did—what did they notice?

JESSICA H. Um, *down,* a lot of that, you know. Um. Just, *a*'s were a big thing. You know, *down*'s the—

BJ Uh huh. The [awz] ("aws").

JESSICA H Yeah exactly. No, no one said *yinz* or anything like that. Except in jest, but um, it was, yeah.

BJ It's interesting that people would notice. You know, you don't have a really
strong local accent compared to some people, but—

JESSICA H. Yeah. Yeah, but it was, it was significant enough them to notice,
though. An—and you think in a educa—in an educational setting it sort of
goes away, everybody sort of blends together, but, it—there were still
some words that everybody picked out pretty quickly, so—

BJ Mm-hmm. *Pop.*

JESSICA H. Mm-hmm, mm-hmm.

The dialect-comparing activity Jessica describes occurs at a time when identity talk is at a premium, as students get to know their new classmates. It draws
on and reinforces the idea that dialect and place are linked: accents are treated as
automatic consequences of people's places of origin. (The idea that dialect could
index other aspects of social identity, such as class, does not arise and would
probably derail the activity if it did.) In this activity, regional accents apparently
consist of features drawn from the kinds of lists found in folk dictionaries and on
T-shirts. The features of Pittsburgh speech Jessica describes in answer to my
question about what the other students "noticed" are the ones that are the most
common in written representations of local speech: monophthongal /aw/ ("ah"),
mainly in the word *down*, the pronoun *yinz*, and the term *pop* (rather than *soda*)
for a carbonated soft drink. These are not the same as the most common features
of unselfconscious Pittsburgh speech, and neither monophthongal /aw/ nor *yinz*
are actually features of Jessica's unselfconscious speech, nor are they features she
uses to do unselfconscious sociolinguistic marking. In this environment, where
accents are "fun" and no longer linked with class or correctness, region is no
longer indexed by the use of local-sounding variants in everyday interaction, but
in performances of a person's knowledge of the sociolinguistic stereotypes that
constitute "Pittsburghese," in the self-conscious construction of social identity.

Indexical Layering in the History of Pittsburghese

As we have seen in this chapter, linguistic forms that can be heard in the Pittsburgh area have meant different things at different times. As a result, the same
nonstandard pronunciation, the same word, or the same bit of grammar can
mean different things to different people, and sometimes different things to the
same person, depending on the context. As a way of modeling what goes on
when different ways of speaking come to have different social meanings, I
evoked the concept of enregisterment. Enregisterment is the process by which
a particular linguistic form, or a set of linguistic forms, gets linked with a social
meaning by virtue of some ideological schema according to which the linkage
makes sense.

Before the 1940s, speaking English meant speaking English like a Pittsburgher, since Pittsburghers were the only linguistic models other Pittsburghers had. With a few small exceptions, which will be discussed in a later chapter, nobody noticed that Pittsburghers spoke English differently than Americans anywhere else. Since Pittsburghers did not notice the differences between Pittsburgh English and any other kind of English, they could not attribute any meaning to such differences. At this stage, Pittsburgh speech (as distinct from English in general) had no social meaning for Pittsburghers. Pittsburgh speech had not yet been enregistered as a distinctive way of speaking with a distinctive set of social meanings. What was important for immigrant newcomers to the city, starting in the twentieth century, was to learn English, since the difference between English and their homeland language did have social meaning, even if the difference between Pittsburgh English and any other kind of English did not. Through the work of churches and fraternal organizations, the European languages of the immigrants' homelands were ideologically linked with tradition, religion, family, and neighborhood. Speaking English was ideologically linked with being an American and practically linked with getting a good job, understanding what was going on at union meetings, and, for some children no doubt, being able to translate for their parents. Speaking English with a foreign accent evoked both sets of ideas. A person with an accent was old-fashioned, fresh off the boat, not yet American. So immigrants who were young enough and the children of immigrants learned to speak the English of their longer settled peers, not the accented English of their parents.

Once Pittsburghers started to become socially and geographically mobile, they were in a position to notice differences between their speech and others, and these differences were at first enregistered according to cultural schemas linking them to class and place. According to one widespread schema, some ways of speaking are more correct than others. To Pittsburghers whose teachers did not themselves have local accents, this set of ideas would be explicitly circulated at school and reinforced by the fact that (better educated) teachers sounded different from their (less educated) students.

When Pittsburghers started to notice that better educated people were less likely to use words like *yinz* or pronunciations like *dahntahn*, they could try to avoid local variants if they wanted to sound educated. Pittsburghers who were in a position to hear people from other neighborhoods or with different jobs, perhaps by virtue of contacts women made in new kinds of jobs or contacts young people made in public schools with multineighborhood catchment areas, drew on the idea that class and speech vary together and became able to attribute *yinz*, *dahntahn*, and other forms to class and neighborhood differences. They could then try to use such forms less when they wanted to sound cosmopolitan or sophisticated.

Through a similar process, Pittsburghers who traveled began to be able to notice that they spoke differently than people elsewhere, and the ideological schema that links place and speech (the idea that people from different places talk differently) led them to link their forms with home and others' forms with elsewhere. Pittsburghese has come to represent Pittsburghers' identity; it represents what makes them similar to each other and different from non-Pittsburghers. For some people who experience Pittsburghese this way, it is enregistered primarily with place. A college student raised in a white-collar suburb can claim to speak Pittsburghese as a way of engaging with, and distinguishing herself from, fellow students. For other younger people, Pittsburghese is now enregistered with place and class: it represents a particular kind of gritty, postindustrial, working-class toughness that seems real and hip.

To model how the social meanings of language forms change, Michael Silverstein (2003) uses the concept of "indexical order." A form that is regularly used in a particular context—say, for example, the fact that people use the "dropped-g" form of words ending in <ing> in more casual situations—can come to evoke, or "entail," that context, so that "dropping the g" can help to make a situation more casual. This can happen if members of the community in question start to notice the correlation between g-dropping and casualness, thereby enregistering with a way of speaking associated with social meaning (whether they actually talk about this meaning or just share it by example). In Silverstein's terms, the "n-th-order" link between casualness and g-dropping becomes an "n+1-th-order" link.[7] The same form can be reinterpreted again, so that the n+1-th-order link becomes an (n+1)+1-th-order link. For example, if members of the community noticed that people speaking casually dropped their g's, they might start to associate g-dropping with people who often speak casually, so that g-dropping could be part of a linguistic style a person adopted if he or she wanted to sound like a casual, relaxed sort of person. At the same time, community members could interpret the correlation between g-dropping and casual speech as an index of sloppiness, enregistering g-dropping with a speech register associated with carelessness. And so on.

To put this more simply, language forms can come to have multiple social meanings at multiple levels. This means that a community of speakers engaged with one another in mutual endeavors (a "community of practice," in other words[8]), may draw on a whole "field" of indexical links to evoke and create meaning as they interact (Eckert 2008). A community of practice may be a high school clique, an academic discipline, a family, a study group, an online community, or a workplace, and everyone participates in multiple communities of practice at the same time and over the course of their lives, sharing different indexical fields with different communities.

If everyone in Pittsburgh belonged to the same community of practice, then we could talk about the range of meanings that Pittsburghese has had over time and has now as an indexical field. But Pittsburgh is a city of over 300,000, a metropolitan area of over a million. It is not a community of practice; most Pittsburghers never engage with most other Pittsburghers in any mutual activity at all. Thus, not all Pittsburghers link speech forms to the same meanings or to the same indexical fields of meanings. The same forms mean different things to different Pittsburghers. This is because different Pittsburghers have experienced Pittsburgh speech in different contexts and in the context of different sets of ideas, making different n-th-order indexical links that have evolved into different $n+1$-th-order links according to different ideological schemas. It is hard to generalize about the social meanings of Pittsburghese, either at one time or over time: indexical order looks rather disorderly from a citywide perspective, and a satellite view of the area would display many indexical fields. What we would see instead, if we had a time-depth, citywide view of Pittsburghese, would be more like a series of overlapping strata, a set of layers, accreting over time, each representing one way of understanding local speech. A person born at one time experiences Pittsburghese, over the course of a life, in one set of ways; a person born at another time experiences Pittsburghese in another set of ways, which may or may not overlap with those of the first person. A person in one neighborhood, or in one social class, or in one occupation, experiences Pittsburghese differently than a person in another.

In the following chapter, we explore in more depth how particular linguistic forms come to have particular social meanings for particular individuals, and how people's senses of what it means to use these forms are related to how they themselves speak. We turn, in other words, from a macroscopic, broad-stroke look at the sociolinguistic history of the city to a microscopic investigation of the sociolinguistic histories of several individual Pittsburghers.

4

Perceiving Pittsburghese

In chapter 3, I sketched a chronological account of sociolinguistic change in Pittsburgh by describing the different ways in which Pittsburgh speech has been enregistered over time. This historical process, I claimed, caused new ways of imagining the social meaning of local speech to be superimposed on older ways, such that Pittsburgh speech now means different things to different generations of Pittsburghers. Many Pittsburghers fit into this picture well, hearing and using features of Pittsburgh speech in the ways this model would lead us to expect, with older people remembering a time when there may have been ethnic varieties of English in Pittsburgh, but Pittsburgh speech as a whole had no social meaning; middle-aged people linking Pittsburgh speech with class and correctness; and younger people hearing Pittsburgh speech as indexing place, firmly enregistered as a regional dialect. It makes sense, in other words, to talk about the relatively discrete ways in which features of Pittsburgh speech can be enregistered for people born at different times and growing up in different sociolinguistic worlds.

On the level of demographic groups—sets of people defined by birth year—it is possible to predict how Pittsburgh speech is enregistered, and the history of Pittsburgh provides a good explanation for this. From this perspective, the social history of Pittsburghese looks clear and orderly. On the level of the individual, however, things are more complex and less orderly. Individuals' sociolinguistic worlds are inevitably different from each other. Because people use and experience language in the course of unique life histories, no two people's sociolinguistic biographies—the sets of utterances they have heard, contexts in which they have interacted, and explicit and implicit generalizations they have made about how bits of language map onto the social and material world—are exactly alike. Furthermore, many Pittsburghers experience Pittsburgh speech in multiple ways, drawing on multiple ideological schemas to make social sense of it. Some of these ideological schemas may be widely shared, but others are the result of more idiosyncratic personal experiences, experiences that have led people to make more idiosyncratic generalizations about how the world works and how language is involved. For many Pittsburghers, Pittsburgh speech has conflicting meanings, which makes them unsure whether they speak it or not, whether it sounds charming or embarrassing, or whether to love it or hate it. Furthermore, many Pittsburghers experience their own speech differently than others experience it: many people are unaware of, or mistaken about, how they sound to others. They are surprised to learn how others hear them and confused about why they sound the way they do.

This chapter explores some of the complexity that enters the picture when we start to think about Pittsburgh speech and Pittsburghese from the perspective of individual Pittsburghers' experience with it. I begin by describing experimental research about how people perceive linguistic differences and their social meanings, including an experiment that was designed to explore Pittsburghers' attitudes about Pittsburghese as a whole. I then turn to a field experiment that asked Pittsburghers to talk about the social meanings of particular ways of pronouncing particular sounds. As we will see, most people answered the questions in predictable ways, but there were surprising exceptions, which I explore further in four case studies. I then discuss the concept of "dialect awareness," the various things it can mean to know that you or others speak a dialect. I look at how Pittsburghers talk about the moment they became aware that something about their speech sounded different to others. Finally, I take a step back from the details to discuss what we can learn from taking a phenomenological approach to language change, an approach that starts with a close look at the sociolinguistic experiences of individuals rather than with generalizations about the sociolinguistic worlds of groups.

Pittsburghese versus Standard English: A Matched Guise Experiment

Perceptual dialectologists (Preston 1989; Niedzielski and Preston 1999; Long and Preston 2000) use a variety of experimental tasks to explore the social meanings of linguistic forms from the point of view of hearers. One of the best known of these techniques, borrowed from social psychologists (Ryan and Giles 1982), is called a "matched guise" experiment. In a matched guise task, people listen to two versions of the same passage, sentence, or word that are identical except for the linguistic phenomenon under study. For example, one "guise" might be in one language, the other in another language, with both guises read by the same bilingual speaker, so that everything is kept constant except for the language. Alternatively, one guise might include a slightly different pronunciation of a particular word than the other does, or a version of a sound that has been mechanically lengthened, shortened, or altered in some other way. Experiment participants are then asked to rank, rate, or describe the two guises, often along axes selected by the experimenter like "friendly—unfriendly" or "stupid—intelligent." The results are interpreted as measures of the participants' attitudes about the two alternatives. Such attitudes are, of course, based on how hearers perceive the social meanings of the different guises.

In research she did for her MA in linguistics at the University of Pittsburgh, Christina Gagnon (1999) used the matched guise technique to explore Pittsburghers' attitudes about Pittsburghese. Gagnon first asked a number of Pittsburghers to read aloud a passage that was meant to include a range of words pronounced either in ways that might sound like neutral or standard American English, or in ways characteristic of Pittsburgh speech. Words like *outside, downtown*, and *route* could have monophthongal [a:] ("ah") or diphthongal [aw] ("aw"); words like *fire* and *retired* could have [ay] ("ay") or [a:] ("ah"); *pole* could be pronounced with a more standard-English [o] or an [ʊ] like the one in *pull*, and so on. The passage was as follows:

> A phone wire snapped yesterday causing a giant fire just outside of downtown Pittsburgh near exit 3 of Route 28. The fire was reported by a retired steel worker on his way to pick up his daughter from school. He stopped at the nearest Giant Eagle to make the call to 911. Police say that the telephone pole was hit by a car whose wheel fell off going ninety miles an hour. The smoke from the fire changed the color of the sky from blue to black all the way from the North side to Mount Washington until a late afternoon rain shower helped to put out the fire before it spread to a nearby beer brewery.

One of the readers recorded the passage twice, once with a Pittsburgh accent and once with a more neutral American English accent. (The other speakers' accents ranged from less to more standard sounding, but the readings by these speakers were included only as fillers, meant to distract Gagnon's subjects from noticing that the two guises she was really interested in were read by the same person.) Gagnon recruited eighty-two Pittsburghers of various ages to listen to the recordings and evaluate them, using a series of 6-point rating scales. Some of the traits on which the subjects rated the guises had to do with social status, or how successful a person is perceived as being in the world at large. For example, subjects were asked to place the voices somewhere between "poor" and "wealthy," "successful" and "unsuccessful," "unmotivated" and "motivated," and "educated" and "uneducated." Other traits had to do with social solidarity, or how successful a person is perceived as being in a local group ("friendly" vs. "unfriendly," "unneighborly" vs. "neighborly," "fun" vs. "boring," and so on). Gagnon found that, on the whole, Pittsburghers preferred the more standard-American-English guise to the more Pittsburghese one when it came to both status and solidarity traits. However, while the subjects rated the Pittsburghese voice low and the neutral voice high on status traits (the Pittsburghese voice was heard as poor, unsuccessful, unmotivated, unintelligent, and uneducated, while the standard voice was heard as wealthy, successful, motivated, intelligent, and educated), they rated both voices relatively high on the solidarity traits. The Pittsburghese voice, in other words, was heard as friendly, neighborly, fun, likeable, and trustworthy, as was the more standard-English voice.

Gagnon's study was fairly small and, as she points out, there were ways it could have been improved. (For one thing, it was difficult to find someone who could really read the passage in two different ways, since people who can speak both with a Pittsburgh accent and with a more neutral-sounding accent do not usually do both in the same contexts.) But it points clearly to Pittsburghers' love-hate relationship with Pittsburghese and the way in which Pittsburghese can sound either bad or good and sometimes, for some people, both. The social meanings of Pittsburghese have changed over time, but newer social meanings have not replaced older ones. Rather, Pittsburghese means multiple things to Pittsburghers now, and some of these meanings conflict with each other.

What Does "Hahs" Sound Like?

Like Gagnon's study, much of the research that uses the matched guise technique gauges attitudes to languages or varieties of language as a whole rather than to particular sounds or words (Tucker and Lambert 1969; Ryan and Giles 1982). However, a growing body of research uses experimental techniques to study exactly which differences carry social meaning (Thomas and Reaser 2004), what kinds of contextual conditions affect these judgments (Niedzielski 1999), and which elements of the speech signal are responsible for perceptual differentiation (Friedland, Bartlett, and Kreutz 2004). Taken together, these studies show that people really can hear small differences between one way of pronouncing a sound and another way as having social meaning, as we have been assuming they do.

In my adaptation of the matched guise technique, I asked participants to listen to single-sentence guises, called "sentence versions," which differed only in the pronunciation of a single sound in a single word. All the sentences that participants listened to were spoken by the same speaker, who recorded two versions of each sentence. For example, one of the pairs of sentences was this:

Version a. "She's wearing a winter [koʷt]," with *coat* pronounced in a standard-English way.
Version b. "She's wearing a winter [koˠt]," with *coat* pronounced with the fronted /o/ ("kewt") sound sometimes heard in Pittsburgh.

In one pair, neither of the two versions included a Pittsburgh variant; one of the variants was the neutral, general American English one and the other one was a less standard pronunciation which is actually unusual in Pittsburgh. Participants in the sentence versions task were thirty-six people who had participated in my sociolinguistic interviews in three Pittsburgh-area neighborhoods. Participants heard each sentence version twice. The order of presentation of the two versions of the sentence—standard version first versus nonstandard version first—was random, although it was the same for each subject. There were ten pairs of sentences. After they heard each pair, I asked the participants if they heard a difference between the two versions. If they said they did, I then asked them a series of questions that were meant to elicit the social meanings of the feature that sounded different in each version. The questions were these:

a) Which version is more like the way a Pittsburgher would say the sentence?
b) Which version is more like the way somebody working class would say the sentence?
c) Which version is more like the way a younger person would say the sentence?
d) Which version is more like the way a girl or woman would say the sentence?
e) Which version is more correct?

Questions (a)–(d) were asked in rotating order, starting with question (a) for the first pair, question (b) for the second pair, and so on, and starting with a different question with each participant. Question (e), "Which version is more correct?" was always asked last, so that people's judgment about correctness would be less likely to affect their answers to the other questions. For each question, participants could answer "version (a)," "version (b)," or "neither one." Comparing the results for three of the sentence pairs with the predictions I had made about how people would respond to them showed me that the participants were, in fact, making the kinds of distinctions I hoped they would make, not, for example, identifying all the less standard-sounding features as local or choosing answers at random.[1]

We now turn to the responses to question (a) "Which version is more like the way a Pittsburgher would say the sentence?" in connection with the pair of sentence versions that involved /aw/-monophthongization. This was the eighth of the ten sets of sentence versions, so the participants had already had considerable practice with the task. The two sentence versions were these.

Version a. "We bought a [haws]," with *house* pronounced the way most speakers of American English pronounce it.
Version b: "We bought a [ha:s]," with *house* pronounced something like "hahs," the way that is sometimes identified with Pittsburghese.

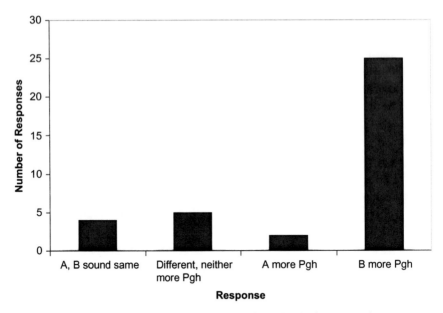

Figure 4.1 Responses for the Matched Guise Task for /aw/. Choice A is the diphthongal variant ("aw"). Choice B is the monophthongized variant ("ah"). Pgh stands for Pittsburgh.

As figure 4.1 shows, twenty-five of the thirty-six respondents said that the sentence version with the monophthongal "hahs" variant of *house* sounded more like the way a Pittsburgher would say it. Four said that [haws] and [ha:s] sounded the same, and five heard a difference but said that neither sounded more like a Pittsburgher. Two people, surprisingly, said that [haws] ("house") was the more Pittsburgh-sounding variant.

With the help of my colleagues Dan Baumgardt and Scott Kiesling, I then compared these results with how the same thirty-six people pronounced this variable in my interviews with them. Every time there was a syllable that could have been pronounced with an [aw] sound (as in "house") or an [a:] sound (as in "hahs"), we noted how it was in fact pronounced. We gave each pronunciation a score of 1, 2, or 3, with 1 designating clearly diphthongal ("house"), 3 clearly monophthongal ("hahs"), and 2 in between. It turned out, as figure 4.2 shows, that there was a statistically significant relationship between the degree of *diphthongal* pronunciation in a participant's own speech ("house") and the likelihood that that person would select response B, identifying the *monophthongal* pronunciation of *house* ("hahs") with Pittsburgh speech.[2]

The gray bars in figure 4.2 represent four groups of people, and the black line represents how many people there were in each group. The height of the bars corresponds to what percentage of the group's spoken /aw/-sounds were of the more Pittsburgh variety (more like "hahs," in other words). The left-hand bar

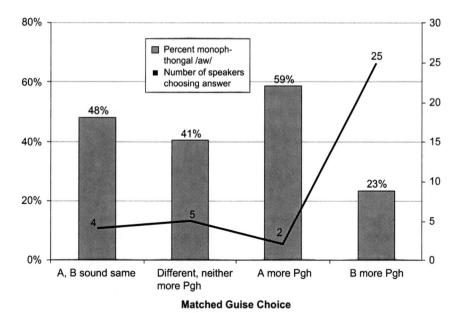

Figure 4.2 Comparison of the Number of Responses on the Matched Guise Task (Line) with the Amount of Monophthongization in Speakers Choosing Each Option (Bars). Pgh stands for Pittsburgh.

represents the four people who said they did not hear a difference between the two versions of the word *house*. On the average, those people pronounced words like *house* with the Pittsburgh variant ("hahs") 48 percent of the time. Moving to the right in the figure, the five people who said the two versions sounded different, but that neither version sounded more like the way a Pittsburgher would say the word, themselves pronounced words like *house* more like "hahs" 41 percent of the time, on the average. The third bar represents the two people who said that the "hahs" version of the sentence sounded *less* like a Pittsburgher than the more general American English version. These people themselves used this variant: during the interviews with me, they pronounced words like *house* in a more monophthongal way ("hahs") most of the time. The largest group (twenty-five people) is represented by the final bar. These people said that "hahs" sounded more like the way a Pittsburgher would say the word. Given the fact that lists of Pittsburghese sounds, words, and phrases inevitably include the "hahs" pronunciation, this does not seem surprising. However, these people themselves did *not*, for the most part, pronounce words like *house* that way. In other words, people who associate monophthongal /aw/ with Pittsburghese speech are unlikely to use this feature in their own speech.

Given these findings, it looks as if people who sound the most like Pittsburghers (at least with respect to how they pronounce words like *downtown*, *out*, and *house*) cannot be doing this because they want to sound like Pittsburghers, since they do not hear a difference between the two ways of saying words like these, they do not think either option sounds more like a Pittsburgher, or they think the more standard option is the one Pittsburghers use. On the other hand, people who do think that "dahntahn," "aht," "hahs," and so on sound local do not actually pronounce words like these that way. So we need to ask not only what do Pittsburghers sound like, but also which Pittsburghers sound like Pittsburghers, and to whom do they sound that way?

Four Case Studies

Linguistic features that become the subject of overt comment as to their social meaning typically become less frequent and eventually stop being used (W. Labov 1972b, 180). For example, the more often people in New York are told, and tell each other, that "Toity-toid Street" is how older, less-educated New Yorkers pronounce *Thirty-third Street*, the less likely it is that New Yorkers will continue to pronounce this word, and words like it, this way. This might help explain the overall finding of my sentence version experiment: speakers who choose monophthongal /aw/ (the "hahs" variant) as the local-sounding variant on the perception task may have done so at least in part because it is very stereotyped, linked with Pittsburghese over and over again on T-shirts, coffee mugs, and the like. If this is the case, then it is not surprising that these speakers are unlikely to have the feature in their speech. However, as we saw, about a quarter of the speakers who hear monophthongal /aw/ as local *do* monophthongize /aw/, and 30 percent of my sample did *not* hear monophthongal /aw/ as local. Stereotyping cannot enter into an explanation of why they behave as they do with respect to this feature. To understand these findings, we need a more nuanced account of how social meaning and the pronunciation of words with the (aw) sound in them are connected. For this, we turn to case studies. We explore the social meaning (if any) of this feature to four individual Pittsburghers on the basis of their use of it and how they talk about it. As we will see, for one of these individuals monophthongal /aw/ has no social meaning. For the others, monophthongal /aw/ has a variety of meanings, not all of which are connected with local identity.

In the final part of my interviews, I invited participants to talk about local speech by asking the question, "Have you ever heard of Pittsburghese?" Almost everyone who was involved in the sentence versions task said they had. If they said "yes," I then asked for a definition and some examples. If they said "no," I introduced the topic of Pittsburgh speech in some other way. So both here and, spontaneously, in other parts of the interview, participants provided metalinguistic talk (that is, talk about language) that sheds direct light on how linguistic form and social meaning are linked for them, and some of this talk was about monophthongal /aw/ in particular.

Table 4.1 **Matched Guise Responses of Case-study Speakers and Degree of Monophthongization in their Speech**

Speaker	Matched guise response	% monophthong	(#/N)
Esther R.	[haws] and [ha:s] sound the same	100.0%	(19/19)
Lydia H.	[haws] and [ha:s] sound different, neither sounds more Pittsburgh	7.7%	(5/65)
Dennis C.	[haws] sounds more Pittsburgh	62.0%	(111/179)
Jason E.	[ha:s] sounds more Pittsburgh	57.0%	(57/100)

Further, the sentence versions task itself elicited spontaneous talk about the prompts and their meanings, and this talk was also recorded. In what follows, I discuss four speakers, each of whom made a different choice on the sentence versions task. Only the last of these speakers linked /aw/-monophthongization with the projection of a local identity, and he is able to use the feature for this purpose only in fairly self-conscious, performed speech. For the others, monophthongal /aw/ and localness are linked in a variety of other ways or not linked at all.

The speakers and their responses are summarized in table 4.1. The first column gives the pseudonym of the speaker, the second tells how he or she responded to the two versions of *house* in the sentence version task, and the third gives figures about how often the person used the "hahs" version of such words in his or her own speech. The percentage is given first, followed by the number of words pronounced with a monophthongal [a:] sound ("ah") in the interview and the number of words that could have been pronounced that way. For example, Esther R. said that the two versions of the word *house* sounded the same. In my interview with her, she used nineteen words that could have been pronounced with one or the other variant of the (aw) sound, and she pronounced all nineteen with the monophthongal variant, for a percentage of 100.

ESTHER R.: [HAWS] AND [HA:S] SOUND THE SAME

Esther R., who was born in 1917, represents the first group in figure 4.1, those who said they could not hear a difference between the monophthongal ("hahs") and diphthongal ("house") variants of /aw/ in *house*. On average, people in this group were about equally likely to use monophthongal and diphthongal /aw/ in a given word, but Esther R. used the nonstandard monophthongal variant 100 percent of the time in the interview.

For Esther R., local speech forms do not function as indexes of social identities. In the interview, she claimed never to have heard of Pittsburghese and said she did not think there is a local accent.

4.1 *Never heard of Pittsburghese*

BJ So, let me ask you if you ever heard of the term "Pittsburghese." No ((responding to head gesture))? Um-hm. Do you think people here have an accent that's different from other places?

ESTHER R. No, I don't think so.

BJ You don't think so? Um-hm.

ESTHER R. To me, it didn't, you know, it doesn't—

BJ But so, there aren't any—

ESTHER R. Yeah.

BJ Particular words or expressions—

ESTHER R. No.

BJ or anything that people think, people think—

ESTHER R. No, I don't think so.

Later in the interview, she did claim to use some local words, like *redd up* ('to tidy'), and to know people who use *yinz*. However, she linked these forms only to the personal identities of individual speakers, as she did here:

4.2 *Ann always said* yinz

BJ Do you know people who would say *yunz* or *yinz*?

ESTHER R. Huh? I've heard of that.

BJ Um-hm. Yeah.

ESTHER R. ((To her son, who was also participating in the interview.)) You know who I often think about using that word? Ann. Remember?

DON R. Yes.

ESTHER R. She always used that word.

BJ Um-hm.

ESTHER R. That's his sister-in-law. My sister-in-law.

Esther R. appears never to have thought about local forms in terms of ideological schemas linking them to localness, standardness, region, gender, or any other larger social category. People like Esther R., who were educated in Pittsburgh schools in the early or mid-twentieth century, are likely to have been told that certain local grammatical features were incorrect, if they were told anything about the difference between how Pittsburghers and other people talked. But since their teachers had local accents and used local forms, features of Pittsburgh speech that involved pronunciation and the use of local words tended to receive little or no attention. This means that students of this era may not associate local speech forms with any social meaning. In Esther R.'s environment, as in the environments of most Pittsburghers, the pronunciation of /aw/ can be observed to be correlated with class, gender, and place of origin, as well as with the degree to which a person's life experience involves local practices (Kiesling et al. 2005). But people like Esther have had no reason to make these sorts of observations. Nothing in Esther's environment has called her attention to these correlations or invested them with meaning. Thus, Esther does not perceive the difference between monophthongal and diphthongal variants of /aw/, and this variable carries no social meaning for her.

LYDIA H.: [HAWS] AND [HA:S] SOUND DIFFERENT, NEITHER SOUNDS MORE PITTSBURGH

The second group in figure 4.1, those who claimed to hear a difference between the two variants but said that neither sounded more like the way a Pittsburgher would say the word, is represented by Lydia H., who was born in 1920. Her interview speech is even more standard with respect to the (aw) variable than the combined score for people who responded this way. In 93.3 percent of the instances in which she could choose a diphthongal ("house") variant or a monophthongal ("hahs") one, she chose the former. When I presented her with the nonstandard version of (aw), she remarked, "I haven't heard anybody say that."

Lydia H. does, however, think that there is a local dialect. When she talked about it, she drew on an ideological schema that is reflected in the folk dictionary (McCool 1982) she reported purchasing ("They have a Pittsburghese book I picked up from Borders"). As we can see in the following extract, this schema links regional dialect with word choice rather than grammar or phonology: "Well, sometimes people put the *an' at* ((*and that*)) . . . they'll say '*an' at*'". She also drew on a schema that links standardness with grammar and usage, including the prohibition of sentence-final prepositions: "Well, and often people put prepositions at the end of the sentences and that, that bothers me," she said. This, she claimed, was the result of her education: "Having been steeped in English writing composition, I know that's not something you do."

4.3 "People put prepositions at the end of the sentences"

    BJ You've said several times that the only thing that's not typical about you is that you don't use some of those—

    LYDIA H. *Yinz.*

    BJ Pittsburgh words. *Yunz.*

    GEORGE H. (LYDIA H.'S HUSBAND) ((Laughs))

    BJ What, what?

    LYDIA H. Pittsburghese, they have a Pittsburghese book I picked up from Borders.

    BJ Um-hm.

    LYDIA G. That's why I'm not gonna . . . I should read it just to see what it says. ((Laughs))

    BJ Um-hm. So what does, what else, besides *yunz*, would you identify?

LYDIA H. They'll, they'll put the—Well, and often people put prepositions at the end of the sentences and that, that bothers me. Of course, having been ((chuckles)) been steeped in English writing composition, I know that's not something you do.

Pronunciation does not enter into the set of resources that, for Lydia, can function as indexes of nonstandardness or regionally marked speech. When asked whether she has ever been told she has an accent, Lydia H. recalled being told by a teacher at her elite college that Pittsburgh had "the second worst speech in all of the United States." However, because she considered herself well educated and linked standardness to education, she did not seem to take this to suggest that her own pronunciation, or that of other Pittsburghers, might sound nonstandard.

As I noted, if people of Esther R. and Lydia H.'s generation had features of Pittsburgh speech called to their attention in their youth, they were likely to have been grammatical ones. For Lydia H., who does hear the difference between the two variants of /aw/ but identifies neither one as more local, word choice and grammatical choice can carry social meaning, but pronunciation does not. At least two ideological schemas are in play for her: one that links region and word choice, the way folk dictionaries like the McCool book typically do, and one that links differences in grammar with differences in education and correctness, the way teachers traditionally did (and do). Lydia H. shares the latter schema with many other Americans (Preston 1996, 54–59), who hear differences in language as differences in correctness. In Lydia's linguistic world, locally hearable forms are indexes of incorrectness, not localness. Furthermore, since correctness, in her experience, is relevant mainly in connection with writing, she links differences in word choice and grammar with degrees of correctness but not differences in pronunciation.

People of Esther and Lydia's generation tended to grow up in ethnically segregated neighborhoods. Working-class children, like Esther, who were the offspring of southern and eastern European immigrants, often attended schools run by ethnic Catholic parishes, which meant that they were not exposed to people who talked differently than they did until high school or later. Upper-middle-class Pittsburghers like Lydia were less likely to attend Catholic schools and more likely to attend private college-preparatory academies catering to the children of the Protestant elite. In both cases, though, their peer groups contained few people who spoke differently than they did, at least until they left Pittsburgh to attend a university (as Lydia did, but not Esther). In general, people who do not hear local forms as bearing social meaning, or whose ideological schemas about local speech link it exclusively to correctness, thus tend to be older and to have lived in more dense, multiplex social networks than other Pittsburghers.

DENNIS C.: [HAWS] SOUNDS MORE PITTSBURGH

Dennis C., born in 1950, chose the more standard, diphthongal variant as the one most likely to be the way a Pittsburgher would say the word *house*. In his interview with me, Dennis's rate of monophthongization is close to the average for people who made this choice: 38 percent of his tokens of (aw) were diphthongal ("aw"), but most (62 percent) were monophthongal ("ah").

As he carried out the sentence versions task, Dennis C. expressed strong opinions about the social meaning of alternative pronunciations. In other words, unlike Lydia H., he did use pronunciation as a resource for interpreting social meaning. Dennis C. said he was unaware of having an accent while he was growing up and still has trouble acknowledging that others hear him as having one. As he put it:

4.4 "I was never aware"

DENNIS C. Actually, I was never aware that . . . we had any particular accent. Words like *slippy* and *redd* something, I thought these were just normal. I didn't realize that people didn't use those words in other parts of the country. I knew that down south they had this accent, but I never, I never thought of myself, as having—Even to this day, I have a hard time thinking of myself as having an accent.

If he does "slur" some words, as he put it, he claimed that doing so had never hurt him: "I don't believe [having an accent has] hurt me anyplace that I've gone to get a job. No one's ever said to me that they couldn't understand me, or anything like that. I never had anybody make fun out of me."

Unlike Esther R. or Lydia H., Dennis C. does link local speech with pronunciation. However, he has a positive attitude about the local accent and, perhaps because of this (cf. Niedzielski 1999), he hears the more standard form as local, despite his own use of the nonstandard form. During the matched guise task, Dennis C. said that he hears the local form as rural. Because it is important to know not just what he said in this excerpt, but how he pronounced some words, I have put phonetic transcriptions of those words in parentheses.

4.5 "The second one sahnds horrible."

BJ Alright, just a couple more here.

RECORDED VOICE Sentence 8. a. We bought a house ([haws]). We bought a house ([haws]). b. We bought a house ([ha:s]). We bought a house ([ha:s]).

BJ All right. Which, is one of those, well you know what the questions are now, wh—

DENNIS C. Well, "hau—" ([ha]) well, the second one sounds ([sa:ndz]) horrible.

BJ Uh-huh.

DENNIS C. "House" ([haws]). But then again now I don't know maybe that's . . .
see I'm not always aware of of my own Pittsburgh accent. "House" ([haws]),
"house" ([ha:s]), that, I don't, that doesn't sound, that sounds terrible, not
Pittsburgh.

BJ Does, does it, it doesn't sound local to you.

DENNIS C. It doesn't sound local to *me*.

In line 4, Dennis C. claims that the monophthongal version of *house* "sounds
horrible" (in the process monophthongizing the /aw/ in *sounds*). He then starts
to admit that the "horrible" version might in fact be the Pittsburgh one, the one
he uses himself: "I'm not always aware of my Pittsburgh accent." But after repeating the monophthongal variant ("hahs"), he asserts that it "sounds terrible,
not Pittsburgh." As he repeats what he apparently hears as the monophthongal
prompt, he actually produces it diphthongally first and then monophthongally:
""House" ([haws]), "hahs" ([ha:s]), that . . . sounds terrible, not Pittsburgh." Together with the fact that he monophthongizes almost invariantly in other words
with the /aw/ sound in them—*sound(s)* ("sahnds"), *out* ("aht"), and *pronunciation*
("pronahnciation")—this suggests that he does not have control over how he
pronounces words with the /aw/ variable. Thus he cannot be using monophthongization to project localness or any other aspect of identity, even though
other people might hear him as doing so. When I probed further, he claimed that
he thinks [ha:s] ("hahs") sounds like "some hillbillies, somewhere out in the hills
somewhere, some strange thing from Ligonier" (the mountain town where his
father worked for a time), "certain pronunciations common to the country folk
for some odd reason."

Because they tend to have local accents and use local words and grammatical
structures, Pittsburghers of the post–World War II generation tend to hear and
contribute to two ways of talking about Pittsburgh speech. On one hand, they
hear and participate in discourse about Pittsburgh speech that links local forms
with incorrectness. On the other hand, they hear and participate in discourse
about Pittsburgh speech that links local forms with nostalgia and pride. Someone like Dennis C., who knows he has a local accent because he has heard people
say he does but cannot hear or control it, represents one of the outcomes for
people of this generation. The ideological schema on which Dennis bases his interpretation of monophthongal /aw/ is, as we have seen, an idiosyncratic, personal one: "hahs" sounds like hillbilly talk. For Dennis C., unlike Esther or Lydia,
pronunciation is an indexical resource, but he hears the local variant as rural and
does not link it with Pittsburgh. The particular ideological schema he brings to
bear, in which forms are heard to differ based on how "hillbilly" or "redneck"
they are, is based in his personal history. While this schema is salient for many
Americans, it is not often adduced in Pittsburgh, where people rarely contrast
urban with rural speech or allude to Pittsburgh's Appalachian setting.

The ideological schema that Dennis C. brings to bear on the linguistic variation he perceives in his environment links linguistic variability and geographic place, according to the belief that dialects map naturally onto places (Johnstone 2004). Even though he cannot produce the two variants at will, Dennis C. hears the difference between them and attributes it to where a speaker is from. However, unlike some other Pittsburghers and in accordance with very personal experience (the way his father talked and his strongly positive, sometimes defensive attitude about Pittsburgh), he does not link the regional form to Pittsburgh, hearing it instead as rural and identifying the more standard variant with the city. This schema is linked with an ideology of urbanness that evaluates it positively in comparison with ruralness.

For people of Dennis C.'s generation, links between linguistic form and social meaning are unstable and variable. These Pittsburghers tend to toggle among multiple ways of thinking about local speech, making multiple links between local forms and social identities, depending on the context. The same person, in the same conversation, can identify local forms both as embarrassing and as charming; middle-aged Pittsburghers tend to claim local accents (whether they have them or not), but their attitudes about sounding local are ambiguous.

JASON E. [HA:S] SOUNDS MORE PITTSBURGH

Jason E. was born in 1986. He was a high school senior when I interviewed him. In most respects, his speech did not sound local; his score for /aw/ monophthongization was 57 percent, but this was mainly because he talked fast. In the perception task, he identified the sentence version with [ha:s] as the one that sounds more like the way a Pittsburgher would say it. Thus, he is in the largest group in figure 4.1. Though he is a native Pittsburgher, Jason E. claimed not to speak the local dialect. Nevertheless, he was eager to discuss and perform both what he called "the actual accent of the Pittsburgher" and "the words that we use and no one else uses." Jason E. also showed that he associated monophthongal /aw/ ("ah") with local identity in the interview, where this was the first feature he used to exemplify Pittsburghese as an accent. When he performed Pittsburghese, he relied on words that include the /aw/ sound to make his point about both accent and usage. This part of the conversation started after I asked him to define "Pittsburghese." The "ah" versus "aw" variable is not the only one I discuss; here are the others:

The pronunciation of *down* as [dæ:n] ("Dan") and *house* as [hæ:s] ("hass" as in "hassle")

Rounded low back vowel in *Knox*, [nɔks] ("knaughks") and *John*, [dʒɔn] ("Jaughn").

Fronted /o/ in *pierogie*, [pəroʷˤgi] ("pierewgi")

4.6 "Welcome to Knox's Pierogie House"

JASON E. It's a—I wouldn't say it's a language, it's a—like a—what's the word—um, a, dialect, unique, to, this, area. ((As if reciting a dictionary definition.))

BJ And what is—what are some things, what are some examples of it?

JASON E. Uh well, you have—I think there's two—two things that make it up. There's, uh, the actual accent of the Pittsburgher, and then there's, the words, that we use and no one else uses. And you know the accent would be like, instead of saying "down" you'd say "dan" ([dæ:n]), or you know— Uh, also the way you, the way you use words, which I guess fits into the second category. You know, "Dan ([dæ:n]), Welcome to, Max—" like "Knox's Pierogie House ([nɔksəz pəroʷˤgi hæ:s])." You know, that, that kind of thing. Or instead of saying "I'm going to this place" they say "I'm goin' dan ([dæ:n]) blah blah blah."

BJ "Dahn ([da:n]) street." *Dahn* ([da:n]), yeah.

JASON E. "I'm goin' dahn ([da:n]) the street. I'm going dahn ([da:n]) a John's ([dʒanz]) hahs ([ha:s])."

BJ "Dahn Jaughn ([da:n dʒɔn])— dahn a Jaughn's hahs ([da:n ə dʒɔnz ha:s])."

JASON E. "Dahn Jaughn's hahs ([da:n dʒɔnz ha:s])." Yeah.

BJ Mm hmm.

JASON E. Yeah. I hate—It's a really ugly accent I think.

The first actual example Jason E. gave was the local pronunciation of *down* represented in the respelling "dahn." After repeating the pronunciation of this single word, he offered a phrase that included a local-sounding restaurant name: "Welcome to Knox's Pierogie House." This phrase seems designed as an illustration of Pittsburghese pronunciation, as it includes three words that can be pronounced in a distinctively Pittsburghese way: *Knox*, *pierogie*, and *house*. Jason pronounced all three the local way: he rounded the low back vowel in *Knox*, (so that it sounded something like "knaughks," to people who can hear the difference), fronted the /o/ in *pierogie*, (so that it sounded something like "pierewgi") and monophthongized the /aw/ in *house* (so that it sounded something like "hass" at first, later on like "hahs"). As his illustration of Pittsburghese went on, Jason E. continued to use a monophthongal [a:] sound, working it repeatedly into the performance in the words *down* and *house* and supplementing it with other phonological features.

To Jason E., as to Mary H., monophthongal /aw/ sounded incorrect; Jason E. also called the local accent "ugly." Although he did once include himself in the group that uses Pittsburghese, using the pronoun *we* in "the words that **we** use that no one else uses," he also did a great deal of work in the interview to distance himself from local speech, which he claimed not to speak. He even misperformed monophthongal /aw/ (as [æ:] as in *ran* rather than [a:] as in "hahs") the first few three times he said *down* and the first time he said *house*, until I modeled the actual local pronunciation. Localness and social stigma are explicitly linked for Jason, and monophthongal /aw/ is explicitly linked with both.

Younger people like Jason have grown up in an environment in which few of their peers use features that could make them sound local in unselfconscious speech. At the same time, though, everyday talk and material artifacts like T-shirts repeatedly connect local forms with a stereotypical, nostalgia-linked local character type. They have also grown up in an increasingly diverse environment: attending racially integrated schools, traveling more, and more likely going to universities in other areas. Thus, they are more likely to have interacted with and accommodated to peers who did not have Pittsburgh accents.

Jason E., like many other people his age, experiences the ideology that links regional forms to local identity mainly through widely circulating media (on T-shirts, in folk dictionaries, and the like) where locally hearable forms are treated as "folk culture artifacts" (Preston 1996, 59–72). Dennis Preston suggests that particular linguistic variants can rise to the level of folk-linguistic awareness as they acquire "performance potential" by being part of a folkloristic framework. In such a schema, regional forms like monophthongal /aw/ function as "traditional items of knowledge that arise in recurring performances" (Abrahams 1969, 106, quoted in Preston 1996, 59). Like most performances, Jason's attempts to perform local variants, including /aw/-monophthongization, are imperfect. Together with what he says about regional speech, these performances show that for him, regional forms are indexically linked to a stereotypical local identity. As a middle-class, half-African-American adolescent, Jason does not aspire to this identity, and he does not use socially meaningful regional forms in unselfconscious speech, where they might sound uneducated to someone like Lydia or rural to someone like Dennis. Note, however, that he is the only one of these four speakers who can use more regional-sounding forms to sound more like a "real" Pittsburgher. A subset of locally hearable forms serve Jason as resources for showing that he has insider knowledge about the city, even if he does not self-identify as or sound like a stereotypical Pittsburgher.

Jason is not alone among his age group in using local forms to display local knowledge, like imitating stereotypical Pittsburghers. Like Jason, younger middle-class Pittsburghers tend to distance themselves from people who use local forms in everyday speech (and they tend to use many fewer local forms in their own speech). Young Pittsburghers like Jason have access to both the more negative social meaning of monophthongal /aw/ as an index of incorrectness or carelessness and the more positive, nostalgic, social meaning of (other people's) monophthongal /aw/ as both an index and a symbol of Pittsburgh. For these Pittsburghers, certain stereotypical pronunciations, words, and structures are available for performances of and allusions to localness that mock the stereotypical working-class Pittsburgher of the industrial era, and in so doing, project, and are heard by their peers as projecting, local knowledge and postindustrial urban hipness. This is the generation that has founded a literary magazine, modeled on the *New Yorker*, ironically named the *New Yinzer*. For them, the social meaning of local forms is relatively regimented and orderly: in their sociolinguistic world, a small subset of the forms that their parents may interpret either as nostalgic reminders of their youth or as signs of a lack of education, or in some other way, have come to be identified with a stereotypical local character type exemplified by Stanley P. Kachowski, the character created by radio DJ Jim Krenn. We look at this character and his speech in detail in later chapters. For now, it is enough to note that this persona is sometimes referred to as a "Yinzer," a term derived from the local pronoun *yinz*.

Coming to Dialect Awareness

Describing Pittsburghers' sociolinguistic worlds from the perspective of individuals' experience suggests that the historical changes I described in chapter 4—the movement of Pittsburgh speech over several centuries from a western Pennsylvania accent that nobody noticed to a noticeable dialect called "Pittsburghese"—has not been as smooth as is suggested by a more abstract community-level representation. In particular, change has disrupted some Pittsburghers' senses of self and language more than others'. The process has called Dennis C.'s identity into question in a way that has not happened to older or younger people. The sociolinguistic world Dennis C. has experienced has been semiotically chaotic.

This chapter serves as a reminder that social meaning carried by a linguistic form from the point of view of a hearer may not be the same as the meaning of that feature to the speaker, and that different people hear different forms as having social meaning as a result of different becoming-aware experiences. People who hear Dennis C.'s or Esther R.'s speech, full of /aw/-monophthongization, may hear them as projecting Pittsburgh identity, but neither Dennis nor Esther would interpret this feature that way in someone else's speech. (Esther would not notice it, and Dennis would think the speaker sounded rural.) If we do not specify whose perspective we are taking when we talk about the social meaning of local speech in a community like Pittsburgh, we may be guilty of what literary critics call the "intentional fallacy," the fallacy of attributing readers' interpretations to authors' intentions. In other words, a nuanced account of sociolinguistic change should describe such change not just from the perspective of "society" but also from the perspective of individuals' experience, since it is at the interface of social order and individual experience that meaning making occurs.

We cannot specify the meaning of a particular variant for all speakers in a community, no matter how we define the community. I have shown that the social meaning of the sounds, words, and structures that can be heard in Pittsburgh varies from speaker to speaker, and that some speakers have more than one way of interpreting locally hearable forms. This does not mean that we cannot create models of how social meanings articulate with larger social categories, or that we cannot explain why those meanings arise and how they spread. But we need to supplement approaches that aim to generalize about the social meanings of linguistic forms (like the one I took in chapter 3) with a framework that supports multiple, layered, and even contradictory, meanings in a speech community. It is people's lived experiences that create meaning. Since every speaker has a different history of experience with pairings of meaning and form, speakers may have many different senses of the potential social meanings of particular forms. Social meaning (like meaning in general) is forged in individuals' experience of their particular sociolinguistic worlds, in the course of the linguistic life experiences that make each person's language unique.

However, precisely because Pittsburgh speech, and particular features of Pittsburgh speech, means different things to different people, differences among people's ways of speaking sometimes become the object of attention. Something happens that makes a particular difference noticeable. I talked in the previous chapter about the large-scale social and historical processes that make people like Dennis C. come to think that they speak a dialect. These forces are put into play when people become mobile, socially and geographically, putting Pittsburghers into contact with people who speak differently than they do. If we think about things on this larger scale, it is tempting to see "dialect awareness" as something that simply happens to people when they are exposed to dialects. As we have seen, however, just listening to someone with a different accent is not enough to make a person notice the differences or to associate the differences with an "accent" (rather than, for example, hearing them as personal idiosyncrasies). We do not automatically interpret every unfamiliar pronunciation or word we hear as evidence that we are listening to an unfamiliar dialect.

Despite what people often think, differences between dialects are not obvious. One reason for this is that there are limits on what people are able notice when it comes to the details of language (Silverstein 1981; Preston 1996). For one thing, it is more likely that people will be able to notice words that carry social meaning than that they will notice sounds that do. For example, it is more likely that people will notice that Pittsburghers use *yinz* than that they will notice that Pittsburghers pronounce *house* as [ha:s] ("hahs"). This is because *yinz* refers to something (whoever is being addressed), whereas the use of monophthongal /aw/, on its own, does not refer to anything. Many of the linguistic features that linguists would characterize in phonological terms, as regular substitutions of one sound for another (like [a:] for [aw]), are described by Pittsburghers as words: *dahntahn, hahs, aht*. For another thing, people obviously cannot notice a difference they cannot hear. For example, to most Pittsburghers *cot* and *caught* sound exactly the same, so they are not aware of the fact that they pronounce words like these differently than many other Americans do, with the sound of *caught* (for those who can hear the difference) rather than with the sound of *cot*.

However, even with limitations like these, humans can learn to attend to all sorts of linguistic differences if they are listening for them. Fortunately, we are not listening for every possible difference all the time. If we were, we would be overwhelmed by the job of figuring out what we were hearing and what it could mean. For language to work, some differences have to be attended to, others ignored. Children learn to talk by gradually learning what differences to attend to and what kinds of difference they make: Does the difference between *shoes* and *juice* matter? What difference does it make whether someone pronounces the first of these words with a fronted /u/ ("shewz") or with a non-fronted /u/ ("shooz")? In order for a linguistic difference to be attended to, something has to happen to make it visible. Somebody has to produce a shoe when you were asking for juice; something has to happen to suggest that one kind of person says "shewz" and a different kind of person says "shooz." In one way or another, linguistic differences have to be pointed out and given meaning in terms of cultural schemas. This can happen in many ways: someone can fail to understand someone else; someone can tell someone else that they sound funny; someone can get into an argument with someone else about the correct way to say something; someone can read in a textbook or on a souvenir T-shirt that people from such and such a place speak such and such a dialect. In one way or another, the difference must be evaluated, given meaning.[3] This is why people who have lived in Pittsburgh for decades can claim never to have heard anyone with a Pittsburgh accent.

Just as different Pittsburghers hear and interpret Pittsburgh speech in different ways, different people become aware of Pittsburghese in general, and features of Pittsburghese in particular, in different ways. Sometimes family members point out people's Pittsburghese to them. Sometimes people notice in school or college, or by moving to another city later on, that features of their speech are different from those used elsewhere. Sometimes it is the media: a book like the Sam McCool dictionary, a newspaper article, or a radio or video parody. Sometimes all it takes for people to become aware of their accents is to hear their own voices on the telephone answering machine. And sometimes it was I, the interviewer, asking about some word or form an interviewee had never thought about before, that made people I talked to suspect they spoke Pittsburghese. Through metalinguistic practices like these, social meanings for a subset of variable forms in a speech community may start to circulate and become increasingly similar from speaker to speaker. To put it another way, people do not notice things simply by opening their eyes or ears wider. People teach each other what to notice and what it means by realigning them toward a particular ideological schema in which it makes sense to notice these things and attribute certain meanings to them. In the chapters to follow, we look at a number of ways in which this happens in Pittsburgh.

5

Linking Language and Place
in Interaction

In earlier chapters, we have seen how the idea of Pittsburghese arose and evolved, and how Pittsburghese came to be linked with Pittsburgh and Pittsburgh's identity. I concentrated in chapter 3 on the historical, economic, and ideological factors that encouraged Pittsburghers to notice things about the way they talked and attribute meaning to these things, and on how the meaning of Pittsburghese has changed over time, first indexing working-class identity or incorrectness, eventually indexing place and place identity. Sounding like a Pittsburgher, whether this means having a Pittsburgh accent, being able to imitate one, or both, can now have a variety of meanings. In chapter 4, I showed that features of Pittsburgh speech mean different things to different people, depending on their own particular sociolinguistic histories.

In this chapter and the chapters to follow, I explore how the sets of ideas and activities that constitute Pittsburghese circulate among people in Pittsburgh and elsewhere. How do people learn what Pittsburghese is and what it means? How do people come to share ideas about what you can do with speech forms that have come to sound like Pittsburgh? How does being a Pittsburgher get associated in so much popular discourse with speaking Pittsburghese? The short answer is this: Pittsburghers teach each other about Pittsburghese as they talk to each other; as they tell stories; as they perform on and listen to the radio; and as they write, read, and react to newspapers and magazines. People make claims and counterclaims about what Pittsburghese does and what it consists of as they sell, buy, and use Pittsburghese t-shirts, decorative license plates, talking dolls, and coffee mugs; and as they create, watch, and comment on online videos and podcasts. The possibility for enregisterment arises every time someone uses a particular linguistic form in a context in which the form can be linked with a social identity. The nature of these contexts—who uses what forms, in what ways, in which media, to what audiences—helps determine which forms get enregistered in which ways. For example, as we will see, talk about Pittsburgh speech typically arises in the context of talk about Pittsburgh, so the words and the sounds and bits of grammar represented in words that are made available for dialect enregisterment are often ones associated with Pittsburgh places and lifestyles.

In order to see how enregisterment happens in the course of social life, we need a model of how people create language, and ideas about language, as they interact. This requires us to consider the ways in which language is REFLEXIVE—always about itself. It also requires us to consider the METAPRAGMATIC things people do as they speak to show how their words should be interpreted.

Reflexivity and Metapragmatics

Enregisterment is the linking of linguistic form and social meaning in the context of a schema of ideas that allows the linkage to make sense. I have traced the history of enregisterment that has given rise to the multiple meanings that Pittsburgh speech has today for different people and in different contexts. But how does enregisterment actually happen? How do correlations between form and context become meaningful? To step back for a moment from Pittsburgh, how do people come to share the idea that, in the United States, people who pronounce /æ/ as [a] (as in "bahth" for *bath*) can sometimes sound upper class? How do we learn that words like *heretofore* are examples of "legalese"? How does *wicked*, used as an adverbial intensifier in phrases like *wicked good*, get associated with New Englanders, and how does *hella*, used the same way, get associated with Northern California youth? On a very general level, the answer is surprisingly simple: people learn to hear linguistic variants as having social meaning by being told that they do, and they continue to share ideas about meaning as long as they keep telling each other about them.

We are able tell each other about the meanings of linguistic forms because language is reflexive—language is always about itself, no matter what else it is also about. Every utterance is an example of how an utterance can be structured, how it can sound, and what it can accomplish. Every time we say something we are potentially modeling to our hearers what someone with the identities that are being oriented to at the moment would say, and how that person would say it. As Talbot Taylor puts it, "We ourselves are the sources of our own verbal regularity" by virtue of "the normative character of the situated events of linguistic production" (1977, 165). We are particularly aware of this when we are careful how we talk around children, knowing that we are modeling appropriate ways of talking. But speech is a model of speech in other contexts, too: how you talk is always a model of how someone like you talks in the situation at hand.

Connections between linguistic form and meaning can be highlighted as people interact. Such highlighting strategies are sometimes referred to under the rubric of METAPRAGMATICS (Silverstein 1993). Metapragmatics (from *meta*, above or about, and *pragmatics*, the actions people perform through their talk) encompasses all the ways in which an utterance can be *framed* (Goffman 1986; Tannen 1979; 1993) or *contextualized* (Gumperz 1982; 1992), that is, linked with a particular context. Forms can be metapragmatically linked with social identities explicitly, in utterances like, "You know you're from Maine if you say *wicked* instead of *very*," or "She sounds like such a nerd." Slightly less direct metapragmatic links can also involve words or phrases that refer to social identities.

Here is an example of how this can work. In answer to a question about a clematis vine, someone suggested two different pronunciations:[1] [kləmæˈDəs] (roughly "kluMADus," as an American would say it) and [klɛˈməDəs] ("KLEmadus"). A third pronunciation was introduced by another speaker who said, "It's [kləmaˈDəs] ("kluMAHDus") if you're in the garden club." With this move, she invited her listeners to enregister the pronunciation [kləmaˈDəs] ("kluMAHDus") with a social identity (being "in the garden club"). Being in a garden club is associated with expertise in the area of plant-name pronunciation, but it is also associated with the upper-class snobbery that can be evoked in the United States by pronouncing words like BATH with [a] ("ah") rather than [æ] (the vowel sound in *mad*.) Saying, "It's [kləmaˈDəs] if you're in the garden club" could be heard as making the metapragmatic claim that [kləmaˈDəs] is the correct pronunciation, or it could be heard as making the metapragmatic claim that [kləmaˈDəs] is the snobbish pronunciation, or both.

Not all metapragmatic activity is explicit talk about talk. Perhaps the most basic metapragmatic practice has been called "text metricality." The idea of text metricality originated with linguist and philologist Roman Jakobson (1960). Jakobson pointed out that in traditional poetic language in Europe and elsewhere, terms with similar meanings appear in parallel places, that is, as parts of similar or identical structures. Rhyme and meter are common types of parallelism in traditional poetry; grammatical parallelism is common in oratory. Parallelism provides a frame in which the item or items that differ from line to line are highlighted and semantically juxtaposed. Because the items occur in the same context, we are led to compare or contrast them. As Deborah Tannen (1987) points out, people collaboratively create text metricality in spontaneous everyday talk, reusing bits of others' sounds and grammar so that the places where their contributions differ—the places where they are contributing something new—pop out. And just as text metricality can draw on and create links between denotational meanings (connecting love with doves on countless greeting cards, for example, by using the words *love* and *dove* as a rhyming pair), it can create indexical links between form and social meaning. Think again about the clematis example above. Here is the interchange. The apostrophes follow syllables that are stressed.

5.1 "What's that one called?"

Ruth: What's that one called?

Anne:	That's called	[kləmæˈDəs] or [klɛˈməDəs],	depending how you pronounce it.
Bess:	It's	[kləmaˈDəs]	if you're in the garden club.
		pronunciation	*identity attribution*

Anne's and Bess's contributions, framed in parallel structures, collaboratively set up two slots: a slot for possible pronunciations of the name of the vine, and a slot for attributing pronunciations to personas. Anne's generic *you* suggests that the alternative pronunciations she proposes, "kluMADus" and "KLEmadus" have no social meaning ("depending how you pronounce it"). Bess is able to take advantage of the structure that has been set up to suggest a third alternative pronunciation, "kluMAHDus" with the British-sounding "bahth" vowel, and link this pronunciation with a stereotypical persona, the knowledgeable but snobbish garden club member. (Note how this move also positions Bess as an expert, but without linking her own identity to the garden club stereotype.)

If we think of a "text" as any kind of interaction rather than only a verbal exchange, and if we extend the notion of parallelism to include more loosely structured juxtapositions, we can use the idea of text metricality as a cover concept for other ways of proposing enregisterments between linguistic forms and social identities. "Interactional texts" are more often than not multimodal, involving verbal discourse but also modes of dress, carriage, or gesture. A person who uses a particular form while looking a particular way can link the linguistic form to the look, if co-participants are somehow invited to attend to the form and make the link. Written texts and pictures can also function metapragmatically, inviting readers and viewers to enregister linguistic form with social identity.

In the rest of this chapter, we look at how metapragmatic activity happens in three kinds of interpersonal interaction: in online talk among strangers, in a face-to-face talk among family members, and in stories people tell in the course of conversation. In all three activities I will describe, it is useful for the people who are interacting to use or to mention features of Pittsburgh speech and to talk about what they mean, how they sound, or who uses them. As we will see, using or mentioning local speech in particular ways can help people establish the right to talk or the right to be treated as an expert in the talk, and stories about misunderstandings between Pittsburghers and non-Pittsburghers do not work unless Pittsburgh speech is presented in certain ways and not others. Pittsburghese has the social meanings it does because talking about Pittsburgh speech has the functions it has.

Pittsburghese Online

In March 2002, my colleague Scott Kiesling and I held the workshop about Pittsburgh speech that I described in chapter 1. A press release about it generated a fair amount of media attention. WTAE-TV, Pittsburgh's ABC affiliate, ran a news item about the workshop. In connection with this, WTAE hosted a moderated online discussion on the topic of Pittsburgh speech. This forum was one of a number of discussion boards about topics or events on which the station's news team had reported that could be accessed from the station's homepage.[2] Would-be contributors registered with Ibsys (Internet Broadcast Systems), which provided Internet services to a WTAE and number of other US television stations. Posts were submitted to the moderators at Ibsys, although the discussion suggests that Ibsys did fairly little censoring. Although Kiesling or I probably spoke to the WTAE reporter, we did not suggest the discussion forum and did not participate in it. Dan Baumgardt and I analyzed the discussion (Johnstone and Baumgardt, 2004), and my discussion here is based on the paper Baumgardt and I wrote.

The prompt for the discussion was "What's your (yunzes') opinion of 'Pittsburghese,' i.e. the dialect indicative of western Pennsylvanians? Also, what's your favorite—and least favorite—term?" Most contributions, particularly at the beginning of the conversation, appeared to respond to another, visually more prominent version of the discussion prompt that also appeared on the first page: "Is Our Local Dialect Charming or Embarrassing?" Our analysis of the discussion board considered the roughly nine-and-a-half month period from its inception on March 22, 2002, until January 10, 2003, when people were still occasionally posting to the forum, although the discussion had almost died out. The part we looked at consisted of 19,253 words; it included 101 participants, who wrote a total of 180 responses.

Particularly at the beginning of the discussion, where responses tended to be directly linked to the discussion question, contributions tended to be quite similar to one another. These two contributions, which I reproduce exactly as they appeared, exemplify some of the recurring topical and structural features:

5.2 *Two typical contributions*
> **Lyn-byrd**: Hey yunz guys! I am also an ex-burgher well actually (Wish)-ington county. Now in VA, Too. When I first went to college at Edinboro I tried to get rid of my accent because other students and even the professors would point it out. Why is it charming to have accent from one region or another?

It should not be embarrassing. It doesn't mean we are not intelligent people.

I am proud of being from the Pix-burgh area. I think that the area is an incredible melting pot of many different cultures.

And if its is such an embarressment to talk this way . . . if we sounds stupid . . . how come i am a univ. prof, and I still say gum bands, pop, and drop the "g" off any word ending in "ing"?

stilesmom: I never realized I spoke Pittsburgheze until my children became older and asked me why I talk funny. Apparently, our teachers spoke the same way and we were never taught the short vowel sounds. I am too old to correct my speaking now. Many years ago, I lived in Rochester, NY and the people knew I was from Pittsburgh, and not only that, they knew I was from McKees Rocks. McKees Rocks has their very own thick Pittsburgh accent. Our dialect is charming and I am proud to speak it!!!!

Their uses of the words "charming" and "embarrassing" show that these participants were both responding to the more prominent version of the prompt: "Is our local dialect charming or embarrassing?" They both touched on many of the themes that recurred throughout the discussion: linguistic features ("Hey yunz guys!"; "the short vowel sounds"), their Pittsburgh origins ("I am also an ex-burgher"; "people knew I was from Pittsburgh"), where in the Pittsburgh area they were from ("(Wish)-ington county"; "McKees Rocks"), and being away from Pittsburgh ("I first went to college at Edinboro"; "I lived in Rochester"). They both provided other details about their backgrounds as well. Both of them touched on other people's attitudes toward dialect ("other students . . . would point [my accent] out;" "my children . . . asked me why I talk funny"), and both assessed their own speech ("I tried to get rid of my accent"; "I am too old to correct my speaking now"). Both contributors included an assessment of Pittsburgh speech that echoed one of the options that the discussion prompt explicitly gave: "It should not be embarrassing"; "Our dialect is charming."

Although there was no inevitable sequence to the moves participants made, the sequences in the above contributions are quite typical. Forum participants often used small personal-experience narratives to establish their right to speak by virtue of their "local knowledge" and as a way of supporting their evaluations of local speech. Then a rationale for the evaluative claim was briefly spelled out. Finally, the participants sometimes provided further reasons in support of the claims they had made.

Lyn-byrd, for example, began by using a local-sounding linguistic item to address the other participants: "Hey yunz guys!" Showing that she[3] knows this form of address constitutes a claim to local identity and an offer of rapport-building solidarity with other locals. Lyn-byrd's subsequent narrative validates this claim by showing that she counts as local by virtue of personal history: "I am also an ex-burgher well actually (Wish)-ington county. Now in VA, Too. When I first went to college at Edinboro I tried to get rid of my accent because other students and even the professors would point it out." Once Lyn-byrd established the right to speak by virtue of local knowledge and experience, she presented an argument, suggesting that regional accents in general can be charming: "Why is it charming to have an accent from one region or another?"

This functions as a segue into Lyn-byrd's explicit argument, which begins with a more direct claim that answers one of the discussion board questions: "It should not be embarrassing." She then made a claim about speakers of the local dialect, which simultaneously serves as a warrant for the claim that local speech should not be embarrassing: "It doesn't mean we are unintelligent people." Her next statement serves as another warrant: "I am proud to be from the Pix-burgh area." In this argument, Lyn-byrd called on local experience (again underlined via a local-sounding form, *Pix-burgh*) to support the claim that people who use local speech should feel proud, not embarrassed. Lyn-byrd then provided a reason for being proud to be a Pittsburgher: "I think it is an incredible melting pot of many different cultures." Finally, she restated the two prior claims, now in an interrogative, conditional form, and closed with evidence supporting both restated assertions: "And if it is such an embarressment to talk this way . . . if we sounds stupid . . . ." As further evidence for the claim that "talking this way" isn't embarrassing, because it doesn't sound stupid, Lyn-byrd invokes another aspect of her identity: her education and occupation: "how come I am a univ prof. and still say gum bands, pop, and drop the "g" off any word ending in "ing"?" These example linguistic features (*gum bands, pop*, and dropping the *g*) work to reestablish a local identity, and hence reinforce Lyn-Byrd's authority.

Like Lyn-Byrd, discussion participants frequently used or mentioned features they claimed were characteristic of Pittsburghese. Table 5.1 lists all the features that were used as examples of or in performances of Pittsburghese.

The most frequently noted phonological feature was the pronunciation of a monophthong [a:] instead of the standard [aw]. Participants sometimes explicitly isolated this sound by putting it in quotation marks (as in "-ahn"), but more commonly, we find the feature in the word *dahntahn*. (A much less frequently mentioned monophthongization is the pronunciation of [a:] for /ay/, as in "pahr.") Participants also noted the laxing of /i/ before /l/, most frequently in reference to the "Stillers" 'Steelers', or when talking about the "still mills." They also repeatedly alluded to the intrusive [r] in "wash" and "Washington." Syllable-level features such as a nonstandard stress (e.g., "UM-brella") were sometimes mentioned, as were eye-dialect constructions such as "d'jeetyet?" 'Did you eat yet?' The second-person plural form *yunz* is the most prominent Pittsburghese lexical item. Then come mentions of a local preference for *pop* over *soda* and *gumbands* ('rubber bands'). Participants also commented on the use of *redd up*

Table 5.1 **Features of Pittsburghese Represented in the WTAE Discussion Forum**

feature	example	# of times
pronunciations		
monophthongization of /aw/	dahn 'down'	25
fast speech	Jeet yet 'Did you eat yet?', woonchu 'won't you'	12
laxing of /i/ before /l/	Stillers 'Steelers'	11
intrusive /r/	warsh 'wash'	10
Southern pronunciation of *creek*	crick 'creek'	5
syllable deletion	'Burghers 'Pittsburghers', frigerator 'refrigerator', hon 'honey'	4
vowels: other	melk 'milk'; wooshing 'washing'	4
monophthongization of /ay/	pahr 'power'	3
deletions of /r/, /h/, /ð/	kohner 'corner', er 'her', ese 'these'	3
nonstandard stress	UM-brella	3
eye dialect (difference is only orthographic)	enuff 'enough', ruff 'rough'	3
schwa deletion	ignernt 'ignorant'	2
stopping of /ð/	mudder 'mother'	2
velarization of /t/ in "Pittsburgh"	Picksburgh 'Pittsburgh'	2
	cookin 'cooking'	1
nonstandard assimilation	sammich 'sandwich'	1
consonants: other	surre 'sure'	1
laxing of /i/ in "eagle"	Giant Iggle 'Eagle'	1
words and grammatical structures		
yinz/yunz		48
pop		22
gumband		13
chipped ham		6
jumbo		6
"we was"		4
needs + PP	The car needs washed.	3
crack me up		1

for 'tidy up'. Finally, some of the words that participants used or mentioned are terms for local products, such as *jumbo* 'bologna'. Grammatical features were mentioned much less frequently. Participants mentioned the plural use of *was* and the *needs* plus past-participle construction, as in "needs washed."

Participants used and talked about these features because doing so was useful, in this conversational context, in several ways. For one thing, using or mentioning a feature of Pittsburghese was a way to establish the authority to describe and evaluate the dialect. A few participants claimed more formal sources of knowledge of Pittsburghese. One mentioned the author of a Pittsburghese dictionary (McCool 1982), another referred to an ongoing academic "study" of local speech (probably the one being planned at the workshop that led to this discussion), and a third mentioned training in linguistics as a source of knowledge about dialects in general. However, local experience, evidenced by previous knowledge of Pittsburghese, was the most commonly adduced warrant for taking part in the conversation.

Some Pittsburghers described themselves as speaking the dialect: "I hafta tell yunz I think the way we talk is neat. I can go anywhere in the country and someone immediately knows where I come from . . . I am Pittsburgh through and through." Other participants explained their knowledge of features in terms of partial exposure: "Well, I was not raised in Pittsburgh, but my sister was raised here." Another group were people who were originally not from Pittsburgh but who claimed familiarity with local dialect forms: "My sons and I have enjoyed 'collecting' words and expressions particular to this area since we moved here . . . in July of 2000." A number of the participants were nonlocals who claimed to be originally from the Pittsburgh area: "I am originally from the 'Burgh, Duquesne to be exact and I must say I think our Pittsburghese is the greatest. I live in Northern Minnesota, on the Canadian border." Other nonlocals noted personal or causal connections between themselves and speakers of the Pittsburgh dialect: "I'm from Canada eh. My girlfriend lives in the Burgh. She's kind of proud of it's uniqueness, in the dialect department." In addition to talking about where they were from, though, participants mentioned particular dialect features. We call this "feature-dropping," since it functions somewhat the way name-dropping does. Feature-dropping was a good way to support evaluative claims about the dialect, and it could help build rapport with the other participants.

Some features that contributors used during their interactions are not typically thought of as Pittsburghese, and mentions or uses of such features functioned to suggest metapragmatically that they should be. When features dropped into contributions were already widely understood to be Pittsburghese, using them worked to enforce existing social meanings. The enregisterment process became explicit when participants engaged in what could be called "vernacular lexicography" (lexicography is dictionary making), or explicit metapragmatic talk about whether particular features should be counted as belonging to the dialect. This is exemplified in the following excerpts:

5.3 Vernacular lexicography
I feel that the non-word *ain't* needs to be included.

[M]y wife informs me that my use of *whenever*, as opposed to just *when*, is Pittsburghese.

Pop is not limited to Pittsburgh.

In contributions such as these, contributors explicitly noted the enregisterment process they were involved in.

Throughout the conversation, participants' talk about regional dialects often segued into talk about place. Many participants' talk about Pittsburghese was as much or more about Pittsburgh as about dialect. Participants like these move from discussing Pittsburghese to commenting on other aspects of Pittsburgh and their relationship to the city:

5.4 From Pittsburghese to Pittsburgh
[I've] been out of [there] for 17 years . . . and still say "melk" instead of milk, gum bands instead of rubber bands, redd up and jaetyet (did you eat yet.) **I can love Pitt when I come home to eat pirogies, hot roast beefw/fries and gravy and permanti bros sandwiches**.

I do call rubber bands as they are called here gum bands . . . Also yins is my plural of ya'll. **I do miss Pittsburgh . . . it's what I call my home!**

Moving from the topic of Pittsburghese to the topic of Pittsburgh required very little conversational work: contributors did not have to make explicit transitions between the topic of dialect and the topic of place.

Not all contributors to the online discussion were enthusiastic about Pittsburgh speech, and there were disagreements, sometimes specifically framed as responses to particular contributions. But interchanges like the one in 5.5 also shifted seamlessly from Pittsburgh speech to Pittsburgh the place, and they show how this shift was enabled by shared ideas about language, place, and identity.

5.5 Disagreeing
kinglarry: Pittsburghese is a joke. It's an embarrassing reflection of laziness in a region trapped in a time-warp!

dish 50: This is in response to kinglarry . . . You must be from cleveland . . . I feel sorry for you, look around in cleveland and what do you see . . . only more cleveland.

The first contribution, by kinglarry, links an evaluation of the dialect to an evaluation of the place, with recourse to a widely shared American ideological schema: the idea that, in general, patterns of talk reflect psychological predispositions, and, in particular, that nonstandard dialects reflect laziness. It is this idea, functioning as the implicit premise of his argument, that allows kinglarry to link the existence of a local dialect with a negative evaluation of the people who speak it, their "laziness," and this allows him to introduce a negative evaluation of the region, "trapped in a time-warp." In response, dish 50 draws on a widely shared schema about how place and identity are linked: people's attitudes are shaped by where they are from ("you must be from cleveland"[4] if you dislike Pittsburgh), partly by virtue of connections between physical geography and mental predispositions (unlike Pittsburgh, Cleveland is flat, which makes it boring, which makes people from there boring).

The fact that the discussion forum draws on and creates ideas about how language is connected to place and identity shapes how it imbues Pittsburgh speech with social meaning. For one thing, it means that many of the terms chosen in illustrations or performances of Pittsburghese are ones that have to do with place and local identity. To give the most obvious example of how place-linked words may be privileged over others, monophthongal /aw/ is represented far more often in the words *town* or *downtown* than in the prepositions in which it is in fact heard more often (due to the frequency of prepositions compared to that of substantives): *about, around, down, out, outside, without*. The fact that Pittsburghese is repeatedly linked to local character and lifestyle is reflected in the number of examples of the dialect that have to do with purported characteristics of local people or practices of local life, like the one in 5.6.

5.6 *Pittsburghese in local life*
> . . . on Saturday we worshed the cars and as kids we were given pop for a treat. we have gumbands in our desk, jeat jumbo, redd up, and then there is the all time great one, nnat

Why do these people engage in this discussion? As I suggested earlier, there are historical and sociolinguistic reasons for enhanced dialect awareness in the Pittsburgh area. Conversations about local speech have both drawn on and enhanced Pittsburghers' awareness of local speech, with the side effect of strengthening its enregisterment with Pittsburgh the place, for some time. Dialect awareness in Pittsburgh is not new, and enhanced attention to local speech has been sparked, as I suggested, by different combinations of factors at different times. Evidence from what happened in this online conversation suggests that geographical mobility and attendant nostalgia for place may have sparked enhanced awareness in the early 2000s.

As we saw in chapter 2, shared ways of experiencing and orienting to physical space arise from shared ways of evaluating and talking about it. As we have seen in this section, individual contributions and exchanges in the WTAE forum moved from the topic of dialect to that of the place with which the dialect is associated and which it helps to define. In short, people talk about Pittsburghese partly because it gives them a way to talk about Pittsburgh.

The evidence suggests, further, that talk about Pittsburgh gave contributors a way to talk about their personal identities with respect to place. Place identity recurs as a theme over and over, in the ways people establish their right to participate by showing how they count as Pittsburghers ("I was born and raised in Pittsburgh"; "I am an ex-burgher") and in the frequent arguments that rest on people's not being Pittsburghers ("You must be from cleveland"; "If you hate [Pittsburgh] so much, what are you doing here?"). As we have seen, participants often linked local identity with personal characteristics like laziness, charm, or friendliness or with a lifestyle they think of as local.

The fact that a great many of the contributors were originally from Pittsburgh but now live elsewhere, and some were from elsewhere but now live in Pittsburgh, suggests that part of the appeal of an online discussion like this is that it provides an outlet for the expression and reinforcement of regional identity in the context of nostalgia. Of the 101 participants, sixty-five provided information in the course of their contributions that allowed us to determine whether they were geographically mobile with respect to Pittsburgh. (They typically did this quite explicitly, by saying things like, "I have lived away from the Burgh for 20+ years," or "we moved here back in July of 2000.") Of these, forty-three (or 43 percent of the total participants, although the percentage would probably be higher if we had relevant information about everyone) were Pittsburghers who were then living elsewhere or had returned to Pittsburgh after living elsewhere. Judging from what they said about how long they had been away, many were people who moved to the South to find work during the 1980s, when, as I noted in chapter 3, the rapid decline in steel production in Pittsburgh resulted in massive unemployment. Seven contributors were non-Pittsburghers who lived in Pittsburgh. (Several of these were students.) Of the participants for whom we can hazard a guess, only fourteen of the sixty-five appear to have lived in the same place all their lives. Thus, at least half the contributors were people who had had their identities called into question by being regional outsiders, and it is clear from many of the contributors' tone that they enjoyed the chance to comment on what felt like an important aspect of their personal life histories. Table 5.2 shows these figures.

One effect of the high percentage of geographically mobile participants on the enregisterment process is that Pittsburghese was often described in comparison with other regional dialects—in particular, of course, those the participants had experienced. Twenty percent of the dialect features mentioned or used in

Table 5.2 **Geographical Mobility of Discussion Participants**

geographic history	number of participants
from Pittsburgh, now elsewhere	38
from Pittsburgh, lived elsewhere, returned to Pittsburgh	5
from elsewhere, lives in Pittsburgh now.	7
total geographically mobile	**50**
lifelong Pittsburgher	12
lifelong non-Pittsburgher	2
total geographically non-mobile	**14**
geographic history unknown	**37**
total	**101**

the discussion exemplify other dialects, even though the original question elicits no cross-regional comparisons. The participants' own comments suggest that their geographical mobility is one of the major factors producing nonlocal forms against which Pittsburghese is defined. The following contributions exemplify how nonlocal dialect forms were typically introduced:

5.7 *Talking about other language varieties*

Living here in Richmond, the people's dialect is southern, and they tend to drop the R's off of the end of their words. ie. River=Riva.

I was born and raised in Pgh., and moved to the south 18 years ago . . . Alas, my kids grew up saying "ya'll" and I still can't get used to it.

If you lived in Canada . . . you would . . . make fun of how they don't pronounce the letter U as in "hows aboot that budday!"

The nonlocal items were ascribed to a variety of places: Atlanta, Boston, California, Canada, Chicago, Cleveland, the East, Florida, Ireland, Massachusetts, New York, Philadelphia, South Carolina, the South, Tennessee, Texas, Virginia, West Virginia, and western Pennsylvania. But the ones cited most frequently are associated with the southern United States. The only nonlocal pronunciation feature mentioned more than once is the southern raising of /ɛ/ to /ɪ/ before nasals in words such as *pen* (which then sounds like *pin*), and the most commonly mentioned nonlocal lexical form is *y'all*, which is adduced seventeen times, far more frequently than any other item from another region.

Geographic mobility affects dialect enregisterment in Pittsburgh in that it calls attention to regional differences in speech and thus encourages comparison of one dialect with another. The fact that so many of the forum participants were members of the Pittsburgh diaspora of the 1980s also affects the resulting norms in more specific ways. For example, the second-person plural pronoun *yinz* (in any of its spellings: *yunz, younz, yins,* and so on) is the most salient and iconic lexical feature of Pittsburghese. *Yinz* appears in every dictionary-like list of local words, and a local term for a local person is *Yinzer* (also spelled *yunzer*). There may be a connection between this and the fact that many ex-Pittsburghers live in an area in which there is a different nonstandard second-person-plural pronoun, *y'all,* with which *yinz* can be easily contrasted. This sarcastic discussion-forum contribution from a former Pittsburgher shows how easily comparable pronoun forms including *yinz* may enter the discussion more often than other forms because they provide an effective, available way of scaffolding an evaluative argument about Pittsburghese and Pittsburgh.

5.8 "Living among the 'y'allers'"

slaps his forehead Gee, why didn't I think of that? People will start moving back once we CHANGE THE WAY WE TALK! But never mind that "cool" cities like New York and Atlanta still have a significant population that use "youse" and "y'all," respectively, for the second-person plural, becuase "youse" and "y'all" both stem from EDUCATED dialects, right? Pittsburgh will be NOTHING until it contains no dialect whatsoever, right? . . . I live in Georgia, the land of "y'all." Why not try living among the "y'allers" for a few years. You'll appreciate the "yunz" a little more.

Here, the counterparts of yunzers are "y'allers" and "appreciating the 'yunz'" has become a metaphor for appreciating Pittsburgh.

To summarize, the WTAE conversation illuminates the process of dialect enregisterment in several ways. For one thing, it illustrates one procedure for relatively overt metapragmatic talk. As we have shown, participants implicitly and explicitly talk about which particular features count as Pittsburghese and which do not, and about what it means to speak Pittsburghese. They sometimes negotiate about this, pointing out that items people think are local actually aren't or suggesting items they think of as new contributions to the dialect.

Secondly, the conversation illustrates the fact that metapragmatic talk, and the enregisterment that can result from it, always arises in a particular kind of interaction for a particular set of social and rhetorical reasons. Which forms end up being enregistered with the dialect is inevitably a function of the situation in which metapragmatic activity like this takes place. A great deal of what occurred in the discussion forum had to do with establishing who could say things about Pittsburghese that would count as authoritative and on what grounds. Participants talked directly about and made indirect reference to the sources of expertise that can warrant this sort of metapragmatic talk: expertise from scholars and other serious students of the dialect, but mainly the expertise conferred by local experience. You can participate in defining Pittsburghese if you are a Pitts-burgher, particularly if you "grew up speaking that way." Constructing interper-sonal relationships is another important interactional demand in online talk like this, particularly since participants are strangers, and mentioning local-sound-ing words and phrases can sometimes work to build rapport or, conversely, to set people apart. In this kind of talk, participants also have to support the claims they make; as we have seen, there are various ways of doing this, some of which call forth metapragmatic talk that can lead to dialect enregisterment.

Different discursive practices differ in what gives a person authority, what personal relationships are expected to be like and how they are evoked, and how argumentation proceeds. Different constellations of participants, media, and genres may thus give rise to different norms. For example, the activity we have been exploring is "democratic" in a way that other kinds of vernacular norming may not be: anyone with Internet access can participate. It contrasts in this respect with the production of single-authored folk dictionaries like the Sam McCool book and with the sort of metapragmatic work that goes on when sociolinguists talk publicly about regional dialects. It also contrasts with more implicit enregisterment processes that are the focus of much socio-linguistic research, in which the linguistic forms linked to a way of speaking are not explicitly listed and the social meanings of forms are not explicitly articulated.

What ends up being enregistered is also a function of the meaning-making context in which metapragmatic activities like this conversation happen. In this case, people were drawing on and reinforcing familiar ideological schemas link-ing personal identity to physical place, and place (and particular characteristics of place) to dialect, so that place, identity, and dialect seem naturally linked. Their interaction was mediated rather than face-to-face, and the activity they were engaged in was understood as not a serious one. Different ideological con-texts for metapragmatic talk give rise to different ways of arguing for the enreg-isterment of forms with meanings, and hence with different enregistered varieties. For example, as is often noted, language standardization arises in the context of nationalism and the idea that people from different parts of a nation need to share a language, which means that the ideas on which discussions about standards are scaffolded have to do with such things as clarity and correctness rather than with such things as nostalgia, personal identity, solidarity, class, and local pride or embarrassment.

Dialect, Identity, and Authority

As we just saw, if people are talking about local speech, it can be useful to claim the identity of a local-dialect speaker. Doing so can give you the authority to describe and evaluate the dialect. I now turn to an activity not unlike the discussion forum, but one that took place face-to-face, among people who knew each other. This will allow us to look in more depth at how people position themselves vis-à-vis particular speech forms and why. The extract we will examine comes from one of my interviews with Pittsburghers.

In this conversation, a woman in her forties and her thirteen-year-old daughter talked about Pittsburgh speech in an explicitly metapragmatic way. They offered examples of what Pittsburgh speech sounds like and argued about which forms are authentically local and how local forms should sound. As they did this, they used claims about and performances of their own speech as ways of establishing the authority to describe the dialect. The mother, Jen R., positioned herself as knowledgeable about Pittsburghese on the basis of insider expertise—by claiming and displaying that she herself spoke it. Donna R., the daughter, initially positioned herself as more of an outsider—someone who experiences Pittsburghese but doesn't use it. But by adopting this approach, she did not manage to be heard as authoritative; her contributions to the discussion were not taken seriously. So, in the course of the conversation, Donna shifted her stance, eventually agreeing that she was, in fact, a speaker of Pittsburghese. Doing this meant that by the end of the conversation she could share the right to speak with her mother.

In order to make it easier to see how ideas and points of view emerge in the conversation in response to other people's ideas and points of view, I have numbered the contributions to the conversation and used some special conventions of punctuation to represent things about the pacing and timing of the talk. Simultaneous talk (two or more people talking at once) is indicated by square brackets surrounding the words that overlap with someone else's words. Equal signs indicate "latched" talk, when a participant's talk immediately follows the previous participant's, without the slight break we expect.

Jen, the mother, makes routine use of a number of pronunciation variables that make her sound local. Her pronunciation of /aw/ is sometimes monophthongized, with *out* realized as [a:t] ("aht"). She merges and rounds the low back vowels, pronouncing *job* as [dʒɔb] ("jaughb"), for example. She fronts /u/ in words like *move* ("mewv") and sometimes vocalizes /l/. She reduces the diphthong /ay/ to a more monophthongal form when it is followed by /l/ (which is vocalized), as when *while* is realized as [wa:u] (somewhat like "wow"). This is another fairly common local variant. Her daughter Donna has a less local accent; she does not monophthongize /aw/ but fronts /u/ (*two* sounds like "tew", *moves* like "mewves") and /o/, vocalizes /l/ ("owder" for *older*), and merges and rounds the low back vowel, in words like *constantly*. ("caughnstantly"). She uses Pennsylvania Dutch question intonation in dialogue she reconstructs for a woman from the area: !"You guys from Pennsylvania?"

As do most sociolinguistic interviews in the Labovian tradition (Labov 1984), this one included subsections on topics meant to elicit a range of levels of self-consciousness. My summary of Jen and Donna's accents is based on the whole interview, as well as unrecorded talk in other contexts. The topic of accent may well have made them self-conscious about their speech, but in fact they sound very much the same in this segment as elsewhere.

5.9 Jen R. and Donna R. on Pittsburghese

1	BJ	Um. So, have you ever heard of Pittsburghese?
2	JEN R.	Oh yes. I mean, [there's]
3	BJ	[What]
4	JEN R.	that store over on the South Side in um [Station Square that has the] Pittsburghese shirts.
5	DONNA R.	[((Breathes in)) Yeah]
6	BJ	Uh huh=
7	JEN R.	=In fact, I remember when my friend Karen moved out of state, with—her husband's job took them out of state and to many other states. I remember sending her a couple Pittsburghese shirts for them.
8	DONNA R.	Hm.
9	JEN R.	Umm. Yeah, I've heard of [Pittsburghese] definitely. Yeah.=
10	BJ	[Mm-hmm.] =What do you think it is? I mean is it—?
11	JEN R.	I think it's the way we say words.
12	DONNA R.	[((Laughs))]
13	BJ	[Yeah?]
14	JEN R.	I think it's how we say *downtown* and um=
15	DONNA R.	= "down[town"]
16	JEN R.	[*South*] *Side* and,
17	DONNA R.	*Y'all.*
18	JEN R.	*wash* and *iron* and different words and the way Pittsburgh is. There're
19	DONNA R.	*Yinz.*
20	JEN R.	[Just the uh—like]
21	BJ	[*Yinz* is another one.] What, what other ones can you think of? ((to Donna))
22	DONNA R.	Just *y'all* and *yinz.* That's, that's the most, my friends always are saying "y'all" to me.

23	BJ	["Y'all"?]
24	DONNA R.	[Drives] me crazy.
25	JEN R.	"Y'all?"
26	DONNA R.	Yeah, they say "y'all" to me. They say [it's a Pittsburghese]
27	BJ	[And that's a Pittsburgh thing?]
28	DONNA R.	It—that's what they tell me.
29	BJ	Huh!
30	JEN R.	*Younz* is more a Pittsburgh thing than [*y'all.*]
31	DONNA R.	[yeah]
32	JEN R.	*Y'all*'s more like a Georgia, [southern.]
33	DONNA R.	[I was thinking] southern, [but]
34	JEN R.	[Yeah.]
35	DONNA R.	they still say "y'all" to me. And then. Yeah *yinz*. You hear *yinz* a lot.
36	BJ	You do? In—
37	DONNA R.	Yeah, well like our neighbors like two doors down, I'm really good friends with their son. He's a year older than me. And like, he says *yinz* constantly 'cause like both his parents say "yinz," like, "Yinz wanna do somethin'?" or [like] ((laughing)) you know so [I hear that.]
38	BJ	[Mm-hmm.]
39	JEN R.	[We don't use that.]
40	DONNA R.	Yeah, I never said you [used it] but
41	JEN R.	[but] I'm just thinking, I know, um, like, your dad and I don't use that [too often.]
42	DONNA R.	[No.] But I hear it a lot from [them when] I'm over there
43	JEN R.	[Mm-hmm]
44	BJ	[Mm-hmm]
45	JEN R.	Yeah. It's funny.
46	DONNA R.	And you pick up on it. You start to say then, [once]
47	JEN R.	[Sure.]

48	DONNA R.	you're around people so often, you start—I started to say "yinz" to people. ((laughing)) And they're looking at me like, "Okay." ((skeptical, amused voice))
49	DONNA R.	Mm-hmm.
50	BJ	So, would— you don't— you wouldn't say you use any of the, Pittsburghese things?
51	DONNA R.	Not really. No, I don't think so.
52	BJ	Uh huh [probably you— ((indistinct))]
53	JEN R.	[You s—] you do, but you don't reali—. Oh, I know I do. I [say "ahrn"]
54	DONNA R.	[I do?]
55	JEN R.	for "iron."
56	BJ	Uh huh.
57	DONNA R.	["iron"] ((quietly))
58	JEN R.	[I] say "wush, w—wash" for "wash." I [mean]
59	DONNA R.	["Wash."] ((quietly))
60	JEN R.	I don't, I don't pronounce my words as clearly as—
61	DONNA R.	"Wash." ((quietly))
62	JEN R.	or the accent's [on]
63	BJ	[Uh huh.]
64	JEN R.	a different [part]
65	DONNA R.	["Wash."] ((quietly))
66	BJ	Uh-huh.
67	JEN R.	Yeah.
68	DONNA R.	"Wash." ((quietly))
69	JEN R.	"Sahsside" instead of "South Side." ((second "South Side" pronounced with exaggerated care))
70	DONNA R.	"Sahsside."
71	JEN R.	I say "Sahsside." "Dahntahn" instead of "downtown."
72	DONNA R.	"Downtown."
73	JEN R.	I know I, I know I kn— use a lot of Pittsburghese.
74	BJ	Mm-hmmm.
75	DONNA R.	I [probably do], and I don't realize it
76	JEN R.	[I know I do.] Well, when I've been in [different] states, in different cities,

77	BJ	[Mm-hmm]
78	DONNA R.	They'll— they'll say, "You're from Pittsburgh."
79	JEN R.	Yeah, they'll immediately [say,]
80	DONNA R.	[When we were in] South Carolina, right?
81	JEN R.	"You're from Pennsylvania=",
82	DONNA R.	=Yeah. "You're— you're [definite—]"
83	JEN R.	["Are you—], are you from the Pittsburgh area?"
84	DONNA R.	Yeah. ((laughing))
85	BJ	Does that happen to you, too, or=?
86	DONNA R.	=Yeah. I mean, I remember one time, we were in South Carolina visiting my, my uncle and my two cousins and my aunt. And we went to (s—some) store, and we were talking about how like the South kind of moves slow, [you know?]
87	JEN R.	[Yeah,] [God, it drives you crazy.]
88	DONNA R.	[And then she's like] she's like, "You guys from Pennsylvania?" We're like "Yeah." And she's like, "You guys wouldn't happen to be from Pittsburgh, right?" And we're like, "We're from Pittsburgh." And she's like, "Oh, okay. I can [tell by your accent."]
89	BJ	[How did she know?] How do you think she knew?
90	JEN R.	She, she was from the Pittsburgh area. She didn't grow up in Pitt—[yeah. She said, she said she originally—]
91	DONNA R.	[Yea—, I thought she was] from Ohio.
92	JEN R.	Yeah, [but she, she was—]
93	BJ	[(Eastern)] Ohio?
94	JEN R.	Right [but she]
95	BJ	[This area?]
96	JEN R.	she was in Pittsburgh and then they moved to Ohio,
97	DONNA R.	Yeah.
98	JEN R.	and then from Ohio they moved to South Carolina.
99	DONNA R.	[She didn't have the] accent either. She still had like a Pittsburgh accent.

100	JEN R.	[She said that—.] Mm-hmm. Yeah. She didn't [have]
101	BJ	[Mm-hmm]
102	JEN R.	a southern accent at all. She was, like a mom. [You know,]
103	BJ	[Mm-hmm]
104	JEN R.	I would say she was in her early thirties at least.
105	DONNA R.	Yeah.
106	JEN R.	[Uhh maybe forties.]
107	DONNA R.	[I don't really remember.]
108	JEN R.	I don't know. I—I'm a bad judge of age. But, she was from, eh, or grew up in Pittsburgh for a while, moved to Ohio, and then was in South—then they relocated to South Carolina.
109	DONNA R.	[Yeah.]
110	JEN R.	[That's] how she knew. 'Cause she even said that Pittsburgh accent, when you're not around it, when you do hear it, you really pick up on it fast.

Knowledgeability and dialect identity come into play here in a number of ways. At the beginning of the extract, Jen claims the authority to speak on the topic of Pittsburghese with reference to knowing about Pittsburghese shirts and sending one to a friend who has moved away. (The shirts Jen is referring to, produced largely for the tourist and local-nostalgia markets, feature words spelled in ways that suggest a Pittsburgh pronunciation; on the back, there may be a dictionary-like list of words and phrases that are thought to be local. We return to the topic of Pittsburghese shirts in a later chapter.) Authority is independent of dialect identity here. Referring to Pittsburghese shirts is a way of arguing from external authority, a resource that is potentially available whether or not one is a speaker of the dialect. Anyone in the Pittsburgh area has access to Pittsburghese shirts, whether they speak with a Pittsburgh accent or not. Jen supports her knowledge claim ("Oh yes, [I've heard of Pittsburghese]," line 2) with reference to indirect, mediated knowledge about the dialect—she has seen it on T-shirts. She maintains this relatively detached stance for another turn (line 9), "Yeah, I've heard of Pittsburghese, definitely." "I've heard of" locates the knowledge source elsewhere, in what other people say. Then, however, in response to my question "What do you think it is?," Jen switches to a different mode of evidence, taking up my invitation to adopt a stance rooted in personal authority ("I think") and aligning herself with other competent speakers of the dialect ("we"), with "I think it's the way **we** say words."

Jen then begins to list some of these words (lines 14–18): *downtown, South Side, wash, iron*. While continuing to locate the source of knowledge in her own competence ("I think"), she disaligns somewhat from dialect speakers and returns to a more distanced mode of authoritativeness that does not rely on claiming to be a competent speaker of the dialect. She pronounces the words she offers in the standard ways, not with the local pronunciations. Anyone who has read or heard about Pittsburghese could produce these words this way, whether or not they knew how the words sound when they are pronounced by someone with a local accent. Jen pronounces /aw/ as a diphthong in *downtown* and *South Side* ("downtown," "South Side") using the less local-sounding variant. She also pronounces *wash* and *iron* in the standard ways, rather than in the local-sounding variants [wʊʃ] ("wush") or [worʃ] ("worsh") and [arn] ("ahrn"). Nor do the ways she pronounces the words fully reflect what Pittsburghers usually imagine is local about "the way we say [these] words." *Downtown* is typically spelled <dahntahn> on artifacts like T-shirts, the spelling suggesting that the monophthongization of /aw/ is to be attended to, whereas *South Side* is often spelled <Souside>, with a standard, diphthongal /aw/ but with /θ/ (the sound spelled with <th> in this word) missing.

In lines 71 and 73, Jen returns to two of these words, contrasting what she represents as their standard pronunciation with the way she claims to say them. In citing the "standard" forms, she exaggerates the diphthongs in both words and the /θ/ ("th") in *South Side*. In her performance of her own pronunciation, she overdoes what popular local spellings suggest are the local pronunciations, monophthongizing the /aw/ in both words rather than just in *downtown*. Here, Jen claims an authoritative stance in two ways. In citing examples of Pittsburghese in their standard pronunciations, she is doing something that either a speaker or a nonspeaker of the dialect could presumably do, assuming he or she had access to lists of local forms like those on T-shirts or folk dictionaries. In this activity, authoritative stance is independent of dialect identity. But Jen also performs the local pronunciations, an activity that indexes the identity of a competent speaker. She also points to this competent-speaker identity repeatedly in more explicit claims to be an actual user of the dialect, "We don't use that . . . I'm just thinking . . . your dad and I don't use that too often" (lines 39–43); "I know I [use the Pittsburghese things]" (line 55); "I don't pronounce my words as clearly . . ." (line 62); "I know I, I know I kn—use a lot of Pittsburghese" (line 75). Note how in this final extract Jen starts to say she *knows* Pittsburghese, which could signal second-hand access to the dialect, but revises the claim to "I use a lot of Pittsburghese," explicitly claiming to speak it.

To summarize, Jen makes claims to knowledgeability throughout the conversation. Some of these claims involve displaying familiarity with external sources of authority such as Pittsburghese shirts. Sometimes Jen displays this familiarity by citing local forms in a standard-sounding way. At other times, however, Jen claims to be a competent speaker of the dialect, who is knowledgeable about it for that reason. And sometimes performances of competent-speaker dialect identity are embedded in these claims, as in "I say 'ahrn' for 'iron'" (lines 55–57), and "I say 'wush' for 'wash'" (line 60).

Donna, the thirteen-year-old, tries to participate in all these activities. At first, she makes contributions to the conversation that distance her from dialect speakers and locate the source of her knowledge about the dialect in other people. Invited, like her mother, to talk about what she thinks Pittsburghese is, she talks about what other people say it is. In line 17, she suggests an addition to the list of words Jen is building, *y'all*, then, after there is no uptake from her mother or me, another in line 19, *yinz*. I acknowledge this contribution in line 21 and encourage her to offer more. She repeats *y'all* and *yinz* in line 22, and then explicitly adduces her friends as the source of her knowledge about local speech, "My friends always are saying 'y'all' to me," and "They say it's a Pittsburghese [thing]" (line 26). When she continues to be met with skepticism, she makes the same move again: "It—that's what they tell me" (line 28). These claims of knowledgeability are not linked to competent-speaker identity— Donna would have access to this source of knowledge whether or not she claimed to be a speaker of the dialect herself—but rather to external authority. Her mother then rebuts Donna's externally based claim with a dialect-performance move: arguing that *y'all* is not really "a Pittsburgh thing," she pronounces *yinz* not in the stereotypical version represented on T-shirt lists, which would be [yɪnz] ("yinz"), but in an older, more traditional-sounding way, [yʊnz] ("yunz"). She then supplements this with a more distanced move referring to presumably widespread knowledge that does not require dialect identity, "*Y'all*'s more like a Georgia, southern [thing]" (line 32).

Donna continues to argue that *y'all* is local and continues to disalign herself from the local way of talking, contrasting *I* with *they* and positioning herself as the recipient of local speech rather than its initiator, "I was thinking southern, but they still say 'y'all' to me" (lines 33–35). But her mother's competent-speaker knowledge apparently trumps what Donna's friends tell her: Donna retreats to a discussion of *yinz*, which everyone in the interaction agrees is local, "Yeah 'yinz.' **You** hear 'yinz' a lot" (line 35). Using *you hear* rather than *I hear*, she aligns herself, if not with dialect speakers, at least with a group larger than herself. She then provides an extended illustration of her claim to hear *yinz* a lot, which includes a dialect performance ("'Yinz wanna do somethin'?'" line 37). Note that this is not exactly the same kind of performance as Jen's: Donna is imitating other people, not making a claim about her own identity. A performance like this displays local knowledge (she knows how local speech sounds) but falls short of a claim to being a speaker of the dialect.

As the conversation proceeds, however, Donna begins to supplement knowledge claims based on external sources with her mother's more successful mode of arguing by claiming to be a competent speaker of Pittsburghese. In her first claim to actually being a dialect speaker, Donna frames her competence as an automatic, unintentional, and uncharacteristic consequence of being around dialect speakers: "You pick up on it. You start to say then, once you're around people so often, you start—I started to say 'yinz' to people. ((laughing)) And they're looking at me like, 'Okay'" (lines 48–50). In answer to my direct question, however, she then explicitly disaligns herself from other dialect speakers, "Not really. No, I don't think I use any of the Pittsburghese things" (line 53). Her mother steers her toward alignment with dialect speakers, "You do, but you don't realize it "(line 55).

At this point, Donna appears to take the hint that it would be useful to her, if she wants to be a full-fledged participant in the conversation, to act like an actual speaker of Pittsburghese. She begins to reframe her identity in such a way that it becomes useful as a source of knowledgeability, the way Jen's dialect-speaker identity is. One revealing segment begins in line 60, where Jen, listing and performing local forms, makes and tries to illustrate a claim about how she says *wash*. Apparently by mistake, she almost confuses the standard form with the Pittsburghese form, so that the second time she says the word it sounds like the standard [wɔsh] but is apparently meant to be an improved performance of what Jen represents as the local pronunciation, [wʊʃ] ("wush"). Donna, who has just claimed that she does not use "Pittsburghese things" in her speech (line 53), then starts to repeat the word over and over in a low voice: "Wash [wɔʃ]," "Wash [wɔʃ]," "Wash [wɔʃ]," Wash [wɔʃ]," (lines 61, 63, 67, and 70). Donna is apparently trying to imitate the Pittsburghese pronunciation to contrast it with her own. But since Donna picks as her target Jen's second performance, which was actually the more standard-sounding variant "wash," Donna seems to conclude that her own pronunciation is in fact the local one. So after "trying out" *South Side* and *downtown* in a similar manner, she explicitly claims the identity of a dialect speaker in line 77, echoing her mother's earlier wording, "I probably do [use Pittsburghese], and I don't realize it."

Shifting identity in this way means that Donna can now adopt the authoritative position of an actual dialect speaker, the position her mother has been taking. She does this in co-narrating the story about the family's having been identified as Pittsburghers by their accents. This begins as an explicit claim, co-constructed by Jen and Donna, to the identity of a recognizable dialect speaker. Jen starts, "Well, when I've been in different states, in different cities" (line 78), and Donna continues, "They'll—they'll say 'You're from Pittsburgh'" (line 80). Jen then claims she is also recognized by her accent, "Yeah, they'll immediately say 'You're from Pennsylvania'" (lines 81–83). The ensuing narrative, which Jen and Donna tell together in overlapping speech, supports their now mutual claim to being competent, recognizable Pittsburghese speakers. It culminates with thirteen-year-old Donna's voicing of her family, now represented as *we*, and a woman they met in the South: "And we're like, '**We**'re from Pittsburgh.' And she's like, 'Oh, okay. I can tell by your accent'" (line 90).

This conversation illustrates one way in which being a Pittsburgher has become linked with speaking Pittsburghese: showing that you know about Pittsburghese can require that you claim to speak it. All semiotic links between language forms (like *yinz* or *warsh*) and social identities (like being or not being an expert, being a Pittsburgher or not, speaking Pittsburghese or not) arise in interaction, in response to particular prompts (in this case, my questions "Have you ever heard of Pittsburghese? What do you think it is?") and more general needs such as wanting a chance to talk and to be taken seriously. The two are intertwined in a particularly visible way here. Since both the activity (the interview) and the particular topic called for knowledge claims, Jen and Donna had to show that they had the right to make such claims. Since the topic was local speech, claims about and performances of competent-speaker dialect identity were a particularly useful way to signal knowledgeability. That the topic of local speech came up in this case is not surprising: I brought it up as a module in a sociolinguistic interview. But the topic comes up nowadays in many ways.

Once the topic arises, Pittsburghese can become linked with Pittsburgh identity because it can be useful to represent oneself as a speaker of the dialect. Not everyone has the same kind of access to this resource. Jen has a stronger local accent than Donna does, in part for linguistic and cognitive reasons that have nothing to do with authoritativeness. A person like Jen, who can perform local pronunciations, may have an authority-building resource in certain contexts that Donna, who can only say she speaks the dialect, lacks. Discursive activities like the one examined here give the upper hand to more competent speakers of the local dialect. This means that competent dialect speakers like Jen have the advantage in this conversation and ones like it. However, as we have seen throughout this chapter, claiming to be a speaker of the local dialect does not always require anything more than knowing a few local-sounding words.

Narrating Dialect Difference

The excerpt from my interview with Jen and Donna that we have just considered ends with a narrative, produced jointly by the two speakers. In the story, members of the R. family visit a shop in South Carolina and are recognized as Pittsburghers by a saleswoman on the basis of how they talk. Stories like this come up often in conversations among Pittsburghers and among non-Pittsburghers who live in the city or visit it. Some of these stories are, like Jen and Donna's, about being recognized as a Pittsburgher by virtue of something about one's speech. Other stories are about misunderstandings that arise because someone speaks like a Pittsburgher. In narratives like these we can see yet again how the enregisterment of Pittsburghese is shaped by the situations in which people talk about Pittsburgh and Pittsburgh speech. As we will see, the fact that people are telling stories leads them to draw bright-line boundaries between Pittsburghese and other ways of speaking, boundaries that are far more difficult to cross in the stories than they are in real life.

What I mean by a story here is not a fabrication—"telling stories" in this sense is not telling lies. Rather, I am interested in moments in conversation when one person takes the floor for longer than usual to narrate a series of events. Because recollection is always partial and shaped by cultural ideologies about time and action, there is no such thing as a literal recapitulation of events: narratives are always selective, even when they count as "history" (White 1980; 1992). When someone takes up time in an interaction to reminisce, there has to be a reason for it, and the reason has to make it worthwhile for others to keep listening. Providing a good enough reason requires a narrator to select certain things, and not others, to represent as key events. Furthermore, a narrative that people will listen to must have a point, and the narrator (or narrators) must make it clear, throughout the narrative, that the story is worth listening to. These requirements shape conversational stories in a number of ways.

In linguistic encounter narratives by Pittsburghers (like Jen and Donna's story about South Carolina), local speech is evoked in one of two ways. In some, the Pittsburgher is told that some word or bit of grammar he or she uses is nonstandard or at least different from what someone from elsewhere would say. The following story arose as Molly G., a woman in her thirties, answered my interview question, "So, have you ever heard of 'Pittsburghese'?"

5.10 Molly G., "Needs ironed"

MOLLY G. Well, I was in college—((laughing)). This is so embarrassing and this is going to be on the tape. My roommate said, "You know, that isn't proper English." I said, "What?" And she said, "You—you said your shirt 'needs ironed.'" I'm like, "Well, it does."

BJ ((Laughs))

MOLLY G. She said, "Well, it either 'needs ironing,' or it 'needs to be ironed.'" And it never occurred to me . . . I had never been corrected all the way through school even though we stuttered— studied grammar and everything else that . . .

BJ Mm-hmm. Mm-hmm.

MOLLY G. And that's a Pittsburgh thing. ((one second pause)) I—I think.

Another narrative in which a roommate objects to a Pittsburgher's speech comes from my interview with Rob U., who was a graduate student in English when I talked to him:

5.11 Rob U., "Redd up"

ROB U. Yeah, I've definitely said "redd up."

BJ Mm-hmm.

ROB U. You know, because my mom says that all the time, but—You know, my roommate who's not from—my ex-roommate, or whatever, who's not from Pittsburgh and would—hated that word, you know. Like, "Redd up the living-room," or something, you know. "What the hell is that supposed to mean?" . . . He—he—he, you know, he—he would always talk about, you know ((three second pause)) correct ways to say things, more self-consciously, or whatever . . .

As we have seen, people often become aware that Pittsburghers talk differently than other people, or are at least thought to, when they move away from Pittsburgh to university. Kristi G. was a student in her early twenties, talking about an experience at her university in another state.

5.12 Kristi G., "Gumband"

KRISTI G. Um, the only people that, I've really noticed, like, get on me because of my accent is, I called, I asked for a gumband from some kid from Ohio, and he didn't know what that was, and I was like, "A gumband, I need it for this," and so, 'bout five minutes later h—he, like, figured out it was a rubber band, or something like that, so, they got me on that one.

In stories like Jen and Donna's, on the other hand, someone recognizes a Pittsburgher's origin on the basis of his or her accent. Another example comes from a Pittsburgher who recognized a fellow Pittsburgher when they were in the military:

5.13 Patrick I., "Yinz"

PATRICK I. I was in the service, and I met a fella, he said, "I'm from Pittsburgh," I said "What part?" He said, ((laughs)) he says "Greensburg."[5] And I said, "I sure recognize that because I heard you say 'yinz.'"

Another instant-recognition story is set in Las Vegas. The narrator was Delma X., a middle-aged woman; her audience consisted of me and her mother-in-law, Margaret-Ann X. I had just asked them to describe their image of the typical Pittsburgher:

5.14 Delma X., Las Vegas recognition

DELMA X. People who find out you're from Pittsburgh talk about the Steelers and the Pirates. That's really, basically, the only thing they would say, you know unless they are from Pittsburgh. Well, one time, we were in Las

Vegas, another couple and, my husband and I, we were standing in line to go into a um ah, a, play, or a show, I guess it was. And we're talking, and the man in front of us turned around, and he said, "You're from Pittsburgh aren't you?" And we said, "Yes," and I said, "Oh I didn't even say *yinz*!" ((laughter)) But he could tell, by the way we talked, that we were from Pittsburgh. I mea—, he must have be—, I don't remember, but he must have been from Pittsburgh too at one time.

BJ Yeah, isn't that interesting, that people can do that.

DELMA X. And that far away.

Stories about instant recognition can also be set in Pittsburgh, however. Here a middle-aged man looks back on his experience in law school at Duquesne, a Catholic university in Pittsburgh.

5.15 Ted H., law school encounter

BJ Would you describe yourself as a typical Pittsburgher in any way?

TED H. I, I would say so, in many ways. Uh, I remember when I went to law school the first week or so, someone came up to me and said, "As soon as you opened your mouth in class I knew immediately where you were from" ((chuckling)), 'cause he was from Pittsburgh, although he had gone away to school and did not have a Pittsburgh accent, um or whatever. Um, so I think, my manner of speaking is probably somewhat typical, and I think that, uh, this irrational allegiance to Pittsburgh is fairly typical.

Outsiders' stories have to do with communicative difficulties they encounter in Pittsburgh. An example comes from a radio talk show on which I was interviewed (Cullen 2002). The interviewer, Lynn Cullen, moved to Pittsburgh as an adult to take a new job.[6] She introduced the topic of the interview with a narrative.

5.16 Lynn Cullen, "I did not really understand a word"

The first night I ever spent in Pittsburgh, um, I, I had come in to look for an apartment, or a home, someplace to live because I was going to be moving here to live, and there was a horrible blizzard that night, and I found myself snowed in at a Holiday Inn on the Parkway East, and, I just tuned on the TV, thought I might as well watch Channel 4 where I was going to be employed, and the first interview was with a guy who owned a gas station, right off the Parkway. His name was Peewee. ((one and a half seconds)) And Peewee was talkin' to the reporter about how he was knee deep in people coming in off the Parkway, and he couldn't help 'em anymore and there wadn't any gas, and there wasn't any help, and people were stuck, and his tow truck couldn't this and that. ((breath intake)) ((two seconds)) I think that's what he was talking about. I did not really understand a word the man said. And I remember sitting there and thinking, "Is he talking English?" wondering why this wasn't being subtitled.

Another such story has to do with an outsider's more specific communicative difficulty having to do with a pair of words, *towel* and *tile*, that sound the same in some Pittsburghers' speech. I am the narrator in this example; my interlocutor, Raymond T., is a native Pittsburgher.

5.17 Barbara Johnstone, "Replacing the towels."

BJ In fact, one of the first encounters I had when I moved to Pittsburgh was uh, walking, the dog in the—in Frick Park in the morning and there was a gentleman who also walks his dog who's a real estate agent, from Squirrel Hill, he's—We were talking about what we were gonna do during the day, he said that he was gonna have some workmen come in and replace the [talz] ("tahls") in his bathroom.

RAYMOND T. ((Laughing))

BJ I thought, "Why would you need workmen ((laugh voice)) to replace the towels in your bathroom, why couldn't you do that yourself?"

RAYMOND T. ((Laughs))

BJ Turned out he meant the tiles in the bathroom!

RAYMOND T. ((Laughing)) They were heavy [talz]] ("tahls").

BJ They were heavy towels, yeah, ((laughing voice)) yeah.

No two personal narratives of linguistic encounter are identical, and all are based in some way on personal experience. And yet they have elements in common (people who fail to understand each other, people who recognize each other, roommates, and attending a university, for example). How do people learn to tell such stories? One way to think about this is in terms of the plots these stories have in common. Plots are easily reusable scaffolds of meaning on which stories can be built. To describe the plots of the narratives we are looking at, we need a way of abstracting from the particular details of stories in order to talk about their meaningful chunks. For this, it is useful to draw on the system of "morphological" analysis proposed by the Russian folklorist Vladimir Propp. Propp's (1968) technique of "functional analysis" was intended to aid in the classification and comparison of fairytales. A "function" for Propp, "is . . . an act of a character, defined from the point of view of its significance for the course of the action" (21). Functions, in Propp's sense, can be repeated from tale to tale, no matter which character fulfills them, and in a class of stories with the same functions, their sequence is always identical. Propp described the structure of a given fairytale type in a series of Roman-numbered clauses, each encapsulated in a noun such as "interdiction," "flight," or "departure." Annotations following each clause provide descriptive detail and examples. Using Propp's method to describe the plot types exemplified earlier, we arrive at table 5.3.

Thinking about linguistic-encounter narratives in this abstract way highlights similarities and differences among them and points to how they work

Table 5.3 **Functional Analyses of Linguistic Encounter Stories (based on Propp 1960)**

Type 1	Type 2
I. THE TELLER/PROTAGONIST IS A PITTSBURGHER (*initial situation*)	I. THE TELLER/PROTAGONIST IS NOT A PITTSBURGHER (*initial situation*)
II. THE TELLER/PROTAGONIST LEAVES HOME (*move*) 1. The move may be that of a student going to college, someone moving for work, someone going on vacation.	II. THE TELLER/PROTAGONIST COMES TO PITTSBURGH (*move*) 1. The move may be that of a student coming to college, someone moving for work, someone on vacation.
III. THE TELLER/PROTAGONIST ENCOUNTERS AN OUTSIDER (*encounter*)	III. THE TELLER/PROTAGONIST ENCOUNTERS A PITTSBURGHER (*encounter*)
IV. THE TELLER/PROTAGONIST SAYS SOMETHING (*utterance*) 1. Typically, the teller/protagonist says very little, a word or a phrase.	IV. THE PITTSBURGHER SAYS SOMETHING (*utterance*) 1. The Pittsburgher may say very little, a word or a phrase.
V. THE OUTSIDER REACTS (*reaction*) 1. The reaction orients to or comments on some aspect of the form of the teller/protagonist's speech. 2. The reaction can take the form of a correction, indication of failure to understand, or recognition of the Pittsburgher's provenance.	V. THE TELLER/PROTAGONIST MISUNDERSTANDS OR FAILS TO UNDERSTAND (*reaction*) 1. The misunderstanding has to do with some aspect of the form of the Pittsburgher's speech.
VI. THE REACTION CAUSES THE TELLER/PROTAGONIST TO MAKE A GENERALIZATION ABOUT PITTSBURGH SPEECH (*generalization*) 1. Sometimes, this generalization is explicit and functions as the point of the narrative.	VI. THE REACTION CAUSES THE TELLER/PROTAGONIST TO MAKE A GENERALIZATION ABOUT PITTSBURGH SPEECH (*generalization*) 1. Sometimes, this generalization is explicit and functions as the point of the narrative.

ideologically to circulate claims about what counts as Pittsburghese and who speaks it, to link Pittsburghese with place, and to differentiate it sharply from other dialects. For one thing, both plot types require geographic mobility (Function II) and an encounter between a Pittsburgher and a non-Pittsburgher that is usually face-to-face. Encounters by Pittsburghers with outsiders often happen outside Pittsburgh, and encounters by outsiders with Pittsburghers happen in Pittsburgh. Thus, dialect is ideologically linked with place not just in the details in the stories but also on the more abstract level of their plots.

The two story types are different with regard to the social identity of the character encountered (Function III). Pittsburghers' stories (Type 1) tend to name and describe the non-Pittsburgher they encounter in ways that link dialect with place, while non-Pittsburghers' stories (Type 2) tend to name and describe the Pittsburghers they encounter in ways that link dialect with class and ethnicity. In the stories in which the teller/protagonists are Pittsburghers narrating encounters elsewhere, the encounter is often with someone identified as a social peer: students' encounters are with fellow students, for example. Social identities are suggested only indirectly, if at all ("my roommate," "a fella," "the man in front of us," "someone"), with the exception of identities connected with place: "this kid from Ohio." In these stories, then, linguistic difference is correlated with place and not with social identities such as class or ethnicity.

In the Type 2 stories, by contrast, dialect speakers are linked with class identities. Cullen's encounter is with a gas station owner whose identity is further linked with class via his name, "Peewee." In my encounter narrative, I identify my interlocutor as "gentleman" and as "a real estate agent," and further by naming his upper-middle-class neighborhood, "from Squirrel Hill." Although the class differential between outsider and Pittsburgher is maximized in Cullen's story and minimized in mine, both stories link local speech with social class.

Both plot types include a "reaction" function (Function V). In both subtypes, communicative difficulty is sometimes represented as a complete failure to communicate: Cullen's character purportedly "did not really understand a word [Peewee] said," despite the fact that she is able to paraphrase him at length, and wonders whether he is actually "talking English." In Kristi G.'s story, it supposedly took the kid from Ohio "five minutes" to figure out what the narrator was asking for. Rob U.'s roommate wonders, "What the hell is [*redd up*] supposed to mean?," even though the context probably made the meaning clear. In the example with Raymond T., I represented myself as having failed to understand what my neighbor was talking about, wondering aloud why he would need a workman to replace his towels, rather than, as actually happened, figuring out immediately and silently that he must be talking about tiles.

In stories like this, the non-Pittsburgher is represented as someone who does not do the kind of interpretive work that would be expected from people communicating across difference. Rather than drawing on the context to figure out what could be going on, the outsider runs into an interpretive wall. In Molly G.'s story, for example, the roommate purportedly reacts to the narrator's saying her shirt needs ironed not by saying something like, "Yes, it sure does," or "Oh, no, it doesn't," which would be typical friendly responses to Molly's observation, but by pointing out that the phrase "isn't proper English." These narrative representations of communicative difficulty as communicative failure work ideologically to differentiate Pittsburgh speech far more sharply from other ways of speaking than is justified by the empirical facts.

When the reaction function involves recognition of fellow Pittsburghers, as in Jen and Donna's story, the recognition is immediate and unambiguous: "they'll **immediately** say 'You're from Pennsylvania'" (lines 81, 83); "You're **definitely** [from Pennsylvania]" (line 84). Even the wording of Donna R.'s representation of the South Carolina woman's question gets edited in production from a hedged yes/no question to a confirmation-seeking question with the "tag" *right* that projects a much more certain stance: "You guys wouldn't happen to be from Pittsburgh, **right**?" (line 90). Representing the recognition and what is recognized in this way also works to link speech with place and differentiate Pittsburgh speech from other varieties. In Ted H.'s story, the fellow student is represented as saying that he **immediately** recognized where Ted was from, **"as soon as [Ted] opened [his] mouth** in class." And in Delma X.'s Las Vegas story, the man in front of them says, "You're from Pittsburgh **aren't you**?," using a tag-question format that suggests that he is just checking up on something he is already fairly sure of.

The generalization (Function VI) that follows the reaction continues this ideological work. Before a difference between a Pittsburgher's speech and someone else's is noticed, it's completely unnoticeable: "It **never occurred to me**," says Molly G., that *needs ironed* wasn't "proper English." Other narrators whose stories are about not being understood also represent themselves as having no idea why. Kristi G. has no idea why the "kid from Ohio" doesn't understand *gumband* and lets him figure it out. When the difference is noticed, it is linked with place as "a Pittsburgh thing."

Personal experience narrative is perhaps a uniquely effective genre for purposes of dialect enregisterment, because there are interactional reasons for dialect boundaries to be drawn more sharply in this genre than in others, perhaps more sharply than the facts on the ground would justify. The plot types I just described are realized as conversational narratives, told in real time in face-to-face interaction. Thus, as William Labov showed in his groundbreaking analysis of the structure of conversational personal-experience stories (1972e, 354–396, 1981; Labov and Waletzky 1977), they need to be highly *evaluated*. Evaluative material states or highlights the point of the story, why the audience should keep listening and allow the teller to keep talking. Evaluation may occur in clauses that comment on the story from outside: "I did not really understand a word the man said" (8); "This is so embarrassing" (2), or in clauses that attribute evaluative commentary to characters in the story: "I remember sitting there and thinking, 'Is he talking English?'" (8). Alternatively or in addition, evaluation can be embedded in the narrative, in the form of such things as extra detail about characters ("some kid from Ohio"), suspension of the action via paraphrase or repetition ("They'll say, 'You're from Pittsburgh.' / Yeah, they'll immediately say, 'You're from Pennsylvania, are you from the Pittsburgh area?'"), intensifiers ("**bout five minutes** later"; it **never** occurred to me"), or dramatic pauses, as in Lynn Cullen's more rehearsed story.

"I did not really understand a word the man said" makes a stronger bid for interlocutors' continued attention than would "He was a little hard to understand," or "He sounded a little different," even though the latter formulations might be closer to what might actually have happened. In these stories, in other words, the interactional demand for evaluation pushes narrators to exaggerate the differences between their speech and that of the others they encounter and the scale of the interactional difficulty to which these differences give rise. By the same token, Pittsburghers narrating encounters with fellow Pittsburghers elsewhere are interactionally constrained to exaggerate the recognizability of their accent by fellow Pittsburghers. "They immediately knew we were from Pittsburgh" is more dramatic than "After they listened to us for a few minutes, they wondered whether we were from Pittsburgh." This means that narratives like these are particularly well suited for producing and circulating ideological differentiation among (imagined) vernacular dialects.

Pittsburghese in Practice

Pittsburghese is a noun. Because of that, it seems natural to think of it as a thing. This is how people usually think of it: Pittsburghese is "the way we talk," "the words we use," "our language," according to Pittsburghers I spoke with. T-shirts that display lists of words under the heading "Pittsburghese" also treat it as a thing: the kind of thing you could find in a glossary or a dictionary, like a set of technical terms or a language. So do key fobs and rag dolls that play recorded phrases in Pittsburghese the way a foreign-language phrase-book might, along with most of the other Pittsburghese artifacts that are for sale.

In this chapter, however, we have seen that Pittsburghese is also like a verb in some ways. The title of this book, *Speaking Pittsburghese*, is meant to point to the ways in which Pittsburghese is process-like, something people do by speaking, even if it can end up seeming like a thing-like entity. Akin to any language or dialect (Harris 1988; Hopper 1988; Love 2007; Agha 2007b), Pittsburghese is emergent in interaction. It is a shifting set of generalizations people make about things they have heard rather than the preexisting topic of their talk. Pittsburghese is always embedded in human activities like arguing, chatting, or telling stories. Pittsburghese comes up in interaction when people need it. There is an important sense in which Pittsburghese is something people do, not a thing that exists on its own, independent of human habits and practices. Even the most thing-like representations of Pittsburghese, such as a dictionary or a glossary on a T-shirt, would be useless, and would cease to exist, if they were not resources for interactions among people. After all, people buy dictionaries and T-shirts; they give them to other people; they read them or wear them; they talk about them. If people did not use artifacts like these, there would no longer be a market for them, and they would stop being produced.

Furthermore, the uses people make of things shape what things are like. Spoons are concave because they are used for spooning; hammers have heavy, flat-ended heads because people pound things with them. The same is true of Pittsburghese. Because people evoke and create Pittsburgh speech when they are talking about home, Pittsburghese includes the names of local places. Because people evoke it to tell stories about differences, Pittsburghese is sometimes incomprehensible. Because people evoke it in familiar, shared contexts, Pittsburghese includes familiarities like *hon* and ways of evoking shared knowledge like *n'at*. Because people compare Pittsburghese with southern speech, Pittsburghese includes *yinz*.

In all the activities I have described in this chapter—discussing local speech face-to-face, contributing to an online forum about it, and telling stories—people claim to know things about Pittsburghese. Knowing things about Pittsburghese serves social purposes: getting a share in the conversation for Donna R., showing that one has the right to contribute for the online-forum users, and giving one's story a point for the narrators. To put it another way, expertise is at stake in all these activities. People have to show they are experts and that they have acquired their expertise in the right way. Donna's contributions to the discussion were dismissed until she claimed to be an actual speaker of Pittsburghese rather than just knowing about it second hand. Forum contributors had to show they knew about Pittsburghese because they were actually from Pittsburgh or had at least lived there.

In this chapter, the focus has been on expertise in interaction: how people make and use claims to knowledge in particular interactions and to particular situated ends. In chapter 6, we look at expertise through a wider lens. Taking a historical approach to expertise about Pittsburghese and Pittsburgh speech, we explore discussions of Pittsburghese in the print media over the course of the twentieth and early twenty-first centuries. Just as expertise about Pittsburghese means different things in different person-to-person social practices, expertise has meant different things at different times in public discourse.

6

Pittsburghese in the Media

Expertise about Pittsburgh speech has always been up for grabs. People who want to have a say as to what Pittsburghese is and what it means have to show that they have the right to be taken as experts. As we have seen, they do this in various ways. In face-to-face interaction, people can claim expertise about Pittsburghese by showing that they can speak that way, by imitating people who speak that way, or by claiming that they know people who speak that way.

People can claim expertise by listing Pittsburgh words, by asserting that they are from Pittsburgh, or by saying that they live in Pittsburgh. In the WTAE discussion forum, we saw different participants arguing for their expertise in different ways. Outsiders and immigrants to Pittsburgh based their claims to knowledge on cosmopolitan experience, claiming to know how Pittsburghers talked because they had heard people in other places and could compare. Pittsburghers based their epistemic claims on local experience, claiming to know how Pittsburghers talked because they had long heard Pittsburghers talk.

In the discursive activities I have described so far, claims to knowledge about Pittsburghese were rarely based on academic expertise. One participant in the online discussion forum mentioned a college course in linguistics as the source of his knowledge about Pittsburgh speech, and another mentioned linguistic research. Far more often, however, people relied on their life experience as a source of authority to speak. Sometimes, the possibility that academic, professional linguists may *not* be the best source of information about Pittsburgh speech becomes overt. For example, in a 2008 column in the *Pittsburgh Post-Gazette*, a newcomer to the city claimed to have chosen a popular website (discussed later in this chapter) over a scholarly one as a source for information about local speech. After claiming that he "still cannot understand most of the people some of the time" after a year in Pittsburgh, columnist Alan Petrucelli (2008) asserts that "Pittsburghese is a language all its own," echoing a claim that has been made in the press (but which sociolinguists would dispute) since at least 1973 (McGough 1973). Petrucelli then describes how he went about finding out more:

To dig deeper, I decided to find a dialectologist and found one in Barbara Johnstone, professor of linguistics and rhetoric at Carnegie Mellon University. She and her sociolinguist associate, Scott F. Kiesling, associate professor of linguistics at the University of Pittsburgh, have put together a Web site (english.cmu.edu/pittsburghspeech) that offers a compressive [sic] look at the what and why and how and when and who of Pittsburghese. Although it's user-friendly, the site is too academic for me, with occasional "big" words such as "monophthongization" rearing their six-syllable heads.

Important stuff? Yes.

But I jest wanna have fun.

And then I went to www.pittsburghese.com, a marvel of a site that promises I can learn Pittsburghese in a day!

Although Petrucelli finds the linguists' website "comprehensive" (or "impressive") and "important," he does not quote or paraphrase any information from it. Instead, he claims that it is "too academic" and not enough "fun," in contrast to the pittsburghese.com site. The nonstandard spellings in Petrucelli's article make it clear that he has borrowed heavily from the latter site, where Pittsburgh speech is (from a linguist's point of view) conflated with nonstandard speech in general, fast speech ("wanna"), and eye dialect ("jest").

In fact, as we will see in this chapter, academic expertise only entered the Pittsburghese picture in the 1960s. At that point, partly through the efforts of a local linguist, academic research came, for the first time, to be thought of as a source of expertise about local speech. Since then, professional language experts have often been consulted for news reports about Pittsburghese, but they never been treated as the only source of knowledge. Newspaper articles combine the voices of academics with the voices of laypeople via headlines and illustrations, and sometimes by quoting people on the street as sources of knowledge in the same way as they quote language professionals. The author of a very popular folk dictionary first published in 1981 drew on the academic knowledge associated with the history of English and American dialectology, but combined it, via hidden contributions from other people and cartoon illustrations, with the popular knowledge associated with daily life experience. Starting in the 1990s, the development of more interactive online media tugged the center of epistemic balance away from academia. A 1990s website encouraged visitors, no matter who they were, to contribute entries to a list of Pittsburghese words, for example.

As technological changes enabled enhanced interactivity online, expertise about local speech began to be challenged overtly, and academic research was not always treated as the primary source of knowledge. It has become more common in print and online for academic expertise to be explicitly contested, sometimes because, as for Alan Petrucelli, what academic linguists have to say is "not fun enough." Still, academic experts continue to play a visible role in shaping Pittsburghese, and current communication technology, in the form of Wikipedia, has encouraged us to reclaim some epistemic territory.

In this chapter, I explore the history of expertise about Pittsburgh speech and Pittsburghese. I turn from the mostly person-to-person discursive activities I sketched in chapter 5 to published, public discourse—newspapers, a folk dictionary, and a website—to explore how knowledge about Pittsburghese has been claimed and contested over several decades in communications media that differ in some key ways. Tracing shifts over time in accepted sources of expertise about local speech, I focus in particular on how communications media that have become interactive in more and different ways have helped reallocate rights to describe and evaluate local speech and made it possible to contest these rights in different ways. I also pay close attention to the recurring role of professional linguists in shaping popular discourse about Pittsburghese, showing how academic and popular representations of Pittsburgh speech have been intertwined over several decades. I explore how Robert Parslow, a dialectologist on the faculty of a Pittsburgh university, legitimized Pittsburgh speech during the 1960s and 1970s by talking about it repeatedly to the press, inevitably in a simplified and partial way. His descriptions of Pittsburgh speech were taken up in more explicit popularizations of Pittsburghese, of which he wrote one of the first (Parslow 1979). This academic dialectologist may, in fact, have coined the term *Pittsburghese*. A folk dictionary (McCool 1982) that has massively shaped subsequent representations of the variety was written by someone with graduate training in the history of English. By means of a quantitative and qualitative comparison of the content of and the generic conventions adopted in several popularizations, I show how the academic representations of Pittsburghese shaped the first popular ones and how these early representations shaped subsequent ones.

I turn, finally, to an effort by academics to reclaim expertise about Pittsburgh speech, namely a Wikipedia entry on Pittsburgh English. I describe the steps taken by the two linguists who wrote and posted the entry to try to ensure that our expertise, based on years of research, would, at least for a time, trump others'.

What Is Expertise, and Who Are the Language Experts?

As John Heritage, Geoffrey Raymond, and others have shown (Heritage and Raymond 2005; Raymond 2000), people do not bring expertise into interaction as a preexisting right. Whether or not someone is already a designated expert about the matter at hand, expertise always has to be renegotiated as people interact. In an analysis of a TV news program, for example, Raymond (2000) shows how an on-the-scene reporter viewing a traffic accident from a helicopter is encouraged by the studio anchors to describe what is "really" happening, despite the fact that the anchors, with multiple sources of video feed, probably have a clearer view of the situation. This example plainly shows how the role of designated expert may not fall to the person who actually knows the most, if it is even possible to talk about "knowing" in the abstract. Perhaps even more common are cases in which multiple sources of expertise come together to mesh or to collide. Parents are experts about their children by virtue of being their parents, teachers are experts about children by virtue of being their teachers, and parents' and teachers' expertise sometimes clashes. Being a native speaker of a language is sometimes assumed to map onto expertise about the grammar of the language, even though native speakers may be less able to describe their language in the abstract than people who learned it in school. Interdisciplinary scholarship is sometimes assumed to be superior to disciplinary work because of the multiple types of expertise involved.

The rules of engagement for the negotiation of expertise differ from activity to activity, from place to place, and from era to era. Since the eighteenth century, scientific expertise has been defined as expertise produced via systematic empirical procedures, and it has increasingly moved out of the purview of educated laypeople and into the narrower purview of accredited experts in universities and industrial research laboratories. Among these accredited experts are professional linguists. Linguist Roy Harris has explored the history of linguistic expertise in the Western intellectual tradition, tracing the ideas that underlie how mainstream linguists have come to think about their object of study (Harris 1980; 1981; 1987). Because a true science has long been thought to need an empirical object of study, linguists have had to find a way to think of language in general, and languages in particular, as objects (rather than, say, as processes). As Jesper Hermann puts it (2008, 97), "Linguists for a long time rightly regarded themselves as professional guardians of 'language,' and consequently had a vested interest in treating [language] as an independently existing 'thing' they looked after." In doing so, they lost sight of the ways in which, in Paul Hopper's well-known formulation, grammar is emergent rather than a priori (Hopper 1988). That is to say that, for the most part, speakers do not create utterances by deploying the rules of grammar, but rather by repeating, varying, and combining bits of language they have experienced before.[1] But in order to be the sort of "thing" science requires it to be, linguists' object of study has had to be based on abstractions, generalizations based on retrospective analysis of written discourse or discourse that is implicitly treated as if it were written (Harris 1980, 6–13). This has led to the idea that people actually talk and write by deploying the sorts of items and rules that are needed to describe linguistic features and languages as objects (Love 2009).

In daily life, linguists and laypeople alike experience variation among ways of speaking by hearing people talking. No two people or situations are exactly alike from a linguistic point of view, but we tune out most of the ways in which they differ. We may, however, notice metapragmatic signals that particular instances of variation need to be attended to because the presence of one variant versus another makes a difference in meaning of some kind. Variation can make various kinds of difference, sometimes indexing differences in denotational meaning, sometimes differences among speakers' identities, sometimes differences among situations, and so on. A feature that has been indexically linked with a particular social identity or recurring situation is, as we have seen, enregistered. A set of features that have been enregistered with the same identity or situation can come to be thought of as a language variety: a style, a dialect, or a language.

Linguistic anthropologists have widely adopted the framework of "language ideology" (Schieffelin, Woolard, and Kroskrity 1988; Woolard and Schieffelin, 1994) for thinking about cross-cultural ramifications of how people imagine talk, language, and linguistic expertise. Judith Irvine, for example, has written extensively about how Western language ideology shaped the history of African linguistics (Irvine 1995; 2008; 2009; see also Blommaert 2008). In a different post-imperial context (North America), David Samuels (2006) explores how Christianity, through the language ideology required for translating the Bible, shaped the indigenous Apaches' sense of what it takes to be a language expert. Dan Knox (2001) explores how "expert" and "enthusiast" institutions have legitimized and politicized the language and culture of northeastern Scotland, turning them from everyday practices into "spectacles."

Like Knox's, much of this work is focused on the role of political and educational institutions in determining "the boundaries of languages and disciplines" (Gal and Irvine 1995). The same is true of much of the literature on the standardization of English (Agha 2003; Bhatt 2002; Cameron 1995; J. Milroy and Milroy 1985), where the institutions involved include governments, the media, and the educational establishment, as well as the discipline of linguistics. Because standard languages and standard varieties are shaped by the discourses of institutions, they reflect the needs and purposes of institutions like schools, universities, and governments, which are shaped, for better or for worse, by the economic, political, and ideological systems in which these institutions function.[2] Pittsburghese has, by contrast, been shaped largely by laypeople, in a grassroots process that has not always accommodated the institutional voices of linguists and other language professionals. As a result, what counts as Pittsburghese largely reflects the needs and purposes for which laypeople talk about language and the ideologies that shape these needs and purposes.

Newspapers, 1952–1992

A corpus of newspaper articles about Pittsburgh speech dating from the 1950s through the early 1990s shows how popular, person-on-the-street language expertise, based on personal experience and personal observation, came to be supplemented and in some cases replaced by technical expertise based on specialized knowledge and knowledge-producing procedures like scholarly research. Print newspaper reports from this period are minimally interactive. Although readers could write letters to the editor to register support for or to correct the knowledge claims made in an article, the letters were not published with the articles, and there was never any guarantee that a correction would be made. As preserved in the historical record, the newspaper articles are even less interactive. Letters to the editor were not archived together with the articles they responded to, so, as these articles are experienced now, they represent only the voice of the reporter and the people the reporter chose to quote or paraphrase.

There are twenty articles in this corpus. Most are from a collection kept in the Pennsylvania Room at the Carnegie Library of Pittsburgh's Oakland branch. According to librarians there, Rose Demorest, the first head librarian of the Pennsylvania department, probably started the collection. The first newsprint clipping is from 1952, making this the likely date that the archive was started. (Material from before 1952 consists of photocopies of microfilmed articles.) The file consists primarily of newspaper and magazine articles, but it also includes several Pittsburghese glossaries, as well as excerpts from Kurath and McDavid's (1961) *The Pronunciation of English in the Atlantic States*. While a majority of the articles focus on the pronunciation, vocabulary, and grammar of Pittsburgh speech, there are several articles on other language-related topics, such as Pennsylvanians whose first language is Spanish, local proverbs, and American African Vernacular English. Andrew E. Danielson, then a student in a class I was teaching, came across the archive and did the initial analysis (Danielson 2001; Johnstone and Danielson 2001), which I draw on here. Other articles in the corpus are from the files of Patricia Parslow, widow of dialectologist Robert Parslow, to whom I return later in this chapter. All are from local publications and are about Pittsburgh speech. There are four articles from the 1950s, three from the 1960s, seven from the 1970s, four from the 1980s, and three from the 1990–1992 period.

In articles dating from 1952 to 1965, observations about local speech and explanations for its peculiarities are presented in the voice of the article's author and members of the general public, often outsiders who had moved to the city. In either case, claims about local speech are based on personal experience rather than technical expertise. The first article in the corpus (G. G. Love 1952) is a collection of comments about Pittsburgh speech paraphrased from letters to the editor, including observations made by "a woman from Philadelphia who moved here several years ago" and "a man from Minneapolis." Writer Gilbert Love's voice is heard mainly as that of the compiler, although he offers his opinion one time: "Many of us deny that we use those phrases." Another writer describes the observations of "a friend, newly come to Pittsburgh," who, "like all newcomers . . . duly noted the rising inflection which native Pittsburghers employ" (Bernhard 1959). In two articles by George Swetnam (1959a; 1959b), the sole voice is that of the writer, who bases his claims about local speech on his own experience, including noticing a "well-educated friend" use *anymore* in a distinctive way. Articles from the 1950s and 1960s were usually feature articles, accompanied by cartoon illustrations and segregated from the "real" news. These early articles treat features of regional speech largely as curiosities, which are characterized almost exclusively in a disparaging way.

The first article that cites an academic expert is from 1967 (Gleason 1967). The expert was Robert Parslow, then a recently arrived instructor of linguistics at the University of Pittsburgh, whose specialty was dialectology. Once the local press realized that specialized, technical expertise about Pittsburgh speech was available, contributions from language experts began to appear regularly in subsequent reports. Articles about Pittsburgh speech published after 1967 almost invariably cite one or more sources identified as having technical expertise, usually by name: "some expert linguists" (Swetnam 1972); "Anita Panek, secondary English teacher" (Browne 1976); "speech teachers" (Bloom 1977); H. L. Mencken, author of *The American Language* (Bloom 1977); Frederick Cassidy and Joan Hall of the *Dictionary of American Regional English* (McHugh 1979); and other "educators," "scholars," and "local linguists." Starting in the 1980s, when articles began to turn from treating local speech as a curious oddity to talking about when it might actually be appropriate to use, experts came to include job counselors and corporate human relations managers (Braknis 1991; Kloman 1992; Warnick 1990).

However, people on the street continue to be quoted from time to time. Sometimes their views are contrasted with "professional opinion," but in two articles from the early 1990s, ordinary citizens are represented as having the same degree of expertise as technical specialists, only that it arises from a different source, personal experience. In an article about local speech in the Lawrenceville neighborhood (Warnick 1990), all but three of the reporter's sources are identified by means of a similar appositive phrase: Samuel Lewis ("manager of Kay Drug Co. on Butler Street"), Sam McCool ("author of 'Sam McCool's New Pittsburghese'"), Richard Enos ("a Carnegie Mellon University English professor who teaches rhetoric"), Christina Bratt Paulston ("a University of Pittsburgh Linguistics Professor"), Maryanna Baldauf ("a lifelong neighborhood resident"), Bernice Palmiere ("principal of St. John Neumann regional Catholic Elementary School"), JoAnne Eresh ("director of the Pittsburgh School district's division of writing and speaking"), Linda Blackman ("president of The Executive Image, Inc.") The other three sources are people on the street in Lawrenceville, identified by name and age: "George Mihelcic, 19", "Tim Frolini, 17," and "Karl Rogosz, 32"). The only quotative author Warnick uses is "says," and as it is used for all his sources it does not rank them with regard to expertise.

Starting in the 1960s, the newspaper articles in the corpus begin to set textual exposition of "the facts" about Pittsburgh speech (whether the source for these facts be popular or technical) against a visual background of popular representations of the dialect and its speakers. At first these are cartoon illustrations: a man using a picture to explain to a shopkeeper what a "gumband" is (Gleason 1965); a man in a Pittsburgh Pirates baseball cap pointing two people in the direction of a sign saying "Dahn tahn Pittsburgh" (Gray 1968); the outline of Pennsylvania with seven open-mouthed cartoon characters in its southwestern corner and the words "dahntahn," "wants washed," and "ahtside," ('outside') (Gleason 1967); a sports fan surrounded by representations of regional words including "youn's" ('you,' pl.), "red up" ('tidy up'), and "crick" ('creek') (Swetnam 1972). Later there are headlines that include representations of Pittsburgh speech. The first of these appears in 1978 ("Pitt prof finds Pittsburghese a **slippy** subject" [Huzinec 1978]). Others include "This column **needs read**" (Leo 1982); "**We'uns** sure stretch the king's English" (Davidson 1984); "Lawrenceville aside, fewer of **yunz** speak Pittsburghese" (Warnick 1990); "Internet **n'at**" (Gitman 1997); and "Pals send tape **an 'at** to priest in Rome" (Ove 1998).

The role of the popular voice in these representations is ambiguous. When it appears in a headline, the popular voice represented by the respelled words has the effect of framing the more expert voice. The expert cited in the article is talking about something that has already been introduced in the headline in a way that presupposes the local knowledge required to recognize and understand the Pittsburghese forms. The expert's role is framed as that of filling in the background blanks about something that is already known: that *slippy* or *needs x'ed* or *we'uns* are local forms, for example. Since headlines are written after articles are submitted, often by a different writer, it is impossible for the technical expert to contest the popular knowledge they represent (such as the questionable claim that *we'uns* is a Pittsburgh form). When it is in a cartoon, what the popular voice says about local speech is presented as an illustration of what the voices in the article say. If, as sometimes happens, the illustrations represent forms the expert would not consider local, such as eye dialect; terms the expert would not consider technical, such as *Pittsburghese*; or activities the expert would not sanction, such as using jokey respelling as a way of representing nonstandard speech, this is invisible to readers, since the experts are not asked to approve the cartoons.

To summarize, the trend over time in the newspaper articles is clearly toward the privileging of arguments about local speech based on technical expertise over person-in-the-street personal-experience arguments. This is particularly true of the body of the articles, where the reporter is in control of the representation of expertise and where, starting with the first article about Robert Parslow, the voice of a technical expert is more often meant to be taken as authoritative than is that of the layperson, who sometimes has no voice at all. But headlines and illustrations, created by other people, often push against that locus of authority, representing the experts as simply elaborating on things Pittsburghers already knew.

Professional Linguists, I: Robert L. Parslow, 1967–1979

The first professional linguist to take a sustained interest in Pittsburgh speech was dialectologist Robert L. Parslow (1924–1981), who was hired as an instructor at the University of Pittsburgh around 1960. Parslow was working on a doctoral dissertation at the University of Michigan under the supervision of Raven McDavid, editor of the *Linguistic Atlas of the Upper Midwest*, when he was hired at Pitt. Once he finished his PhD, he was appointed assistant professor (Christina Paulston, personal communication, Feb. 19, 2008). Local curiosity about local speech coincided in the late 1960s and early 1970s with Parslow's willingness to legitimize these forms in interviews by explaining their history and referring to them in the aggregate as a dialect. As we will see, however, while many Pittsburghers appreciated Parslow's work, not everyone acknowledged his expertise as superior to their own.

The term *Pittsburghese* first appears in the 1967 article mentioned earlier (Gleason 1967), in which Parslow discusses the place of Pittsburgh speech in the midland dialect region as well as the historical background of the northern United States dialect region. The article's title, "Only in Western Pennsylvania Do You Hear 'Gumband' and 'Needs Washed,'" makes an explicit (if inaccurate) claim for the variety's distinctiveness. The article appears to be the outcome of an interview by writer David Gleason with Parslow. Parslow is introduced as an "instructor in linguistics at the University of Pittsburgh," and the article consists entirely of quotes from Parslow (in quotation marks) and paraphrases of his words. No other voices are heard. The words that are used to introduce Parslow's quotes represent him as authoritative: he "hastens to point out (that the Pittsburgh area doesn't have a monopoly on different ways of writing or saying things)," "knows (that people say things differently, depending on [where they are from])," "explains," "emphasizes," and "reports." Article author Gleason cites the Linguistic Atlas of the United States projects as the source for one claim about US dialectology—"The United States is divided into regions, according to speech habits, in the Linguistic Atlas"—but Parslow is represented as citing no source for any of his claims about Pittsburgh speech or dialect geography in general, representing them, rather, as common expert knowledge, as in this passage:

> "Gum band—for rubber band—is exclusively Pittsburgh, but you will find 'rubber binders' substituted for it in some parts of the country," explains Mr. Parslow. "It's easily explained—the use of the word 'gum,' that is. Rubber is a gummy material. In some places, galoshes, for instance, are called 'gum boots'—for the same reason."

Parslow's certainty is underscored by his use of the simple present ("gum band . . . **is** exclusively Pittsburgh"; "galoshes . . . **are called** 'gum boots'"), and his teacherly stance is further performed in expressions like "you will find" and "it's easily explained." Parslow's voice dominates in two subsequent newspaper articles (Huzinec 1978; McGough 1973), which are about his planned research in Pittsburgh.

However, the newspaper articles' representation of Parslow as the authority on the topic did not keep readers of the articles, both in the local press and via wire service versions of the latter two articles, from writing to offer their own expertise. Professor Parslow saved forty-three letters he received between 1973 and 1979 in response to the McGough and Huzinec articles, many of them with copies of his long, meticulous answers.[3] I cannot be sure that these are all the responses to these articles. However, the fact that they range from multipage letters to notes on postcards, and the fact that the collection includes some letters that Parslow answered and some he did not answer suggest that this may be the complete set. Some writers wrote simply to enclose copies of the United Press International or Associated Press wire service articles, based respectively on the 1973 and 1978 local articles, which appeared in newspapers around the United States, others to offer to work with him or ask for a job doing so. One letter, from a columnist for a suburban Chicago newspaper, describes how she used an article about Parslow as the basis for a request to Chicago-based Pittsburghers to get in touch with her. Several request written information and/or bibliographic citations to use in college reports or school classes. A few include narratives about encountering other ways of speaking, like those described in chapter 5 ("It only took me several months at boarding school to hear myself as 'different' and to set about immediately to erase the 'different.' My three daughters in turn have astonished their roommates when they redd up their cupboards.")

Most often, though, letter writers offer their own expertise in one or more of four ways. Some proffer features of Pittsburgh speech they think Parslow may have missed. For example, one writer wonders, "Have you come across the word 'juke'?" and another notes that "another thing some of us do is to gloss over or omit syllables." Several describe what I have called the Pennsylvania question intonation (chapter 2). A Mrs. H. W. Green sends three handwritten pages of suggestions about things Parslow should study. Another writer notes, "I assume you have also gotten into the German words—the smear case (cottage cheese), clearly derived from schmier kässe [sic]." Second, some letter writers object to items that are included in the articles or definitions of them: "My parents used the term 'redd up' to mean, not so much as [sic] to clean, but as to tidy up a disordered room."

Third, writers offer alternative accounts of the history or social distribution of features. One reader writes, for example, "Apparently, [Pittsburghers] have never been taught how to pronounce combinations of certain vowels, such as o and u and o and w." A professor of political science in Flint, Michigan, who once taught in Pittsburgh, objects to the claim that the mayor's Pittsburgh accent shows that intelligent, educated people use this local standard: "I would quarrel with that, particularly the more formal education they have received. I believe there is a reverse correlation here in terms of the local dialect." Finally, a number of writers point out that things that Parslow (or, quite possibly, reporters paraphrasing him inaccurately) claims are unique to Pittsburgh are in fact not. For example, a British writer objects to a mention in the 1973 article of "the expression 'redd up' as being typical of this area," pointing out that "C. Brontë does use the expression in 'Jane Eyre.'" Another says, "Also believe the RED or READ UP is Pennsylvania Dutch extraction." Another reader writes, "I think I may be able to give you some unexpected assistance by way of the southern Appalachian region" and provides a long list of words and pronunciations he has heard in Martin County, Kentucky. Another notes that "incidentally—lower Delaware people also 'warsh.'"

In letters to the editor sparked by the 1973 article, two writers voiced the opinion that the entire project was misguided. One, from a Betty W. Shields, indirectly refers to Parslow as one of "the same liberal professors who would adhere to and uphold poor and incorrect pronunciation because it has always been spoken and would be the first to agitate for changing the eloquent old English poetic language" and argues that "this is similar to condoning a six-year-old assimilating into his speech the popular four-letter obscenities now in current usage by our college graduates." Ms. Shields ends by wondering, "What state funds are being used, or what foundation was conned into underwriting this bit of ho-hum research?" An Arlene Tegtmeier notes that although she thinks Pittsburghers should be proud of their speech, "with so much strife in the world, one would think Dr. Parslow could find a more beneficial project to busy himself with than studying dialects." These letters elicited a pointed rebuttal letter from Edward M. Anthony, then the chairman of the University of Pittsburgh linguistics department, where Parslow was employed: "Ms. Tegtmeier needs contradicted and corrected . . . Since so much of the understanding between people is achieved through the use of language, it seems to some of us very much in order to study it. I shall resist the temptation to inquire whether the aforementioned Ms. Tegtmeier finds writing letters to the editor the most beneficial project to busy herself with."

What is striking about the lay responses to Parslow's work is their confidence. Readers of the articles about Parslow speak to him as if they were professional colleagues. Correspondents appear to assume that they are interested in Pittsburgh speech for the same reasons as Parslow, that the examples they provide are the kind of data he needs, and that the generalizations they make are the same kinds of generalizations he would make. Although some writers hedge their claims with "it seems to me," "might," "may I suggest," or "I am by no means a linguist," others are extremely direct: "First of all, Pittsburgh is NOT unique 'speech-wise'"; "The early German-Dutch . . . are responsible for the vocabulary, grammar, and pronunciation of Pennsylvanians—not just 'Pittsburghese.'" Suggestions are sometimes phrased as imperatives: "Along with slippy and illigle, don't forget prolly"; "look into the settlements of the ancestors in Lebanon, Lancaster, York—etc." An attorney writes to tell Parslow that "your case is overstated" and to point out that "few people here [in Harrisburg, Pennsylvania] pronounce 'caught' differently from 'cot' or 'egg' differently from 'plague,'" ending his letter by suggesting that Parslow "redd up [his] act."

In his responses, Parslow usually dealt with writers' claims point by point, often referring to scholarly sources such as the *Oxford English Dictionary* and Hans Kurath's dialect atlas research in Pennsylvania. One writer, Norma Farrell McCormack, complained that Parslow had "stolen [her] thunder," as she had been planning to write "a handbook about the City on the Point [Pittsburgh], featuring, of course, the local tongue," and taking "strong exception" to a claim she thought Parslow had made. In his response (April 14, 1977), Parslow explicitly addresses the difference between lay and scholarly understandings of language variation:

> My inclination has always been to encourage amateur dialectologists like you; very often, observers of your ilk have insights that ease the task of the professional linguist . . . It is incumbent on us professional dialectologists, however, to remind the laity that our discipline has evolved into a complex and structured science, with its particular theoretical and methodological foundations.

He goes on to describe his own professional credentials:

> I myself started in 1952 under the tutelage of Hans Kurath and Raven McDavid, successive directors of the Linguistic Atlas of the United States and Canada; and I continued to investigate dialects in Michigan, Massachusetts, and now Pennsylvania.

Parslow's responses often exhibited not the empirical methods of dialectology but the intuition-based methods of the Chomskyan linguistics of his day. In many letters he describes what features he "has" (that is, could use) in his speech or grew up hearing or saying in western Michigan. In doing this, Parslow may have appeared to be basing his claims on the same sort of anecdotal evidence his correspondents were adducing. However, evidence from later lay-linguist interactions on the topic of Pittsburgh speech suggests that the difficulty Parslow had in asserting his professional expertise as different from the expertise of laypeople was not just a result of occasional carelessness. As we will see, professional expertise has continued to be challenged and contested in the same ways.

By the late 1970s, Pittsburghers had come to believe that they or their neighbors spoke a dialect and that the dialect was unique, local, and sometimes even appropriate. Conditions were ripe for this dialect to acquire a dictionary, and dialectologist Parslow was the first to take on this task. In a letter dated May 4, 1979, Parslow, by then promoted to associate professor, agreed to the request of the Pittsburgh Diocesan Holy Name Society to write an introduction to local speech meant for people attending the society's national convention in Pittsburgh that year.[4] The mimeographed booklet he produced, "A Little Guide to Pittsburghese" (figure 6.1), has as its central section a dictionary-like alphabetical vocabulary list representing local pronunciations with nonstandard spellings.

Some representative entries are these:

aht: opposite of in. "Jack Horner pooled aht his thumb"

anymore: now (used in positive statements). "Anymore the Stillers are the best team in the Lig."

ditn't: negative of did. "Youns ditn't warsh younses hands."

jell: a prison. "Richardson designed the County Jell."

Robert Parslow died in 1981 at the age of fifty-seven, before doing any fieldwork or publishing any scholarly research about Pittsburgh speech. But his role in the history of Pittsburghese was significant, if not crucial. Parslow's contributions to public discourse about Pittsburgh speech served to legitimize it for the first time as a "real" dialect, by giving it a history (in the English of the Scotch-Irish) and a dictionary (in the form of lists of Pittsburgh words and their meanings). Once he appeared on the scene, journalists writing about Pittsburgh speech started to consult people they considered experts. Person-on-the-street expertise continued (and continues) to be significant in shaping Pittsburghese, but, since 1967, experts have been seen, at least by the traditional broadcast news media, as the holders of the official stamp of approval and are consulted for every newspaper, TV, and radio report on the topic.

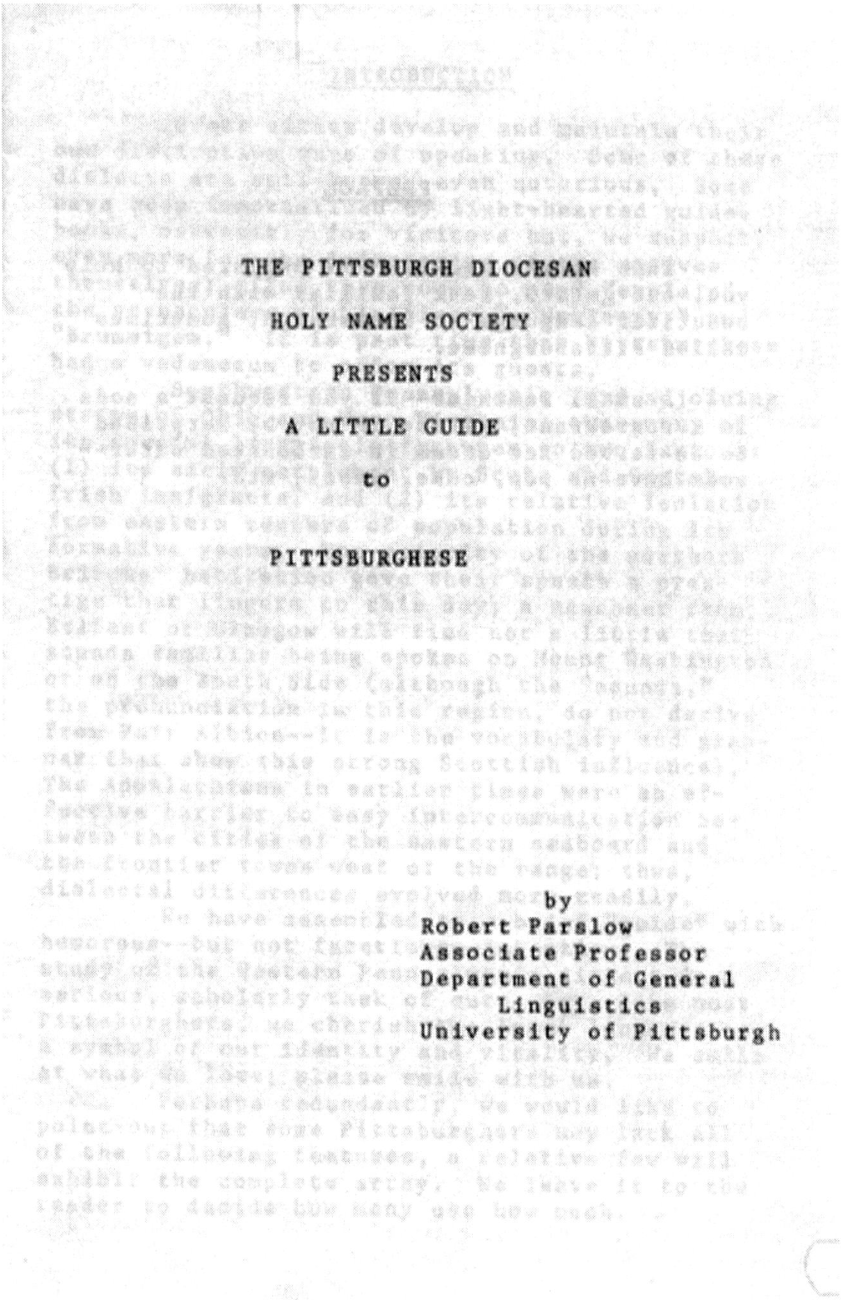

THE PITTSBURGH DIOCESAN

HOLY NAME SOCIETY

PRESENTS

A LITTLE GUIDE

to

PITTSBURGHESE

by
Robert Parslow
Associate Professor
Department of General
Linguistics
University of Pittsburgh

Figure 6.1 Front Cover of Robert Parslow, *A Little Guide to Pittsburghese*.

Sam McCool's New Pittsburghese: How to Speak like a Pittsburgher (1981–Present)

If judged by the extent to which it has been borrowed from, then by far the most influential description of local speech in Pittsburgh is *Sam McCool's New Pittsburghese: How to Speak Like a Pittsburgher* (McCool 1982). (For this reason, *How to Speak* was the source of one of the corpora of Pittsburghese I discussed in chapter 1.) Originally published in 1981, this 39-page paperback book has been available ever since and is widely offered in bookstores and souvenir shops. On the cover (black and gold, the colors of the local sports teams) is a photograph of the downtown skyline of Pittsburgh with cartoon word balloons emanating from four building windows (figure 6.2). In them are the words "worsh," "imp 'n arn," "yunz," and "dahntahn."

Like other such booklets, as well as similar lists contained in newspaper and magazine articles and on websites about Pittsburghese and many other varieties of English, *How to Speak Like a Pittsburgher* combines generic elements of a dictionary with elements of a school vocabulary exercise. Words and phrases are listed in alphabetical order. Each entry consists of the word to be defined, spelled in a way that is supposed to represent how it is pronounced, followed by a short definition and an illustration of the word's usage in a sample sentence. As we saw in chapter 1, the entries in *How to Speak Like a Pittsburgher* contain a combination of semiphonetic respellings like 'cahch', jokey definitions, and references to Pittsburgh places, products, and preferences.

Sam McCool had originally come to Pittsburgh from his home in eastern Pennsylvania to attend college, first at Carnegie Tech (now Carnegie Mellon University) and then at the University of Pittsburgh, where he graduated with a bachelor's degree in English. He then earned an MA in English from West Virginia University, about an hour's drive away, while living in Pittsburgh. McCool had become interested in local speech by virtue of several things. A course in the history of English while working on a PhD in English at Lehigh University taught him to "listen to speech for what it tells us about language" (personal communication, Oct. 24, 2011). As he was growing up in eastern Pennsylvania, McCool's Pittsburgh-bred mother had been the butt of teasing because of her accent, and when he returned to Pittsburgh in 1980 after two years at Lehigh, McCool paid closer attention to Pittsburgh speech than he had before and started telling people they should be proud of the dialect. McCool's wife at the time was from Pittsburgh, and her parents encouraged him to put his new appreciation for local speech to use by producing something about it.

How to Speak Like a Pittsburgher came about when Sam McCool was working as the manager of Goodwill Industries' print shop on Pittsburgh's South Side. McCool thought that the print shop could get extra business, beyond just

Figure 6.2 Front Cover of *Sam McCool's New Pittsburghese: How to Speak Like a Pittsburgher.*

printing flyers and signs for in-house use, by printing books for industry, so in 1981, he wrote and published a small booklet called *How to Speak Pittsburghese* as an example of the kind of thing they could do.[5] According to McCool (interview, Oct. 24, 2011) it seemed to be the "right moment" for a book about Pittsburghese. He thought that then-Mayor Richard Caliguiri's "second Renaissance" economic-development initiatives were going to bring corporate outsiders to Pittsburgh who would be curious about local speech and that insiders might find a booklet about it amusing. Local pride was particularly high due in part to the mayor's efforts and in part to sports success throughout the 1970s and the visibility this had given the city.

With training in English linguistics and experience living and working elsewhere in Pennsylvania and in West Virginia, McCool knew that the words and structures in the booklet were used in other places as well as in Pittsburgh, in an area "which included everything below Erie and west of the central Susquehanna River and . . . west of the Three Rivers along the Ohio and [in] parts of Kentucky, Tennessee, and northern Mississippi and Alabama" (Sam McCool, personal communication, December 2012). But the term *Pittsburghese* was already circulating, and if the list in *How to Speak Pittsburghese* included things people said elsewhere, these were things Pittsburghers were aware of and claimed as their own, so that a booklet about Pittsburghese would capture the attention of the people McCool wanted to reach.

The first edition was a little black-and-gold book with no illustrations, produced as a gift for the members of the Board of Directors of Goodwill of Southwestern Pennsylvania attending a board meeting. McCool knew he was taking the risk that people would find the book insulting. As he put it (personal communication, December 2012):

> most of [the board members] were pillars of the business, religious, and social work communities. I wasn't sure what the reaction would be. I was sure, though, that the topic was provocative, and in light of Pittsburgh's new national prominence as City of Champions, it was worth a shot.

The booklet was an instant success. One of the Goodwill board members showed a copy of it to Roy McHugh, a columnist with the *Pittsburgh Press*, who wrote a favorable review (McHugh 1981).[6] Booksellers, such as Kaufmann's department store and the bookstore chain B. Dalton's, urgently requested copies, and McCool was interviewed on local and national radio and TV for local-color features that appeared on programs like ABC's *Good Morning America*.

The next edition of the book was published in 1982 by Hayford Press and printed by New Image Press on Pittsburgh's South Side. Hayford Press added the artwork—by Dave Hereth, McCool's staff artist at Goodwill—that has continued to appear in subsequent printings. McCool had left Goodwill by this point for a better-paying job. Goodwill claimed copyright to the book and took over publishing it beginning in 1984, continuing to use New Image Press to print it. Goodwill Industries and Sam McCool have shared very modest royalties for the more than forty years the book has been in print.

How to Speak is distributed by Renaissance News, whose website claims that "thousands of this book are printed every six months."[7] Exact sales figures are unclear, but a representative of Renaissance news told McCool in 2012 that they have sold roughly six or seven thousand copies a year since Renaissance took over distributing the book in the late 1980s. The representative claimed that the book was always in demand, selling out before it could be restocked (Sam McCool, personal communication, December 2012). A rough estimate of the number of copies published since 1982, first by Hayford Press and then by Goodwill Industries, falls between two hundred and two hundred fifty thousand (ibid.).

How to Speak Like a Pittsburgher has served as a model and a source for a great deal of subsequent discourse about how Pittsburghers talk. For example, a comparison of How to Speak with a souvenir Pittsburghese T-shirt that was for sale in the late 1990s shows that twenty-six of the thirty-two items on the T-shirt (or 72 percent) are also in the McCool book, and twenty of the twenty-six, or 78 percent, are spelled identically in the book and on the shirt. Further evidence of the book's influence comes from our interviews: almost all of the eighty people we talked to in 2003 and 2004 for the Pittsburgh Speech and Society Project said they either owned the book or had seen it somewhere.

As a print book, How to Speak Like a Pittsburgher represents in most ways the least interactive of communications media. From when the book was first published until at least the mid-1990s, readers had almost no way of responding to it publicly. The Internet has changed this somewhat. A Google search suggests that readers' responses to the book take the form of brief evaluative reviews on booksellers' websites. For example, at the time of writing, How to Speak was available through several booksellers via Amazon.com, and there were four customer reviews on Amazon. The reviews used terms like "cute," "fun," and "humorous," but none responded to particular details of the book's content.

However, a certain degree of interactivity is hidden in the single-authored text. According to McCool (interview, Oct. 24, 2011), once the first, un-illustrated version of How to Speak became a success, people suggested additions. Some of the suggestions were hard to reject, coming, for example, from McCool's superiors at work, and the 1982 edition contains a number of entries that McCool added at others' behest. One of these is "Jeat jet," defined as "an inquiry heard frequently around lunchtime" (McCool 1982, 19), meant to be interpreted as "Did you eat yet?" Others are similar examples of eye-dialect that do not, in McCool's opinion, represent speech features local to Pittsburgh. To me, a linguist, this has always made the book seem oddly multivoiced, as if it vacillated between the expertise of a dialectologist who knew something about the history of American English and the expertise of a layperson who had seen previous representations of nonstandard speech; it was not until I talked to McCool that I understood why.

Because McCool is the only official author of the book, the voice represented in the book is officially his, and most readers are likely not to notice the multi-voiced qualities I thought I detected. Whose voice is this, then? As represented in the (very outdated) post-script called "The Author," McCool is

> a resident of Pittsburgh's Brighton Heights, [who] has a B.A. from the University of Pittsburgh and an M.A. from West Virginia University, both in English literature. When he's not putting friends and acquaintances to sleep with tales of seafarers and discourses on irregular Anglo-Saxon verbs, he practices his Pittsburghese.

To readers who ask themselves who the author is and turn to this page to find out, McCool might seem like an academic of some sort, or at least a language expert—someone who can talk about "irregular Anglo-Saxon verbs." He might also seem like a Pittsburgher—someone who lives in the Pittsburgh neighborhood of Brighton Heights and speaks (or at least "practices") Pittsburghese. The hidden interactivity that was involved in the creation of *How to Speak Like a Pittsburgher*, by virtue of which the book represents lay as well as more scholarly expertise, is arguably reflected in the blurb about the author, in which McCool is represented as coming from both positions, expert and lay. In sum, *How to Speak Like a Pittsburgher* reflects the same sort of combination of official and lay expertise as we saw in the newspaper articles.

Pittsburghese.com (1997–Present)

In the 1990s, the development of more explicitly interactive media enabled the center of epistemic balance to shift. A website called Pittsburghese (http://www.pittsburghese.com) encouraged visitors to contribute entries to a list of Pittsburghese words and phrases. Pittsburghese.com is the work of a local web designer, Alan Freed, who mounted it in 1997 as a way of calling attention to his web-design business (Voice of America 2000; Alan Freed, personal communication, June 27, 2002). The site carries banner ads for small, Pittsburgh-based enterprises such as souvenir wholesalers and photo suppliers. Promising that readers can "learn Pittsburghese in a day," the site includes some "Pittsburghese calisthenics," a "translator," and "audio quiz," as well as a link to a recording of a Voice of America radio program that featured the site (Voice of America, n.d.).

Starting in 2002, a tab called "For Actual Research" linked to a page about my research on the dialect and, from there, to the Pittsburgh Speech and Society website mounted in connection with the research.

The most popular section during the period in question was the "Glossary." Here, visitors could fill in a form on which they listed their name and location and a word or phrase (often spelled in a way that was meant to indicate its non-standard pronunciation) with a definition and an example sentence. Entries appeared on the site in an invariable format exemplified by this one:

> Bawdle **Bottle**. Gimme a bawdle of arn!
> *(Submitted by Hank Smoot, Springfield)*

Contributions automatically appeared on the site unless Freed deemed them obscene. In 2002, the site was getting one thousand visits a day, and the glossary had grown to thousands of items (Fleming 2008).

Although it is not my focus here to evaluate the actual claims people make about local speech in any of the media I am discussing, a look at the subsection called "adjectives" gives a sense of what sorts of things glossary entries did. Twenty-five percent of the adjective entries represented eye-dialect, nonstandard spellings of standard, dictionary pronunciations such as "cawfing" for 'coughing'. Nine percent represented standard pronunciation as it often sounds in actual connected speech as opposed to the dictionary pronunciation: an example is "ig'nernt" for 'ignorant'. Another quarter of the entries appear to represent non-standard usage, but of either a very widespread or a very idiosyncratic nature, as in entries for words like "inneresting" (a widespread nonstandard pronunciation of interesting) or "jiagunda" (possibly a family's or even an individual's term for 'huge'). An additional 25 percent were words that do vary regionally in US English but are not associated with Pittsburgh speech in any other source: "cattywumpus" for 'diagonally across from' or "ascared" for 'scared.' Only a quarter of the entries represent words or pronunciations that are widely understood, by linguists and/or Pittsburghers, to be limited in geographical range and widely heard in the Pittsburgh area, and which we have seen repeatedly in previous chapters. These include "lahsy" ('lousy' with monophthongal /aw/) and "slippy," 'slippery'.

Although the tone of the entries, and that of the site as a whole, was meant to be humorous, it was by no means clear to all its readers and contributors that the activity was intended as a joke. The reporter for the Voice of America who described the site represented it as "entertaining," and her report was set to the background of "The Pennsylvania Polka" and a song about the Pittsburgh Steelers. However, she also represented her discovery of the site as the discovery that the dialect of her youth was real, not just a nostalgic figment of the collective imagination (Voice of America, n.d.). Although the site's designer and webmaster, Alan Freed, later claimed that "there's not a serious word on the whole site" (Freed, e-mail to author, Jan. 30, 2008), he also admitted that "every so often people were taking us seriously." Beginning in 2001 or so, this became clear to me, too, when Freed became aware of my work on Pittsburgh speech and Pittsburghese and started referring queries he got from students to me. (When I told him about the new Pittsburgh Speech and Society website in June of 2002 he immediately created the link to it, and to me, that I mentioned previously.) In other words, students, and perhaps other people as well, thought that the nature of the expertise the site represented was ambiguous: was the person-on-the-street (or person-on-the-World Wide Web) expertise that appeared on the site the kind of expertise you could draw on for, say, a school or university term paper? Freed insisted that the representation of local speech on his website did not represent technical expertise, but some of the site's users either thought it did or did not ask themselves the question.

Around 2003, webmaster Freed turned off the interactive feature that allowed people to contribute new words. According to a newspaper interview, he felt that he had lost control of the site's content: "It got to the point where people were submitting anything Myron Cope [a local sports announcer with a distinctive speaking style] had ever said in his life," Freed was quoted as saying (Fleming 2008). The site is still, as of this writing, accessible, but visitors can no longer experience it as interactive in the same way.

Because anyone could post to it and editorial censoring was minimal, the site diffused expertise about local speech far beyond the few carefully selected local people on the street whose voices appeared in some of the newspaper articles. Anyone with Internet access could, in this medium, claim expertise about local speech simply by posting an entry to the list. Participants were unable to argue for their expertise or explicitly indicate its source. Because the form that created the database entries behind the site constrained what kinds of information posters could provide—name, place, word, definition, and example—the only way posters could make any sort of claim about the source of their expertise about Pittsburgh speech was by listing Pittsburgh or some nearby place as their location. People not in the Pittsburgh area had no other way to support the implicit claim to expertise they made by posting on the site. Nor did this medium afford users any way to contest the expertise that others implicitly claimed.

Professional Linguists, II: The Pittsburgh Speech and Society Project, 2000-2001

The first newspaper article about my research on Pittsburgh speech was published in February 2001. In what follows, I describe how the article came about, what it contained, and how people reacted to it over the following month. The struggle over expertise about Pittsburgh speech and Pittsburghese has not gone away, as we will see, and it manifested in some of the same ways in 2001 as it had decades earlier. In the meantime, however, the social meaning of Pittsburghese had changed, such that speaking Pittsburghese no longer necessarily identified a person as working class or uneducated. Performances of Pittsburghese by people who did not themselves speak with Pittsburgh accents had become common, and such performances were now sometimes seen as displays of affection for and solidarity with Pittsburghers.

The article was sparked by a press release from my university about the class project on monophthongal /aw/ that I described earlier. In the eyes of the public relations officer assigned to the College of Humanities and Social Sciences, the fact that Bhasin, Wittkowski, and I had presented our findings at a conference made it sufficiently newsworthy for such an announcement. In early February 2001, I was interviewed by staff writer Marylynne Pitz from the *Pittsburgh Post-Gazette*. Pitz normally reported on lifestyle and human-interest stories; she was not one of the paper's science writers. She was not from Pittsburgh and, although she knew some of the words that people thought of as local, she had never heard, or at least never noticed, many people with Pittsburgh accents. I was aware during the interview that she was having trouble understanding some of what I was saying about the phonetic variable we had studied, although she had a clear sense in general of the link between Pittsburghese and local identity and a positive attitude about it.

The article appeared on Sunday, February 11, 2001, on the front page of Section C, "The Region" in print, and as the lead story under "Local News" on the *Post-Gazette*'s website. The article is headlined "Patter, patois, or pidgin, it's the talk of the town" (Pitz 2001). The first paragraph is written in Pittsburghese:

> If yinz think Pittsburghese is disappearing, yinz better think again 'n' 'at: Plenny a people in Allegheny Cahny still go aht the hahs t'buy sahrkraht for New Year's dinner or see a tagger at the Picksburgh zoo.[8]

A sidebar, starting directly under a photograph of me, is headlined "Nahns 'n' 'at" and begins "The Web site www.pittsburghese.com needs read if you really want to speak like a native." The sidebar continues with a list of items taken from the pittsburghese.com website described earlier in this chapter. None of the items represent monophthongal /aw/, which was the topic of our research. Scattered throughout the main article are words spelled in such a way to suggest that they are Pittsburghese: "Ahia ['Ohio'] River," "a big dill ['deal']." A quote from the interview claiming that intrusive /r/ (in "warsh" or "Warshington") is common throughout the US midland is followed by "Nuh-uh! Git aht!," an expression of doubtful amazement something like 'No way!' In short, the article intermingles my voice and the voices of Bhasin and Wittkofski (who were also interviewed) with a voice that speaks in Pittsburghese. This voice can be heard as framing, elaborating on, and commenting on what we are represented as saying. For many readers, though, the Pittsburghese voice was interpreted as having emanated from us.

My initial worry was about the inaccuracies in the report. Pitz opened with the claim that "The city's distinctive dialect remains especially popular among working-class guys under the age of 30," when what our research had suggested was simply that one feature of the dialect had not declined among young working-class men as compared to men of their fathers' generation. The use of "popular" seemed particularly troubling. Pitz also referred to the monophthongal /aw/ in words like "dahntahn" [da:nta:n] as "the shortened vowel sound" (when in fact the vowel nucleus is *lengthened* when the glide is reduced), conflated the monophthongization of /aw/ with the monophthongization of /ay/, and suggested that language change was the result of television watching. But readers were not focused on this level of detail, it turned out.

Many of the letters, phone calls, and e-mails I started receiving on the day the article ran did the same sorts of things Parslow's correspondents had done almost thirty years earlier: asked for more information, offered assistance, suggested etymologies for words and reasons for sound changes, pointed out that some of the words the article claimed were local could be heard elsewhere. For the most part, these comments reacted not to the research that the article reported on but to the Pittsburghese in it and, especially, to the sidebar taken from the Pittsburghese.com site. Writers took it for granted that these, too, represented my work. Rosemary P. told me in a phone message that she "may have some information that would be helpful," information that "you happen to know, if you grew up in Pittsburgh." Jared K. e-mailed to asked how "Carnegie" should be pronounced, and Elaine K. wrote with a series of stories about misunderstandings between Pittsburghers and Californians. Chris C. pointed out by e-mail that people on Prince Edward Island, Canada, use "slippy." Karyn C. asked whether I knew where Pittsburghese was most prevalent, noting with a mix of hedging ("unscientific") and certainty ("always," "is") that "it has always been [her] unscientific finding that the accent is most prevalent in the Steel Valley— Homestead, Duquesne, McKeesport, etc." Paul P. wrote a letter suggesting that "gumband" might be the result of Slovak influence, as he had recently learned in a community college class that the Slovak word for rubber is "guma." A history professor from a nearby campus of Penn State University was more confident about his expertise: "While I certainly agree as to the Scots-Irish origin of much that is today labeled 'Pittsburghese', I'm not so sure about the flattened vowels . . . being attributable to the great influx of Eastern European immigrants." His evidence, he said, was that he had heard these sounds in rural areas where there were no immigrants. In an even more confident letter to the editor of the *Post-Gazette* published the following Sunday, February 18, 2001, Dwight

L. Sontum wrote, "I must clarify something I saw in the article on Pittsburghese. The word referred to therein as 'yinz' is actually the rather cleverly devised local word 'youns,' which I believe is a combination of 'you' and the German 'uns.'"

The issue of technical expertise—who knows the facts about Pittsburgh speech, and how to talk about these facts—continued to arise in reaction to the article. A colleague in the history department sent a PhD student of his to talk to me. Peter Gilmore, a historian of local religion, was also an amateur dialectologist who had put together a book called *"Scots-Irish" Words from Pennsylvania's Mountains*. In conversations with Gilmore, I came to see that his highly politicized way of approaching the history of local speech could complicate my less self-consciously political approach: "The problem isn't with the facts so much," I wrote in field notes at the time, "but about what to call the varieties and influences in question." The trouble with *Scots-Irish*, for Gilmore, was that the term conceals the degree of Celtic, Gaelic-language influence in the settlers' speech, which was in any case descended from "Scots" (a sister language of English spoken in Scotland), not "English," as he thought I had been claiming. My field notes reflect my growing sense that expertise would be a continuing issue if I pursued this project further: "For the first time, I'm really having to deal with the differences between different kinds of expertise and how to negotiate among them. Not just popular and scholarly expertise, but also Peter [Gilmore]'s kind of expertise and other sort of intermediate kinds, like that of people who would go to the History Center, consult their website, or read their magazine."

There was another strand to the 2001 correspondence, however, that was not evident during the 1970s: people talked about using Pittsburghese "for fun" and being proud of having it as a linguistic resource. For example, Vanessa N., a recent graduate of Carnegie Mellon who was living in the Washington, DC suburbs, talked about using "some good Yinzer dialect" with her manager at work, a fellow Pittsburgher. "Perhaps when we speak this way for fun," she notes, "it brings some comfort." Her e-mail ends, "Good luck n'at." Readers of the *Post-Gazette* article noticed the stylized, performed Pittsburghese in it (performances that they often took to be mine) as much as the actual report and responded with performances of their own.

On Monday, February 12, the day after the *Post-Gazette* article appeared, an editorial in the *Pitt News* (the University of Pittsburgh's student newspaper) was headlined "Yinz should respect and learn Pittsburghese n'at." The editorial is full of self-conscious written Pittsburghese. (Glosses are in double brackets to distinguish them from other editorial material.) "Something needs clarified for those not born in da Ahrn City" [['something needs to be clarified for those not born in the Iron City']], it starts. "Pittsburghese is a distinct dialect, a unique way of speaking, as refreshing as a nice cold glass of melk [['milk']], and as real and substantial as a jumbo sammich [['bologna sandwich']]." The editorialist continues to play with Pittsburghese, working in as many of the items found on

Pittsburghese.com and other lists of local forms as possible and imagining a course in the language that I could teach with guest speakers like Myron Cope, in which "True Picksburgh-bred [['Pittsburgh-bred']] students could serve as teaching assistants" and "da professors and da TAs [would] need respected. No shooting gumbands [['rubber bands']] n'at." Performing Pittsburghese is, as we have seen before, one way of enacting one's right to evaluate it, and the editorialist does this explicitly:

> [Johnstone's research] needs publicized because it affirms something we Picksburghers have always known, though the rest of yinz may not have realized. It may not be as famous as the Boston twang or Southern drawl, but the Pittsburghese [*sic*] *is* special, and it's about time someone validated it with a serious scientific study. Our language is inseparable from our heritage, just like da jaggers on a jaggerbush are all tangled up n'at [['just like the briars on a briar-bush are all tangled up and so on']]. Instead of trying to worsh [['wash']] out Pittsburghese from the archives of our culture, we should document it and celebrate it.

The editorial is clearly a response to a very local exigency: The University of Pittsburgh attracts students from larger, more sophisticated cities farther east who look down on their Pittsburgh-area classmates, at least in the opinion of the local students. That Pittsburghese is a real dialect shouldn't be too shocking, the editorialist writes, "even if you are a snobby East Coast type who wants everyone to speak all perfect n'at." Only "true Picksburgh-bred students" would be qualified to assist in the new course. But the editorial also reflects, circulates, and reinforces the enregisterment of Pittsburghese as a performable index of identity in the context of the more widely circulating ideas about language, identity, and place that were the topic of earlier chapters. That this was a response by a younger Pittsburgher is not surprising, given that for many such people Pittsburghese is now linked not only to class or correctness but also to Pittsburgh and Pittsburghers' identity.

A newspaper opinion piece by an older writer provides an interesting contrast. In a February 14 column in the *Post Gazette* headlined "Pittsburghers Skip a Syllable or Two," middle-aged columnist Gene Collier takes an ambiguous stance toward Pittsburghese. Collier first narrates a purported misunderstanding from when he was new to Pittsburgh about the meaning of what he heard as "Katy Kay" (radio and TV station KDKA) and a joke about "distillers" ('the Steelers'). He was prompted, he then says, by

> Sunday's excellent piece by Marylynne Pitz in this newspaper, written in loving Pittsburghese and detailing the work of Carnegie Mellon University rhetoric professor Barbara Johnstone and her doctoral students,

who've determined that Pittsburghese, rather than being mercifully homogenized into the standard language, might actually be thriving. Well, git aht.

Following this, Collier lists entries from a "Pittsburghese glossary" he says he has been compiling for several years, "without any academic credentials and without any real purpose." These are almost all eye dialect, phrases respelled in ways that reflect their pronunciation in informal conversational American English speech: "merncy vickle" ('emergency vehicle'), "dineen" ('didn't even'), "gim" ('give him').

Collier intertwines a straightforward evaluation of the article ("excellent") with a more indirect evaluation of what he takes to be the research results (Pittsburghese is not being "mercifully" homogenized into the standard) and a somewhat snide evaluation of the research itself. ("Well, git aht!" suggests that the findings are unsurprising, and "without any academic credentials" suggests that anyone can come up with a useful description of the variety.) On a local cable talk show the next evening, Collier said he was surprised that responses to the column were mostly favorable, which suggests that he was aware of the risk that his list might seem offensive. Yet he describes Pitz's written performance of Pittsburghese in the article as "loving."

To summarize, academic expertise continued to be contested in the 2000s in the same ways it was contested in the 1970s, by readers who were in many cases equally confident that their knowledge would enhance or trump ours, and that academics were engaged in the same endeavor as they were. However, performances of Pittsburghese played a far larger role in the 2000s than they had three decades earlier. As I noted earlier, newspaper articles from the 1970s sometimes included bits of written Pittsburghese in titles and cartoon illustrations. The 2001 article, by contrast, was actually written partly in Pittsburghese, and it was juxtaposed with a list of Pittsburghese items contributed by readers of a website who made minimal claims to expertise and did not have to make any. This development reflects the history of Pittsburghese that I described in earlier chapters. Extended performances of Pittsburghese like the one in the Pitz article could be seen as "loving" in 2001, because semiotic change had re-enregistered Pittsburghese with place, particularly for younger Pittsburghers, and loosened its ties with class.

This development served to complicate negotiations over expertise. While lay people and professional linguists alike would agree that the making and evaluation of knowledge claims about language variety is something that linguistics professors do, making and evaluating performances of Pittsburghese is not. To engage in a performance of Pittsburghese, or even to evaluate one, would be to make a claim to local identity, undermining the professional distance and emotional neutrality by which laypeople and our peers alike judge us as technical experts (Prelli 1997).

But by embedding performances and folk glossaries in representations of linguists' work, reporters can put such performances and lists in linguists' mouths, since many readers cannot distinguish the voices from one another.

A Wikipedia Entry, 2006—Present

The diffusion of the right to create knowledge that we see in the progression from the newspaper articles to the website is often celebrated. However, as Ronkin and Karn (1999), Hill (1995), and others have shown, popular discourse about vernacular speech often enacts racism, classism, and other forms of discrimination, particularly when such discourse takes place among outsiders. This is as true for Pittsburgh speech as it is for any other nonstandard way of speaking. Outsiders are sometimes sensitive to this. Columnist Gene Collier was, as we saw, aware of the possibility that people might object to his glossary, with its implicit claim that Pittsburghers are sloppy speakers. But social prejudice can hide behind "just for fun" talk about linguistic difference in more insidious ways, too. On one of the radio talk shows I was asked to participate in during the month after the *Post-Gazette* article appeared, host Lynn Cullen began with the class-laced story I discussed in chapter 5 about the snow storm, the gas station, and the incomprehensible Pittsburgher with the unlikely name "Peewee." She then claimed that Pittsburgh speech sounded "ignorant" and seemed to expect me, and later the people who called in, to agree. (No one took her invitation, although one caller talked about the effort she had made to lose her Pittsburgh accent.) Cullen's combative style is part of her radio persona as a sophisticated liberal speaking out against Pittsburgh's provincial, conservative culture. She seemed not to realize that the position she was taking vis-à-vis Pittsburghese could be heard as classist, intolerant, and inconsistent with her social and political persona.

Many Pittsburghers are deeply offended by representations of the dialect that suggest they all speak alike, in a stupid-sounding way, and my initial foray into the study of the dialect was the result of a wish to correct some of this widely available misinformation. I turn, then, to an effort by academics to reclaim expertise about Pittsburgh speech. In 2006, Dan Baumgardt and I developed and posted a Wikipedia entry on Pittsburgh English (Baumgardt and Johnstone, 2006). We chose this medium (in addition to a mounting a website) because we knew the people we wanted to reach—students and other young adults—would likely use it before turning to more traditional sources of information. We expected it to be extremely difficult to claim and maintain expertise in a forum that is interactive in new ways and in which expertise is potentially distributed even more widely than in the media discussed in this chapter. It turned out to be relatively easy, for reasons I will touch on below.

A wiki (derived from the Hawaiian word for 'fast') is software that allows people to create and edit web pages quickly and easily; it is typically used for collaborative projects (Pentzold 2007, 2). Wikis consist of a main page, a page on which drafts and edits can be made and transferred to the main page, and often a revision history function that allows users to see every version of the document and compare different versions. Wikipedia entries also have a discussion page where users can comment on the topic or on each other's editing or editorial standards.

Anyone with Internet access can edit a Wikipedia entry and/or contribute to the discussion. This initially created the expectation that expertise, if not irrelevant altogether, would have different sources in this medium than in a print encyclopedia, where topic authors are selected based largely on academic expertise (Bryant, Forte, and Bruckman 2005). It has turned out, however, that the volunteer editors who patrol Wikipedia in fact rely on the citation of scholarly sources as a major criterion for evaluating entries. With three months of time and effort, Baumgardt and I were able to replace the existing article on Pittsburgh English with an entirely different one in which every claim is attributed to a reputable, printed scholarly source, and every study of the Pittsburgh speech that we knew of is cited.

That article has since been edited, but the editing has only made it more technical and limited participation rights in the editing process to people familiar with the relevant scholarly literature. For example, the list of Pittsburgh words on the site has been edited repeatedly to remove entries that were sourced solely to personal experience. In early 2006 (before our revision was posted), there was a discussion of this issue on the discussion page of the Pittsburgh English entry during which one of the entry's regular editors made it clear that local knowledge was not a valid source of expertise ("Personal experience isn't good enough"). Weatherman1126 asked:

> What references are needed for the dialect terms? Most of it is probally [sic] from "experience"/tradition by living in Pittsburgh. (Weatherman1126 15:23, 28 January 2006 [UTC])

Editor angr replied, the same day:

> All information on Wikipedia needs to be verifiable and backed up with published sources. Personal experience isn't good enough. Some dictionaries, such as the American Heritage Dictionary, indicate that word is used only in a specific region, so if you can find a citation from one of those that the word in question is unique to Pittsburgh, then that's citing a source. Published dialect surveys and atlases will also often show what words are used where, so that's another place to look for verification. (Angr 16:14, 28 January 2006 [UTC])

Later, another regular editor threatened to delete all uncited entries in the glossary:

> The vast majority of these terms are not cited. These citations need to be added within the next week or I will be deleting them [the terms]. There is a references section, but that's not the same thing as citing; individual terms need to be sourcable. (Chris Griswold 17:06, 11 July 2006 [UTC])

In sum, despite being in material ways the medium with the most potential for interaction between people with different sources of linguistic expertise, Wikipedia, as it is actually used, is the most insistent that the sole source of legitimate expertise is not only technical but in print. Ironically, the voice of ordinary Pittsburghers—unless they are linguists or can cite the literature of sociolinguistics and dialectology—is even less present than it was in the least interactive of media, the pre-internet print newspaper report.

"Interactivity" and Language Expertise

In research about computer-mediated communication and new media studies, the term *interactive* is often used to describe systems of communication in which the receiver of a message is not just a passive consumer. Exactly what this can entail has proven to be very difficult to pin down. As it is often used, the term *interactive* is shot through with ideological connotations: whatever it actually is, interactivity is a good thing. As Jensen (1999, 161) puts it, "It seems relatively unclear just what 'interactivity' and 'interactive media' mean. The positivity surrounding the concepts and the frequency of their use seem, in a way, to be reversely proportional to their precision and actual content of meaning." A number of scholars have offered typologies of the kinds of interactivity made possible by various communications media and realized in the ways they are used (Jensen 1999; Downes and McMillan 2000; McMillan 2002; Herring 2007; for an overview, see Lister et al. 2009, 21–25). Interactivity can refer to the possibility for users to make changes to the software they use, to edit the texts they read, to converse with other users, or some combination of these, and there can be varying degrees of reciprocity in user-to-user interactivity. Interaction can be synchronous (occurring in real time) or asynchronous, one-way or two-way, anonymous or not; some media allow for the transcript of the interaction to be archived and some do not. And so on.

Three of the four communications media I have discussed allowed for two-way communication between the original message sender and receivers of the message (*How to Speak Like a Pittsburgher* originally did not, although there are now ways of talking about the book online, and McCool has received many letters and e-mails about the book). All were asynchronous, meaning that people were not talking to each other in real time but rather at a temporal distance. All allowed message responders to be anonymous or pseudonymous. Beyond that, the four media differ in ways I have described. The 1990s website forced users to respond using a tightly controlled format; letters to the editor are somewhat constrained in length, but less so in format. In a wiki, users can add to and/or change the original text and talk to one another on a separate page. In consequence, the four media allow for expertise of different sorts to be represented, and some media allow expertise to be contested while others do not. This results, ultimately, in different voices being heard as those of language experts.

In other words, language expertise is distributed, contested, and negotiated differently in different communications media, depending on the material constraints and affordances of the medium and users' ideologically shaped expectations about how, and by whom, it is used. In print newspapers, where reporters have the right to decide what sources of expertise to represent, claims about Pittsburgh speech are attributed first to newcomers, whose authority arises from personal experience, then increasingly to people with various kinds of institutionally sanctioned technical authority, including linguists, although people on the street are also sometimes quoted. On the 1990s website, anyone could act as an expert. The medium afforded no way to indicate the source of one's expertise and no way to contest the expertise of others or the particular claims about Pittsburgh speech that they made. On Wikipedia, expertise is most explicitly contested and most restrictively defined: the only thing that counts is technical expertise, as represented by citations to published scholarly work.

The uses of technology, like the technology itself, are shaped by human meaning systems (Chandler 2000). The technical affordances of a communication medium do not determine what people do with it. Wikipedia provides a clear example of this. In an analysis of linguistic features of Wikipedia and a similar collaborative authoring environment called Everything2, William Emigh and Susan Herring discovered that "the greater the degree of post-production editorial control afforded by the system, the more formal and standardized the language of the collaboratively-authored documents becomes" (Emigh and Herring 2005, 1) "Paradoxically," Emigh and Herring note, "users who faithfully appropriate such systems create homogeneous entries, at odds with the goal of open-access authoring environments to create diverse content" (1).

By the same token, however, there are material constraints on the possibilities for dialect enregisterment. In studies of the discursive construction of standard varieties, this issue often does not arise, since it is assumed that the institutions that control this process, and the ideologies they represent, can make themselves heard. But when language making happens in more grassroots ways, where noninstitutional sources of expertise are in play, as in the case of Pittsburghese, it is apparent that lay and institutional voices compete over access to the conversational floor, and the resulting discourse reflects the tension.

7

Selling Pittsburghese

Another response to the 2001 *Pittsburgh Post-Gazette* article I discussed in chapter 6 came by e-mail from someone called Mike Ellis. Ellis was the webmaster of a site called Slanguage.[1] In the message, Ellis defined slanguage as "regionalisms, slang, dialects, idiolects, and really anything spoken somewhere that also is hopefully funny." Ellis objected to what he took to be our research findings, explicitly basing his objection on a claim to expertise based on the popularity of his website:

> As publisher of one of the internet's most popular websites, www
> .slanguage.com, I must take issue with you and your students [*sic*]
> conclusions regarding Pittsburgh's slang, dialects, etc.
>
> I collect slanguage from people all over the world. Over 12 million
> unique visitors to my site have taught me what the truly local slanguage
> is out there.

Ellis said that the words he thought we had claimed as characteristic only of Pittsburgh were not and listed "the words compiled by you and your students that are not unique to Pixberg." What followed was, oddly, not the list from pittsburghese.com that had appeared with the article, but instead the list that had appeared in Gene Collier's February 14 column in response to the article. Ellis had apparently cut and pasted Collier's list into his e-mail. Ellis signed his e-mail "Mike Ellis, Emperor of Slanguage dot com."

What did the "emperor of slanguage" have to offer? Visitors to slanguage.com in the early 2000s saw the same sort of list of words and definitions that visitors to pittsburghese.com saw, except that the slanguage site also included lists of words purportedly associated with other cities, too. Both sites had been mounted by people who thought they could use playful lists of words that people thought of as regionalisms to sell things. In the case of Alan Freed of pittsburghese.com, it was web design and other advertising services. In the case of slanguage.com, the commercial purpose was less clear, and the site could have seemed as if it had really been mounted just for fun. A visit to the site eleven years later, however, shows that Ellis's purpose was to sell books that he writes and amass e-mail addresses to sell to other advertisers. In 2012, the site carried more book advertisements than actual lists of slanguage, and readers were repeatedly urged to e-mail Ellis with suggested slanguage items (thereby divulging their e-mail addresses to him). Ellis's objection to the *Post-Gazette* article, and to the expertise he thought was being claimed in it, probably had less to do with who had the right to make claims about Pittsburghese than with who had the right to use Pittsburghese for commercial purposes. Pittsburghese added value to his website. For Ellis, as for Freed, Pittsburghese functioned as a commodity.

If Mike Ellis thought that he could establish an exclusive claim to the commercial use of Pittsburghese, he was wrong. Pittsburghese has been for sale since long before 1995, when Ellis mounted his site. Pittsburghese can add economic value not just to websites but also to coffee mugs, T-shirts, shot glasses, beer steins, refrigerator magnets, postcards, talking dolls, key chains, bumper stickers, dog clothing, shirts, and hats. Strikingly, people sometimes base claims about the nature of Pittsburghese on such items. Asked for examples of local peculiarities of speech, one of my interviewees produced a coffee mug decorated with Pittsburghese words. Another interviewee opened a plastic bag he had brought along and dramatically produced a white T-shirt with letters and images in black and gold. The front of the shirt depicted the city's skyline with words like *pop*; *redd up*, *keller*, *hans*, and *sammich* superimposed on it. On the back was a dictionary-like list of words and phrases with definitions and sample sentences. "This," he told us, holding up the shirt, "is Pittsburghese." In an interview we looked at in a previous chapter, I asked Jen R., a speaker of the local dialect, if she had ever heard of Pittsburghese was, and she responded:

> Oh yes. I mean, there's that store over on the South Side, in Station Square that has the Pittsburghese shirts. In fact, I remember when my friend Kathy moved out of state, with—her husband's job took them out of state and to many other states, I remember sending her a couple Pittsburghese shirts for them.

Asked whether she was familiar with the dialect, Jen talked about the T-shirt: "Oh yes, I mean there's that store . . . that has the Pittsburghese shirts."

This chapter has to do with people buying Pittsburghese in the form of T-shirts with Pittsburghese on them, and dolls that speak Pittsburghese. I explore how artifacts like these are produced and consumed and how the buying and selling of Pittsburghese shapes the ways people imagine the dialect. I start with T-shirts bearing words and phrases thought to be unique to Pittsburgh. What people are buying when they buy a Pittsburghese shirt is not only an item of clothing but also the words and images on it. I suggest that Pittsburghese shirts contribute to dialect enregisterment in at least four ways:

they put local speech on display, they imbue local speech with value, they standardize local speech, and they link local speech with particular social meanings.

I then turn to the Yappin' Yinzers, plush dolls named Chipped Ham Sam and Nebby Debbie. When people press the dolls' stomachs, the dolls utter short phrases in Pittsburghese. I explore how the dolls' appearance and their speech work together to shape the persona of the Yinzer. The Yinzer persona embodies (literally, in the bodies of the dolls) a set of ideas about how locality, class, and communicative style are related. At the same time, the persona of the Yinzer connects and reconnects these ideas every time it is evoked. Like Pittsburghese shirts, the Yappin' Yinzers are a standardizing force: They represent a limited number of linguistic forms in the immediate visual context of a limited number of possible meanings.

Pittsburghese Shirts

Pittsburghese shirts, for sale at sidewalk markets, in souvenir shops, and online, often look like the one we were shown by the man described earlier. Figure 7.1 shows the front and back of that shirt.

The shirts are almost always white, black, or a yellow-orange color thought of locally as gold, with printing in white, black, and/or gold. The front typically depicts the cityscape and includes the word "Pittsburghese" (sometimes "Pixburghese")

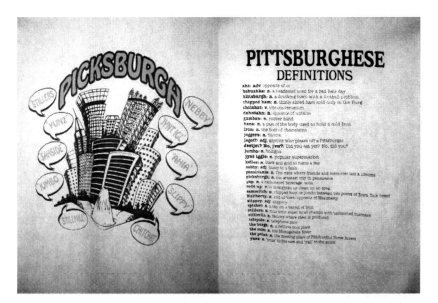

Figure 7.1 Front and Back of a Pittsburghese T-shirt. (Photograph by Barbara Johnstone)

together with a scattering of respelled words meant to represent local pronunciation (*dahntahn* 'downtown', *worsh* 'wash', *jynt iggle* 'Giant Eagle' supermarkets), vocabulary (*gumband* 'rubber band', *redd up* 'tidy up', *slippy* or *slippey* 'slippery'), and sometimes syntax (*needs washed* 'needs to be washed'). On the back there is typically a dictionary-like alphabetical list. Newer designs are often simpler, involving a single black word or phrase on the front of a white shirt: *YNZ*; I'm *surrounded by jagoffs!*

People will pay a lot more for a T-shirt with Pittsburghese on it than they will for a plain one. Online advice for would-be T-shirt printers (How to start a silk screen T-shirt business, n.d.) suggests that a shirt that wholesales for two dollars per shirt can be marked up to four dollars if printed in just one color. People who buy shirts in bulk from a printer can then mark up the price to eight or ten dollars each. (Additional colors would cost more and shirts with more colors would have to be sold for more.) What has happened, locally and in popular culture at large, to enable Pittsburgh speech to add value to a shirt in this way? Under what circumstances can a way of speaking become a commodity available for sale and purchase?

A linguistic variety (a language, a dialect, a way of speaking) is commodified when it is for sale and people will pay to buy it. This can happen in a number of ways. For example, Kira Hall (1995) explores the commodification of intimate-sounding talk by telephone sex workers, who are paid to speak in this style and whose talk is sold to customers who call. Deborah Cameron (2000) discusses the commodification not only of speech styles but also of particular scripted utterances in new-economy jobs like telephone marketing, consumer service, and opinion polling. In jobs like these, highly standardized speech has economic value, and people are paid to produce it. Rudolf Gaudio (2003) explores how conversation is commodified by a well-known coffeehouse chain that sells not only coffee drinks but also an environment in which people can converse as they consume them. Mary Bucholtz shows how linguistic styles can involve ways of talking associated with material goods (Bucholtz 2008). English has become a valuable commodity worldwide, and other languages more locally (Tan and Rubdy 2008). Monica Heller (2003) shows how French-English bilingualism, once associated with Francophone Canadian identity but stigmatized on the economic market, has come to be a valuable commodity in the call-center sector, as call centers locate where bilinguals can be hired.

A useful heuristic for exploring the conditions and processes that have led to the viability of Pittsburghese shirts is anthropologist Arjun Appadurai's (1986) description of the "commodity situation." According to Appadurai, the "commodity situation in the social life of any 'thing' [is] the situation in which its exchangeability . . . for some other thing is its socially relevant feature" (1986, 13). In order to enter into a commodity situation, a "thing" (in our case, the imagined dialect people call Pittsburghese) must historically be in a "commodity phase," it must be a potential "commodity candidate," and it must be in a viable "commodity context" (13–15). In other words, to understand how and why Pittsburghese has become a commodity bought and sold in the form of T-shirts, we need to answer these questions:

1. Commodity phase: When and how did local speech in Pittsburgh acquire the potential for commodification? What set of ideas about local speech had to be in place before people could begin to think of it as having economic value? Answering this question requires taking a historical perspective on the indexical meanings of Pittsburgh linguistic forms.

2. Commodity candidacy: What makes something like local speech a potential commodity? What is the larger cultural framework in which it makes sense to people to buy and sell Pittsburghese? Answering this question requires thinking about more widely circulating ideas about place, identity, and authenticity that shape how vernacular practices like regional speech are evaluated.

3. Commodity context: In what ideological and material contexts can local speech be a viable commodity? Answering this question requires taking a close look at the economics of T-shirt sales and the ideas about T-shirts as a medium of communication that encourages people to produce and purchase Pittsburghese shirts.

COMMODITY PHASE: LOCAL SPEECH FORMS BECOME LINKED WITH THE IDENTITY OF PITTSBURGH

Historically, Pittsburgh speech became a commodity only once it came to index place, not just social class or lack of education. Earlier chapters have told this story in detail. To summarize, most Pittsburghers did not notice Pittsburghese at all until the middle of the twentieth century. At this stage, a T-shirt with Pittsburghese written on it would have been uninterpretable. Once people began to notice some of the sounds, words, and phrases that distinguished the speech of some Pittsburghers from the speech of others, Pittsburgh speech became semiotically linked with social class and education, and people who wanted to sound well-educated and cosmopolitan tried to avoid sounding like Pittsburghers. At that point, and in situations like this, Pittsburghese had negative value and standard-sounding English became a commodity people would buy. People would (and do) pay speech therapists to help them lose their accents. Such people might buy Pittsburghese shirts, if they were available, but they might also feel that displays of Pittsburghese called attention to the words and accents they wanted to lose. Only when it became possible to imagine Pittsburghese as a badge of local identity—when it became possible to claim that Pittsburghese was "the way Pittsburghers talk" or "our way of speaking"—did Pittsburghese acquire the status that made it add value to things like T-shirts.

COMMODITY CANDIDACY: PITTSBURGHESE IS SEEN AS "AUTHENTIC"

One of the many intersecting sets of ideas that make local-sounding speech a potential commodity is the ideology about language, place, and tradition that underlies what Regina Bendix (1988) calls "folklorism." Folklorism is the idea that old, vernacular practices and artifacts are the most authentic. This idea originates in nineteenth-century Romanticism and continues to circulate today. According to the ideology of folklorism, "authentic" folkways are untainted, desirable in a way that newer practices are not, even if newer ways are more practical. Ideas like these lead people to want to preserve old things and old ways of doing things even if—or even to show that—they do not do things that way themselves. In Pittsburgh, as we have seen, being able to cite old words or older forms of local words (*you'uns* rather than *yinz*, for example) can be a useful way of claiming expertise about local speech.

According to the ideology of folklorism, cultural authenticity is also linked with connectedness to place. This is because older social practices last longer in isolated places, where it is less likely that new practices will be imported. People and practices that have never moved, or that have generations of rootedness in a particular geographic area are, according to this set of ideas, better and more authentic than others. When this ideological scheme is in play, Appalachian folk songs collected in remote valleys trump contemporary or even classical forms, Texas roper boots and broad-brimmed hats trump contemporary clothing, and the "Downeaster" accent of traditional Maine or the "Carolina Brogue" of the once-isolated Atlantic-coast islands trump more regional or national varieties.

In Pittsburgh, the display of local speech is sometimes part and parcel of the display of other elements of local cultural heritage, like steelworkers' hard hats, plaques and signs commemorating local people and historical moments, buildings where memorable events occurred, and so on. For example, the Senator John Heinz History Center (Pittsburgh's largest historical museum) has, at times, had a small informational poster about Pittsburgh speech on display. In 2001, the History Center mounted an exhibit on the theme of "Pittsburgh A to Z" meant to accompany the release of a documentary film with the same name by WQED, one of Pittsburgh's public television stations (Sebak 2001). By agreement between the museum and the TV station, the exhibit and the film were both to represent each letter of the alphabet with one word. The two exhibits were curated separately, with no attempt to agree on their choices. However, both the History Center and the filmmaker chose the pronoun *yinz* to fill the slot for Y. This was the only letter on which the film and the museum exhibit overlapped.

Knowing what local linguistic forms mean is sometimes explicitly linked with Pittsburgh authenticity, as in the T-shirt in figure 7.2.

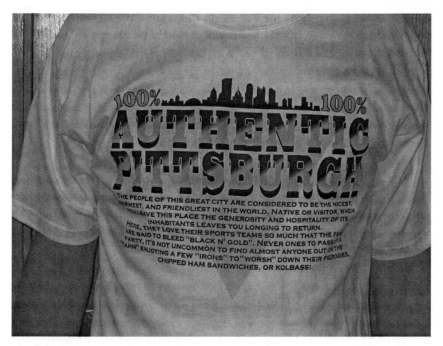

Figure 7.2 "100% authentic Pittsburgh" T-shirt. (Photograph by Barbara Johnstone)

The final sentence of the text on the shirt reads, "It's not uncommon to find almost anyone out on the 'tahn' enjoying a few 'irons' to 'worsh' down their pierogies, chipped ham sandwiches, or kolbassi." Although at first glance the text on this shirt looks as if it is explaining to readers what an authentic Pittsburgher does, in fact, you can only understand the references in this sentences if you already know what "tahn" and "worsh" mean and what an "iron" is (Johnstone forthcoming).

COMMODITY CONTEXT: T-SHIRTS ARE CHEAP AND PEOPLE KNOW WHAT TO DO WITH THEM

When the right historical and ideological factors are in place, economic and technological factors must also line up in such a way to make Pittsburghese shirts viable as a commodity. First, it must make sense in the context of local resources and practices to sell and buy T-shirts with words and images printed on them. People who see Pittsburghese shirts for sale must know how to consume them. That is, they must know how to interpret them, and they must know who might wear them and in what contexts. In Pittsburgh as elsewhere in the United States, T-shirts are often purchased and worn because of their "badging" function (Kelly 2003; Symes 1987). T-shirts identify their wearers with the people or social practices that are evoked by the images on the shirts. People actually wearing the shirts are not much in evidence in Pittsburgh, perhaps because there is relatively little need for a person in Pittsburgh to "badge" the fact that he or she is a Pittsburgher. Ex-Pittsburghers living elsewhere and tourists who have visited the city have a greater use for the identity badging afforded by the shirts. People who live in Pittsburgh buy the shirts, but, like Jen R., they often send them as gifts to people who no longer live in the city. The fact that there are a great many such people, due to the massive out-migration from Pittsburgh that started in the 1980s, means that there is a continuing market for the shirts.

Second, elements of the shirts' design must be available. The designers of Pittsburghese shirts draw heavily for the shirts' content on Internet lists of Pittsburghese words like the ones on www.pittsburghese.com. The shirt in figure 7.3 borrows a well-known phrase, "I'm surrounded by idiots" and reworks it with a local word, *jagoff*.

Ideas for the shirts' visual design are also borrowed and reused. Black and gold are the colors of the city's sports teams and the city shield and flag; they are almost compulsory for any item alluding to local identity. Images of the downtown cityscape have been featured on Pittsburghese shirts since they were first produced. Other elements of visual design are also borrowed. As Miller (2002) points out in a study of T-shirts produced by fans of the rock band Phish, there is a tradition in and outside the United States of playful T-shirts featuring

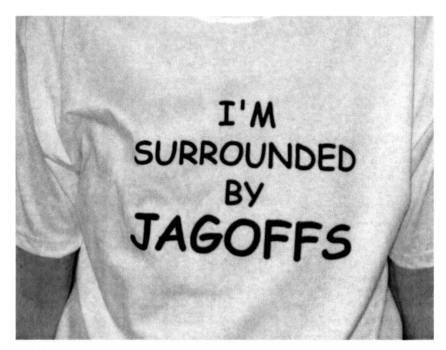

Figure 7.3 "I'm surrounded by jagoffs" T-shirt. (Photograph by Barbara Johnstone)

images borrowed from elsewhere and humorously reshaped. During the 1990s, for example, automobile bumper-stickers that identify vacation spots in a design borrowed from European country-identification stickers became common in the Pittsburgh area and elsewhere in the United States. OBX, black text on a white background and enclosed in a black-bordered oval, means the Outer Banks, and HHI means Hilton Head Island, both popular beach destinations for Pittsburghers. The T-shirt in figure 7.4 borrows this design and reworks it with a designation based not on a place-name abbreviation but on the Pittsburghese word *yinz*.

Third, producing and selling Pittsburghese shirts must be economically feasible so the shirts seem affordable. The availability of wholesale T-shirts at low cost, together with inexpensive reproduction technology that is locally accessible, makes the shirts relatively disposable, so people are willing to purchase them without much forethought. Dealers' overhead costs are low, since the shirts can be produced nearby and are often sold from folding tables and open-air booths on the street. In sum, it makes economic sense both to sell Pittsburghese shirts and to buy them.

PITTSBURGHESE SHIRTS AND THE ENREGISTERMENT OF PITTSBURGH SPEECH

Pittsburgh shirts both require and contribute to the enregisterment of local speech forms as a dialect. Enregisterment is a precondition for Pittsburghese shirts for two reasons. First, the shirts appeal to people who are able to hear

Figure 7.4 "YNZ Pittsburgh" T-shirt (Photograph by Barbara Johnstone)

Pittsburgh speech as different from other varieties and who link Pittsburgh speech not with working-class or incorrect speech as much as with authentic local identity. Second, they require already-available lists of linguistic forms identified with Pittsburghese, and they require purchasers to be familiar with the practice of respelling words to make them sound local. As I have argued earlier, these conditions are met only when a set of local forms has been enregistered, and in particular only when their indexicality has moved beyond pointing only to class and education.

But the enregisterment of Pittsburgh speech with Pittsburgh the place is also an outcome of the production, distribution, and consumption of Pittsburghese shirts. For one thing, Pittsburghese shirts put local speech on display on sidewalk tables, in shops, and on bodies. Second, Pittsburghese shirts link local speech with social and economic value. T-shirts were once men's underclothes, and many people who buy or wear them think they are appropriate only for casual-dress situations. Pittsburghese shirts are also relatively inexpensive. This both mirrors and suggests the idea that Pittsburgh speech has limited value but may be appropriate in some contexts.

Third, Pittsburghese shirts help standardize Pittsburghese, the imagined dialect. This is by virtue of how similar they are to one another and to representations of Pittsburgh speech in other media, such as online lists and the well-known folk dictionary that I described earlier (McCool 1982). When asked where they get their ideas, T-shirt vendors sometimes refer to "lists on the Internet." This degree of similarity is made possible in large part by the fact that Pittsburghese shirts are often bought and sold in a grassroots, person-on-the-street market which is not quite legitimate, if not quite illegitimate. Trade marking is rare and designers and vendors are unlikely to sue one another for copying their ideas, word lists, or designs.

Finally, Pittsburghese shirts, and the economic practices in which they participate, lend specific meanings to local speech. They link dialect and place by juxtaposing local words on images of the city, sometimes directly, as when local words are enclosed in speech balloons emanating from downtown windows (figure 7.5; see also figure 7.1).

As noted, the shirts' colors—the city's colors and those of the city's professional football, baseball, and hockey teams—also link the speech forms represented on the shirts with the city of Pittsburgh. In addition, the words that are included and the way words are defined on backs of many shirts serve also to link the forms with local practices. Of the thirty-one items listed on the back of the shirt depicted in figure 7.1, thirteen (arguably more if one includes indirect allusions to the city) are forms that are explicitly linked with the Pittsburgh area, by virtue of how they are defined ("sold only in the Burg"; "used to hold a cold Iron") or by virtue of the fact that they are included at all ("blitzburg"; "the point").

Figure 7.5 Speech Balloons and Cityscape on the Front of a Sweatshirt. (Photograph by Barbara Johnstone)

blitzburgh: n. a drinking town with a football problem

chipped ham: n. thinly sliced ham sold only in the Burg

hans: n. a part of the body used to hold a cold Iron [Iron City is a Pittsburgh beer]

jagoff: n. anyone who pisses off a Pittsburger [*sic*, Pittsburgher]

jynt iggle: n. a popular supermarket [Giant Eagle]

keller: n. black and gold to name a few [color]

picksburgh: n. the greatest city in pensivania [Pennsylvania]

sammich: n. chipped ham or jumbo between two pieces of Town Talk bread [chipped ham or bologna sandwich made with bread from a local bakery]

spicket: n. a tap on a barrel of Iron [spigot]

stillers: n. four time super bowl champs with unfinished business [Steelers, Pittsburgh's professional football team]

the burgh: n. a helluva cool place

the mon: n. the Monogahela [*sic*, Monongahela] River

the point: n. the meeting place of Pittsburgh's Three Rivers

The venues where Pittsburghese shirts are sold and the people who sell them reinforce the idea that local speech is casual and fun, linked with working-class habits and in some cases even a bit shady. They are sold at airport newsstands and gift shops where tourists congregate, but probably more than anywhere else in the wholesale market area called the Strip District, now also a destination for "ethnic" ingredients and fresh meat and seafood sold in rundown but charming old buildings; a cafe where Italian can still be heard; and a number of upscale kitchen-supply and home-decorating stores and restaurants. Pittsburghers of Italian heritage go to the Strip to shop for Italian breads, cheeses, and pastry; seafood for the traditional seven-fishes Christmas Eve dinner; and grape juice for wine making. There are also shops selling Greek, Arab, Asian, Polish, and Mexican ingredients and prepared foods. On the sidewalk, takeaway food, flowers, and a variety of other items, such as inexpensive clothing and jewelry, are sold from folding tables. On any Saturday, at least three T-shirt vendors open up or set up shop; one in an old, windowless storefront, one at a permanent wooden booth, and at least one at a folding table. Their location is thus associated experientially with traditional food ways and with an informal, leisurely way of shopping for fun, in a somewhat grubby but comfortable environment. The Strip experience attracts tourists, reminds Pittsburghers of their heritage, and encourages impulse buying. This makes it an ideal site for the sale of Pittsburghese shirts.

The merchandise with which Pittsburghese shirts are juxtaposed on tables and hanging displays also reinforces its connection with local vernacular practices. Especially prominent are sports T-shirts, particularly ones celebrating the Pittsburgh Steelers. Some shirts combine Pittsburghese and sports imagery, for example by displaying the word "Stillers" ('Steelers') in a design that evokes the official look of the team typography. T-shirts that say "We got Rings N'at" and "Yinz Got 5?" refer to the team's national championship victories in ways that include Pittsburghese forms. Pittsburghese shirts are sometimes sold alongside shirts that disparage Cleveland, Pittsburgh's traditional sports rival.

The production and circulation of Pittsburghese shirts is one of the many ways in which many Pittsburghers, ex-Pittsburghers, and visitors come to share ideas about what Pittsburgh speech consists of and what it means. It is also evidence that this process has been going on for some time. Appadurai's heuristic provides a useful way of exploring the details about what makes Pittsburghese shirts viable. It would no doubt also be useful for exploring the circumstances under which other media for Pittsburghese have been produced, circulated, and consumed, although the details would be slightly different for coffee mugs or postcards than for T-shirts.

The Yappin' Yinzers

The Yappin' Yinzers are plush dolls. One, called Chipped Ham Sam, represents an adult male , and the other, Nebby Debbie, an adult female. At ten inches (25.4 centimeters) and nine inches (23 centimeters), respectively, they are smaller than most dolls designed for children, and the battery-powered plastic sound module accessible through an opening in their backs adds to their unsuitability as toys. Each time one of the dolls is squeezed in the middle, the sound module plays a sentence uttered by someone using a Pittsburghese accent, highlighting one or more Pittsburghese words or phrases. The dolls are produced and sold by Colloquial Enterprises, LLC, which is based in Bethel Park, Pennsylvania, a suburb of Pittsburgh. They are manufactured in China. They can be ordered online at http://yappinyinzers.com/ and are available in some Pittsburgh gift shops. They cost about $20.00 each or about $35.00 for both if purchased together. The male doll, Chipped Ham Sam, went on sale in 2007; the female one, Nebby Debbie, a year or two later.

Figure 7.6 is a screenshot of the yappinyinzers.com homepage (captured on May 23, 2012) that shows the dolls' heads and upper bodies and how they are presented on the site. The web page's design enregisters the dolls with place and local practice in ways we have seen repeatedly. The primary colors on the page are black and gold, and the dolls are superimposed on a photograph of part of Pittsburgh's downtown skyline. A stylized version of the skyline can also be seen around the small image at the bottom center, which can be read as a cartoon representation of Chipped Ham Sam holding a cheeseburger and a mug of beer and wearing a Pittsburgh Steelers football jersey and helmet. The dolls are also linked with Pittsburghese, via their designation as "yappin' Yinzers"—*yappin'* 'yapping' is the somewhat sound-symbolic designation of a quality of

Figure 7.6 Homepage of the Yappin' Yinzers Website (http://yappinyinzers.com/)

voice or a style of speech—via the phrase on the homepage, "Da yinz nowum-sayin'?" (Do you know what I'm saying?) and via their names. "Chipped ham" (a kind of sandwich meat that was invented and sold by a Pittsburgh-area dairy-store chain) is often on lists of Pittsburghese words and phrases. Pittsburghers sometimes report not knowing that it was a regional item until they ordered it or looked for it somewhere else, an experience that, as we have seen, enregisters words with places. "Nebby" is an adjective of northern English and Scotch-Irish origin meaning nosy. The link between Pittsburghese and the dolls' identity is made even tighter through the text-metrical rhyming of "chipped ham" and "Sam" and "nebby" and "Debbie." (Before Nebby Debbie actually appeared on the market, the producers sometimes referred to the promised female doll as Nebby Nancy, which would have drawn on alliteration rather than rhyme to link the two terms.)

Unlike T-shirts, Chipped Ham Sam and Nebby Debbie represent imaginary people, and they talk. Because they have bodies, clothes, facial features, hairstyles, voices, and even personal histories in the form of biographies on small cards that come with them, they highlight some aspects of the Pittsburghese story that we have not yet paid much attention to. The dolls package Pittsburghese with particular lifestyles and biographies in ways that other artifacts do not or do less. For one thing, they put the connection between Pittsburghese and social class front and center, forcing us to consider what social class is; how it intersects with ethnicity, gender, and other aspects of Pittsburghers' identity; and how it is linked to Pittsburgh's identity as a collective. For another thing, what Sam's and Debbie's voices sound like and what they say lead us to consider how a particular rhetorical stance toward the world is implicated in how people understand Pittsburghese.

THE YAPPIN' YINZERS REPRESENT "CHARACTEROLOGICAL FIGURES" OF SOCIAL IDENTITY

Chipped Ham Sam and Nebby Debbie represent what Asif Agha refers to as characterological figures. Agha suggests that a linguistic feature or a set of features can be linked via enregisterment with what might be also called a persona: a way of being and acting associated not just with a social identity in an abstract sense but also with its embodiment in a character, imagined or actually performed (Agha 2007a, 177).[2] The characterological figure in question is the Yinzer. Sam and Debbie are not, in other words, just dolls that happen to speak in Pittsburghese. They are "yappin' Yinzers." Their Pittsburghese is part and parcel of the fact that they are Yinzers. The Pittsburghese that emerges from the sound module when the dolls are squeezed is one of the things that identifies the dolls as Yinzers, and the Yinzerishness of their voices, their appearances, and the life stories they come with identifies their speech as Pittsburghese.

The term *Yinzer* appears to have emerged sometime during the 1960s, possibly in high school slang. I discuss the word's history further in chapter 9. Here, rather than asking what the word can mean in general, I ask what it means to say that Chipped Ham Sam and Nebby Debbie are Yinzers. What can be read from the way this characterological figure is embodied in these plush dolls about what a Yinzer is and about the relationship between Yinzerness and Pittsburghese?

For one thing, the dolls' appearance links them to the characterological figure of the Yinzer and the Yinzer figure to them. Both dolls are meant to look like white people. Chipped Ham Sam has blond yarn hair in the style known as a mullet. Nebby Debbie's hair is brown, pulled back from her face except for a few bangs on her forehead. Both dolls have large, open mouths, extending almost from ear to ear. Sam's abdomen is exposed, attention drawn to it via a plush ball representing his navel. Debbie wears gold hoop earrings and lots of makeup: mascara, yellow eye-shadow, bright red lipstick, and rust-colored fingernail and toenail polish. She is wearing a black mesh top over a sleeveless gold T-shirt, dark green track-suit pants with orange stripes along the outside seams, and high-heeled black mules. Sam has on a Steelers jersey with the number 0 and the name "yinzer" on the back where a player's name usually goes. He is wearing blue cut-off shorts, gold and black socks, and shoes that resemble construction boots.

The front of the card that comes attached to each doll's arm identifies the doll as a Pittsburgher. The top two-thirds of the page have the words (in gold) "yappin' Yinzers," superimposed on a photo of the Pittsburgh downtown skyline as seen from the Point (at the confluence of the Allegheny and Monongahela Rivers). Under this, in very small type, is "Pittsburghers with personality," and under this is the doll's name in a larger type size. The claim that the dolls have "personality" suggests that they are to be seen as larger than life in some ways, but it also points to how they evoke personas. Inside each card on the left-hand page is a set of three bulleted "quick facts" about each doll. On the right-hand page is the heading "9 Hilarious Pittsburgh Sayings" with three of the doll's utterances reproduced in speech balloons emanating from skyline building windows. We return to the "sayings" shortly.

The "quick facts" about Chipped Ham Sam are these, as they appear in the card:

—Born of Polish and Ukrainian parents (with whom he will most likely always reside) on October 12, 1975—exactly 9 months to the day from the Lombardi trophy's first arrival in the "burgh."
—Given the nickname "Chipped Ham" because of his insatiable desire for barbequed chipped ham sandwiches, a local delicacy.
—A fanatical supporter of Pittsburgh sports, Sam can usually be found screaming at a television at one of his favorite South Side watering holes.

Sam is identified in ethnic terms as having Eastern European parents. He is identified as a fan of Pittsburgh sports and implicitly as the child of sports fans, conceived right after the Steelers' first national championship. (The Lombardi trophy is held by the winners of the year's Super Bowl.) He is identified as being in younger middle age (born in 1975, which means that he would have been thirty-four in 2007 when he was created). He lives with his parents. He is identified by what he eats (chipped ham sandwiches) and that he drinks (at South Side watering holes, or bars). "South Side" links him with an older working-class neighborhood and with its transformation into an area where people now go to drink. And he is identified as someone who "screams at a television."

The quick facts about Nebby Debbie are the following:

—A life-long resident of the Pittsburgh borough of McKees Rocks and almost a graduate of the local high school, Debbie has found recent fame as the top nail stylist in the area. Her signature rhinestone-leopard nail art is most requested by her loyal customers, followed by black-and-gold zebra stripes.

—You can find Debbie trolling for love on most Friday and Saturday nights at various Station Square, Strip District, and Mt. Washington hot spots, as well as anywhere the city puts on fireworks or is giving away bobbleheads.

—Boy is Debbie nebby. She seems to know interesting little tidbits about everyone in town, and if she feels she is missing any of the scoop, believe me, she'll ask.

Debbie is not identified in ethnic terms, but instead in terms of what neighborhood she is from (McKees Rocks), her education ("almost" a high school graduate), her profession (successful nail stylist), and the tastes of her professional clients (rhinestone-leopard and black-and-gold nail designs). Like Sam, Debbie is linked with social practices and consumption, but these involve sex (trolling for love), spectacle (fireworks), and the consumption of things (bobblehead dolls), rather than sports and the consumption of food and drink. Both dolls are identified in ways that evoke a style of communication, Sam by "screaming at [the] TV" and Debbie by being nosy ("nebby"), gossiping ("seems to know interesting little tidbits about everyone in town"), and being unafraid to dig for information ("believe me, she'll ask").

The communicative style that is both evoked and suggested by the Yappin' Yinzers is also enacted in their actual speech, in the form of the prerecorded utterances that play when their voices are activated with a squeeze. Although both are advertised as coming with nine "hilarious Pittsburgh sayings," Debbie actually comes with eleven. In the next chapter, I perform a more detailed analysis of the phonetic features of some performances of Pittsburghese. Here, where the phonetic details are less crucial for the analysis, informal phonetic spelling suggests how the yappin' Yinzers sound.

7.1 *The "sayings" of Chipped Ham Sam*

1. *What yinz doin' ewver dere?* ['What are you (pl.) doing over there?']
2. **Come off it, fer cryin' aht lahd!** ['Come off it, for crying out loud!']
3. *Hows come yinz ain't watchin' 'e game?* Pixburgh's on. ['How come you (pl.) aren't watching the game? Pittsburgh's on.']
4. Jeez ewh man! ['Jeez oh man!']
5. Nuh-uh! ['No!']
6. **Quit jaggin' arahnd!** ['Quit fooling around!']
7. *Jinz eat jet?* I'm gettin' hungry fer a sammich. ['Did you (pl.) eat yet? I'm getting hungry for a sandwich.']
8. I'm going dahn the Sahth Side to drink some Irons n'nat. ['I'm going down to the South Side to drink some Iron City beer, and things like that.']
9. I'm taking the trowey dahntahn. ['I'm taking the trolley downtown.']

7.2 *The "sayings" of Nebby Debbie*

1. Jeat yet? ['Did you eat yet?']
2. You ain't gonna believe this; I just saw whutsername with whutsisface. ['You aren't going to believe this; I just saw what's-her-name with what's-his-face.']
3. **How 'bout yinz redd up them rewms before comp'ny comes ewver?** [How about if you (pl.) clean up those rooms before company comes over?']
4. **Yinz better settle dahn!** ['You (pl.) had better settle down!']
5. **Watch out when yinz go outside, it's col' out there today**. ['Watch out when you (pl.) go outside. It's cold out there today.']
6. I hafta go da the bafroom. ['I have to go to the bathroom.']
7. **Yiz ain't 'upposed to be aht, yinz are grahnded!** ['You (pl.) aren't supposed to be out. You (pl.) are grounded (i.e., confined to the house).']
8. **You're 'upposed to put a gumband arahnd it**. ['You're supposed to put a rubber band around it.']
9. I ain't payin' no hundert dowers fer 'at! ['I am not paying a hundered dollars for that!']
10. What's gewin' on? ['What's going on?']
11. **Git atta tahn!** ['Get out of town!']

The Pittsburghese word represented most often in both Sam and Debbie's speech is *yinz*, 'you (pl.)', which is heard eight times in the twenty utterances. Versions of *Jeat jet?* 'Did you eat yet?, Have you eaten yet?' appear in both dolls' repertoires. Other lexical items often associated with Pittsburghese are *Irons* 'Iron City beer', *n'at* 'and things like that', *redd up* 'tidy up', and *gumbands* 'rubber bands'. *How's come* 'why, how come' and *nuh-uh* [nʌ'ʔʌ:], an emphatic 'no!' are also sometimes found on lists of Pittsburghese. Both dolls use *ain't*, and there is one instance of negative concord in Nebby Debbie's speech ("I ain't payin' no hundert dowers fer 'at!"). Phonologically, the dolls' speech sounds casual, with lots of elided syllables and sounds. Both voices use Pittsburgh accents, though somewhat inconsistently. Of the many words in the utterances that could showcase the area's characteristic monophthongal /aw/ (*down*, *out*, *outside*, *grounded*, *around*, *loud*, and *downtown*), not all are actually monophthongized every time. Both speakers use fronted versions of the vowel in words such as *over*, *going*, and *oh* ("ewver," "gewin," "ewh") and Debbie's voice fronts the /u/in *rooms* ("rewms"). Each script includes a word that showcases /l/-vocalization, *trolley* ("trowey") for Sam and *dollars* ("dowers") for Debbie, and both voices strongly vocalize these /l/s. In *bafroom*, Debbie is represented as using /f/ for /θ/.

The speech acts performed by these utterances lean heavily toward the directive. The bold-faced items listed in 7.1 and 7.2 are all things a person could say to get someone else to do something. These include "Come off it," "Quit jaggin' around," "Yinz better settle down," and so on. Of the twenty utterances by both dolls, eight (arguably nine, if "What's going on?" is taken as a suggestion that the addressees stop what they are doing) are directives. Almost half the time, in other words, the Yappin' Yinzers tell other people what to do and what not to do.

Nebby Debbie's audience is also called up by what she says. "Whutsername" and "whutsisface" suggest that she is accustomed to talking to people she knows well, that is, people who will be able to identify who is being talked about. All but one of her directives represent instructions that adults (especially mothers) address to children: instructions to tidy up, settle down, put on warm clothes before going outside, and get back in the house.

Another attribute of the Yinzer speech style, as it is figured in the dolls, is a distinctive tone of voice. This occurs only in the male doll's speech in the places that are italicized in the list of 7.1. In these places, the pitch and volume of Chipped Ham Sam's voice are raised. The effect of this higher, louder voice is to make him sound aggrieved and petulant.

Table 7.1 pulls together all the characteristics of the Yappin' Yinzer dolls that have been discussed. As represented via these dolls, the Yinzer character is highly gendered. Male Yinzers, the dolls suggest, go to bars to eat and drink, females to find romance. Male Yinzers like sports; female Yinzers like the fireworks that sometimes follow sports events and the souvenir bobblehead dolls that are sometimes given away there. Male Yinzers wear an outdated hairstyle from the 1980s; female Yinzers wear a lot of makeup. Males yell at the Steelers; females yell at their children. But there are also many commonalities, especially in how their speech styles are represented.

Who, then, is the prototypical Yinzer, as this character is figured in the Yappin' Yinzer dolls? He or she is a white Pittsburgher who does things in Pittsburgh, a sports fan or at least a wearer of the team colors. A Yinzer

Table 7.1 **Characteristics of the Yappin' Yinzers**

	Chipped Ham Sam	*Nebby Debbie*
physical appearance	**white-skinned** **big-mouthed** blonde has a protruding belly	**white-skinned** **big-mouthed** brown-haired
clothing, bodily adornment	mullet hair style **wears black and gold**: Steelers jersey, black and gold socks cut-off jeans shorts construction boots	long hair, bangs **wears black and gold**: black mesh top, gold t-shirt track suit pants mules with heels gold hoop earrings make up and nail polish
place	**Pittsburgher** **frequents local places**: the South Side	**Pittsburgher** from McKees Rocks **frequents local places**: Station Square, the Strip District, Mt. Washington
profession	[not specified]	nail stylist
ethnic/cultural identity	**yinzer** Ukrainian-Polish	**yinzer**
lifestyle/consumption practices	parents were sports fans lives with his parents is a sports fan eats chipped ham sandwiches goes to bars	her customers like rhinestone-leopard, black and gold fingernail styles likes to troll for love likes fireworks likes bobblehead dolls
communicative style	**yaps** **is uninhibited**: screams at the TV **says *yinz* and *Jeat jet?*** **has a Pittsburgh accent** **sounds casual** **sounds nonstandard** **directs people to do things** sometimes sounds aggrieved	**yaps** is nosy gossips **is uninhibited**: is not afraid to ask **says *yinz* and *Jeat jet?*** **has a Pittsburgh accent** **sounds casual** **sounds nonstandard** **directs people to do things** talks to people she knows well, to children

dresses casually. A Yinzer uses Pittsburghese words and sounds like a Pittsburgher. A Yinzer has a big mouth, and when he or she opens it, the voice that
emerges is casual and sometimes nonstandard. A Yinzer is uninhibited, not
afraid to tell people what to do. A Yinzer yaps.

COMMUNICATIVE STYLE AND WORKING-CLASS IDENTITY

Knowing what we do about Pittsburgh's history and about how people talk
about Pittsburgh, and judging from what the dolls look like, how they are
described, what they say, and how they say it, we might be tempted to say that
the Yinzer character is working class. But what would this mean? Neither
Chipped Ham Sam nor Nebby Debbie is explicitly identified as working class.
Sam is not assigned a job, a trade, or a profession in the biography that accom-
panies him. Debbie is identified as a nail stylist, which means that she may be
an independent operator, not a salaried worker. Neither doll is dressed in work
clothes (although Sam wears what might be work boots). The dolls' income is
not specified. Nothing they say is explicitly related to socioeconomic class. And
yet there are reasons to claim that consumers are meant to think of the Yinzer
figure, as it is represented in the dolls, as working class. One of these reasons is
their communicative style.

Scholars continue to debate about how to define social class, and this is not
the place to rehash the entire debate. The view I adopt here is similar to that of
other ethnographers of the postindustrial "working class" (Dunk 1991; Foley
1990; Fox 1997; Lindquist 2002; Weis 1990). According to these scholars and
the like, the social identities associated with class result from the material circumstances of work (one's relationship to the means of production, whether as
hourly wage-earner, on one end of the spectrum, or as owner and/or investor on
the other), as well as the ideology that shapes how a person makes sense of those
circumstances. Social class is thus both an economic and a cultural phenomenon.
People's understanding of their place in the economic system, and what that
entails when it comes to how to act, talk, and think, is shaped by models that
circulate as people perform class identity in interaction with others. People have
various ways of talking about this aspect of social identity, some of which do not
involve using the term "working class" at all, and "working-class culture" can
take a wide variety of forms. Still, the concept of class is useful, even if the people
we study may not overtly orient to it. In a capitalist economy, the need to work
(or not), along with the kind of work one does, shapes how people think and talk
about identity, just as biology shapes (but does not determine) how people
understand gender and sexuality, and physical appearance shapes how people
understand race. As Julie Lindquist explains it in the introduction to an analysis
of working-class rhetorical practices, "Implicit in my claim to take as my subject
'working-class culture' is the assumption that shared cultural experiences (and

the narrative processes and products of these experiences) are linked to material conditions" (2002, 5).

One aspect of the working-class experience is opposition. As Thomas W. Dunk puts it in his study of a "working man's town" in Ontario, Canada, "Class happens because of the common experiences of a group of people whose interests are different from *and usually opposed to* the interests of another group" (1991, 27, emphasis mine). This may be opposition rooted in competing economic interests, as in the classical Marxist account. This is the sort of opposition that leads to labor unions; to negotiations over wages, hours, and working conditions; and to strikes. Or it may be opposition rooted in struggles against the hegemonic dominant ideology circulated in bourgeois institutions and practices like education, as presented in more recent interpretations of Marxism (Gramsci 1971; E. P. Thompson 1966; Williams 1982). This is the sort of opposition that leads working-class teens to reject school culture (Weis 1990; Eckert 1996; 2000; 2004) and adults to value low-culture activities like team sports that involve group physical activity over high-culture intellectual ones like theater or ballet (Dunk 1991, 90–91). It is the sort of opposition that leads working-class arguers to value the "common sense" that arises from lived experience over "formal, theoretical knowledge that is not immediately applicable to work and to action" (Lindquist 2002, 99).

Linguistic anthropologist Douglas Foley (1989) takes this argument a step further, suggesting that class differences in postindustrial settings are fundamentally differences in expressive style. Foley combines Jürgen Habermas's (1984) insights about how communication is affected by modern economic life with Erving Goffman's (1959; 1981b; 1986) analyses of "the performance of self." Goffman claimed to be describing how social interaction always works, everywhere, and was apparently uninterested in how inequality could be created and perpetuated in interaction. Foley, however, sees Goffman as "an ethnographer of communication in late capitalist society, despite [Goffman's] claims to universality" (Foley 1989, 149). Foley points out that "Goffman's empirical descriptions of communication look very like what Habermas calls instrumental action" (152). Habermas's work critiques modern, bureaucratic, knowledge and service economies, where ways of speaking have become increasingly regimented. What Habermas calls "instrumental rationality," geared toward efficiency, productivity, and profit, requires people to perform elaborately constructed identities in highly staged, instrumental interaction, where "traditional normative ideals about doing what one says and being sincere and truthful become less of a constraint on communicative action" (Foley 1989, 155) than the ability to manage one's identity by playing the kinds of language games that Goffman describes. For Foley, working-class social identity is "stigmatized," in Goffman's terms, because traditional working-class expressive norms are different from and opposed to those of the "normal" social actors Goffman describes. As Foley describes it (151):

Two generalized class roles are routinely enacted in recurring everyday situational speech performances. Bourgeois/petit bourgeois actors typically assume they are leaders with "normal" identities and superior speech, who have the right to speak often and in an official manner. Standard, official speech is authoritative and proper. Proper, polite speech and etiquette become a strategic weapon in their everyday communication . . . Conversely, working-class actors assume they are outsiders and subordinates with "stigmatized" identities and inferior speech . . . Unofficial speech is often nonstandard, informal, and lacking in politeness forms. Impolite speech becomes an unstrategic form of expressiveness that either meekly enacts the subordinate, stigmatized role of outsider, or openly, hostilely rejects it. These more open, dialogic speech practices help preserve the dual role and identity of an uncultured, inferior outsider and rebel.

The working-class actor Foley describes here maps almost exactly onto the Yinzer persona. Located outside the new economy and its regimented modes of speech, the Yinzer can speak freely, using casual, nonstandard, regionally marked speech forms, speaking directly, telling people off, gossiping, and yelling. But the Yinzer is also frustrated, petulant, and sometimes whiny. Her kids misbehave; his team makes idiotic plays on the football field. Yinzers have big mouths and are not afraid to open them, but when they do, they yap powerlessly, like miniature dogs that think they are big and strong.

As enregistered in artifacts like these dolls, Pittsburghese is not just a set of words and phrases, but an expressive stance associated with a particular working-class style, shaped by a particular economic history. The dolls embody a stance that is both oppositional and powerless, embedded in a specific set of consumption practices, communicative needs, and vocal styles. While Pittsburghese T-shirts enregister words and meanings with place and to a certain extent with local practice, the dolls much more explicitly enregister Pittsburghese with a specific stance toward the world: the stance of the Yinzer. In this they severely limit the possible meanings of speaking Pittsburghese. The Yappin' Yinzers help standardize not only what counts as Pittsburghese but also who speaks it, what they say, and how they sound when they say it. Artifacts like these, and the activities in which they are used and referred to, re-enregister Pittsburghese with social class, but now in a new way, as part of the ongoing shift in the social meaning of Pittsburghese that I will discuss in chapter 9. Rather than evoking the working-class lifestyle of the (nostalgically tinted) past—lunch pails, chipped ham sandwiches, falling asleep on the "cahch" after work—the Yappin' Yinzers evoke a (partly imagined) working-class persona of the present.

BUYING NOSTALGIA

Why, then, would anybody buy one of these dolls? To put it in Appadurai's terms, what makes the Yinzer identity a candidate for commodification? Foley's analysis suggests a way to answer this question. As we have noted, working-class expressive culture has been described as oppositional. Working-class actors like the Yappin' Yinzers resist the expectations of lifestyle and speech style that are tied to the kinds of nonphysical labor that are increasingly the only option: the expectations that one finish school, speak properly and politely, and so on. They resist the commodification of speech in the form of the scripts that a call-center employee has to read, the put-on friendliness of mall-store employees, the carefully managed speech style of the well-trained teacher or manager, the untrustworthy identity performance of lawyers. They resist what Foley refers to as the "theft of communicative labor" in "an overly administered world of manufactured symbols and identities" (Foley 1989, 156). Working-class expressive style makes a claim to a certain kind of authenticity, to the realness of people who are not putting on elaborate performances of self.[3]

But "such expressions of cultural resistance may also become commercialized" (Foley 1989, 156). This happens when the Yinzer persona, once linked causally with the experience of being working class, gets unlinked from the actual conditions of labor and appropriated as a second-order symbol of local authenticity. Once this happens, people start to use the term *Yinzer* for anyone from or even just living in Pittsburgh. TV reporters and teachers—members of the speech-regimented new economy—can now put on a Yinzer persona when they perform Pittsburghese: leaning forward, raising their voices, speaking in a higher pitch, complaining, giving orders, and calling people jagoffs. People buy Yappin' Yinzer dolls because they make fun of the Yinzer's crudeness and lack of sophistication, but also, I suggest, out of nostalgia for an imagined time when people could speak their minds and sound like whoever they were; an imagined time when there was no need for the kind of persona management that is now required in the new economy. What gets lost, or at least obscured, in the process, is the way that the Yinzer style reflects and reacts to the brute facts of physical wage labor and the frustration of being part of economic system in which, in the end, labor was powerless to forestall economic disaster. Also obscured is the fact that these voices do not actually emanate from people like Sam and Debbie—people who actually run nail salons and wear construction boots—but rather from entrepreneurs, sufficiently removed from the kind of life Sam and Debbie lead that they can reflect on it and sell it to people who experience Pittsburghese in the same mediated way. Actual Sams and Debbies probably do not even hear their own accents.

8

Performing Pittsburghese

The most widespread, dominant social meanings of Pittsburghese are much more visible and shareable in the 2010s than ever before. Due to media coverage and to Pittsburghese T-shirts, talking dolls, and the like, it is now possible to learn about Pittsburghese and its social significance without ever actually hearing anyone who has a Pittsburgh accent or uses local words or structures. Fewer people actually have Pittsburgh accents than before, and the economic changes that are leading to the leveling of the local dialect into a broader, regional one also mean less daily contact between younger, middle-class Pittsburghers and older, working-class ones. Your lawn may now be mowed by someone with a Spanish accent rather than someone with a Pittsburgh accent, and the people serving you coffee are more likely to be young baristas at chain cafes than lunch-counter ladies who call everyone "hon." People who are in a position—by virtue of their age, origin, or personal history—to hear local speech used in everyday, unselfconscious ways can still take it to mean various things about its speakers or fail to notice it at all. But public discourse about local speech invariably identifies it as Pittsburghese and treats it as the authentic voice of the city. Pittsburghese is amusing. For some people it is cool in a retro, gritty way and, for most people, it is linked with insidership and pride.

What you might hear now, instead of people speaking with Pittsburgh accents, are people performing Pittsburghese, putting on what they think of as local words, structures, accents, and personas, thus showing that they know how Pittsburghers sound, whether the performers actually sound that way themselves in nonperformed, real life. The voices of the Yappin' Yinzer dolls are recordings of people performing Pittsburghese. Performances of Pittsburghese help enregister a particular set of sound, words, and bits of grammar with the social identity of Pittsburgh and Pittsburghers, just as do the conversations, newspaper articles, and artifacts we have explored. But while oral performances of Pittsburghese have a great deal in common with the practices we have discussed up to now, they are different in an important way. The processes we have looked at in previous chapters—conversations about Pittsburgh

speech, negotiations over expertise in the media, the production and consumption of artifacts like T-shirts and dolls—all have the effect of standardizing
Pittsburghese and restricting its social meaning. Oral performances can do this
too. On the other hand, however, oral performances can also expand the inventory of possible local forms and loosen the semiotic links between local-
sounding speech and particular social meanings. In other words, performances
can act as a centrifugal force in the process of enregisterment, counteracting,
to some extent, the centripetal, standardizing, focusing force of things like folk
dictionaries and T-shirts.

Performances of Language

People's response to language is always partly aesthetic. We are always attending
to how language sounds (or looks on the page) as well as attending to what is
being said. Language that looks or sounds better may be more persuasive, more
memorable, more effective, better at creating conversational rapport (Tannen
1989). In this sense we could say that speaking and writing always involve performance. We could also say that all language is performance in the sense that
we are always putting forth some sort of persona, playing some sort of part. But
there are times when speakers and hearers are especially attentive to what talk
sounds like. There are times when we judge speakers not only on the basis of
what they say but also on the basis of how they say it, times when it is considered fair to comment on someone's delivery, not just the meaning of their words.
It is considered fair to evaluate verbal performance not just on the basis of
whether it is true, understandable, or effective, but also on the basis of the
details of its form: its words, its structures, its sounds, how it is acted out.
Speech that is performed calls attention to and takes responsibility for its multivoiced quality, the way, in other words, in which the speakers' "normal" voice is
juxtaposed with a performed voice that may represent some other person or
persona (Bakhtin 1981; Bauman and Briggs 1990; Bauman 1977). As Richard
Bauman describes it (1977, 11):

> Performance as a mode of spoken verbal communication consists in the
> assumption of responsibility to an audience for a display of communi-
> cative competence . . . From the point of view of the audience, the act of
> expression on the part of the performer is thus marked as subject to
> evaluation for the way it is done . . . Additionally, it is marked as avail-
> able for the enhancement of experience, through the present enjoy-
> ment of the intrinsic qualities of the act of expression itself. Performance
> thus . . . gives license to the audience to regard the act of expression and
> the performer with special intensity.

Speakers can move back and forth between relatively performed and relatively nonperformed speech. Sometimes a small chunk of speech in an otherwise non-performed stretch of talk suddenly strikes people as artistic or clever or funny because of its form, and it is commented on. For example, an unintentional rhyme might call forth, "Hey, I'm a poet and I don't know it!," and an unintentional pun might elicit an audience's groans or the speaker's quick acknowledgment of the pun: "so to speak."

Performances of enregistered varieties of speech like languages and dialects are often referred to as "stylizations" (Coupland 2001; 2007; Rampton 1999). The use of the verb "stylize" calls attention to the fact that there is a difference between speaking in a certain way and performing someone speaking that way, between having a certain style and temporarily adopting someone else's style. In fact, what people sound like when they are doing these two kinds of things may be quite different. In studies of US whites and blacks who were instructed to imitate each other's speech, as well as northerners instructed to imitate southerners, Dennis Preston and Nancy Niedzielski (Niedzielski and Preston, 1999; Preston, 1992; 1996) showed that people may control the details of others' dialects with varying degrees of accuracy, from a linguist's point of view. Greg Guy and Cecelia Cutler illustrate this point in their case study of the speech of an upper-middle-class white youth who identified with hip-hop culture and tried to sound black. They found that the teen had absorbed some of the unconscious rules that dictate how words are pronounced in African American English, but that he applied these rules in some cases where African Americans would not (Guy and Cutler 2011). As we will see, people trying to sound like Pittsburghers (as well as Pittsburghers trying to sound like people from elsewhere) also get it "wrong" in many ways.

People perform stylized ways of speaking for many reasons. A shift into a stylized version of another language or variety can signal a shift in footing or a change in point of view, for example. Ben Rampton (1995) studied London schoolchildren from various backgrounds who make brief excursions into languages and varieties other than the ones associated with their own ethnic group. Rampton focused on the micro-interactional uses of such switches, pointing out, for example, that they occur at moments of social tension or at the boundaries between activities. Children know how to perform stylized Punjabi, Afro-Caribbean English, or Cockney because they interact with native speakers of the languages. Nik Coupland (2001) talks about a Welsh radio announcer who interpolates stereotypically Welsh-sounding words, cultural references, and phonological variables, as well as a Scottish-sounding phrase and an American-sounding one, into his humorous monologue. The function of these switches is, says Coupland, "to project shifting social personas and stances" (347), by which he means orientations to the material at hand, one more authoritative and standard sounding, one more personal, local, and Welsh sounding.

The kinds of linguistic shifting that go on when people stylize others' speech are often talked about as if they were conscious choices. For example, as I found in an earlier project, Texas women who sometimes adopt a "Southern Belle" style of speaking often talk about "turning on the Southern charm" and describe what they can accomplish by doing this (Johnstone 1999). As we will see, however, people are not actually aware of everything they are doing when they imitate someone else. Speakers may not even be able to reflect on or talk about dialect features that they do control accurately (Preston 1996, 64). Stylizations are often set off from the surrounding speech: the speaker's voice quality may change, or the pitch may move upward or downward, and sometimes stylizations are explicitly identified as quotes.

In an earlier chapter we looked at a brief performance of Pittsburghese, Jason E.'s illustration of "the actual accent of the Pittsburgher" in "Knox's Pierogie Hahs." Younger Pittsburghers like Jason often perform bits of Pittsburghese, and they often talk about doing this. Here, in an interview with me, a musician in his twenties describes two reasons a person might break into stylized Pittsburghese: to entertain friends from elsewhere, and as a mildly subversive, "ironic" activity by young retail workers and restaurant servers. Daniel D. is talking about a trip to England with a youth choir he directed, then about coming back to Pittsburgh after college.

8.1 Ironic Pittsburghese

> DANIEL D. When I got to England and I met up with my, two friends in particular, I started speaking in Pittsburghese to them and they were like, "We can't understand a word you're [saying]." And I said, "Well, yeah.". . . And it's funny, when I first came back to Pittsburgh and started waiting tables, a lot of the kids that I was working with would just do it, just ironically . . . They just literally change their accent and just, you know, kind of, just ironically, just for fun, you know, just to joke around.

Just as with the adolescents Rampton studied, dialect stylizations can also annoy adults, as described here by a thirteen-year-old girl talking about her Lebanese-American grandmother, to the laughter of some classmates and me:

8.2 "Yinz, yinz, yinz"

> MIRIAM X. One time [my grandmother] got really mad at me for, I don't even remember, oh, I was irritating her. I kept saying, "Yinz, yinz, yinz." And

she was like, "You better stop it right now." And I was like, "Yinz, yinz, yinz." And she got a wooden spoon out. Oh, I swear I used to get beat with a wooden spoon when I was a baby. But anyway, my grandma got a wooden spoon out; she started speaking Lebanese and was chasing me around a tree.

Speakers imitating other dialects sometimes adopt stereotyped personas associated with the dialect in question (Coupland 2001; 2007; Preston 1996). In other words, rather than performing a way of speaking, they may be acting out a stereotype, and performing that persona might entail speaking in a particular way. The speakers who were recorded for the Yappin' Yinzer dolls may well have been aiming to sound like Yinzers rather than to speak in Pittsburghese. In other words, speaking Pittsburghese may have come along with sounding like a Yinzer, rather than the reverse.

The bits of talk that I analyze in the rest of this chapter are meant to illustrate some of the ways it can sound, and some of the things it can mean, to speak with a regional accent. First, we look at a story in which someone with a Pittsburgher accent imitates someone from Texas. Although his performance of the "typical Texan" sounds like other performances of Texanness, it does not sound like someone speaking in a Texas accent. Instead, Dave O. speaks in his native Pittsburgh accent throughout. This illustrates how different a stylized performance of an accent can be from how the accent sounds in everyday use by someone who uses it natively, and it shows how difficult it can be to override habits of pronunciation learned as a child. Then we turn to a bit of conversation between me and another man from Pittsburgh who is not self-consciously performing any other accent or persona, but rather speaking in a voice he means me to take as his own. Dennis C. is someone who could be heard as a Yinzer: he has a strong local accent and a strongly local sense of identity, and he can sound petulant and combative. From his point of view, however, he is not speaking as a Yinzer or performing a character. He is just being himself. We can see this if we look at the details of his pronunciation.

Dennis C.'s speech provides a baseline for comparison with a third bit of talk, this time a story in which a Pittsburgher performs the voice of a Yinzer. Even though this storyteller is himself a Pittsburgher, and thus probably has more experience with Pittsburgh accents than Dave O. does with Texas accents, his performance of the Yinzer character is not much closer to the mark than Dave O.'s is, if the mark is an accurate imitation of the accent in question. Instead, Josh G. adopts a stereotypical, stylized voice associated with the Yinzer character, a voice that actually does not draw on characteristics of Pittsburgh speech except in one word.

Finally, we turn to two longer, more complex performances by professional actors. Each one includes a character who could be taken as a Pittsburgher but who could also be heard in other ways. Exploring the details of the two radio skits shows how performances can create new links between ways of sounding and social meanings as well as drawing on familiar links.

"General Gus": A Pittsburgher Speaking as a Texan

In the course of sociolinguistic interviews I conducted in Pittsburgh, people often imitated other people's accents. These imitations were usually intended as illustrations of how Pittsburghers talk, something interviewees knew I was interested in. But interviewees also sometimes imitated other dialects. One example occurred during story a Pittsburgher I call Dave O. told about a visit to a San Antonio racetrack, where he and his friend bet on a horse named General Gus. Twice during the story, Dave broke into a stylized imitation of a Texan he met at the track. Linguistic analysis of the General Gus story clearly shows that if a good imitation is one that approximates a native, people are sometimes not very good at imitating other dialects. On the level of pronunciation, Dave's two performances of Texanness provide better data about a Pittsburgh accent than about a Texas one. The imitations serve as a good illustration of the staying power of early-formed linguistic habits and the difficulty of learning a second way of speaking without having earlier learned ways of speaking interfere with it.

Yet, even though it is not accurate, the stylized Texas accent being performed here is recognizable. The imitation does not sound like a Texan, but it does sound like other imitations of Texans. Sounding like a Texan in this stylized sense does not mean adopting a Texas accent,[1] but rather deploying a few key structural devices and features of voice quality in order to perform a stereotypical Texas character. Doing this draws on and reinforces a set of rules or norms that are quite different from those involved when southerners sound southern or when people talk about southern speech. Dialect styling is not just a matter of adopting or exaggerating the normal features of a dialect as it is used in routine ways, but rather, at least in some cases, a matter of adopting a specialized set of performance norms that overlap only slightly, if at all, with the norms that shape routine uses of the dialect.

The storyteller, Dave, was a man in his early fifties who, when his elder brother died, gave up a career in the military in order to take over the working-class tavern that had been in the family for four generations. He is married to a Taiwanese woman he met when he was in the Air Force, whom he mentions. As a bartender, Dave is a professional raconteur, and he repeatedly took the floor during the interview for long humorous narratives. This is part of a series of stories about traveling to events connected with his former military life. In the transcript, I have noted words that illustrate nonstandard or local-sounding features of his language. In line 25 and again in line 43, he imitates a Texan who is a character in the story. The story arose as Dave and I were talking about differences between southerners and northeasterners like us, and Dave recalled a trip to San Antonio for the retirement of a former colleague.

8.3 *General Gus*

1	DAVE O.	When I went down [to San Antonio] for the uh, retirement ceremony, my father didn't go on that one. My wife was supposed to go, but after I bought her ticket, her mother came down with a fatal disease over in Taiwan, uh, cervical cancer.
2	BJ	Oh, yuck.
3	DAVE O.	So she went back there and, it was a long death. It was over six months, so sh—.
4	BJ	Mmm.
5	DAVE O.	The talk in the neighborhood was poor Dave's wife left him and he, he wouldn't admit it.
6	BJ	((laughs))
7	DAVE O.	((laughs)) ((indistinguishable)) 'Cause they—
8	BJ	God, you can't talk them out of that, huh?
9	DAVE O.	Nah, so you know, Barb, I'm—So, I took my buddy, uh, one of the guys at the bar that likes military stuff, and he was my guest when we went for the retirement ceremony. 'N we got there a day ahead of time and they had a big party the night before the official ceremony and we had like five hours to kill, so we went to the racetrack, as you could see, we like that type of stuff. An' uh, there was a horse running in the first race called General Gus.
10	BJ	((laughs))
11	DAVE O.	So we bet the farm on General Gus, 'cause we're there to see a general retire.
12	BJ	((laughs))
13	DAVE O.	((laughs)) And uh,
14	BJ	((laughs))
15	DAVE O.	((claps once)) horses take off, and they're running down, and General Gus shoots to the lead.
16	BJ	Uh huh.

17	DAVE O.	And he makes the first bend, he shoots to the lead, he's coming down the backstretch, he's widening his lead, he's, now they're making the clubhouse turn! Now he's coming down— And th—we sh—we got a sure winner!
18	BJ	Yeah.
19	DAVE O.	And there's this Texan sittin' next to us, with a, typical Texan, cowboy boots, hat,
20	BJ	Mm-hmm.
21	DAVE O.	and he got a straw, that's going up and down when he talks.
22	BJ	((laughing)) Uh huh.
23	DAVE O.	Big belt buckle. Just out of the movies.
24	BJ	((laughs))
25	DAVE O.	And he says ((imitating the Texan)), **"Y'all do know that that there horse got to run around the track twice."**
26	BJ	((laughs))
27	DAVE O.	((laughing)) It was a two-mile race.
28	BJ	((laughing)) So you thought you'd won, and—
29	DAVE O.	It's, this horse was so tired
30	BJ	It was only a—
31	DAVE O.	running so fast, I think he's still running.
32	BJ	((laughs))
33	DAVE O.	((laughs)) General Gus. ((laughs)). He went down the tubes.
34	BJ	So I hope you didn't put too much money on it.
35	DAVE O.	Too much money for it.
36	BJ	((laughs))
37	DAVE O.	It was a hunch.
38	BJ	Yep, well.
39	DAVE O.	But the Texan. You talk about th—, then just—,
40	BJ	The—
41	DAVE O.	The reason, it—it popped into my mind, was, his, his so— slow Texan drawl was,
42	BJ	Mm-hmm.
43	DAVE O.	((imitating the Texan)) **"Y'all do know that there horse got to run around the track twice."**
44	BJ	((laughs))
45	DAVE O.	I'll remember that for the rest of my life, that drawl.

Like many other Pittsburghers, Dave merges the low back vowels and pronounces the resulting vowel in a rounded realization, as in [fɔther] or [pɔpped] ("faughther," "paughpped"). He fronts the /o/ in go ("gew") and over and know and /u/ in do and boots ("biuts"). His central vowel /uh/ is lowered in stuff, buddy, and so on, and he vocalizes /l/ in words like kill, General, buckle, and drawl. In hours he monophthongizes /aw/ ("ahrs"). Before /l/ and /r/, but not elsewhere, he also monophthongizes /ay/ (mile sounds like "maw," tired like "tarred"). This is also typical of Pittsburgh speech. He pronounces "didn't" in one of the many not-quite-standard ways you can hear it pronounced in Pittsburgh, [dɪŋko] ("dink ko"). He also often deletes interdental fricatives (the sounds spelled with <th>) or pronounces them as the stop vowels /t/ or /d/: "back 'ere," "ina neighborhood," "shoots to duh lead." This is a stereotypical feature of northeastern working-class speech.

Dave's two imitations of the Texan (in the highlighted lines 25 and 43) sound very much alike. Both involve several departures from the style of the rest of story. Particularly in the first imitation, Dave's delivery is stretched out and slowed. He has the Texan address the two Pittsburghers as "y'all," which is not a native form for Dave, and he stresses that pronoun. He also has the Texan say "that there" instead of the more standard "there." However, Dave's accent in the imitations is exactly the same as in the rest of the story, with fronted /u/ in do; fronted /o/ in know; stopped /ð/ in that, that, there, and a rounded low back vowel in got. He fails to duplicate even the most stereotypical feature of southern phonology, monophthongal /ay/, saying [tways] ('twice') rather than the more stereotypically Southern-sounding [twahs] ("twahs").

Since the imitation does not sound like a Texan from the point of view of pronunciation, and since many Texans do not say "that there" or speak particularly slowly, we would have to say that Dave's is not a very accurate imitation of a Texas accent except in that it includes y'all (although Texans do not typically need to call attention to the fact that they're using y'all the way Dave does). Yet the imitation clearly works in its context: I laughed, as I am sure many other people have. In the terminology of narrative studies, the imitation is an effective evaluative device. It calls attention to a key moment in the plot, the moment at which the protagonists' error is revealed. We might also note that what Dave is doing here is not so much stylizing Texas speech as performing a persona. He is not being any Texan, but what he calls a "typical" Texan, whom he describes in lines 19–23. With cowboy boots, a hat, a big buckle on his belt, and a piece of straw in his mouth, the Texan is "right out of the movies."

A Pittsburgher Speaking in His Own Voice

For people who have Pittsburgh accents, like Dave O., nonstandard pronunciations, words, and structures may be the only choice they have. Their use of more local forms may be invariable, because it is dictated by linguistic or cognitive facts or because the speaker has no other variant available. Even when he is imitating the speech of a Texan, Dave uses Pittsburgh vowels and consonants exactly the way he always uses them. This is true even when it comes to the most stereotypical aspect of Southern pronunciation. Even though Dave himself pronounces *retire* as "retahr," the way someone with a Southern accent would, when Dave as the Texan says *twice* it sounds like "tways," not "twahs"—because in Dave's native accent the diphthong /ay/ is only pronounced /a:/ ("ah") before /r/ and /l/, not before /s/.

From the perspective of hearers, of course, any nonstandard word, pronunciation, or structure can potentially sound like a signal of localness, whether or not speakers can control their use of the form and whether or not the form is in fact local. As I noted in chapter 4, hearers may orient to people who sound local as instantiations of a stereotypical local identity (such as Yinzer or working-class male), whether or not the speaker is aware of or has any control over his or her accent. But in the conversation we turn to now, the fact that Dennis C. uses language forms that could be heard as markers of a Pittsburgh identity does not get taken up in the interaction. Dennis C. sounds like a Pittsburgher to me, but at this stage in our conversation neither Dennis nor I had commented on Dennis's accent or reacted to it in any other way. In fact, in a conversation like this, calling attention to another person's pronunciation or usage could derail the interaction. In conversations like this, talking as a local does not mean adopting a stereotypical set of local-sounding features but rather staying within one's own unselfconscious, everyday repertoire of linguistic forms. From Dennis's perspective, it was his personal identity rather than a stereotypical regional character or way of speaking that was potentially on display.

Dennis C. was a fifty-three-year-old teacher and accountant whom I interviewed. In each interview I tried to find a way to get the interviewee to talk at length in a relatively unselfconscious way. In Dennis's case, I discovered that local politics made him voluble, very much in keeping with his strongly local orientation. Dennis has lived in the same Pittsburgh neighborhood all his life and is active in its historical society and the most conservative, tradition-oriented of its civic groups, and his feelings about the artists and designers who are gentrifying and revitalizing the neighborhood, but also changing it, are mixed.

Dennis C.'s speech is characterized by a number of the phonological features associated with Pittsburgh speech. His pronunciation of the diphthong /aw/ is variable: anywhere except at the ends of words, but especially before the nasal sounds "m," "n," and "ng," it is sometimes monophthongized, so that *downtown* can sound like [da:nta:n] ("dahntahn"). For another thing, /o/ is often fronted, so that *over* may sound like "ewver." The low back vowels /a/ and /ɔ/ are merged, and the resulting vowel is often pronounced with o-shaped lips, such that *not* sounds more like "naught" than like "gnat." Further, /l/ is often vocalized, so that *smaller* is pronounced somewhat like "smower." The vowels in *really* ("ruhlly"), *stuff*, and *want* are all somewhat lowered and Dennis employs *it* in one instance, rather than the more standard *there*, as the subject of a sentence that asserts the existence of something ('*It* was more people in this city when I was a kid').

8.4. Downtown

1	DENNIS C.	And then the downtown [dawntawn], the way they have, emphasized the downtown [dawntawn], over [oˤvr] the past twenty thirty years as opposed [əpoˤzd] to the neighborhoods. I believe they've abandoned the neighborhoods to a large extent.
2	BJ	Mmm-hmm.
3	DENNIS C.	And there's a lot [lɔt] of emphasis on downtown [da:nta:n] and then the stadiums, things of that sort.
4	BJ	Mmm-hmm.
5	DENNIS C.	And I really [rʌʷi] am very disappointed uhhhhh in the city. 'Cause it's not a big—this is a small [smaʷ]—actually it's getting, it's growing smaller [smaʷɚ] as the years go [goˤ] on. It was—more people in this city when I was a kid
6	BJ	Mmm-hmm.
7	DENNIS C.	than are here now. So I, I think they need to get away from this attitude that Pittsburgh is Chicago [ʃəkɔg oˤ], New York. We're not. We're a small [smaʷ] little city. And I think they should take advantage of that fact.
8	BJ	Yeah, yeah. So, uh ((two second pause)), wh—if you could change local politics, what would, what would you want to do?
9	DENNIS C.	I would, I would, well I would throw out [a:t] everybody that's in there right now. I w—I would not [nɔt] have a Democrat or a Republican. I'd like to see somebody independent in there, running the city.
10	BJ	Mmm-hmm.
11	DENNIS C.	Uhhhhh,
12	BJ	And you think they should, just give up on downtown, or what what should they do?
13	DENNIS C.	No, I—downtown [da:nta:n]. They maybe they should give up on downtown [da:nta:n] to a certain extent to maintain. I—People do not go downtown [dawntawn], I would think they would get this in their heads, for one thing.

14 BJ   Mmm-hmm.

15 DENNIS C.   There's a lot [lɔD] of reasons, parking. Ahhh, downtown
                  [dawntawn] ((air intake)). I am shocked [ʃɔkt] sometimes
                  on Saturday,

16 BJ   Mmm-hmm.

17 DENNIS C.   you go downtown [da:nta:n], pan handlers, bums, [and]
                  it's not [nɔD] a pleasant, it's, it's not [nɔt] pleasant

18 BJ   Mmm-hmm. Mmm-hmm.

19 DENNIS C.   I know [noˤ] policemen that I know [noˤ] that tell their
                  wi—they don't want their wives going downtown
                  [da:nta:n] shopping [ʃɔpɪŋ] downtown [da:nta:n].

20 BJ   Mmm-hmm.

21 DENNIS C.   I mean, I don't know [no] if it's quite that bad, but, it
                  doesn't ((sighs)).

22 BJ   Mmm-hmm.

23 DENNIS C.   I was, I went downtown [dawntawn] on a weekday one
                  time. Usually I'm not [nɔt] downtown [dawntawn] on
                  a weekday. And this was about ten o'clock [klɔk] in the
                  morning. I saw nothing but panhandlers and people
                  standing on corners drinking liquor out of bags.

24 BJ   Yeah. Mmm-hmm.

25 DENNIS C.   And it's just, it's it's. I—I think the downtown [dawntawn],
                  I think they need to accept the fact that it's not [nat] going
                  to come back the way it once was.

26 BJ   Mmm-hmm.

27 DENNIS C.   The reality [riæʷəDi] is, people are going to th—. It's easier
                  to—you can park easier

28 BJ   Mmm-hmm

29 DENNIS C.   and I, I, I, I think they have to accept that fact,

30 BJ   Mmm-hmmm.

31 DENNIS C.   which I don't think they they want [wʌnt] to.

32 BJ   Yeah. Well, I, no, they obviously don't want to yet, but

33 DENNIS C.   I just don't think they, we—

34 BJ   I mean, I think it's the people who work down—I mean
                  whatever s—stays open down there, is just because

35 DENNIS C.   Yeah, oh yes, yes.

36 BJ	the people who work there go shopping during their lunch break,
37 DENNIS C.	Yes.
38 BJ	That's basically it. And then there's
39 DENNIS C.	that's what it—
40 BJ	the Cultural District, which, is a whole different
41 DENNIS C.	Right, that's a different
42 BJ	it's a totally different thing, and that's really nice, that's
43 DENNIS C.	Yeah that.
44 BJ	I think that works really well.
45 DENNIS C.	That part of it works, uhhh the businesses, and then you're right. And that's why, when I, I kind of laugh when they talk about [aba:t] taxing the people [pipl] living outside [awtsayd] the city. They oughtta be on their hands and knees thanking these people [pipʷ], 'cause they are keeping the downtown [da:nta:n], the stores and restaurants, they're, they're what keeping, they're—they are the ones keeping that open [oˤpn], that
46 BJ	Mmm-hmm.
47 DENNIS C.	that work downtown [dawntawn]=
48 BJ	right
49 DENNIS C.	And I, I can't see tax—, and then you want to tax them, and oh, I, I. We need to—, I think the—, we need a new m— mayor, ((laughing)) and a whole new city council [ka:nsl], I
50 BJ	((laughing)) Well, we're not getting that this time.
513 DENNIS C.	No, we're not [nat] gonna get that this time, and probably not [nat] in the near future either. ((laughing))

Dennis C. is speaking as a Pittsburgher here, talking about and demonstrating his local experience ("when I was a kid") and local knowledge in part to establish his right to be heard on the topic of local politics. Research linking topic and dialect style suggests that a topic less evocative of his local identity might call forth a less local-sounding accent (Eckert 2000). But he is not performing a Pittsburgh accent. He does nothing to make himself accountable for the quality of his speech, and the conversation is not about local speech or local identity. Dialect is correlated with and thus, for some interlocutors, in some circumstances, may index Dennis's local expertise and his attitude about localness. There are people like Dennis in his generation, working class in origin but college educated, who no longer live in their childhood neighbor-hoods and whose accents are not potentially as local sounding, to some extent because they have made different identity choices. On the other hand, though, a great deal of what might make Dennis's phonology sound local is not under his control or in his awareness and could thus not be performed or talked about.

Dennis's speech provides a model of the kinds of variability that are often found in spontaneous, vernacular talk by Pittsburghers with working-class roots and mostly local life experience. Monophthongal /aw/ occurs in several different words (*downtown, outside, about, council*) but it is variable from instance to instance in particular words. For example, *downtown* sometimes sounds like "dahntahn" and sometimes like "downtown," although if one syllable is monoph-thongized the other almost invariably is, too. Vocalization of /l/ is also variable, in one case because of the first sound in the following word (*people living*, where the initial /l/ in *living* precludes vocalization of the final /l/ in *people*). The low back vowel tends not to be rounded in the word *not* ("naught"), and it does tend to be rounded elsewhere, but, as with each other feature, this is variable, as is the fronting of /o/. Dennis C.'s way of pronouncing *really* is often mentioned when people talk about what Pittsburghers sound like. His pronunciation of *want* and his use of existential *it* are more idiosyncratic.

The norms reflected in Dennis's speech are statistical norms (he talks the way many Pittsburghers do), but they are also the kinds of norms that actually shape people's behavior, the community norms Milroy describes (1992). The social network in which Dennis grew up was the dense, multiplex kind in which people interact with many other people from their neighborhood and in multiple ways. This kind of social network tends to enforce local norms. However, the statistical fact that Dennis C. sounds like other people also has to do with more strictly linguistic and cognitive factors, such as the chain shifts whereby the pronuncia-tion of one phoneme is partly dictated by the pronunciation of another, and the difficulty of learning to distinguish between words that, for you, are homonyms, the way *cot* and *caught* are for Dennis. We could say that Dennis talks the way he does because he grew up speaking that way and, for reasons having to do with his personal history and his personality, he has not felt the need to try to change how he talks.

"The Mayor of McKees Rocks": A Pittsburgher Speaking as a Yinzer

Performing a stereotypical Pittsburgh persona is quite different from speaking the way Dennis does. An extract from my interview with Josh G., a twenty-eight-year-old journalist and musician, illustrates some of the differences. Here, nonstandard forms are used to make more explicit claims to insider knowledge or to alter the interpretive frame, accomplishing shifts in perspective, voice, point of view, or footing. The shift into Pittsburghese is meant to be noticeable: it is signaled with laughter, changes in voice quality, and other "keys to performance" (Bauman 1977). Although it is meant to be noticed, it is not necessarily meant to be commented on. Performances like these represent both the speaker's personal identity and that of a stereotypical other, and they signal the speaker's stance vis-à-vis that other.

Josh's personal orientation and life experience are less local than Dennis's, and he speaks here less as a native Pittsburgher (though he is one) than as a representative of a younger, more mobile, more globally oriented cohort. This part of the conversation had to do with resistance, on the part of some residents of older working-class neighborhoods, to gentrification, and the condescending attitudes that sometimes give rise to such resistance. Josh's accent is less local sounding than Dennis C., sounding, although, like Dennis C., he fronts /o/ in words like *moved* ("mewved"), vocalizes /l/, and merges and rounds the low back vowel in a word like *rocks* ("raughks"). In the course of a brief narrative, he contrasts people like himself ("a friend of mine" and "an artist") with a representative old timer, the mayor of a rundown mill town to which young artists and professionals are beginning to be attracted by virtue of the inexpensive real estate there. The mayor of McKees Rocks is presumably someone like Dennis C.: a politically active longtime resident, who, in the context of a city council meeting, probably adopts a relatively careful style. But the character Josh creates sounds like Dennis C. only in that he monophthongizes /aw/ in *town*.

8.5 *The Mayor of McKees Rocks*

1 JOSH G.   Yeah you'll get that attitude, a friend of mine moved to, bought a house in McKees Rocks because it was only fifteen thousand dollars.

2 BJ   Mmm-hmm, yeah.

3 JOSH G.   Uhh, but he, he goes to the community meetings every week now, he's really active and that makes him one of very few people in McKees Rocks that's active. But he said, uh, when when when uh, the artist from the Community Mural Project was there, uhm, this was, months ago, now it's done but, before that, ((swallows)) she had uh come eh to the, with the, to the mayor and the council there and said "What, needs to be done to heal this town?" You know which was,

4 BJ   "Heal this town!" ((sarcastically))

6 JOSH G.   you know, that's how, right. Right, right you and I laugh. Uhh but eh, but at the same time, the mayor immediately responds "There ain't nothin' wrong wid' [wɪd] dis [dɪs] tahn [taːn]!" ((lower, gruffer-sounding voice))

7 BJ   ((laughs))

8 JOSH G.   And ((laughing)) you know and so there's, you know I guess there's that there's that tension there.

With the exception of pronouncing the word *town* as [taːn] ("tahn"), Josh's imitation of the mayor (in line 6) employs not more Pittsburgh features but more nonstandard features of the kind that index working-class speech throughout the United States: *ain't*, multiple negation ("ain't nothing wrong"), the stopping and voicing of /θ/ in *with* ("wid"), and the stopping of /ð/ in *this* ("dis"). Josh also adopts a lower pitched, grittier sounding way of speaking known as "creaky voice" or "vocal fry." The performance is also signaled by means of a long, suspense-building introduction with a fairly formulaic way of introducing the story's punch line: "Uhh but eh, but at the same time, the mayor immediately responds . . ."

His performance of the mayor of McKees Rocks accomplishes several things for Josh. First, demonstrating that he knows what a local person sounds like lends credibility to Josh's self-presentation in a way his own much less salient Pittsburgh accent may not. It helps establish his authority to describe and evaluate local life, in the context of an interaction (the interview) in which he was invited to participate by virtue of being local. Second, the switch from his "own" dialect to the mayor's helps shift Josh's footing from third-person narrator to first-person character. Third, the switch in dialect helps key the shift into performance.

"Sounding like a Pittsburgher" is modeled in two very different ways here: in Josh's speech in his own voice (and in that of the artist), and in his performance of the mayor's speech. The first of these—Josh's own place identity as created and potentially signaled by his accent—represents one process by which a particular set of linguistic features can become differentiated from other features and linked with local identity. This enregisterment process is also exemplified by Dennis C.'s dialect use in example 8.4. Just as Dennis could be heard as an example of how Pittsburghers talk, so could Josh. This is why I interviewed them, in fact: I was looking for examples of how Pittsburghers talk. Aspects of how Dennis talks (such as how he says "downtown") have in fact become enregistered as Pittsburghese, while Josh's accent would not sound particularly Pittsburghy to most Pittsburghers. This is not to say, though, that the way Josh talks could not start to sound Pittsburghy.[2]

The mayor character represents another enregistration process, and it enregisters a different set of features. The sets of features drawn on in each of these activities—those that are heard in Pittsburghers' speech, and those that are heard in performances of Pittsburgh speech—may overlap, but they are not the same. In other words, the two activities enregister different sets of norms, norms for speaking as a Pittsburgher and norms for sounding like a prototypical Pittsburgher. The first activity—simply being a Pittsburgher speaking—displays and gives rise to Pittsburgh speech in all its diversity. The second activity—performing as a Pittsburgher—displays and gives rise to Pittsburghese. A thorough description of Pittsburgh speech—how people from Pittsburgh talk—would have to encompass both Dennis's and Josh's nonperformed, everyday, vernacular accents. A description of spoken Pittsburghese—what people do when they try to sound like Pittsburghers in performances—would encompass only the kinds of things Josh does when he is imitating the mayor.

Performing Pittsburghers on the *DVE Morning Show*

To explore in more depth what people can accomplish with performances of Pittsburghese, we turn now to two self-conscious broadcast performances of speech and social identity. We look at two comedy sketches performed by a team of radio DJs. Both sketches revolve around characters who talk in ways that can be taken to sound local, thus potentially enregistering features of their speech with Pittsburghese. But the characters' speech can be taken to index other things about them, too, including gender, class, profession, and personal identity. I ask whether dialect enregisterment works differently in these high performances than it does in other genres. How do the facts that the sketches are created and performed by professional actors, clearly framed as humorous performances, and broadcast via radio and Internet to a wide audience shape how the sketches draw on and create links between linguistic form and social meaning? To answer this question, I explore what social identity or identities are being evoked or created (and thus what kinds of enregisterment are being proposed) in each sketch and what linguistic forms can be said to be doing this semiotic work.

Performances such as these can mean different things to different hearers. In fact, they are designed to do this. Unlike the cultural artifacts I discussed in previous chapters, this kind of broadcast comedic performance creates multiple possibilities for the enregisterment of unexpected linguistic forms, so that different audience members may draw on different cultural schemata to make these forms meaningful. By linking locally occurring forms to multiple models of speech, behavior, and action, performances like these can act as a centrifugal force. In other words, these performances expand the set of potential meanings of particular language forms. The skits we will examine link language forms with new or additional ways of speaking, and they superimpose different cultural schemata that can be indexed by the same forms. They thus counteract the focusing, centripetal force of enregisterment activities, like many of the ones we explored earlier, that standardize Pittsburghese by limiting the number of forms enregistered with it and reducing the range of their meanings. The construction of humorous personae like the ones in the skits can enregister particular linguistic forms in multiple overlapping ways, some linked to place and some not, sometimes aligning different cultural schemata with one another but sometimes juxtaposing conflicting schemata. Broadcast humor like this must appeal to a wide audience; it has to be funny in different ways to different people.

The material we look at consists of two comedy skits performed by the cast of WDVE radio's *DVE Morning Show*. WDVE's programming is geared particularly to young and middle-aged men. The station is the radio broadcaster for the Pittsburgh Steelers games and was the long-time source of the distinctive and beloved voice of play-by-play announcer Myron Cope. The music is rock from the 1970s, 1980s, and 1990s. The station's website offers links to slide shows that include "Wind Blown Skirts," "Sexy World Cup Fans," and "Busty Boxing Babes," as well as photos of cheerleaders and attractive young female station "crew members" at the most recent Pittsburgh Steelers game. The *Morning Show* airs during commuting hours, 6:00 a.m. to 9:00 a.m. On the show, music, news, and traffic and weather reports are interspersed with skits performed by Jim Krenn, Randy Baumann, and other station crew members and guests. The skits are typically two to three minutes long.

The skits I analyze here were reproduced on a CD released around 2000 (it is undated) that was sold in local record stores to raise money for charity. They were originally performed on the *Morning Show*. One, called "Mother," is (or can at least be heard as) a parody of a song by the same name by Pink Floyd. The other is a "Commentary" performed by Jim Krenn, the *Morning Show*'s star DJ, playing the fictional WDVE station manager Stanley P. Kachowski.

MOTHER

This skit was performed by Randy Baumann, singing and playing the guitar, and Cris Winter (a female member of the *Morning Show* crew), who played the Mother character. I focus on Winter's performance here, though the lyrics sung by Baumann are included in the transcription. Many regular listeners will hear the song as a take-off on a song of the same name by Pink Floyd, released on the album called *The Wall*. The lyrics of the song are based loosely on those of the Pink Floyd song, and the choruses are the same as the Pink Floyd ones. *The Wall* is a collection of dark-toned songs performed in the character of a disillusioned overdosing rock star who wants to wall himself off from the world; the original "Mother" depicts a bleak back-to-the-womb fantasy. In the skit, lines of the now parodically sentimental song about the singer's mother alternate with spoken-word illustrations by a Mother character voiced by a female member of the show's crew. The parody invites *Morning Show* listeners to recognize the skit as a take-off on the Pink Floyd song, although not all actually do, and people who do not get the Pink Floyd connection can still enjoy the skit. A great deal of the potential humor of the skit has to do with the mismatch between the sentimental-sounding song lyrics and the persona of the Mother character who illustrates them, and noticing this does not depend on knowing the original song.

In my analysis of the skit, I explore the potential social meanings of the linguistic choices Cris Winter makes as she voices the Mother character. Of the many possibilities, I will focus on three: Winter could be said to use linguistic variation to sound like a mother, to sound working class, and/or to sound local. I use the following typographic conventions to highlight the sets of features I will discuss in what follows: elements of the performance that might index a mother's style are underlined, elements that might index a working-class persona are italicized, and elements that might index a Pittsburgh identity are in boldface. Phonetic features that could be semiotically associated with Pittsburgh are also transcribed phonetically. (I have not tried to highlight every feature that could conceivably be taken as an index of one or another of these three styles, only the ones I will discuss.) Some features can index more than one social identity. The phonetic features I will be discussing are as follows:

Monophthongal /aw/, so that *slouch* can be pronounced [slaːtʃ] ("slahch")
Fronted /o/, so that *over* can be pronounced [oˢvər] ("ewver")
Lowered, rounded low back vowel /a/, so that *soccer* can be pronounced [sɔkər] ("saughker")
Vocalized /l/, so that *old* can be pronounced [oʷd] ("owd")
Deletion of /ð/, so that *that* can be pronounced as [æt] ("'at")
Alveolar-*ing*, so that *smoking* can be pronounced as [smoˢkɪn] (smewkin')
Elided pronunciations of *going to* [ɡʌnə], *have to* [hæftə], *let me* [lɛmi] ("gonna," "hafta," "lemme," etc.)

8.6 "Mother"

1	RANDY BAUMANN (RB)	*Mother says I better sit up straight.*
	MOTHER (M)	You're *gonna* [ɡʌnə] get curvature of the spine like <u>your Uncle Lou</u> don't [don] **slouch [slaːtʃ]**!
2	RB	*Mother tells me not to make that face.*
	M	<u>If you keep *makin'* [mekɪn] **'at [æt]** face you're *gonna* [ɡʌnə] freeze like **'at [æt]**!</u>
3	RB	*Mother calls me out by all my brothers' names.*

M	Jim, Frank, Charlie, Gar-, whatever the hell your name is, get **over [oˤvr]** here!
4 RB	*Oooh ahh, mother drives to all the games.*
M	*Git [gɪt]* your ass in the car I *haveta [hæætə]* pick up your sister at **soccer [sɔkər]** after I **drop [drɔp]** you **off [ɔf]** at **karate [kərɔdi]**!
5 RB	*Mother told me to eat all I took.*
M	<u>There's kids starvin' in Africa *that'll love [ðæDllʌv] them* Brussels sprouts [sprawts]!</u> Ain't **yinz** paid no *[no]* attention to that Sally Struthers[3] commercial?
6 RB	*Mother made it clear she wasn't my cook.*
M	**Ohh [o:ˤ]**, you don't *[dõ]* like Brussels sprouts [sprawts]? Well feel free to order **off [ɔf]** the menu! We have Like It, or Lump It.[4]
7 RB	*Mother always spit on tissues to clean my face.*
M	Come here, your face is filthy. *Lemme [lɛmi]* get that crud **off [ɔf]** it!
8 RB	*Ooooh ahh Mama hates a messy place.*
M	What the hell happened in here? What if *company [kʌmpni]* comes over [ovr]?
9 RB	*Hush , now baby, baby, don't you cry.*
M	If you're *gonna [gʌnə]* cry, I'm *gonna [gʌnə]* give *ya [yə]* something to cry about [abawt].
10 RB	*Mama's gonna be your alarm clock for you.*
M	*Git [gɪt] outta [aDə]* bed!
11 RB	*Mama will be your doctor too.*
M	Put Vick's[5] **on [ɔn]** your chest!
12 RB	*Mama's gonna wait up until you get in.* *Mama will always find out where you've been.*
M	Were you down [dawn] **at'ta [ætə]** park *drinkin'[drɪŋkɪn]* Boone's Farm?[6]
13 RB	*Mama's gonna make sure your underwear's clean.*
M	So [so] help me, if you get in an accident *and [n̩]* you **got [gɔt]** skid marks in your underwear I'm *gonna [gʌnə]* die.
14 RB	*Ooooh, babe, ooooh, babe, oh babe, you'll always be baby to me.*

M	<u>No matter how **old [oᵂd]** you get you'll still be my baby</u>, and you're **not [nɔt]** too **old [oᵂd]** for a *lickin' [lɪkɪn]*!
15 RB	*Mother caught me out back getting . . . high.*
M	Were **you'unz** behind the garage **smokin' [smoˆkɪn] pot [pɔt]**?

The Mother identity is clearest on the level of topic and word choice. The sung part of the skit sets the character up as a mother, depicting her doing things mothers do. She tells her children to sit up straight, chauffeurs them around, spits on tissues to clean their faces, and occasionally gets their names wrong in the heat of the moment. Among the many things the mother character does that could be taken to index that she is speaking as a mother, she uses the kin terms *your uncle* (line 1) and *my baby* (14); reuses formulas that many listeners would associate with a stereotypical mother ("If you keep making that face you're going to freeze like that"; "There are kids starving in [part of the world] that would love that [food item child isn't eating]"); and adopts sing-songy intonation in "No matter how old you get you'll still be my baby" (14). The Mother character is both typical and atypical: her behavior departs sometimes from the sentimental cultural schema of good motherhood with which her audience is familiar (and which is evoked in the lyrics) and teeters on the brink of the cultural schema of the bad mother, who shouts, curses, and threatens to hit. Yet she reminds some listeners of their mothers and others of themselves as mothers, sometimes because they too act in some of these ways but would not publicize the fact.

It would be hard to imagine anyone understanding or appreciating this skit without noticing at least some of the ways in which the social identity of the mother is played with. But there are a number of possible ways of hearing where this mother is located in class and space. For one thing, she could be a working-class mother. Linguistic variants that sound working class to at least some Americans include voice quality (low pitch, relatively monotone intonation), grammatical features such as multiple negation ("Ain't yinz paid no attention"), *git* [gɪt] for *get*, the alveolar ("in'") variant of *'ing* (mak[ɪn] in line 2, starv[ɪn] in 5, drink[ɪn] in 12, lick[ɪn] in 14, and smok[ɪn] in 15), and elision associated with fast, casual speech (*gonna* [gʌnə], *haveta* [hætə], *that'll love* [ðæDllʌv], *lemme* [lɛmi] 'let me', *comp'ny* [kʌmpni]) 'company'. Likewise, the deletion and stopping of interdentals (*that* [æt], *the* [ə], *them* [dɛm], and so on) is in its distribution both working class and local and can be heard either way. References to class- and gender-linked practices like drinking Boone's Farm might also encourage a hearing of the character that evoked working-class speech style and, possibly, enregistered some of these features with it.

For another thing, this mother could sound like she is from the Pittsburgh area. Winter makes a gesture toward this reading of her character's identity at the very beginning. In the (stressed) last word of the first line she pronounces *slouch* with monophthongal /aw/, as [slaːtʃ]. Winter does not monophthongize /aw/ in every possible environment in the skit, so that, to someone who can hear this variant as different from the standard variant, it may stand out perceptually when she does. Of five opportunities to monophthongize /aw/, Winter does so only once. Interestingly, she does *not* monophthongize the /aw/ in *Brussels sprouts*, thus failing to take advantage of another phrase-final, stressed, "phono-opportunity," to use Nik Coupland's apt term (Coupland 1985), to display the feature. This inconsistency could be taken to index the fact that Winter does not monophthongize /aw/ in her "real" (unselfconscious, everyday) persona.

Another widely recognized index of a Pittsburgh identity, as we have repeatedly seen, is to use *yinz* or *you'unz*, rather than *you*, as the second-person plural personal pronoun. Winter does this twice. Another feature of the performance that could sound local, at least to some listeners, is the fronting of /o/. Like monophthongal /aw/, this feature is variable in Winter's performance. Of ten opportunities to front /o/, Winter does so four times, all in particularly audible places where the fronting is likely to stand out: "Get over [oˤvɹ̩] here!" in line 4, "Ohhh [oːˤ], you don't like Brussels sprouts?" in line 6, "No matter how old [oˤʷd] you get" in line 14, and "Were you'unz . . . smokin' [smoˤkɪn] pot?" in line 16. Vocalization of /l/, a feature of local speech that outsiders often notice, occurs only twice in Winter's performance, both times in the same word—*old* [oʷd], in "no matter how old you get," line 14.

Line 8 includes the words *soccer* and *karate* in stressed, phrase-final and in one case line-final position. Winter pronounces both with the rounded low back vowel, [ɔ], that linguists identify as characteristic of the Pittsburgh area. To an outsider's ear it may sound as if soccer and karate had been chosen, rather than other activities mothers could drive children to, precisely because they provide opportunities to showcase this vowel ("saughker," "karaughte"). However, Pittsburghers do not notice this feature of local speech, since it is the result of a merger and thus sounds the same to them as the other, more widespread variant of this vowel in North America. So local listeners could not, for the most part, hear this as an index of local identity. Winter pronounces the merged low back vowel this way invariably, throughout the skit, which suggests that it may not be part of the performance from her point of view, either. Still, it is hearable to a non-Pittsburgher as evoking a Pittsburgh identity.

To sum up, Winter's character is likely to be taken as a mother by any listener. This means that aspects of the way Winter talks evoke and create one or more cultural schemas of motherhood. The linguistic forms she uses may already be enregistered as indexes of one or another of these schemas for a given listener. For another listener, the performance may enregister them. For most listeners, what happens is probably a mix of the two processes: they hear certain forms as familiar indices of models of motherhood, while other forms become associated with motherhood for the first time. Additionally, some listeners may take the Mother character to be a Pittsburgher. Some may take her to be working class. Some may hear Cris Winter in her public persona as Cris Winter the DJ, in addition to hearing the character she creates in this skit.

The fact that the mother voice alternates with lines of a song highlights the contrast between the voice (or voices) represented in the song and the voice (or voices) represented in the spoken lines. This juxtaposition also contributes to the enregistration process by which features of the mother's speech become linked with social identities. But this does not work the same way for every listener. Some may hear the skit as a comment on the Pink Floyd song, so that the mother schema evoked in the original song becomes overlaid with the ones evoked in the parody. For some, the performance may overlay a mother schema on a Pittsburgher schema, so that the song is about what a Pittsburgh mother is like. Or the song could be interpreted as a depiction of a working-class mother, or as a comment on all mothers, or as a parody of one's own mother. In other words, the language of the performance, on all levels, can potentially be or become enregistered with multiple cultural schemata. Likewise, multiple listenings (for people who own the CD or download the song) can enregister the same forms in different ways for the same listener.

STANLEY P. KACHOWSKI/JIM KRENN

The skit called "Stanley P. Kachowski and Gore" instantiates a subgenre of *Morning Show* skits that is familiar to regular listeners: Jim Krenn's Stanley P. Kachowski character makes regular appearances on the show. Stanley P. Kachowski is presented as the "station manager" of WDVE. Although he is sometimes represented as barging in on the DJs in the studio, at other times he performs monologues which are framed as prerecorded editorial commentary about current events. The one under consideration here is of this sort. This skit was originally broadcast during the 2000 US presidential campaign, when then Vice President Albert Gore was running against George W. Bush to replace Bill Clinton as president, with Senator Joseph Lieberman as Gore's running mate. It takes off from a recent visit to Pittsburgh by presidential candidate Gore and vice presidential candidate Lieberman. The monologue revolves in part around a pun on "Tipper," Gore's wife's name.

There are at least three kinds of enregisterment that could be going on in the turns produced by Jim Krenn, who plays the Stanley P. Kachowski character. First, Krenn could be heard as representing Kachowski as having a Pittsburgh accent. Second, Krenn could be heard as representing Kachowski as having a stereotypical working-class, male lifestyle. Third, Krenn could be heard as representing himself as himself, in a performance of his own public persona consistent with audiences' expectations. All three of these activities involve the use of nonstandard speech forms that reinforce the content of the skit. Randy Baumann plays the role of the announcer, who introduces and concludes the monologue. Baumann also breaks away from this role and into his public persona as Randy Baumann, on occasion.

I use the following typographic conventions to highlight the sets of features I will discuss in what follows: In Baumann's lines, elements of the performance that might index formality are underlined. In Krenn's lines, elements of the performance that might index a working-class male style are italicized and elements that might index a Pittsburgh identity are in bold-face. As with the Winter skit, phonetic features I discuss are also transcribed phonetically. Again, I have not tried to highlight every feature that could conceivably be taken as an index of one or another of these three styles, only the ones I will discuss. The phonetic features to be discussed are as follows:

Lowering of /ɛ/, so that *commentary* can be pronounced [kaməntɛˇri] ("commentehry")

Monophthongal /aw/, so that *Kachowski* can be pronounced [kətʃaːski] ("Kachahski")

Fronted /o/, so that *know* can be pronounced [noˍw] ("kneu")

Fronted /u/, so that *boom* can be pronounced [buˍm] ("bium")

Lowering of /ʌ/, so that *stuff* can be pronounced [stʌˇf] ("stuhff")

Lowered, rounded low back vowel /a/, so that *not* can be pronounced [nɔt] ("naught")

Vocalized /l/, so that *politics* can be pronounced [pɔʷɪtɪks] ("powitics")

Deletion or stopping of /ð/, so that *that* can be pronounced as [æt] ("at") or *those* as [doˍz] ("doz")

Alveolar *–ing*, so that *partying* can be pronounced as [pɔrdiyɪn] ("partyin'")

Elided pronunciations of *got to* [gɔDə] ("gotta"), *on the* [ɔnə] ("ona"), *want to* [wanə] ("wanna," etc.)

8.7 *Stanley P. Kachowski and Al Gore*

1	ANNOUNCER (A)	And now with a <u>commentary [kaməntɛˇri]</u>, please welcome <u>General Manager of WDVE, Mr.</u> Stanley P. Kachowski [kətʃawski].
2	STANLEY P. KA-CHOWSKI (SPK)	Hey, *Stanley P.* **Kachowski [kətʃaːski]** , P is for **politics [pɔʷɪtɪks]**, you **know [noˍ]** Gore is in **town [taːn]**, what a go—, oh what a great time we had, I *gotta [gɔDə]* tell *ya [yə]*. I'm **not [nɔt]** really **political [pɔʷɪtɪkʊʷ]** or anything like *that [æt]*, you **know [noˍ]**, it's just that you **know [noˍ]** we were *partyin' [pɔrdiyɪn]*, they're, everybody's *sayin' [seɪn]* how, you **know [noˍ]**, he's boring and **stuff [stʌˇf]**, *this guy ain't boring*, he's crazy! Hey I'm *tellin' [tɛlɪn]* y-, Randy, he's a **wild [waˍd]** man! He's a **wild [waˍd]**—
3	A	Well that goes s- against his image, <u>I would say, Stan</u>—
4	SPK	Did you see *on the [ɔnə]* news they sai—who endo—who endorsed *them [əm]*, Franco Harris[7], did you see that?

5	A	No.

6 SPK   Yeah, Franco [fræŋko] Harris **come [kʌˇm] out [aːt]** 'n [n̩] endorsed *them [əm]*. And he's **wild [waʷd]**, they didn't have it *on the [ɔnə]* news but then Van Morrison[8] came **out [aːt]** on the other side and endorsed *them [əm]* and did you see "He inhales! He inhales!"[9]

7 A/RANDY BAU-   ((laughs))
   MANN (RB)

8 SPK   You **know[noˤ]** and Gore's just throwing **[θroˤwɪn]** his arms up in *the [ɪni]* air, and **stuff [stʌˇf]**. So we **go [goˤ] down [daːn]** *there's [ərz]* me, *there's [ərz]* Gore, *there's [ərz]* Lieberman, right and you **know [noˤ]** what we do we **hop [hɔp]** in my pea-green Vega, you **know [noˤ]**,

9 A/RB   The three of you?

10 SPK   *'cause [kʌˇz] we want to [wanə] be inconspicuous [ɪnkənspɪkiəs].* So, **don't [dõˤ]** worry, **don't [dõˤ˺ ʺ]** worry, I have my my **Foster [fɔstɽ]** Grants **on [ɔn]**, my my sunglasses, just to give that, you **know [noˤ]**, little look of the,

11 A/RB   Secret Service[10]

12 SPK   Secret Service, *kind of [kajnə]* look, you **know [noˤ]**, and, uh, the cookie sheets[11] *that [ət]* that I have, riveted *on the [ɔnæ]* you **know [noˤ]**, fender areas of my pea-green Vega to pass

13 A/RB   ((laughs))

14 SPK   inspection *for [fɽ]* emissions test,[12] pretty sure ***those are [doˤzɽ]* bullet [bʊʷət]**-proof. But anyway, so we're driving, we go **down [daːn] Club [klʌˇb]** Elite,[13] OK, we **go [goˤ]** in there, and and Gore looks at me and says "Stanley, your **money's [mʌˇniz] no [noˤ]** good in **Club [klʌˇb]** Elite, *'cause [kəz]* I'm like *getting [gɛDɪn]* all *kind of [kaynə]* cash from people for this campaign thing, I'll just write it into one of those campaign fundraisers **accou—[akã̃ː]**."[14] "Oh [o], OK." It's (Terry Weigel's?)[15] last night, you **know [noˤ]**, so (I'm like) "Whoo, let's **go [goˤ]** in!" So he, th—an—, and Gore, let me tell you *something [sʌˇmm̩]*, he saw all (Terry Weigel's) **movies [muˤviz]**, too, by *the [də]* way, Inferno [ɪnfərno] being his favorite.

15 A   Big fan.

16 SPK

Big fan. So anyway we **go [goˁ]** in *there [ɛr]* and we're, you **know [noˁ]** Albert gets us some great seats and we're sitting *there [ɛr]* and next thing you **know [noˁ]**, Terry Weigel **comes [kʌˇmz] over [oˇvɹ̩]** *to [də]* Gore, you **know [noˁ]**, and he **goes [goˁz]**, "Hey, I may be *running [rʌnɪn]* for president but I but right now I'm already *vice* president."[16] You **know [noˁ]**, so next thing you **know [noˁ]**, he's *getting [gɛʔn̩]* a lap dance. They're *screaming [skrɪmɪn]*, **crowd's [kraːdz]** *screaming [skrɪmɪn]*, all of a **sudden [sʌˇdn̩]** you **know [noˁ]**, they're getting in—the **crowd's [kraːdz]** even *getting [gɛʔn̩]* into it (watching this), they're *yelling [yɛlɪn]* "[tɪpɹ̩, tɪpɹ̩, tɪpɹ̩]!" *And then [ənɛn]* he **pulls [puʷz] out [aːt]** twenty **dollars [dɔʷərz]**, you know [no] he s—, he just sticks it *in the [mə]* g-string, and *screaming [skrɪmɪn]* "[tɪpɹ̩]!" he gets another twenty ou—ti—'tip—' puts it in right *in there [mɛr]*, (they) yell "[tɪpɹ̩]!" you know [no] the whole crowd [krawd] (and) "Tipper Gore's *in the [mə]* doorway!"

17 A/RB

((laughs))

18 SPK/JIM
    KRENN (JK)

"She's *in the [mə]* doorway!" ((A/RB laughing)) The **crowd [kraːd]** was *trying [traym]* to help him **out [aːt]**! ((A/RB laughing)) **You'unz** should have *[ʃʊdə]* seen the look **on [ɔn]** his face! Oh [o], my good—, he **jumped [dʒʌˇmpt] up [ʌˇp]**, he just **[dʒʌˇst]** went, ((A/RB laughing)) she grabbed him by *the [di]* ear and just twisted it and **boom [buˁm]**, he was just [dʒɪst], he was **gone [gɔn]**. *Me and [miːn]* Lieberman just [dʒɪst] looked at each other, we went **down to [daːnə]** Primanti's **got [gɔt]** a kosher capicola *[kæpəkolə] and [n̩]* cheese *and [n̩]*, you know [no], just [dʒɪst] **polished [pɔʷɪʃt]** *that [æt]* **off [ɔf]**, *and that [næt]* was the end *of the [ədə]* night, we just [dʒɪst], we couldn't help but laugh though. He'll recover, **don't [dõˁ]** worry. I don't [dõ] know [no] who I'm *voting [votɪn]* for yet, but I tell *you [jə]* what, ((A/RB laughing)) I'll vote [vot] for him for partier *of the [ədə]* year. This is Stanley P. **Kachowski [kətʃaːski]**, *reminding [rimaynɪn]* you [yu], tipping is good (?) ((SPK/JK laughing))

19 A/RB

For a written transcript of <u>Mr. Kachowski's [kətʃawskiz]</u> statements, send a self-abused, stomped antelope to WDVE, <u>Pittsburgh [pʰɪtsbök]</u>.

The skit begins with a phrase of classical music reminiscent of the Elgar "Pomp and Circumstance," which is familiar to many Americans as the music played at graduation ceremonies, and with the voice of an announcer played by Randy Baumann, who sets a formal scene by saying, "And now with a commentary, please welcome General Manager of WDVE, Mr. Stanley P. Kachowski." The music continues to repeat throughout the performance. Baumann's use of Kachowski's full title and the honorific "Mr." enhances the scene setting, as do the announcer's low-pitched, relatively monotone, evenly spaced voice and the lowered /ɛ/ he produces in *commentary* [kamɑntɛᵛri], which can be heard as an attempt to pronounce the word the way it is spelled or to sound vaguely British. What follows would constitute a complete violation of the expectations set up by the introductory framing, if much of the audience did not actually expect something like it.

To represent Kachowski as speaking with a Pittsburgh accent, Krenn voices him in such an accent, drawing on stereotyped links between a subset of locally hearable nonstandard phonological features and local identity. As mentioned, one of these is the monophthongization of /aw/. The name Kachowski (which Krenn, of course, chose for his character) is itself a phono-opportunity for the production of this variant, with /aw/ in its stressed syllable. Krenn has Kachowski start by saying the name, monophthongizing the /aw/: [kɑtʃaːski]. Also close to the beginning of the skit is the word *town*, which is a stereotypical environment for /aw/-monophthongization when it occurs in the word *downtown* ([daːntaːn]) (Johnstone, Bhasin, and Wittkofski 2002). Unlike Winter, however, Krenn is consistent having Kachowski monophthongize /aw/: of fifteen occurrences of /aw/ in Kachowski/Krenn's speech in the skit, thirteen are monophthongal, one is partly monophthongized, and only one is diphthongal. Like the Mother character, the Kachowski character employs other features that can be associated with Pittsburgh speech, by insiders and/or by outsiders: *you'unz*, fronted /o/, a rounded low back vowel, and vocalized /l/. Like Winter, Krenn produces the rounded variant of the low back vowel invariantly. His /o/-fronting is, however, much more consistent than Winter's. As noted above, Winter's Mother character fronts /o/ only in particularly audible words, and less than half the time, whereas Krenn's Kachowski fronts /o/ in twenty-nine out of forty possible cases, or almost three-fourths of the time. In Krenn's skit, it is the *non*-fronting of /o/ that is unusual. Nonfronted /o/ occurs in unstressed syllables of proper names (*Franco*, lines 4 and 6, and *Inferno*, line 14), in "Oh, okay," (line 14) where he is quoting his character, in particularly fast speech (two instances of *you know* at the punch line of the "tip her/Tipper" joke, line 16), and in the word *capicola*, line 18. Krenn stops fronting /o/ at the end of the skit, in line 18, where *you know*, *don't know* (twice), and *vote* all have nonfronted /o/. At this point Krenn is arguably moving out of the Kachowski persona and into the Jim Krenn the DJ persona. Additionally, Krenn almost invariably lowers /ʌ/ in words like *stuff*, *just*, and *something*, and he sometimes fronts /u/. Neither of these features of Pittsburgh speech is part of Winter's performance.

"Stanley P. Kachowski," a stereotypical Polish-immigrant name, evokes a working-class persona. Features of Krenn's speech that might point to his character's being working class include some of the same features we saw in Winter's performance of the Mother: elision (*gonna* [gʌnə], *on the* [ɔnə], *of the* [əjə]), alveolar *-ing*, and deleted or stopped interdentals. Nonstandard syntax can also be enregistered with a working-class male schema: nonstandard negation in "this guy **ain't** boring," a nonstandard preterit form in "Franco Harris **come** out and endorsed them." Krenn can also rely on the content of the skit: "partying" at a strip club, being "wild," going to Primanti's (a popular sandwich shop) for a late-night meal. In line 10 of the skit, Krenn has Kachowski pronounce *inconspicuous* in a slow, somewhat labored, hypercorrect way, [ɪnkənspɪkiəs] ("inconspickious"), that suggests that the word is not part of Kachowski's everyday lexicon.

Representing Kachowski as driving "a pea-green Vega" is a succinct way for Krenn to invite the inference that the Kachowski character is later-middle aged and from working-class roots. Chevrolet Vegas were produced in the 1970s; they were inexpensive and sporty looking and appealed to young men of limited means, like the working-class generation that came of age in 1970s Pittsburgh, when steelmaking jobs were quickly disappearing. They were also unreliable, it turned out, now considered candidates for "the worst Detroit car ever" (Newman 2008), and the pea-green color soon looked dated. Someone driving such a car (not to mention imagining that baking sheets are bulletproof) is represented as hapless to listeners who get the reference. This sort of haplessness goes along with the Yinzer persona with which Krenn can be taken as playing. The reference to "kosher capicola and cheese" sandwiches can be heard as another such tightly packed, multivoiced indexical, simultaneously pointing to the facts that Joseph Lieberman (an observant Jew) eats only kosher food, that a sandwich combining cheese and meat could not be kosher, that the real Jim Krenn knows these things, and that the fictional Stanley Kachowski is oblivious to them.

Performances of fictional personas are inevitably superimposed (Goffman 1986, 156–157 uses the apt term "laminated") on the actors' performances of their own public personae. As Bakhtin (1981) showed, performances are always "double-voiced" in that the voice of the performer is always intertwined with the voices of the characters being performed. It is clear in the data at hand, both from the ethnographic evidence and from linguistic details, that the public persona of Jim Krenn the WDVE DJ is hearable to many people who listen to Stanley P. Kachowski skits. For one thing, it is hearable to some listeners that Jim Krenn, unlike Cris Winter, has a Pittsburgh accent. Although they both draw on the same repertoire of features that can be heard as voicing Pittsburgh-sounding personas in their performances, Krenn is, as we have seen, much more consistent in using these features throughout the performance than Winter is. While Winter performs Pittsburgh speech by selectively (and inconsistently) deploying particularly salient features of the dialect like monophthongal /aw/, fronted /o/, and *you'unz*, Krenn's performance includes both salient features of local speech and ones that are not. In addition, Krenn's speech is characterized by a phonological variant that Winter does not use. Krenn's /ʌ/, in words like *stuff, come, club,* and *something,* is almost invariably lowered. This means that Krenn's speech, unlike Winter's, displays both elements of the Pittsburgh chain shift described by Labov et al. (2005). Although lowered /ʌ/ is never commented on or self-consciously worked into performances of local speech, listeners who are familiar with the gestalt that is a Pittsburgh accent and who have heard Krenn in situations in which he is not performing Stanley P. Kachowski may in fact know that he always sounds like a Pittsburgher, even if his performance is not as exaggerated as in the Kachowski role. People who know about him (which is fairly likely in the case of fellow Pittsburghers, since Krenn has often been profiled in the press) know that he grew up in a working-class family in an old, working-class, inner-city neighborhood. Thus, it is very likely that at least some listeners will hear not just a fictional character but Jim Krenn the radio DJ as well.

In fact, some of the potential for humor in the *DVE Morning Show* skits has to do with the fact that the parodic double-voicing calls attention to itself. In general, the fact that Krenn, Baumann, and their colleagues are local celebrities means that local listeners are likely to know who is doing the performances on the show and what to expect in the performances. This means that the fact that there are authorial voices behind the characters' voices is harder to overlook than it is in the routine double-voicings of everyday conversation. In particular, the skits often play with the fact that laminations of personas projected as "real" and personas projected as "fictional" can come unstuck, so that the performer slips between the voice of his character and a voice that can be heard as his or her own. In the Stanley P. Kachowski skit, this is heard to occur in the lines I have labeled with two sets of initials, those of the performer and those of his character. Lines 1–11 contrast Randy Baumann speaking in character as the announcer (A) with Randy Baumann speaking as Randy Baumann the DJ (RB).

In line 1, as noted, Baumann speaks in a formal style, pronouncing *commentary* with a stylized lowered vowel in the final syllable and adopting formal diction. In line 2, Kachowski addresses the announcer as Randy ("I'm telling y—, Randy, he's a wild man!"). The fictional announcer could be fictionalized Randy Baumann doing part of his DJ job, or Jim Krenn could be slipping out of the Kachowski character to address Baumann the way he would if Krenn were not in character as Kachowski. Baumann treats this turn as having been spoken in character, though, and, in line 3, Baumann responds in character as the announcer, addressing Kachowski ("Stan," or possibly a cut-off "Stanley"), not

Krenn (who would be "Jimmy"), and sticking to the careful diction ("I would say") of the announcer character.

In line 7, however, Baumann responds to the Kachowski turn of line 6 by laughing, something the announcer would not do. Here, in other words, Baumann has come unstuck from the announcer, slipping out of an announcer persona and into a Baumann persona. He does likewise in his subsequent two turns, interjecting a request for clarification in line 9 and adopting a more casual tone than the announcer's (you as [yə]), and interjecting to assist Krenn in his improvisation by suggesting a phrase, "secret service," in line 11.

At the end of the skit, however, the Randy-the-DJ persona and the announcer persona become completely intertwined. Baumann speaks in the announcer's formal diction, referring to the other speaker as "Mr. Kachowski," pronouncing the article *a* as [ɛi] rather than [ə], and pronouncing *Pittsburgh* as [pʰɪtsbök], vocalizing the /r/ in such a way as to suggest formal British speech to many Americans. He voices a formula that was once often heard at the end of commentaries of the sort being played on here: "For a written transcript . . . send a self-addressed, stamped envelope." But his play on the words of this formula ("a self-abused, stomped antelope") evokes the Randy Baumann persona, the persona of the comic DJ. Krenn stays in character as Kachowski throughout most of the skit. But in his final turn, he, too, can be said to break partly into Jim Krenn persona, no longer fronting /o/ and laughing because Kachowski's story is so funny.

Slippages like these can serve as cues to performance, reminders that something double-voice, reflexive, and artful is going on. They can also point to the improvisational quality of the performance, in that things can spontaneously become so funny that the actors "crack up," falling out of character. When they do, they fall into other characters, however—themselves as they present themselves on the *DVE Morning Show*, Jim Krenn and Randy Baumann the drive-time DJs.

To sum up, features of Krenn's and Baumann's speech, like the features of Winter's speech discussed previously, can be heard in multiple ways, or, to put it another way, enregistered according to multiple cultural schemata. A feature that evokes (and helps construct) a Pittsburgh persona may also evoke (and help construct) a working-class persona, or it may evoke both, thus serving to overlay and align Pittsburgh and working-class identities. The same feature, or the distribution of the feature across the skit, may also enregister the feature with the Jim Krenn persona, reminding listeners (or creating the impression) that Krenn is a working-class Pittsburgher. Alternatively, a person could hear this skit and find it funny because of the joke about Al and Tipper Gore, oblivious to how the skit plays on characterological stereotypes. And there are many other references, overt and covert, to identities and events that may be juxtaposed in new ways, for some listeners.

Performance, Pittsburgh Speech, and Pittsburghese

In chapter 1, I argued that Pittsburgh speech, as a linguist would describe it, is not the same as Pittsburghese. Pittsburgh speech is how people from Pittsburgh talk. Pittsburghese is how people (in Pittsburgh and elsewhere) think Pittsburghers talk. The words and phrases that people talk about when they argue about Pittsburghese or tell stories about Pittsburghese are drawn from a set of words and phrases that represents this set of ideas about how Pittsburghers talk. So are the words and phrases on T-shirts and the ones uttered by Chipped Ham Sam and Nebby Debbie. Pittsburghese is stylized Pittsburgh speech.

In this chapter, I examined several oral performances of Pittsburghese. If people imitating Pittsburghers sounded exactly like people with Pittsburgh accents, there would be no particular reason to be interested in performances of Pittsburghese. However, as we have seen, stylizations of others' speech are not reproductions of others' speech styles. Dave's stylization of the Texan at the racetrack misses the target in more ways than not, if the target is how Texans actually speak. But stylizations do not need to be reproductions. If an American can evoke the stereotype of a pompous British person simply by pronouncing *bath* as "bahth" and dropping a few r's, there is no need to adopt a real British accent. Furthermore, at least in most cases, stylizations could not be reproductions. Learning to speak perfectly in a foreign language or accent is something that only young children and, perhaps, some trained actors can do. Contrasting Dennis's unselfconscious Pittsburgh accent with Josh's performance of a stereotypical Pittsburgher reminds us how different Pittsburgh speech can be from Pittsburghese.

Oral performances like these highlight the creative potential of performances of Pittsburghese. Whereas conversations about speech, dialect dictionaries, T-shirts, and the like tend to narrow and standardize the list of things that count as instances of Pittsburghese, oral performances, and the *Morning Show* skits in particular, tend to open up new possibilities for the enregisterment of locally hearable linguistic forms. The defining feature of linguistic performance is that it calls attention to itself, putting on display not only what the message means but also how. Performers ask not just, "What does it mean that I am saying these words?" but also "What does it mean that I am saying these words *this way*?"

In the case of the *DVE Morning Show* skits, audiences are implicitly asked to reflect on what it could mean that a mother character has a Pittsburgh accent, what it could mean that she also sounds working class, and how good mothers and bad mothers are related; why the station manager would sound like a working-class man, why an announcer would try to sound British, and what it says about Jim Krenn that he sounds the way he does. Not all audience members are asked the same questions—if one cannot hear a rounded low back vowel, then this feature could not mean anything—and no one is given answers. Thus, the skits act as a centrifugal force, mixing characters and voices up in new ways and opening up new possibilities for the social meaning of familiar forms. The use of nonstandard or otherwise unexpected forms in performances can reinforce existing form-meaning links, call existing links into question, or create new links, and which combination of these possibilities actually occurs depends on who is listening.

9

The History of *Yinz* and the Outlook for Pittsburghese

The second-person plural pronoun *yinz* has been a semiotic resource in Pittsburgh ever since colonial-era Scotch-Irish immigrants brought it to the area. Its use then is still one of its uses now: in address to two or more people. In the course of the twentieth century and the beginning of the twenty-first, however, *yinz* has acquired new ways of meaning, such that it is now one of the most often cited examples of Pittsburghese, and one of the most visible icons of localness in Pittsburgh. *Yinz* appears on bumper stickers and T-shirts that say things like "Yinz are in Steeler Country." It is used as a graffiti tag (figure 9.1).

Yinz has become a productive morpheme. That is to say that *yinz* is now an element of meaning that can be used in new ways, as it is in words like *Yinzer*, *Yinz-burgh*, or *yinz play*. *Yinz* shows up when people want to claim they are Pittsburghers and when Pittsburghers address the world as Pittsburghers. It can show that someone is an insider. Some spectators at the 2012 Saint Patrick's Day parade in downtown Pittsburgh wore T-shirts that said "Yinz, I'm Irish" or "Irish, yinz?" These slogans point to the wearer's being a Pittsburgher—knowing the insider term to use with fellow Pittsburghers—as well as being "Irish"—an ethnic designation that is accurate for many Pittsburghers and playfully adopted by many others every April 17. The text on a T-shirt that was for sale for a time at the Andy Warhol Museum made the insider/outsider distinction transparent: "we say yinz/you say you all."

Yinz can also be used by outsiders to address Pittsburghers, as on a sign at a protest during the G-20 summit meeting that was held in Pittsburgh in 2008. The sign read "Yinz' live in a police state." The spelling "yinz'," with a final apostrophe, suggests that the sign writer was not from Pittsburgh, where the word is never spelled that way. Alternately, *yinz* can leave it ambiguous whether the addresser is a Pittsburgher or not. For example, a newspaper report on a set of podcasts about Pittsburgh speech was entitled "Yinz can learn about Pittsburghese online—Podcasts provide origins of the city's most colorful words" (Fleming 2008a). Whether or not the headline writer was a Pittsburgher, the

Figure 9.1 Yinz as a Graffiti Tag (Photograph by Barbara Johnstone)

use of *yinz* in the headline suggests that the podcasts will be of interest to Pittsburghers.

In the pages that follow, I trace the semiotic history of *yinz*, starting from when it was an unremarked feature of vernacular Pittsburgh speech, with no social resonance, and ending in 2012, when *yinz* could still be heard in Pittsburghers' unselfconscious vernacular speech but was also a key feature of Pittsburghese, talked about, performed, and otherwise deployed more than any other Pittsburghese word. Exploring the more strictly linguistic history of the word, I show how traces of its derivation have been erased as people have reanalyzed its internal structure and changed its spelling. This has meant that the range of grammatical roles this word can play has broadened. Using the model of meaning and meaning change I elaborated earlier in the book, I explore how *yinz* became enregistered with correctness, class, and localness, paying particular attention to the role of talk and material artifacts in this process. I then describe how this set of social meanings has been taken up into a new semiotic order, such that *yinz* can now index youthful urban hipness. In the process of laying out the multiple orders of meaning in which *yinz* now makes different kinds of sense to different people in Pittsburgh, I recapitulate some of the book's major themes.

Many languages have distinct pronouns that mean 'you' in the singular and 'you' in the plural (more than one 'you', in other words): French has *tu* (singular) and *vous* (plural), German has *du* (singular) and *ihr* (for famil-iars) or *Sie* (the more formal option) for plural, and so on. When English-speakers use pronouns to point to themselves or to people they are not talking to, we, too, use different forms to distinguish between singular and plural. In the first person, we use the singular *I* and the plural *we*; in the third person we use *he, she, it* (singular) and *they* (plural) However, due to a set of historical accidents, standard English has only one form, *you*, for referring to the person or people being addressed. *You* does double duty in standard Eng-lish as both the singular and the plural form. This leaves a gap in the English inventory of pronouns, and, at least in more casual speech, English-speakers often try to fill this gap.

The form that became *yinz* was first brought to America by Scotch-Irish im-migrants (Montgomery 2002; 2006). As we saw in chapter 3, these were mainly the descendants of Protestant people from Scotland and northern England who had been settled in northern Ireland beginning in 1610. During the nineteenth century, when many Irish speakers switched to speaking English, they found the gap in the English pronoun system problematic, because the Irish language has both a singular second person pronoun, *tu*, and a plural one, *sibh*. In response, these speakers coined a variety of English-based second-person plural forms, including *you all, yous, youns, yiz*, and *you ones*. Subsequent Irish speakers of English, as well as the Scotch-Irish who lived alongside them in northern Ireland, inherited these forms and brought them along when they emigrated. Beginning in the early eighteenth century, as we have seen, hundreds of thou-sands of people from northern Ireland migrated to America, and a second wave of emigration, mainly from Ireland's more southern counties, followed the potato blight that caused widespread famine in the 1840s and 1850s. *Y'all*, a contracted form of *you all*, is now used across the southern United States. Other forms are used in other places where Irish or Scotch-Irish people settled. The word now spelled "yinz" in Pittsburgh is a contracted form of *you ones*. *You ones* (often spelled "you'uns") is used not only in the Pitttsburgh area but also else-where in the Appalachian Mountains, where it often actually sounds more like [yuənz] ("you'unz").

A form of *you'uns* has thus been used in the Pittsburgh area since the early eighteenth century, and the word continues to be used elsewhere in Appalachia. However, most Pittsburghers think that *yinz* is unique to the Pittsburgh area. They are not aware that the word they think of as "yinz" is related to *you'uns*. *Yinz* has become disconnected from its linguistic history through three related pro-cesses. For one thing, the pronunciation of the form has changed, from [juənz] ("you'unz") to [jʊnz] ("yunz") to (for some speakers) [jɪnz] ("yinz"). This change is still in progress, and people argue about how the word should sound. Nowa-days, however, the argument is mainly between [jʊnz] and [jɪnz], as is suggested in this excerpt from an e-mail:

My wife and I lived in Pittsburgh from 1974–1977, and our son has lived there for the last eight years. I remember the word to be "yunz," but he claims that it's more properly "yinz." He cites another word, "yinzer," in defense of this. My argument is that the word was likely "you-uns," contracted to become "yunz." (Devlin Gualteri, e-mail to author, Jan. 21, 2011)

The writer notes (correctly) that the word started out as "you-uns" and remembers it being pronounced in a way that sounded closer to that, while his son thinks the "proper" pronunciation is "yinz." Another e-mail correspondent (Pete Peterson to author, Jan. 6, 2011) complained to me about "the misuse of 'yinz' [rather than 'yunz'] by those who want to talk the working-class lingo."

Gualteri's son's perspective reflects a second development in the linguistic history of *yinz*, namely that people now tend to understand *yinz* as a single unit of meaning rather than two. Jason E., the seventeen-year-old interviewee from whom we heard in chapter 4, said that he "didn't get" yinz, because "it's not a contraction"—in other words, not a shortened form of "any words": "I don't really even get [yɪnz]," said Jason, "'cause it doesn't make any sense, it's not a contraction, because it's not any words, 'yinz' is not a 'you'—." To put it in more technical terms, people like Jason E. have reanalyzed the morphology, or internal structure, of *yinz*, imagining it as monomorphemic (a single, indivisible unit of meaning) rather than bimorphemic (two units of meaning).

Finally, the spelling of the word has changed in ways that reflect these developments and at the same time help push them forward. Because *yinz* is nonstandard, it does not have an official, dictionary-approved spelling, and people have been free to write it various ways. The spelling of *yinz* is an easily sparked topic of discussion in Pittsburgh. Variants include <yunz,> <yins,> <you'uns,> and <youns> or <younz.> People tend to suppose that there is a correct spelling, but they are not sure what it is, and they explain the variability in the word's orthography (which can easily be observed) with reference to variability in its pronunciation; they imagine, in other words, that people must spell the word differently because they pronounce it differently.

The most frequent spelling is now <yinz.> A Google search conducted in April 2011 (figure 9.2), uncovered far more uses of <yinz> together with the word *Pittsburgh* than of <yunz,> <younz,> or <you'uns.> While earlier spellings, such as <you'uns> preserved traces of the history of the word (treating it as a contraction and spelling *you* the standard way), reading from right to left on the chart in figure 9.3 shows how the spellings have become more and more phonetic: more and more based on how the word sounds, not where it comes from. <Younz> preserves a trace of the fact that part of the word was once *you*, but spells the rest the way it sounds: <unz.> <Yunz> and <yinz> have lost this trace of history and are even more phonetic.

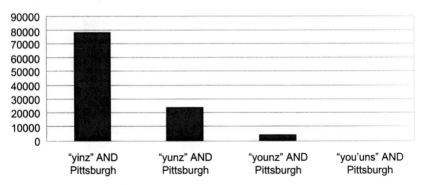

Figure 9.2 Spellings of *yinz* on the World Wide Web: Google Search April 12, 2011.

How has *yinz* come to mean so many things? For one, personal pronouns occur frequently in talking and writing, and they both reflect and reinforce distinctions among categories of people that can easily spark controversy. English personal pronouns have a history of becoming controversial because of social meanings with which they become enregistered. One example is the now un-fashionable "generic" use of *he* (as in "Each of the students opened **his** book"). In other contexts, *he* indexes biological maleness or cultural masculinity, and once the distinction between generic *he* and some other option (*he or she, s/he, they*) was enregistered with gender it came to sound as if it suggested that the typical or default person was male. The distinction between *I* and *we* can carry social meaning, too, as when individuals use *we* to refer to themselves—the "royal *we*" that caused a furor when used by not royal Prime Minister Margaret Thatcher after the birth of her son's first child ("**We** are a grandmother").

More specifically, though, the semiotic history of *yinz* tracks the semiotic history of Pittsburghese in general. In order for *yinz* to be associated with one way of talking as opposed to some other way of talking, Pittsburghers first had to become aware that not everybody uses *yinz*. As we saw in chapter 4, until around the middle of the twentieth century, Pittsburghers rarely noticed that they used a form that was different than anyone else's. We heard from Dottie X., born in the late 1920s, who said that as a child, she "never even heard" *yinz*, despite the fact that she and everyone around her used it in everyday speech.

To model how *yinz*, together with other features of Pittsburghese, moved from being an unremarked, unremarkable feature of Pittsburgh speech to being a meaningful choice that could express social meaning, I introduced the idea of enregisterment (Agha 2003; 2007a): the linking of a linguistic feature (a word, sound, or bit of grammar) with a social meaning (a persona, situation, or iden-tity). The social meanings of linguistic features are enregistered according to "ideological schemas"—in other words, local ideas about language and society and how the two are related.

For example, a very widespread ideological schema is that there are "better" and "worse" ways of talking. American children learn from caregivers and teachers that some words are "bad," that in some situations (if not all) you need to speak "properly," and that some ways of saying things "sound better" than others. In Pittsburgh, people who noticed that they sometimes heard *yinz* and sometimes *you* as the plural pronoun mapped this difference onto the idea that some ways of talking are better than others: *you* started to be heard as better, *yinz* as worse.

Yinz has also been enregistered with social class. It is thought of as a feature of working-class speech. This has happened partly through people's lived, everyday experience. The people in the next neighborhood, who all worked in the steel mill, might have sounded different from people in your neighborhood. This might have caused you to enregister the way the people in the other neighborhood talked with the fact that they were working class. Material artifacts like the Yappin' Yinzers also help enregister *yinz* with social class. Chipped Ham Sam says *yinz* often and looks like a stereotypical working-class Pittsburgher.

Yinz has also been enregistered with correctness, however, so that even people with working-class roots that they are proud of will deny that they use it. Jen and Donna, the mother and daughter we heard from in chapter 5, talked about *yinz*. The daughter claims that the neighbors say yinz "constantly." Her mother responds with, "We don't use that! . . . Your dad and I don't use that too often."

In addition to being semiotically linked with class and with incorrectness, *yinz* has also been linked with place, as perhaps the most iconic feature of Pittsburghese. Leaving a Giant Eagle grocery store in September 2007, I passed three employees on break. One of them used *yinz* in an unselfconscious way, in addressing the other two. Rather than responding to what she had actually said, another of the employees responded with, "Yinz. Yes, that's Pittsburgh." Other Pittsburghers agree. A blogger writing about the word claims that "any Steelers fan will tell you that 'yinz' is pure Pittsburghese."[1] A young man I interviewed agreed, telling me, "Probably the number one prime example of Pittsburghese is 'yinz.'" And an entry under Pittsburghese on UrbanDictionary.com, a site where users post definitions of new and nonstandard words, says this: "Emblematic of Pittsburghese is 'yinz' as the plural of 'you', with 'yunz' as a variant."[2]

Yinz has become "emblematic of Pittsburghese" partly because many Pittsburghers now live in places where people use a different form, *y'all*, in the same contexts. Over the course of repeated interactions with southerners, the pattern this creates—a pattern I referred to in chapter 3 as text metricality—comes to highlight the contrast. The fact that different people use different words in the same contexts, to do the same thing—address multiple hearers—points up the possible semiotic value of *yinz* beyond its meaning as a pronoun. Several posts in the WTAE discussion forum (chapter 5) allude to this. "Alas, my kids grew up saying 'ya'll' and I still can't get used to it," wrote someone who "moved to the south eighteen years ago." The discussion took place in 2002, which means that this participant left Pittsburgh in 1984, exactly when the massive contraction of the steel industry forced so many young Pittsburghers out, and the fact that this person has grown children suggests that she or he was part of that cohort. Another participant said that he "live[s] in Georgia, the land of ya'll," and suggests that others "try living among the 'y'allers' for a few years. You'll appreciate the 'yunz' a little more."

Yinz has also been further reanalyzed. In addition to being used as a personal pronoun, it can now be used as an adjective, prefix, or suffix, to modify a noun. In these uses, *yinz* means "Pittsburghy," somehow connected to Pittsburgh or typical of Pittsburgh. For example, "Yinz Play" was the name of an exhibit at the Pittsburgh Children's Museum in 2010. This was not meant as an imperative ("Yinz, play!") but rather as a chance to find out more about Pittsburgh by playing. *Yinz* served as an adjective modifying the noun *play*. The exhibit included an area called "Pittsburghese Illustrated Word Play," where, according to the *Pittsburgh Post-Gazette*, children could "place Pittsburghese phrases and famous quotes in the mouths of such images as Troy Polamalu [a Pittsburgh Steelers football star] and Mister Rogers [once the host of a popular television show for children.] For example, Andy Warhol might ask to go 'dahntahn', with Mr. Rogers responding 'Nuh, uh!'" (Chapman 2010). (The artist Andy Warhol was from Pittsburgh and is much celebrated there.)

There were other Pittsburghy activities as well. "Other elements of the exhibit," said the *Post-Gazette*, "allow visitors to create their own version of a Primanti Brothers' sandwich, pretend to paddle a kayak, and do much more." Primanti Brothers' overstuffed sandwiches have become an emblem of localness; kayaking is a recent and often advertised possibility on the now cleaner rivers. Also involving *yinz* used as an adjective is the Yinz Teddy Bear, a plush bear, for sale online, dressed as a Pittsburgh Steelers football fan.

"Yinz float" (figure 9.3) is the label of a picture of three people in a boat just big enough for them, a cooler, and some fishing gear. The photo appears in a Flickr stream by an amateur photographer, David Kent, called "simple pleasure" (Kent 2009). The scene is the Monongahela River. Taken from above as the boat passed under a bridge, the picture shows the boaters looking relaxed, the two young women in bikinis sunbathing, the older man, shirtless, at the tiller of the outboard motor, in his other hand a beverage can in a foam "beer koozie." One of the women sits in a folding lawn chair. *Yinz* suggests that they are Pittsburghers, engaged in a typical Pittsburgh activity.

As a prefix or suffix, *yinz* is used to modify nouns in words like "Yinzburgh" (an exhibit at the Carnegie Science Center consisting of photographs of unidentified

Figure 9.3 "Yinz Float" (Photograph by David Kent, used with permission)

Pittsburghers, together with activities aimed at getting visitors to think about their family's history and the history of industry), as well as YinzPitt and Yinz Sports (websites about Pittsburgh). YinzBlog was a section in the *Pittsburgh City Paper* consisting of excerpts from blogs about the city. A blog on the website iheartpgh.com in 2012 was called Questyinz.[3] Readers were invited to submit "questions about Pittsburgh or life in Pittsburgh."

As noted, a Yinzer is a stereotypical Pittsburgher. *Yinzer* can be used disparagingly or fondly, depending on who uses it to label whom, but it is increasingly used in the latter way, as a claim to localness. In 2003–2004, I asked all my

Figure 9.4 Yinzer as Part of a Shop Name. (Photograph by Barbara Johnstone)

interviewees whether they were familiar with the term *Yinzer*. Older people tended not to recognize the word, while younger people did. McCool's Pittsburghese dictionary, published in 1982, does not include *Yinzer*, and *Yinzer* does not appear in the corpus of print representations of Pittsburgh speech I assembled between 1997 and 2000. Over the course of the 2000s, the word *Yinzer* has become more and more visible, and its appearance in the final volume of the *Dictionary of Regional American English* (Joan Houston Hall 2012) has given it an official seal of approval, in some people's eyes.[4]

A July 2012 Google search yielded more than 223,000 hits for *Yinzer*. Photos tagged Yinzer tend to be of male sports fans, sometimes drinking (or drunk). Figure 9.4 shows *Yinzer* used in the name of a shop that sells sports team T-shirts, additional gear for fans, and other Pittsburgh souvenirs. Yinzerparty. com provides "Street Style and Nightlife Photos of Portland and Pittsburgh." The site's name invites readers to imagine that the blogger is from Pittsburgh, not from Portland.

However, the term is also used in many contexts that do not call up sports and parties, contexts in which it appears simply to mean "Pittsburgh." *The New Yinzer* is a literary magazine founded in the early 2000s by a group of people in their twenties. (The name is a take-off on *The New Yorker*, a prominent

US literary magazine.) The website makes an explicit link between the "new Yinzer" and "Pittsburgh's newly emergent identity:"

> Welcome to the fall 2011 issue of Pittsburgh's literary magazine, The New Yinzer.
>
> Our mission is to question, develop, and embody Pittsburgh's newly emergent identity via literary discourse.
>
> We provide regional writers with a working classroom to cultivate writing from fresh idea to finished product on the page and on stage.[5]

A 2011 *Pittsburgh Post-Gazette* review of the new album by a Pittsburgh rapper was headlined, "Miller pounds out a show for Pittsburgh's Yinzers." Pittsburgh's Penn Brewery produces an India Pale Ale called "Cheeky Yinzer." *Yinzer* has itself become a productive morpheme in words like the blend "Yinzercation" (a blog about the Pittsburgh public schools). Yinzermakover.com was the domain name of a website about an online contest, held in 2008, described in a Facebook announcement as "Pittsburgh's Biggest Fashion Disaster: What Yinz Shouldn't Wear."

The links between *yinz* and its social meanings have been forged in the kinds of activities I described in the second half of this book: in conversation and storytelling, in the media, on artifacts that are for sale, and in performances both fleeting and carefully designed. The visual artifacts in figure 9.5, for example, invite viewers to enregister *yinz* with local identity in various ways. On the T-shirt in figure 9.5, *yinz* is superimposed on the Pittsburgh skyline and further linked with the city via the colors black and gold and by virtue of the T-shirt's title: Picksburgh. On the motor scooter, a souvenir sticker of the kind that usually indicates a place name (like OBX for the Outer Banks) says "YINZ" where a viewer might expect "PGH." The Subway Sandwich drink dispenser that thanks "yinz" for visiting Pittsburgh was in the airport, where people arriving at the concourse where it was located might encounter *yinz* as one of their first Pittsburgh experiences.

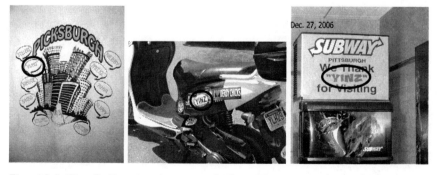

Figure 9.5 Visually Enregistering *yinz* with Place (Photographs by Barbara Johnstone).

The social practices through which *yinz* has been enregistered as incorrect, as working class, as Pittsburghy, and as an emblem of "rust belt chic" (Doig 2012) have been shaped by the history of the city and its people, which has in turn been shaped by the physical geography of the area.

What does *yinz* mean now, in the second decade of the twenty-first century? *Yinz* is a second-person plural pronoun. *Yinz* is a noun prefix or suffix, or an adjective. *Yinz* is a noun. *Yinz* sounds incorrect. *Yinz* is a working-class word. *Yinz* is a Pittsburgh word. *Yinz* is hip. In short, people use *yinz* in many different activities, each of which draws on and reinforces a different overlapping set of ideological schemas. *Yinz* is enregistered in multiple ways. It is a resource, in different ways, for different publics in Pittsburgh. Its meanings are both layered in time and dispersed in social space, so that, depending on when and where a person is socially located, some meanings are available and others are not.

Older uses of the word can sometimes be seen through newer ones: *yinz* can sound working class partly because it can sound incorrect; it can sound Pittsburghy partly because it can sound working class. *Yinz* is sometimes a window on the past, its newer meanings laminated on its older ones. Sometimes, though, for some people, newer social meanings have replaced older ones. A college student from out of state uses *yinz* in a bar, as a way of showing that he fits in, unaware of its other social resonances; his Pittsburgher friend cringes, hearing an embarrassing allusion to the uneducated Pittsburghers of the past. A colleague who reads an online forum for video gamers noticed that one contributor called himself "Yinzer Slayer" and asked whether that meant "Yinzer who slays" or "one who slays Yinzers." Yinzer Slayer's reply was scaffolded on an older meaning: "slayer of Yinzers—I hate the stupidity that some willfully ignorant people around Pittsburgh display on a regular basis. Some people take 'Yinzer' as a term of endearment, I don't." People who *do* take Yinzer as a term of endearment might, on the other hand, pay for an item made by jeweler Sharon Massey, who designs, produces, and sells silver pendants, earrings, cuff links, and other wearable products in the shapes of Pittsburghese words or with Pittsburghese words on them. Massey markets her Yinzer pendant to people who are "proud to be a Yinzer" (Massey, n.d.).

Massey's jewelry can link Pittsburghese with a variety of social meanings, depending on who buys it for whom and who wears it. The fact that Massey's pendants, belt buckles, and earrings are experienced on the bodies of people who wear them rather than on the bodies of standardized dolls like Chipped Ham Sam, or in the visual context of the fronts and backs of T-shirts, opens up the possibility that the words they represent may be taken into new orders of indexicality, given meaning according to new cultural schemata. Unlike the Pittsburghese on T-shirts, Pittsburghese as jewelry need not be visually linked with images of the city, local names and activities, or aspects of visual design (like color) that look Pittsburghy. Unlike the Pittsburghese uttered by the

Yappin' Yinzer dolls, Pittsburghese jewelry is not directly linked with the persona of the Yinzer. If, for example, a pendant that says Yinzer were worn by a youthful hipster, it could link Pittsburghese to a different sort of social identity than that of the Yappin' Yinzer dolls, still perhaps evoking the Yinzer identity in a more ironic, detached way, or perhaps not. Like the oral performances we looked at in chapter 8, the jewelry serves as a centrifugal force, pushing *yinz* into new semiotic domains.

From Remembered Locale to Imagined Persona

One of the biggest surprises for me as I have pieced together the history of Pittsburghese has been the huge role played by the baby boomers, the generation of Pittsburghers and ex-Pittsburghers who were born after World War II and who became working-aged in the 1980s. This cohort of Pittsburghers has been the bridge generation, anchored both in Pittsburgh speech and in Pittsburghese. In their lifetimes and with their participation, economic and social history, ideas about language, and the history of western Pennsylvania speech came together with communication technology to put Pittsburghese in place.

Stories about language change are often stories about young people, and part of the Pittsburghese story traces the baby boomers' youth in a still-industrial Pittsburgh where high union wages and the highway building boom of the 1950s and 1960s made it possible for their parents to move from Lawrenceville to the suburbs or from East Pittsburgh to Forest Hills. Their parents had grown up sounding like Pittsburghers, unaware of how they sounded and what it could mean to sound one way or another, but these Pittsburghers, more aware of other ways of speaking because they were more mobile, linked Pittsburghese with class and knew it could sound uneducated and sloppy. They try not to say "dahn-tahn" or *yinz*. Still, they know they have Pittsburgh accents, because people have told them so. They grew up reading articles about Pittsburghese in the newspapers and still today get recognized as Pittsburghers by how they talk. As we have seen, they grew up thinking of themselves as Pittsburghers, too, not as immigrants or the children of immigrants.

Huge numbers of baby boomers were forced away from Pittsburgh when the economy contracted in the 1980s. Many of them moved to the "sun belt," a group of southern and southwestern states that were attracting industry in part because of lower labor costs. Coincidentally, personal computers were just becoming widely available, first in workplaces, then in homes. By the early 1990s, many younger adults were comfortable with e-mail, and by the mid-1990s they were exploring the World Wide Web. Still young or in early middle age, the ex-Pittsburghers quickly caught on to personal computing and used it to keep in touch with home and talk about home. As we have seen, this involved talking about how Pittsburghers talk. They continue to do so, perhaps even more now that their children are grown and they have more time for nostalgia.

The children of this generation grew up with Pittsburghese. Those in the diasporic "Steeler Nation" may have seen Pittsburghese or heard it discussed, mainly on football Sundays, but it is unlikely that they are interested enough in it to carry on in their parents' online footsteps. Those who grew up in Pittsburgh may still speak with their parents' unselfconscious Pittsburgh accents. On the other hand, if their parents moved up socially and economically, they probably speak in a more leveled, regional-sounding way, maintaining some features of the way their parents speak (they pronounce words like *not* with the rounded low back vowel, words like *school* with a vocalized /l/) but not the features that have come to sound Pittsburghy. These people are probably able to talk about Pittsburghese, though, and they may use it playfully to claim a local or insider identity. The in-migration to Pittsburgh by college students and young professionals means that these Pittsburghers are joined by people who learn to talk about Pittburghese, even use bits of it, but who relatively rarely hear anyone speaking with a Pittsburgh accent. If they do, they may not even recognize it.

The people who enregistered a subset of Pittsburgh words, phrases, and sounds as Pittsburghese in the latter half of the twentieth century typically had personal memories of childhoods in Pittsburgh, and the Pittsburghese of the twentieth and early twenty-first century included many forms that evoked activities and artifacts they associated with their youth. Lists of Pittsburghese from those years included local place names and local products as well as distinctive words, and these tended to be embedded in phrases and sentences that evoked the past. The people who generated these lists and argued over their contents knew many people who actually used these words and sounds, people who really sounded like Pittsburghers, and the experience of being recognized by their accents made them sensitive to the sounds of local speech. Thus, lists of Pittsburghese from the 1980s, 1990s, and early 2000s tended to represent a variety of local pronunciations, in iconic words like "dahntahn," "Stillers," and "Giant Iggle," but also in less iconic contexts like "still mill" ('steel mill') and "cahch" ('couch').

The Pittsburghese that has been created by and for the baby boomers is shaped by the idea that Pittsburghese is linked to the Pittsburgh of the remembered past. It is an aspect of Pittsburgh's cultural heritage, albeit rarely acknowledged as such in more official kinds of talk about the city. It has become unloosed from the kind of social evaluation that can make it shameful to have an actual Pittsburgh accent or provincial to use Pittsburgh words. *Pittsburgh Post-Gazette* columnist Brian O'Neill, writing in 2004, gave voice to this idea in an e-mail to me in which he suggested that he had used a local-sounding term in one of his columns because "'rubber bands' has no authority over 'gum bands.'" This is to say that the standard, "correct" form (*rubber bands*) no longer trumps the local form (*gum bands*). Given that most people in the United States, most of the time, use *rubber bands* instead of *gum bands*, the world in which O'Neill's claim makes sense is a world in which the local is as good as the global. Pittsburghers no longer live in such a world, but many miss it.

As the realm of discourse about Pittsburghese becomes further and further disconnected from the realm of people who speak the way Pittsburghers speak, the repertoire of Pittsburghese items has shrunk and standardized. Older Pittsburghese T-shirt designs, with ten or more words on the front and a longer list on the back, are now sold next to newer designs, which tend to play with a single Pittsburghese word: "I'm surrounded by jagoffs," "YNZ", "Drink up, yinz bitches," "Stillers," "We got [Super Bowl] rings n'at." An apparently self-published 2012 book called *Yinzer Bible* (Anon 2012) includes a "Pittsburghese Dictionary" that is different from earlier ones in some telling ways. Some of the entries appear to be copied from the lists that circulate via the McCool dictionary, T-shirts and other artifacts, and online. Others, however, suggest that the list maker was not very familiar with the way Pittsburghers talk. *Redd up* is spelled "Red-up" and wrongly defined as "to get ready," and *hoagie* is misspelled "hogie." Most of the other entries are eye dialect: "picknick" for *picnic*, "rilly" for *really*, "grahj" for *garage*, and so on. The monophthongal /aw/ sound is spelled <aaw>, <ah>, <awh>, and <ha>, which suggests that the writer of the list may not be sure what it actually sounds like. But the new dictionary includes one item that is missing from earlier lists: "Yinzer," defined as, "The beloved Pittsburgher who speaks Pittsburghese and follows the culture."

Particularly for people who do not remember the Pittsburgh of the 1950s and 1960s, the meaning of Pittsburghese is shifting. Pittsburghese is being enregistered not with the city's identity in general but more specifically with the persona of the Yinzer. As I noted in chapter 7, the Yinzer figure represents a style of communication as well as a lifestyle; Yinzers are forthright, loud, and directive because they are free of the need to control their speech for the new economy. They are also frustrated and petulant. They call people jagoffs, rant ineffectively about the "Stillers," and yell at their kids. When I ask older people to explain what Pittsburghese is, they list words and phrases; when I ask younger people, they break into performances of the Yinzer, often leaning forward, raising their voices, sounding a bit aggressive. Speaking Pittsburghese, for them, is not so much a matter of knowing local speech forms that evoke the past as a matter of putting on a speech style that evokes a stereotypical working-class character.

It has been argued that economic and cultural developments have diminished the relevance of place in human lives. According to Robert N. Bellah and his colleagues (Bellah et al. 1985), contemporary Americans inhabit "lifestyle enclaves" rather than communities centered around common experience of place. The instability of meaning in general and the threat to meaningful places in the modern world is often said to be the result of rapid change and mobility (Ogilvy 1977). Edward Said (1978, 18), for example, speaks of the "generalized sense of homelessness" experienced by the globally mobile. According to sociologist Anthony Giddens (1991), the dynamism of modern life has the effect of separating place from space, removing social relations from local contexts. Once social life becomes "disembedded" in this way, "place becomes phantasmagoric" (Giddens, 1991, 146), "much less significant than it used to be as an external referent for the lifespan of the individual" (147). The world is no longer just the physical world in which a person moves through.

But it is also claimed that local, place-based community still has a role to play, albeit a changing one. Giddens points out how people attempt to "re-embed the lifespan within a local milieu" (1991, 147), such as through attempts to cultivate community pride. Cultural geographers who continue to focus on traditional cultures and traditional aspects of culture recognize the continued persistence and importance of traditional sources of meaning such as localness (Entrikin 1991, 41). That localness can still be valued can be seen in activities aimed at perpetuating or even creating it. Local contexts of life may still be tied to human identity in more immediate ways, too. As Stuart Hall points out (1991, 33–36), globalization is not, after all, a new phenomenon, and "the return to the local is often a response to globalization . . . It is a respect for local roots which is brought to bear against the anonymous, impersonal world of the globalized forces which we do not understand." Face-to-face community is knowable in a way more abstract communities are not: one "knows what the voices are. One knows what the faces are" (35). In sum, it is increasingly difficult to predict exactly how the local will articulate with an individual's life.

In exploring one of the ways in which Pittsburghers articulate experience with place, I hope I have said something new about the meaning of place in human lives. Due to a particular set of geographical, economic, linguistic, and ideological circumstances, people in Pittsburgh grabbed onto language as a way of defining themselves, and arguments about what Pittsburgh means continue to be framed as arguments about Pittsburghese. (A controversy over whether the *Post-Gazette* should continue to allow its writers to use the word *jagoff* erupted as I was writing this chapter. On the surface it was about the meaning of a word, but the argument actually had as much to do with the meaning of the city's history.) The set of circumstances that produced Pittsburghese has coincided nowhere else. There are similar stories, but none identical. This is the sociolinguistic history of a particular spot on the planet at a particular time. In telling the story of Pittsburghese, I hope to have opened up some new ways of thinking about what regional dialects are and what they mean at a time when mobility appears to be erasing difference.

Notes

Chapter 1

1. Some people prefer the term *Scots-Irish* because of contemporary usage: a person from Scotland is a Scot and Scotch is a drink. However, *Scotch-Irish* is the term these people used for themselves, and so it is the term I use in this book. See Montgomery (2001) for more on the nomenclature issue.
2. See Johnstone and Kiesling (2008, 13–14) and Thomas (2003) for more detailed acoustic descriptions of glide-reduced diphthongs in American speech in general and Pittsburgh in particular.
3. There is a website devoted to the distribution of forms of *soft drink* in the United States at http://www.popvssoda.com/.

Chapter 2

1. For critiques of the notion of autonomous languages (and, by extension, dialects) as objects, see Hopper (1988), Harris (1981), and N. Love (2009). Eckert and McConnell-Ginet (1992) and Rampton (1998) critique the idea of the clearly bounded, homogeneous speech community.
2. Human geography has to do with the connections between space and human activity in general and has involved work in various theoretical and methodological frameworks. See Johnston, Gregory, and Smith (1986).
3. See also Tuan (1977). Other influential humanistic geographers include Entrikin (1976, 1991), Relph (1981), and Buttimer (1979).
4. Linguists in other research traditions, including Lyons (1977), Halliday (1970), and Jakobson (1960), by contrast, talked about connotative meaning as well as denotative meaning.
5. http://www.slanguage.com/.

Chapter 3

1. On the history of the Scotch-Irish, see Blethen and Wood (1997), Chepesiuk (2000), Dunaway (1944), Leyburn (1962), and Kirkham (1997).
2. Dunaway (1944, 41) estimates that 250,000 immigrants came during the eighteenth century alone, which would make the total higher.
3. Byington uses *Slav* "as a general term to include Magyars and Lithuanians, as well as those belonging to the Slavic race" (12, n. 1). The book includes drawings and photographs that purport to represent typical Slavic faces, usually contrasted with the faces of non-Slavs.
4. These people would most likely not have been Scotch-Irish but rather Catholics from what is now the Republic of Ireland, displaced as a result of the potato famine and its aftermath in the mid-nineteenth century.

5. *Gumbander* is derived from the Pittsburghese *gumband*, 'rubber band.' As we have seen and will see again, words for Pittsburgh identities are often derived from words that are associated with Pittsburghese.

6. Steeler bars are marketed to Pittsburgh Steelers fans, who gather there to watch games. They usually feature Steelers- and Pittsburgh-themed decorations, foods, and beers. Several online lists identify Steeler bars all over the United States and in many other parts of the world.

7. Ochs (1992) describes the same process as a shift from "direct" to "indirect" indexicality. For a more thorough discussion of these ways of thinking about how indexical meaning changes, see Johnstone, Andrus, and Danielson (2006).

8. The idea of the community of practice originates in learning theory (Wenger 1998) and was brought into sociolinguistics by Penelope Eckert (Eckert and McConnell-Ginet 1992; Eckert 2000).

Chapter 4

1. In addition to (aw), I explored responses to the variables (oh), (ow), and (aeh) (in Labov's 1972e notation). For the (oh) variable, the [ɔ] allophone is the one that can be heard locally, but since the low back vowels (oh) and (o) are merged for Pittsburghers, one would expect them not to be able to hear the difference. For the (ow) variable, I expected Pittsburghers to be able to hear the difference between a fronted [oʷ˂] and a nonfronted [oʷ] but not to identify either as "more like a Pittsburgher," since this feature is not subject to local stereotyping. For (aeh), the nonstandard version was the nonlocal one, so I expected subjects to identify the *standard* version with Pittsburgh. My expectations were borne out in all cases.

2. Chi-square = 334.58, df=6, p<=.001.

3. Agha (2007a, 189) puts it this way: "The value of speech and other object-signs is not a disembodied abstraction. The cultural values of enregistered signs become empirically observable when they are articulated by sensorially accessible meta-signs (including utterances) that typify these values." This happens in many ways, both in linguists' discourse about language and in nonlinguists'.

Chapter 5

1. The IPA symbol D represents the "flapped" sound of /r/ in American English, when /r/ occurs in between two vowel sounds.

2. Most news websites no longer offer this kind of forum. Instead, readers or viewers are invited to post comments.

3. We cannot be completely sure of participants' sex on the basis of their screen names, which they choose. But rather than using "he or she," which would reflect this fact, I will use the pronouns that the screen names suggest. This makes the text more readable.

4. There is a traditional rivalry between Pittsburgh and Cleveland, Ohio.

5. Greensburg is a city thirty-five miles south of Pittsburgh which is not usually thought of as part of Pittsburgh. Here again, as we saw happening with Johnstown in chapter 3, Pittsburgh can subsume a much larger area than just the city or its metropolitan area, at least for the purposes of language.

6. Unlike the names I use for my research participants, this is not a pseudonym. Cullen was speaking in public, on the radio, on an eponymous talk show that anybody could have recorded.

Chapter 6

1. Beginning learners of foreign languages may piece together sentences by deploying rules they have learned in advance, but this is the exception, not the norm, and it does not result in fluent face-to-face interaction but rather contributes to a language game of a different sort.

2. Sociolinguists have often pointed out, for example, how the idea of "standard" languages, linked to the enterprise of nationalism, serves the needs of the powerful and marginalizes less powerful people's ways of speaking. Deborah Cameron's (1995) *Verbal Hygiene* is an accessible example. Monica Heller's (2011) *Paths to Postnationalism* critiques ideas about language associated with neo-liberalism. See also Piller and Cho (2013).
3. I am grateful to Priscilla Parslow for showing these to me and allowing me to make copies of them.
4. According to Priscilla Parslow, the request had come from a former student of his.
5. McCool's book looked similar enough to Parslow's booklet to make members of Parslow's family suspect that McCool had borrowed from Parslow (Patricia Parslow, personal communication). A comparison of the two texts suggests that this is unlikely, at least on the level of words and definitions: while thirty-three of the fifty-seven words in the Parslow list (or 57.9 percent) are also in McCool's list, only 27.7 percent of the total items on McCool's list are defined or exemplified the same way on Parslow's list. Structurally, the two dictionaries are very similar, but Parslow and McCool could have been drawing independently on previous instantiations of this folk-dictionary genre from elsewhere. (Hilliard and Wolfram describe folk dictionaries dating from the 1960s, e.g., Freeman 1961; neither Parslow nor McCool invented the genre.) Further, although McCool knew of Parslow, he had not met him or studied with him.
6. McHugh had previously written an article for the paper on Frederic G. Cassidy and the *Dictionary of American Regional English* (McHugh, 1979), which suggests that he was already interested in local speech.
7. http://www.renaissancenewsinc.com/regional/proddetail.php?prod=0615223974, accessed March 16, 2012.
8. 'If you think Pittsburghese is disappearing, you better think again, and so on: Plenty of people in Allegheny County [where Pittsburgh is located] still go out of the house to buy sauerkraut for New Year's dinner or see a tiger at the Pittsburgh zoo'.

Chapter 7

1. www.slanguage.com.
2. Agha borrows the term "figure" from Erving Goffman (Goffman 1981a). In his discussion of participant roles, Goffman uses this term to identify personas evoked in interaction that are clearly different from the persona of the "animator" speaking the words. A figure could be the past self of someone telling a story or the character played by an actor on stage.
3. Coupland (2003, 424) refers to this as "authentic language 5": the everyday use of "authentic" with regard to language when "language is deemed to express personal authenticity, in accordance with the moral prescription that people should 'be themselves.'" People who orient to this moral prescription may organize social life "on the assumption that some groups of speakers are more trustworthy, honest and straightforward than others." Along with Bucholtz (2003), Coupland rightly points out that we need to think critically about the meaning of authentic, whether referring to sociolinguists or to the laypeople we study. From an ethnographic point of view, however, there is no question that authenticity is a relevant concept in Pittsburgh and that it is associated both with traditional ways of doing things (authenticity based on "historicity," as Coupland puts it) and with ways of doing things that are considered to be real and unmediated (authenticity based on "ontology," in Coupland's terms). Johnstone (forthcoming) explores the meaning of the T-shirt that says "100% Authentic Pittsburgh."

Chapter 8

1. In fact, Texans speak with many different accents, as research by Guy Bailey and others makes clear (Bailey 1991).
2. To a linguist like me, Josh does sound like a Pittsburgher because of the way he pronounces certain vowels. According to the ideological scheme I draw on as a linguist when

I talk about accents, Josh's pronunciation of the low back vowel and his vocalization of /l/ both identify him as a Pittsburgher.

3. Sally Struthers: an actress known and satirized for appearances in late-night TV commercials raising money for poor children in developing countries.

4. "Like it or lump it": Eat it or go without. Here the Mother character uses the two phrases *like it* and *lump it* as if they were the names of menu items.

5. Vick's: mentholated petroleum jelly, a traditional remedy.

6. Boone's Farm: inexpensive flavored apple wine.

7. Franco Harris: A former Pittsburgh football star who often makes public appearances in the area.

8. Van Morrison: An international rock/blues star of the 1970s–1990s.

9. "He inhales!": A reference to a well-known political faux pas, when then US presidential candidate Bill Clinton told an interviewer that he had tried marijuana in his youth but "didn't inhale."

10. Secret service: the plain-clothes guards who protect the president and other political figures whose jobs put them at risk. Members of the secret service stereotypically wear dark glasses.

11. Cookie sheets: flat metal baking pans.

12. "Pass inspection for emissions test": In Pennsylvania, automobiles must be inspected annually to ensure they are safe ("pass inspection"). They must also pass an "emissions test" that measures pollutants emitted by the car. Krenn has conflated the two kinds of tests here.

13. Club Elite: a Pittsburgh night club where strip-tease is performed.

14. "Campaign fund-raisers account": Money donated by members of the public to support a political campaign. It would be highly questionable to use such money to entertain at a strip club.

15. Terry Weigel: presumably a star in pornographic films.

16. *Vice* president: The stress on the word *vice* brings out the potential ambiguity of "vice president," making it hearable as meaning "the president of vice."

Chapter 9

1. http://www.grammarphobia.com/blog/2011/02/yinz.html, accessed July 17, 2012.

2. http://www.urbandictionary.com/define.php?term=pittsburghese, accessed July 4, 2012.

3. http://iheartpgh.com/quest-yinz/, accessed July 3, 2013.

4. If *Yinzer* did not start with a letter that is close to the end of the alphabet, it would not have appeared in *DARE*, whose earlier volumes were all published before the word came onto the scene.

5. http://www.newyinzer.com/archive/fall2011/tocindex.html, accessed July 3, 2013.

References

Adams, M. (2000). Lexical doppelgängers. *Journal of English linguistics, 28*, 295–310.

Agha, A. (2003). The social life of a cultural value. *Language and communication, 23*, 231–273.

Agha, A. (2007a). *Language and social relations.* New York: Cambridge University Press.

Agha, A. (2007b). The object called language. *Journal of English linguistics, 35*, 217-235.

Alim, S. (2004). *You know my steez: An ethnographic and sociolinguistic study of styleshifting in a Black American speech community.* Chapel Hill, N.C.: Duke University Press, for the American Dialect Society.

Allen, H. B. (1973). *The linguistic atlas of the Upper Midwest.* Minneapolis: University of Minnesota Press.

Anon. (2012). *Yinzer bible: Pittsburgh N'@: If you don't understand go back to Cleveland!* (second edition.). Lexington, KY: publisher not listed.

Appadurai, A. (1986). Introduction: Commodities and the politics of value. In A. Appadurai (Ed.), *The social life of things: Commodities in cultural perspective* (pp. 3–63). Cambridge, UK: Cambridge University Press.

Auer, P. (2005). The construction of linguistic borders and the linguistic construction of borders. In M. Filppula, J. Kemola, M. Palander, & E. Penttila (Eds.), *Dialects across borders* (pp. 3–30). Amsterdam/Philadelphia: John Benjamins.

Auer, P., Hinskens, F., & Kerswill, P. (Eds.). (2005). *Dialect change: Convergence and divergence in European languages.* Cambridge: Cambridge University Press.

Ayers, E. L., & Onuf, P. L. (1996). Preface. In E. Ayers & et al. (Eds.), *All over the map: rethinking American regions.* Baltimore: Johns Hopkins University Press.

Bailey, G. (1991). Directions of change in Texas English. *Journal of American culture, 14*, 125–134.

Bakhtin, M. M. (1981). *The dialogic imagination.* (C. Emerson & M. Holquist, Trans., M. Holquist, Ed.). Austin: University of Texas Press.

Bauman, R. (1977). *Verbal art as performance.* Rowley, MA: Newbury House.

Bauman, R., & Briggs, C. (1990). Poetics and performance as critical perspectives on language and social life. *Annual review of anthropology, 19*, 59–88.

Baumgardt, D., & Johnstone, B. (2006). Pittsburgh English. *Wikipedia.* Retrieved August 18, 2010, from http://en.wikipedia.org/wiki/Pittsburgh_English.

Beal, J. (2009). "You're not from New York City, you're from Rotherham": Dialect and identity in British indie music. *Journal of English linguistics, 37*, 223–240.

Beal, J. C. (2010). Enregisterment, commodification, and historical context: "Geordie" versus "Sheffieldish". *American speech, 84*(2), 138–156.

Bean, J. M. (1993). "True grit and all the rest": Expression of regional and individual identities in Molly Ivins' discourse. *Journal of southwestern American literature, 19*, 35–46.

Bellah, R. N., Madsen, R., Sullivan, W. M., & Swidler, A. (1985). *Habits of the heart: Individualism and comitment in American life.* Berkeley: University of California Press.

Bendix, R. (1988). Folklorism: The challenge of a concept. *International folklore review, 6*, 5–15.

Bensman, D., & Lynch, R. (1988). *Rusted dreams: Hard times in a steel community*. Berkeley and Los Angeles: University of California Press.

Bernhard, A. (1959, December 4). Pittsburgh speech has its own differences. *Pittsburgh post-gazette*, p. 2.

Bhatt, R. M. (2002). Experts, dialects, and discourse. *International journal of applied linguistics*, 12(1), 74–109.

Blethen, H. T., & Wood, Jr., C. W. (1997). Introduction. In H. T. Blethen, C. W. Wood, & T.D. Fraser (eds.), *Ulster and North America: Transatlantic perspectives on the Scotch-Irish* (pp. 1–14). Tuscaloosa and London: University of Alabama Press.

Blommaert, J. (2008). Artefactual ideologies and the textual production of African languages. *Language & communication, 28*, 291–307.

Bloom, S. (1977). Everyone talks funny but us. *The Pittsburgher*, 1(3), 39, 79.

Bodnar, J. E. (1977). *Immigration and industrialization: Ethnicity in an American mill town, 1870-1940*. Pittsburgh PA: University of Pittsburgh Press.

Bodnar, J. E. (1979). Immigration and modernization: The case of Slavic peasants in America. In M. Cantor (Ed.), *American working-class culture: Explorations in American labor and social history* (pp. 333–360). Greenwood Press.

Bodnar, J. E. (1987). *The transplanted: A history of immigrants in urban America*. Bloomington & Indianapolis: Indiana University Press.

Bodnar, J. E., Simon, R., & Weber, M. P. (1983). *Lives of their own; Blacks, Italians, and Poles in Pittsburgh, 1900-1960*. Urbana and Chicago: University of Illinois Press.

Boissevain, J. (1974). *Friends of friends: Networks, manipulators, and coalitions*. Oxford: Blackwell.

Bourdieu, P. (1977). The economics of linguistic exchanges. *Social science information, 16*(6), 645–668.

Bourdieu, P. (1991). *Language and symbolic power*. (Gino Raymond & M. Adamson, Trans., J. B. Thompson, Ed.). Cambridge MA: Harvard University Press.

Braknis, G. (1991, December 3). Straight talk: Slang can derail job interview, stifle career. *Pittsburgh press*, pp. 1, 3.

Britain, D. (2002). Diffusion, levelling, simplification and reallocation in past tense BE in the English Fens, *Journal of sociolinguistics* 6(1), 16–63.

Browne, J. (1976, December 20). Our towne. *Pittsburgh post-gazette*, p. 1.

Brumberg, S. F. (1986). *Going to America, going to school: The Jewish immigrant public school encounter in turn-of-the-century New York City*. New York: Praeger.

Bryant, S. L., Forte, A., & Bruckman, A. (2005). Becoming Wikipedian: Transformation of participation in a collaborative online encyclopedia. In *Proceedings of GROUP '05* (pp. 1–10). Presented at GROUP '05, Sannibel Island, Florida, USA: Association for computational machinery.

Bucholtz, M. (2003). Sociolinguistic nostalgia and the autentication of identity. *Journal of sociolinguistics, 7*, 398-416.

Bucholtz, M. (2008). Shop talk: Branding, consumption and gender in American middle-class youth interaction. In B. McElhinny (Ed.), *Words, worlds, and material girls: Language, gender, globalization* (pp. 371–402). Berlin: Mouton de Gruyter.

Buttimer, A. (1993). *Geography and the human spirit*. Baltimore, MD: Johns Hopkins University Press.

Buttko, B. (2001). *Klondikes, chipped ham, & skyscraper cones: The story of Isaly's*. Mechanicsburg, PA: Stackpole Books.

Byington, M. F. (1974). *Homestead: The households of a mill town*. (S. P. Hays, Ed.). Pittsburgh and London: University of Pittsburgh Press.

Cameron, D. (1995). *Verbal hygiene*. London/New York: Routledge.

Carrell, M. (1910, December 12). Pittsburg's sayings and proverbs. *Pitttsburg dispatch*, p. 7.

Chambers, J. K., & Trudgill, P. (1998). *Dialectology*. Cambridge: Cambridge University Press.

Chandler, D. (2000). *Technological or media determinism*. University of Aberdeen. Retrieved from http://www.aber.ac.uk/media/Documents/tecdet/tecdet.html

Chapman, J. (2010, January 29). "Yinz Play": It's just a 'Burgh thing. *Pittsburgh post-gazette*. Retrieved from http://www.post-gazette.com/stories/sectionfront/life/yinz-play-its-just-a-burgh-thing-231039/#ixzz1zwVPH3Ys

Chepesiuk, R. (2000). *The Scotch-Irish: From the north of Ireland to the making of America.* London, Jefferson, NC: McFarland.

Coupland, N. (1985). "Hark, hark, the lark": Social motivations for phonological style-shifting. *Language and communication,* 5, 153–172.

Coupland, N. (2001). Dialect stylization in radio talk. *Language in society,* 30(3), 345–375.

Coupland, N. (2003). Sociolinguistic authenticities. *Journal of sociolinguistics,* 7, 417–431.

Coupland, N. (2007). *Style: Language variation and identity.* Cambridge, UK: Cambridge University Press.

Cowie, J. R., & Boehm, L. (2006). Dead man's town: "Born in the U.S.A.," social history, and working-class identity. *American quarterly,* 58(2), 353–378.

Crowley, G. J. (2005). *The politics of place: Contentious urban redevelopment in Pittsburgh.* Pittsburgh PA: The University of Pittsburgh Press.

Crowley, T. (2012). *Scouse: A social and cultural history.* Liverpool: Liverpool University Press.

Cullen, L. (2002, February 22). Interview with Barbara Johnstone. WPPT Pittsburgh.

Danielson, A. (2001). *Talking about Pittsburgh speech: Representations of "local" speech features in Pittsburgh's print media.* term paper, Carnegie Mellon University.

Davidson, J. (1984, December 30). We'uns sure stretch the King's English. *Pittsburgh press,* p. 4.

Dickey, L. W. (1997). *The phonology of liquids.* PhD dissertation, University of Massachusetts, Amherst.

Doig, W. (2012, May 12). Rust Belt chic: Declining Midwest cities make a comeback. *Salon.* Retrieved from http://www.salon.com/2012/05/12/rust_belt_chic_declining_midwest_cities_make_a_comeback/singleton/

Dorian, N. (1994). Varieties of variation in a very small place: Social homogeneity, prestige norms, and linguistic variation. *Language,* 70, 631–696.

Dorian, N. (2010). *Investigating variation: The effects of social organization and social setting.* Oxford: Oxford University Press.

Downes, E. J., & McMillan, S. J. (2000). Defining interactivity: A qualitative identification of key dimensions. *New media & society,* 2(2), 157–179.

Dunaway, W. F. (1944). *The Scotch-Irish of colonial Pennsylvania.* Chapel Hill: University of North Carolina Press.

Dunk, T. W. (1991). *It's a working man's town: Male working-class culture in northwestern Ontario.* Montreal and Kingston: McGill-Queen's University Press.

Dyer, J. (2002). "We all speak the same round here": Dialect levelling in a Scottish-English community. *Journal of sociolinguistics,* 6, 99–116.

Eberhardt, M. (2008). The low back merger in the Steel City: AAE in Pittsburgh. *American speech,* 83, 284–311.

Eckert, P. (1996). (ay) goes to the city: Exploring the expressive use of variation. In G. R. Guy, C. Feagin, D. Schiffrin, & J. Baugh (Eds.), *Towards a social science of language: Papers in honor of William Labov, Vol. I: Variation and change in language and society* (pp. 47–68). Amsterdam/Philadelphia: John Benjamins.

Eckert, P. (2000). *Linguistic variation as social practice.* Oxford: Blackwell.

Eckert, P. (2004). Variation and a sense of place. In C. Fought (Ed.), *Sociolinguistic variation: Critical reflections* (pp. 107–118). New York, Oxford: Oxford University Press.

Eckert, P. (2008). Variation and the indexical field. *Journal of sociolinguistics,* 12(4), 453–476.

Eckert, P., and S. McConnell-Ginet. (1992). Think practically and look locally: Language and gender as community-based practice. *Annual review of anthropology,* 21, 461–490.

Eckert, P. and J. R. Rickford. (2001). *Style and sociolinguistic variation.* Cambridge, New York: Cambridge University Press.

Ellis, M. Slanguage. www.slanguage.com/ Accessed Feb. 21, 2001.

Emigh, W., & S. Herring (2005). Collaborative authoring on the web: A genre analysis of online encyclopedias. In *Proceedings of the thirty-eighth Hawai'i international conference on system sciences (HICSS-38).* Los Alamitos: IEEE Press. Retrieved from http://ella.slis.indiana.edu/~herring/wiki.pdf.

Entrikin, J. N. (1991). *The betweenness of place: Towards a geography of modernity.* Baltimore: Johns Hopkins University Press.

Fairclough, N. L. (1992). *Discourse and social change.* Cambridge: Polity.

Fasold, R. (1980). The conversational function of Pennsylvania Dutch question intonation. Presented at the New Ways of Analyzing Variation (NWAV), Ann Arbor, MI.

Fitch, J. A. (1989). *The steel workers.* Pittsburgh PA: University of Pittsburgh Press.

Finnegan, R. (1988). *Tales of the city: A study of narrative and urban life.* Oxford: Blackwell.

Fleming, A. (2008, January). History: Yinz can learn about Pittsburghese online - Podcasts provide origins of the city's most colorful words. *Pittsburgh city paper.* Retrieved from http://www.pittsburghcitypaper.ws/gyrobase/Content?oid=oid%3A41403

Foley, D. (1989). Does the working class have a culture in the anthropological sense? *Cultural anthropology, 4*(2), 137–163.

Foley, D. (1990). *Learning capitalist culture: Deep in the heart of Tejas.* Philadelphia, PA: University of Pennsylvania Press.

Fox, A. A. (1997). "Ain't it funny how time slips away?" Talk, trash, and technology in a Texas "redneck" bar. In B. Ching & G. W. Creed (Eds.), *Knowing your place: Rural identity and cultural hierarchy* (pp. 105–130). New York and London: Routledge.

Francis, W. N. (1983). *Dialectology: An introduction.* Essex, UK: Longman.

Fraser, T. G. (1997). Foreword. The Ulster-American heritage symposium: A retrospect. In H. T. Blethen, C. W. Wood, & T. D. Fraser (Eds.), *Ulster and North America: Transatlantic perspectives on the Scotch-Irish* (pp. vii–x). Tuscaloosa and London: University of Alabama Press.

Fridland, V., Bartlett, K., & Kreutz, R. (2004). Do you hear what I hear? Experimental measurement of the perceptual salience of acoustically manipulated vowel variants by Southern speakers in Memphis, TN. *Language variation and change, 16,* 1–16.

Gagnon, C. L. (1999). *Language attitudes in Pittsburgh: "Pittsburghese" versus Standard English* (MA Thesis, Linguistics). University of Pittsburgh.

Gal, S., & Irvine, J. T. (1995). The boundaries of languages and disciplines: How ideologies construct difference. *Social research, 62,* 967–1001.

Gaudio, R. P. (2003). Coffeetalk. *Language in society, 32,* 659–691.

Giddens, A. (1991). *Modernity and self-identity: Self and society in the Late Modern age.* Stanford, CA: Stanford University Press.

Giles, H., Taylor, D. M., & Bourhis, R. (1973). Towards a theory of interpersonal accommodation through language: Some Canadian data. *Language in society, 2*(2), 177–192.

Gitman, M. (1997, January 20). Internet "n" at: Web site pools the finer points of Pittsburghese. *Pittsburgh post-gazette,* pp. 1, 2.

Gleason, D. (1965, May 30). What's that you said. *Pittsburgh press,* p. 4.

Gleason, D. (1967, June 18). Strictly Pittsburghese: Only in Western Pennsylvania do you hear "gum band" and "needs washed." *Pittsburgh press,* p. 3.

Goffman, E. (1959). *The presentation of self in everyday life.* Garden City, NY: Doubleday Anchor Books.

Goffman, E. (1981a). Footing. In *Forms of talk* (pp. 124–159). Philadelphia: University of Pennsylvania Press.

Goffman, E. (1981b). *Forms of talk.* Philadelphia, PA: University of Pennsylvania Press.

Goffman, E. (1986). *Frame analysis: An essay on the organization of experience.* Boston: Northwestern University Press.

Gorter, D. (Ed.) (2006). *Linguistic landscape: A new approach to multilingualism.* Clevedon, UK: Multilingual Matters.

Gramsci, A. (1971). *Selections from the prison notebooks.* New York: International Publishing.

Granovetter, M. (1973). The strength of weak ties. *American journal of sociology, 78,* 1360–1380.

Gray, J. (1968, July 14). Dialect in dilemma. *Pittsburgh press,* p. (illegible).

Gumperz, J. J. (1982). *Discourse strategies.* Cambridge, UK: Cambridge University Press.

Gumperz, J. J. (1992). Contextualization and understanding. In A. Duranti & C. Goodwin (Eds.), *Rethinking context: Language as an interactive phenomenon* (pp. 229–252). Cambridge: Cambridge University Press.

Guy, G. R., & Cutler, C. A. (2011). Speech style and authenticity: Quantitative evidence for the performance of identity. *Language variation and change, 23,* 139–162.

Habermas, J. (1984). *The theory of communicative action.* T. McCarthy (Trans.). Boston: Beacon Press.

Hall, Joan Houston (Ed.). (2012). *Dictionary of American regional English, Volume V: Si-Z*. Cambridge, MA: Harvard University Press.

Hall, K. (1995). Lip service on the fantasy lines. In K. Hall & M. Bucholtz (Eds.), *Gender articulated: Language and the socially constructed self* (pp. 183–216). New York and London: Routledge.

Hall, S. (1991). The local and the global: Globalization and ethnicity. In A. D. King (Ed.), *Culture, Globalization, and the World-system* (pp. 19–39). Basingstoke, UK: MacMillan.

Halliday, M. A. K. (1970). Language structure and language function. In *New horizons in linguistics*. Harmondsworth, UK: Penguin.

Hardy, T. (2000). *Far from the madding crowd*. London: Penguin.

Harris, R. (1980). *The language-makers*. Ithaca, NY: Cornell University Press.

Harris, R. (1981). *The language myth*. New York: St. Martin's Press.

Harris, R. (1987). *The language machine*. Ithica, NY: Cornell University Press.

Heller, M. (2003). Globalization, the new economy, and the commodification of language and identity. *Journal of sociolinguistics, 7*, 473–492.

Heller, M. (2011). *Paths to post-modernism: A critical ethnography of language and identity*. Oxford: Oxford University Press.

Heritage, J., & Raymond, G. (2005). The terms of agreement: Indexing epistemic authority and subordination in talk-in-Interaction. *Social psychology quarterly, 68*(1), 15–38.

Hermann, J. (2008). The "language" problem. *Language & communication, 28*, 93–99.

Herold, R. (1990). *Mechanisms of merger: The implementation and distribution of the low back merger in eastern Pennsylvania* (Ph.D. dissertation, Linguistics). University of Pennsylvania.

Herold, R. (1997). Solving the actuation problem: Merger and immigration in eastern Pennsylvania. *Language variation and change, 9*, 149–164.

Herring, S. C. (2007). A faceted classification scheme for computer-mediated discourse. *Language@ Internet, 1*. Retrieved from http://www.languageatinternet.de/articles/2007/761/index_html/

Hill, J. H. (1995). Junk Spansh, covert racism, and the (leaky) boundary between public and private spheres. *Pragmatics, 5*, 197–212.

Hilliard, S., & Wolfram, W. (2003). The sociolinguistic significance of folk dictionaries. Presented at the Southeastern Conference on Linguistics, Washington D.C.

Hindle, D. (1975). *Syntactic variation in Philadelphia: Positive anymore* (Pennsylvania working papers on linguistic change and variation, Series 5, Vol. 1). Philadelphia, PA: U.S. Regional Survey.

Hindle, D., & Sag, I. (1973). Some more on "anymore". In R. Fasold & R. W. Shuy (Eds.), *Analyzing variation in language: Papers from the second colloquium on ways of analyzing variation* (pp. 89–111). Washington D.C.: Georgetown University Press.

Hoerr, J. P. (1988). *And the wolf finally came: The decline of the American steel industry*. Pittsburgh PA: University of Pittsburgh Press.

Hoffman, M., & Walker, J. A. (2010). Ethnolects and the city: Ethnic orientation and linguistic variation in Toronto English. *Language variation and change, 22*(1), 37–67.

Hopper, P. J. (1988). Emergent grammar and the a priori grammar postulate. In D. Tannen (Ed.), *Linguistics in context: Connecting observation and understanding* (pp. 117–134). Norwood, NJ: Ablex.

How to start a silk screen t-shirt business. (n.d.). Retrieved May 17, 2012, from http://www.ehow.com/how_4913339_start-silk-screen-tshirt-business.html

Huzinec, M. (1978, November 21). Pitt prof finds Pittsburghese a slippy subject. *Pittsburgh press*, p. 2.

Ingham, J. N. (1989). Steel city aristocrats. In S. P. Hays (Ed.), *City at the point: Essays on the social history of Pittsburgh* (pp. 265–294). Pittsburgh and London: University of Pittsburgh Press.

Irvine, J. T. (1995). The family romance of colonial linguistics: Gender and family in nineteenth-century representations of African languages. *Pragmatics, 5*, 139–153.

Irvine, J. T. (1996). Language and community. *Journal of linguistic anthropology, 6*,

Irvine, J. T. (2008). Subjected words: African linguistics and the colonial encounter. *Language & communication, 28*(4), 323–343.

Irvine, J. T. (2009). Stance in a colonial encounter: How Mr. Taylor lost his footing. In A. Jaffe (Ed.), *Sociolinguistic perspectives on stance* (pp. 53–72). Oxford, New York: Oxford University Press.

Jakobson, R. (1960). Concluding statement: Linguistics and poetics. In T. Sebeok (Ed.), *Style in language* (pp. 350–377). Cambridge, MA: MIT Press.

Jaworski, A., and C. Thurlow. (Eds.) (2010). *Semiotic landscapes: Language, image, space.* London: Continuum.

Jensen, J. F. (1999). "Interactivity"—Tracking a new concept in media and communication studies. In P. A. Mayer (Ed.), *Computer media and communication: A reader*, 160–187. Oxford: Oxford University Press.

Johnston, W. G. (1901). *Life and reminiscences from birth to manhood of Wm. G. Johnston.* Pittsburgh: William G. Johnston Co.

Johnston, R. J., Gregory, D., & Smith, D. M. (1994). *Dictionary of human geography.* Oxford: Blackwell.

Johnstone, B. (forthcoming). "100% Authentic Pittsburgh": Sociolinguistic authenticity and the linguistics of particularity. In T. Breyer, V. Lacoste, & J. Leimgruber (Eds.), *Indexing authenticity.* Berlin: De Gruyter Mouton.

Johnstone, B. (1990). *Stories, community, and place: Narratives from middle America.* Bloomington: Indiana University Press.

Johnstone, B. (1995). Sociolinguistic resources, individual identities and the public speech styles of Texas women. *Journal of linguistic anthropology, 5,* 1–20.

Johnstone, B. (1999). Uses of Southern speech by contemporary Texas women. *Journal of socio-linguistics, 3,* 505–522.

Johnstone, B. (2004). Place, globalization, and linguistic variation. In C. Fought (Ed.), *Sociolinguistic variation: critical reflections* (pp. 65–83). New York: Oxford University Press.

Johnstone, B. (2009). Stance, style, and the linguistic individual. In A. Jaffe (Ed.), *Stance: Sociolinguistic perspectives* (pp. 29–52). New York, Oxford: Oxford University Press.

Johnstone, B. (2010). Language and geographical space. In P. Auer & J. E. Schmidt (Eds.), *Language and space: An international handbook of linguistic variation* (Vol. 1: Theories and methods, pp. 1–18). Berlin: De Gruyter Mouton.

Johnstone, B., & Baumgardt, D. (2004). "Pittsburghese" online: Vernacular norming in conversation. *American speech, 79,* 115–145.

Johnstone, B., Andrus, J., & Danielson, A. E. (2006). Mobility, indexicality, and the enregisterment of "Pittsburghese." *Journal of English linguistics, 34*(2), 77–104.

Johnstone, B., & Bean, J. M. (1997). Self-expression and linguistic variation. *Language in society, 26,* 221–246.

Johnstone, B., Bhasin, N., & Wittkofski, D. (2002). "Dahntahn Pittsburgh": Monophthongal /aw/ and representations of localness in southwestern Pennsylvania. *American speech, 77,* 148–166.

Johnstone, B., & Danielson, A. (2001). "Pittsburghese" in the daily papers, 1910–2001: Historical sources of ideology about variation. Presented at New Ways of Analyzing Variation, 30, Raleigh, NC.

Johnstone, B., & Kiesling, S. F. (2008). Indexicality and experience: Exploring the meanings of /aw/-monophthongization in Pittsburgh. *Journal of sociolinguistics, 12*(1), 5–33.

Joseph, J. E., & Taylor, T. J. (Eds.). (1990). *Ideologies of language.* New York: Routledge.

Kelly, M. (2003). Projecting an image and expressing identity: T-shirts in Hawaii. *Fashion theory, 7,* 191–212.

Kent, D. (2009). *yinz float.* Retrieved from http://www.flickr.com/photos/simple-pleasure/4196741382/

Kerswill, P. (2005). Migration and language. In K. Mattheier, U. Ammon, & P. Trudgill (Eds.), *Sociolinguistics/Soziolinguistik: An international handbook of the science of language and society,* 2nd edn (pp. 2271–2285). Berlin: Mouton DeGruyter.

Kerswill, P., & Williams, A. (2000). Creating a new town koine: Children and language change in Milton Keynes. *Language in society, 29*(1), 65–115.

Kiesling, S. F., Andrus, J., Bhasin, N., & Johnstone, B. (2005). Local orientation and local-sounding speech in Pittsburgh: Complicating the picture (poster). Presented at New Ways of Analyzing Variation (NWAV) 34, New York, NY.

Kiesling, S. F., & Wisnosky, M. (2003). Competing norms, heritage prestige, and /aw/-monoph-thongization in Pittsburgh. Presented at New Ways of Analyzing Variation (NWAV) 32, Philadelphia, PA.

King, R., & Wicks, J. (2009). "Aren't we proud of our language?" Authenticity, commodification, and the Nissan Bonavista television commercial. *Journal of English linguistics, 37*(3), 262–283.

Kirkham, G. (1997). Ulster Emigration to North America, 1680-1720. In H. T. Blethen, C. Wood, and T. G. Fraser (Eds), *Ulster and North America: Transatlantic perspectives on the Scotch-Irish* (pp. 76–97). Tuscaloosa and London: University of Alabama Press.

Kloman, H. (1992, February). The truth and consequences of Pittsburghese: How you say downtown can affect your career. *Pittsburgh magazine,* 40–43.

Knox, D. (2001). Doing the Doric: The institutionalization of regional language and culture in the north-east of Scotland. *Social & cultural geography, 2*(3), 315–331.

Kurath, H. (1945). German relics in Pennsylvania English. *Monatsheft fuer deutsche Unterricht, 37,* 96–100.

Kurath, H. (1949). *A word geography of the eastern United States: Based upon the collection of the Linguistic atlas of the eastern United States.* Ann Arbor: University of Michigan Press.

Kurath, H., Bloch, B., & Hansen, M. L. (1939). *Linguistic atlas of New England* (Vols. 1–3). Providence, RI: Brown University Press, for the American Council of Learned Societies.

Kurath, H., & McDavid, R. I. (1961). *The pronunciation of English in the Atlantic States: Based upon the collections of the linguistic atlas of the Eastern United States.* Ann Arbor: University of Michigan Press.

Labov, T. G. (1998). English acquisition by immigrants to the United States at the beginning of the Twentieth Century. *American speech, 73*(4), 368–398.

Labov, W. (1972a). The isolation of contextual styles. In *Sociolinguistic patterns* (pp. 70–109). Philadelphia: University of Pennsylvania Press.

Labov, W. (1972b). On the mechanism of linguistic change. In *Sociolinguistic patterns* (pp. 160–182). Philadelphia: University of Pennsylvania Press.

Labov, W. (1972c). *Sociolinguistic patterns.* Philadelphia, USA: University of Pennsylvania Press.

Labov, W. (1972d). Hypercorrection by the lower middle class as a factor in linguistic change. In *Sociolinguistic patterns* (pp. 122–142). Philadelphia: University of Pennsylvania Press.

Labov, W. (1972e). Some principles of linguistic methodology. *Language in society, 1*(1), 97–120.

Labov, W. (1981). Speech actions and reactions in personal narrative. In D. Tannen (Ed.), *Georgetown University round table on language and linguistics* (pp. 219–247). Washington DC: Georgetown University Press.

Labov, W. (2001a). The anatomy of style shifting. In P. Eckert & J. R. Rickford (Eds.), *Style and sociolinguistic variation* (pp. 85–108). Cambridge: Cambridge University Press.

Labov, W. (2001b). *Principles of linguistic change: Social factors.* Malden, MA; Oxford, UK: Blackwell.

Labov, W., Ash, S., & Boberg, C. (2005). *Atlas of North American English: Phonetics, phonology and sound change.* Berlin, New York: Mouton/deGruyter.

Labov, W., & Waletzky, J. (1967). Narrative analysis: Oral versions of personal experience. In J. Helm (Ed.), *Essays on the verbal and visual arts* (pp. 12–44). Seattle: University of Washington Press.

Landry, R., & Bourhis, R. (1977). Linguistic landscape and ethnolinguistic vitality: An empirical study. *Journal of language and social psychology, 16,* 23–49.

Leith, D. (1997). *A social history of English.* 2nd. ed. London: Routledge.

Leo, P. (1982, June 21). This column needs read. *Pittsburgh post-gazette,* p. 4.

Levinson, S. C. (1983). *Pragmatics.* Cambridge: Cambridge University Press.

Leyburn, J. G. (1962). *The Scotch-Irish: A social history.* Chapel Hill: University of North Carolina Press.

Lindquist, J. (2002). *A place to stand: Politics and persuasion in a working-class bar.* Oxford, New York: Oxford University Press.

Lister, M., Dovey, J., Giddings, S., Grant, I., & Kelly, K. (2009). *New media: A critical introduction* (2nd. ed.). London: Routledge.

Long, D., & Preston, D. R. (2000). *Handbook of perceptual dialectology.* Vol. 2. Amsterdam: John Benjamins.

Love, G. (1952, January 18). What we say. *Pittsburgh press,* p. 23.

Love, N. (2009). Science, language, and linguistic culture. *Language & communication, 29,* 26–46.

Lyons, J. (1977). *Semantics,* Vol. 1. Cambridge: Cambridge University Press.

Massey, S. (n.d.). Jewelry for her. *Http://www.jewelrynat.com/*. Retrieved July 9, 2012, from http://www.jewelrynat.com/p/jewelry.html

Maxfield, E. K. (1931). The speech of south-western Pennsylvania. *American speech*, 18–20.

McClymer, J. F. (1982). The Americanization movement and the education of the foreign-born adult, 1914–25. In B. J. Weiss (Ed.), *American Education and the European immigrant, 1840–1940* (pp. 96–116). Urbana: University of Illinois Press.

McCool, S. (1982). *Sam McCool's new Pittsburghese: How to speak like a Pittsburgher*. Pittsburgh: Hayford Press.

McDavid, R. I., O'Cain, R. K., & Dorrill, G. (1979). *Linguistic atlas of the middle and south Atlantic states*. Chicago: University of Chicago Press.

McElhinny, B. (1999). More on the third dialect of English: Linguistic constraints on the use of three phonological variables in Pittsburgh. *Language variation and change*, 11, 171–195.

McGough, M. (1973, October 15). Pittsburghers have a dialect all their own. *Pittsburgh post-gazette*, p. 22.

McHugh, R. (1979). He scotches Pittsburgh monopoly on "yunz". *Pittsburgh press*, p. 2.

McHugh, R. (1981, February 2). Chitchattin' dahntahn inna still city. *Pittsburgh press*.

McMillan, S. J. (2002). Exploring models of interactivity from multiple research traditions: Users, documents, and systems. In L. A. Lievrouw & S. Livingstone (Eds.), *Handbook of new media: Social shaping and consequences of ICTs* (pp. 163–182). Thousand Oaks, CA: Sage Publications.

Meining, D. (1978). The continuous shaping of America: A prospectus for geographers and historians, *American historical review*, 83, 1186–1205.

Mendoza-Denton, N. (2008). *Homegirls: Language and cultural practice among Latina youth gang*. Malden, MA: Blackwell Publishing.

Miller, S. J. (2002). Phish phan pholklore: identity and community through commodities in the Phish parking lot scene. *Midwestern folklore*, 28, 42–60.

Milroy, J., & Milroy, L. (1985). *Authority in language: Investigating language prescription and standardization*. London and New York: Routledge and Kegan Paul.

Milroy, L. (1987). *Language and social networks*. Oxford: Basil Blackwell.

Mock, B. (2005, 10.26/11.02). Slightly shorter shot: A black Republican finds a few more supporters than usual. *Pittsburgh City Paper*, p. 8.

Modan, G. (2007). *Turf wars: Discourse, diversity, and the politics of place*. Malden, MA: Blackwell.

Mohl, R. A. (1982). The International Institutes and immigrant education. In B. J. Weiss (Ed.), *American education and the European immigrant: 1840–1940* (pp. 117–141). Urbana: University of Illinois Press.

Montgomery, M. (1989). Exploring the roots of Appalachian English. *English world-wide*, 10, 227–278.

Montgomery, M. (2001). Eighteenth-century nomenclature for Ulster emigrants. *Journal of Scotch-Irish studies*, 2, 1–6.

Montgomery, M. (2002). The structural history of y'all, you all, and you'uns. *Southern journal of linguistics*, 26(1), 19–27.

Montgomery, M. (2006). *From Ulster to America: The Scotch-Irish heritage of American English*. Belfast: Ulster Historical Foundation.

Montgomery, M., & Kirk, J. M. (2001). "My mother, whenever she passed away, she had pneumonia": The history and functions of whenever. *Journal of English linguistics*, 29(3), 243–249.

Mufwene, S. S. (1996). The founder principle in creole genesis. *Diachronica*, 13(1), 83–134.

Mugerauer, R. (1985). Language and environment. In Seamon, D. and Mugerauer, R. (Eds.) *Dwelling, place and environment: Towards a phenomenology of person and world*. Dordrecht: Martinus Nijhoff.

Murray, T. E. (1993). Positive anymore in the Midwest. In T. C. Fraser (Ed.), *"Heartland" English: Variation and transition in the American Midwest* (pp. 173–186). Tuscaloosa and London: University of Alabama Press.

Murray, T. E., Fraser, T., & Simon, B. L. (1996). need + past participle in American English. *American speech*, 71, 255–271.

Murray, T. E., & Simon, B. L. (2002). At the intersection of regional and social dialects: The case of like + past participle in American English. *American speech*, 77(1), 32–69.

Myers, G. (2006). Identifying place: Where are you from? *Journal of sociolinguistics*, 10(3), 320–343.

Newlin, C. M. (1928). Dialects on the western Pennsylvania frontier. *American speech*, 4(2), 279–302.

Niedzielski, N. (1999). The effect of social information on the perception of sociolinguistic variables. *Journal of language and social psychology*, 18, 62–85.

Niedzielski, N., & Preston, D. R. (1999). *Folk linguistics*. Berlin: Mouton.

Ochs, E. (1992). Indexing gender. In A. Duranti & C. Goodwin , *Rethinking context: Language as an interactive phenomenon*, 335–358. New York: Cambridge University Press.

Oestreicher, R. (1989). Working-class formation, development, and consciousness in Pittsburgh, 1790–1960. In S. P. Hays (Ed.), *City at the point: Essays on the social history of Pittsburgh* (pp. 111–150). Pittsburgh: University of Pittsburgh Press.

Ogilvy, J. (1977). *Many dimensional man: Decentralizing self, society, and the sacred*. New York: Oxford University Press.

Ove, T. (1998, January 19). Pals send tape an'at to priest in Rome. *Pittsburgh post-gazette*, pp. 1, 2.

Overstreet, M. (1999). *Whales, candlelight, and stuff like that: General extenders in English discourse*. Oxford, New York: Oxford University Press.

Parslow, R. (1979). *The Pittsburgh Diocesan Holy Name Society presents a little guide to Pittsburghese*. Pittsburgh PA: Pittsburgh Diocesan Holy Name Society.

Pavlenko, A. (2002). "We have room for but one language here": Language and national identity in the US at the turn of the 20th century. *Multilingua*, 21, 163–196.

Pederson, L., McDavid, R. I., & Leas, S. (1986). *Linguistic atlas of the Gulf States*. University of Alabama: The University of Alabama Press.

Peirce, C. S. (1960). *The collected papers of Charles Sanders Peirce*. (C. Hartshorne & P. Weiss, Eds.) (Vols. 1–5). Cambridge: Harvard University Press.

Pentzold, C. (2007). Fixing the floating gap: The online encyclopaedia Wikipedia as a global memory place. Presented at Collective memory and collective knowledge in a global age: An interdisciplinary workshop, Centre for the study of global governance, London School of Economics. Retrieved from http://www.lse.ac.uk/Depts/global/EventsPDFs/MemoryWorkshop/FixingtheFloatingGap_ Pentzold.pdf

Petrucelli, A. W. (2008, December 1). A fresh look: Speaking clearly in Pittsburghese. *Pittsburgh post-gazette*. Retrieved from http://www.post-gazette.com/pg/08336/931482-51 .stm#ixzz0wOodb9UL

Piller, I., & Cho, J. (2013). Neoliberalism and language ideology. *Language in society*, 42, 23–44.

Prelli, L. J. (1997). Rhetorical construction of scientific ethos. In R. A. Harris (Ed.), *Landmark essays on rhetoric of science: Case studies* (pp. 87–104). Hillsdale, NJ: Hermagoras Press, an imprint of Lawrence Erlbaum Associates, Publishers.

Preston, D. R. (1982).:'Ritin' fowklower daun 'rong: Folklorists' failures in phonology, *Journal of American folklore*, 95, 304–26.

Preston, D. R. (1985). The Li'l Abner syndrome: Written representations of speech. *American speech*, 60, 328–337.

Preston, D. R. (1989). *Perceptual dialectology*. Dordrecht: Foris.

Preston, D. R. (1992). Talking black and talking white: A study in variety imitation. In Joan H. Hall, N. Doane, & D. Ringler (Eds.), *Old English and new: Studies in language and linguistics in honor of Frederic G. Cassidy* (pp. 327–355). New York: Garland.

Preston, D. R. (1996). Whaddayaknow? The modes of folk linguistic awareness. *Language awareness*, 5, 40–74.

Prichard, L. K. (1989). The soul of the city: A social history of religion in Pittsburgh. In S. P. Hays (Ed.), *City at the point: Essays on the social history of Pittsburgh* (pp. 327–360). Pittsburgh: University of Pittsburgh Press.

Propp, V. (1968). *Morphology of the folktale*. Austin: University of Texas Press.

Rampton, B. (1995). *Crossing: Language and ethnicity among adolescents*. London: Longman.

Rampton, B. (1998). Speech community. In J. Verschueren, J. O. Ostman, J. Blommaert, & C. Bulcaen (Eds.), *Handbook of pragmatics*, 1-34. Amsterdam: John Benjamins.

Rampton, B. (Ed.). (1999). Styling the "other": (Theme issue). *Journal of sociolinguistics*, 3, 421–556.

Raymond, Geoffrey. (2000). The voice of authority: the local accomplishment of authoritative discourse in live news broadcasts. *Discourse studies*, 2(3), 354–379.

Ronkin, M., & Karn, H. E. (1999). Mock Ebonics: Linguistic racism in parodies of Ebonics on the Internet. *Journal of sociolinguistics*, 3, 360–380.

Rotstein, G. (2004, December 26). Scattered abroad: Many of the thousands of Pittsburghers who left yearn to return. *Pittsburgh post-gazette*. Retrieved from http://www.post-gazette.com/pg/04361/432153.stm

Ryan, E. B., & Giles, H. (1982). *Alttitudes towards language variation: Social and applied contexts.* London: Edward Arnold.

Said, E. (1978). *Orientalism.* New York: Vintage Books.

Samuels, D. W. (2006). Bible translation and medicine man talk: Missionaries, indexicality, and the on the San Carlos Apache Reservation. *Language in society*, 35(04), 529–557.

Sauer, C. (1925). The morphology of landscape. *University of California publications in geography*, 2, 19–54.

Schegloff, E. A. (1972). Notes on a conversational practice: Formulating place. In E. A. Schegloff & D. Sudnow (Eds.), *Studies in social interaction* (pp. 75–119). New York: The Free Press.

Schieffelin, B. B., Woolard, K. A., & Kroskrity, P. V. (Eds.). (1988). *Language ideologies: Practice and theory.* New York: Oxford University Press.

Schilling-Estes, N. (2002). On the nature of isolated and post-isolated dialects: innovation, variation, and differentiation. *Journal of sociolinguistics*, 6, 64–85.

Schneider, E. (1986). "How to speak Southern": An American English dialect stereotyped. *Amerikastudien*, 31(4), 20–33.

Seamon, D. (1979). *A geography of the lifeworld: Movement, rest, and encounter.* New York: St. Martin's.

Searle, J. R. (1969). *Speech acts: An esay in the philosophy of language.* Cambridge: Cambridge University Press.

Sebak, R. (2001). *Pittsburgh A to Z.* Documentary, WQED Public Television, QED Communications.

Shields Jr., K. (1985). Germanisms in Pennsylvania English: An update. *American speech*, 60, 228–237.

Silverstein, M. (1981). The limits of awareness. Southwest Educational Development Laboratory, Vol. 84. Austin, TX: Southwest Educational Development Laboratory.

Silverstein, M. (1993). Metapragmatic discourse and metapragmatic function. In J. A. Lucy (Ed.), *Reflexive language* (pp. 33–58). Cambridge: Cambridge University Press.

Silverstein, M. (1994). "Cultural" concepts and the language-culture nexus. *Current anthropology*, 45(5), 621–652.

Silverstein, M. (1995). Shifters, linguistic categories, and cultural description. In B. G. Blount (Ed.), *Language, culture, and society: A book of readings* (pp. 187–221). Prospect Heights, IL: Waveland Press.

Silverstein, M. (1998a). The uses and utility of ideology. In B. B. Schieffelin, K. A. Woolard, & P. V. Kroskrity (Eds.), *Language ideologies: Practice and theory* (pp. 123–145). Oxford: Oxford University Press.

Silverstein, M. (1998b). Contemporary transformation of linguistic communities. *Annual review of anthropology*, 27, 410–426.

Silverstein, M. (2003). Indexical order and the dialectics of sociolinguistic life. *Language and communication*, (23), 193–229.

Silverstein, M. (2005). Cultural knowledge, discourse poetics, and the performance of social relations. In A. Makkai, W. J. Sullivan, & A. R. Lommel (Eds.), *LACUS forum XXXI: Interconnections* (pp. 35–54). Houston: LACUS.

Soja, E. W. (1989). *Postmodern geographies: The reassertion of space in critical social theory.* New York: Verso.

Steinbeck, J. (1980). *Travels with Charley: In search of America.* New York: Penguin Books.

Swetnam, G. (1959a, March 8). Pittsburgh's peculiar proverbs. *Pittsburgh press*, p. 3.

Swetnam, G. (1959b, September 6). Pittsburgh patois. *Pittsburgh press*, pp. 4–5.

Swetnam, G. (1972, October 15). Your talk tells tales. *Pittsburgh post-gazette*, pp. 10–11.

Symes, C. (1987). Keeping abreast with the times: Towards an iconography of T-shirts. *Studies in popular culture, 12*, 87–100.

Szmrecsanyi, B. (2010). Geography is overrated. In S. Hansen, C. Schwarz, P. Stoeckle, & T. Streck (Eds.), *Dialectological and folk dialectological concepts of space*. Berlin: Walter de Gruyter.

Tan, P. K. W., & Rubdy, R. (Eds.). (2008). *Language as commodity: Global structures, local market-places*. London and New York: Continuum.

Tannen, D. (1979). What's in a frame? Surface evidence for underlying expectations. In R. Freedle (Ed.), *New directions in discourse processing* (pp. 137–181). Norwood, NJ: Ablex.

Tannen, D. (1986). Folk formality. In *Proceedings of the twelfth annual meeting of the Berkeley Linguistics Society* (pp. 246–60). Berkeley, CA: Berkeley Linguistics Society.

Tannen, D. (1987). Repetition in conversation: toward a poetics of talk. *Language, 63*, 574–605.

Tannen, D. (1989). *Talking voices: Repetition, dialogue, and imagery in conversational discourse*. Cambridge: Cambridge University Press.

Tannen, D. (Ed.). (1993). *Framing in discourse*. New York, Oxford: Oxford University Press.

Taylor, T. (1977). *Theorizing language: Analysis, normativity, rhetoric, history* (2nd ed.). Bingley, UK: Emerald Group Publishing Limited.

Tenny, C. (1998). Psych verbs and verbal passives in Pittsburghese. *Linguistics, 36*(3), 591–597.

Thomas, E. R. (2003). Secrets revealed by Southern vowel shifting, *American speech, 78*, 150–170.

Thomas, E. R., & Reaser, J. (2004). Delimiting perceptual cues used for the ethnic labeling of African American and European American voices. *Journal of sociolinguistics, 8*, 54–87.

Thompson, E. P. (1966). *The making of the English working class*. New York: Vintage Books.

Thompson, W. (2011, October 2). "The Pittsburgh we're from isn't there anymore": For many displaced NFL fans, their teams are their only way back home. *ESPN*, 121–126.

Trudgill, P. (1972). Sex, covert prestige and linguistic change in the urban British English of Norwich. *Language in society, 1*(2), 179–195.

Trudgill, P. (1983). Acts of conflicting identity: The sociolinguistics of British pop song pronunciation. In *On dialect: Social and geographical perspectives* (pp. 141–160). Oxford: Blackwell.

Trudgill, P. (1986). *Dialects in contact*. Oxford/NY: Basil Blackwell.

Trudgill, P. (2006). *New-dialect formation: The inevitability of colonial Englishes*. Oxford:Oxford Unversity Press.

Tuan, Y.-F. (1974). Space and place: Humanistic perspective. In C. Board, R. J. Chorley, P. Haggett, & D. R. Stoddart (Eds.), *Progress in geography* (Vol. 6, pp. 211–252).

Tuan, Y.-F. (1977). *Space and place: The perspective of experience*. Minneapolis: University of Minnesota Press.

Tucker, R. W. (1934). Linguistic substrata in Pennsylvania and elsewhere. *Language, 10*(1), 1–5.

Voice of America. (n.d.). *Pittsburghese*. Retrieved from http://www.unsv.com/voanews/wordmaster/scripts/2009/09/22/.

von Schneidemesser, L. (2003). Settlement history in the United States as reflected in DARE: The example of German. *American speech, 77*, 398–418.

Wales, K. (2006). *Northern English: A social and cultural history*. Cambridge: Cambridge University Press.

Warnick, M. S. (1990, July 15). Lawrenceville aside, fewer of yunz speak Pittsburghese. *Pittsburgh press*, pp. 1, 4.

Watt, D. (2002). "I don"t speak with a Geordie accent, I speak, like, the Northern accent': contact-induced levelling in the Tyneside vowel system. *Journal of sociolinguistics, 6*, 44–63.

Watt, D., & Milroy, L. (1999). Phonetic variation in three Tyneside vowels: Is this dialect level-ling? In P. Foulkes & G. J. Docherty (Eds.), *Urban voices: Accent studies in the British Isles* (pp. 25–46). London: Arnold.

Weber, M. P. (1989). Community-building and occupational mobility in Pittsburgh, 1880-1960. In S. P. Hays (Ed.), *City at the point: Essays on the social history of Pittsburgh* (pp. 361–384). Pittsburgh PA: University of Pittsburgh Press.

Weis, L. (1990). *Working class without work: High school students in a de-industrializing economy*. New York: Routledge.

Wenger, E. (1998). *Communities of practice: Learning, meaning, and identity*. Cambridge: Cambridge University Press.

White, H. (1980). The value of narrativity in the representation of reality. In W. T. J. Mitchell (Ed.), *On narrative* (pp. 1–23). Chicago: Univeristy of Chicago Press.

White, H. (1992). Historical emplotment and the problem of truth. In S. Friedlander (Ed.), *Probing the limits of representation: Nazism and the"final solution"* (pp. 37–53). Cambridge MA: Harvard University Press.

Williams, R. (1982). *The sociology of culture*. New York: Schocken Books.

Woolard, K. A., & Schieffelin, B. (1994). Language ideology. *Annual review of anthropology, 23,* 55–82.

Yeager, M., & Skowron, J. (2009). *Greg and Donny Have an accent*. Retrieved from http://www .youtube.com/watch?v=k4jn1L-riak

Zelinsky, W. (1995). Cultural geography. In E. Miller (Ed.), *A geography of Pennsylvania* (pp. 132–153). University Park: Pennsylvania State University Press.

Index

Figures, notes, and tables are indicated by f, n, and t following the page number.

CPSIA information can be obtained at www.ICGtesting.com
Printed in the USA
LVOW06s1525081215

465958LV00006B/952/P